# GURDJIEFF IN TIBET

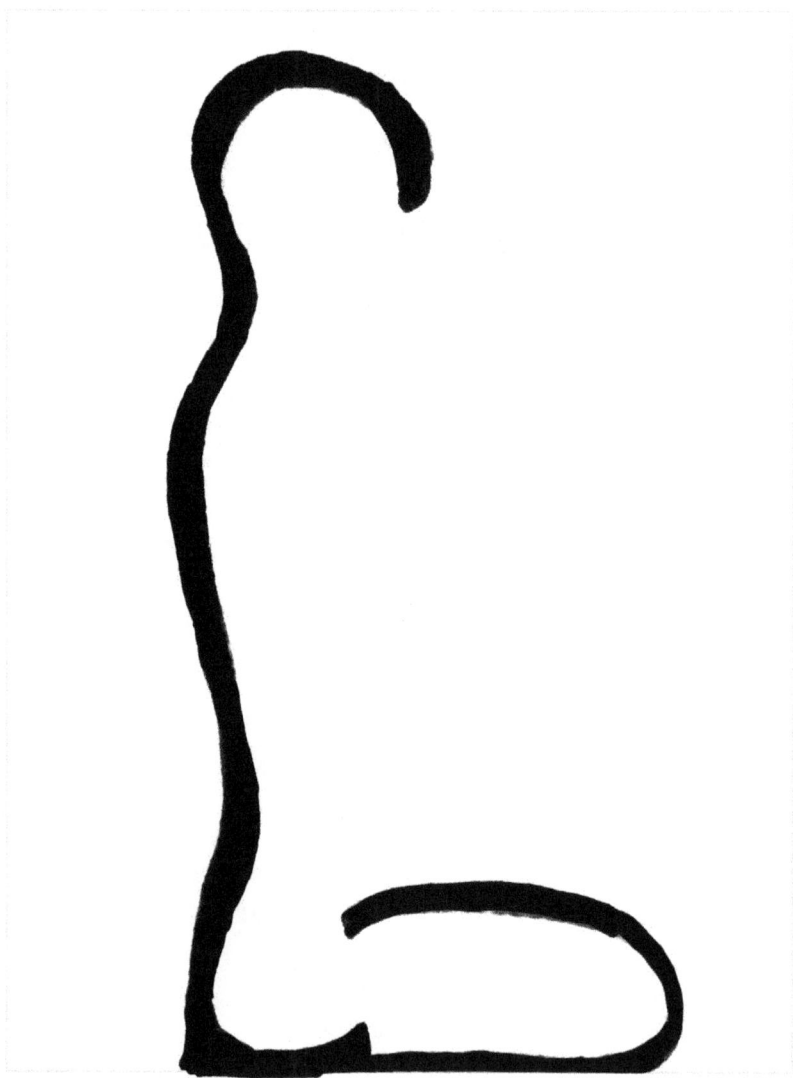

Ink drawing made by Gurdjieff

# GURDJIEFF IN TIBET

by

Layne Negrin

*Always and Everywhere*
*2025*

ISBN: 978-0-9741079-0-5

Dust jacket art from a painting by Yahne Le Toumelin titled "Lac Danakasha," copyright © Matthieu Ricard, is reproduced here with his permission.

The frontispiece, an untitled ink drawing by G. Gurdjieff, copyright © Damon Lindbergh, to whom it was gifted upon his birth by Annette Herter, a pupil of Gurdjieff and his parent's group leader, is reproduced here with his permission.

Other credits follow their inclusion.

Always and Everywhere Books and Publishing, LLC
always-and-everywhere.com
layne@always-and-everywhere.com
457 Classon Unit 8
Brooklyn NY 11238

*For the many friends I
made during the journey
of researching the subjects
in this book, especially
Yahne and Sophie.*

# TABLE OF CONTENTS

Foreword..........................................................................................................i
Preface ..........................................................................................................1

## Part One: The Quest of Urgyen Tag

Introduction to Part One ..................................................................... 9
A Seeker of Truth.................................................................................. 13
*The History of the Institute* by G. Gurdjieff .................................... 19
Skridlov.................................................................................................. 25
*Conscience* by W. M. Flinders Petrie................................................. 33
Magical Tibet ........................................................................................ 35
In Search of Shambhala ...................................................................... 41
*A Conversation with Chatral Rinpoche* by William Segal.................... 47
Brother Asiman .................................................................................... 61
Turkestan Tiger .................................................................................... 65
The Chief of Seven ............................................................................... 73
*Beelzebub in Tibet* by G. Gurdjieff .................................................... 83
*Advice* by Dudjom Lingpa .................................................................. 87
A Breeze of Grace................................................................................. 89
Sarmung................................................................................................ 93
*A Tibetan Ritual* by G. Gurdjieff ...................................................... 105
Prince Lubovedsky ............................................................................... 111
*Third Voyage to Lhasa* by Ovshé Norzunov...................................... 119
Soloviev................................................................................................. 133
The Abbot .............................................................................................. 145
Dying Like a Dog .................................................................................. 149
*Silver Is Poison* by Tsewang Norbu ................................................. 153
Dzogchen Rinpoche.............................................................................. 157
*Freedom* by The Fifth Dzogchen Rinpoche ...................................... 159

Two Sons.................................................................................... 163
*The Sacred Site Known as Halashiri* by The Sixth Shechen Rabjam.... 171
The Self-Tamers........................................................................ 175
Dance ....................................................................................... 179
*An Encounter with Gurdjieff's Institute* by Alfons Paquet .................. 187
Cuisine ..................................................................................... 191
Medicine ................................................................................... 195
A Modern Marpa ........................................................................ 201
*Milarepa* by Solange Claustres ................................................... 205
Phowa ....................................................................................... 211
Return to Tibet?........................................................................ 213

## Part Two: Children Seeking Their Roots

Introduction to Part Two............................................................ 217
Sausage .................................................................................... 221
*The German Translation of the* Bardo Thödol by Louise March.......... 229
A Special Secretary .................................................................... 237
*Taking Refuge in the Work* by Paul Anderson .............................. 247
*Relaxing with Presence* by Chögyal Namkhai Norbu ..................... 253
Saru-san.................................................................................... 261
*Energy from High* by William Segal............................................. 271
*This!* by Soen Nakagawa........................................................... 273
Mademoiselle Pourquoi............................................................... 281
*Meditation with the Guru* by Arnaud Desjardins............................ 289
*Impermanence* by Kangyur Rinpoche .......................................... 293
Maverick ................................................................................... 299
*Striving* by Paul Beidler ............................................................ 305
*Sangha Life* by Gosung Shin ..................................................... 307
Mr Hazard................................................................................. 313
*Gurdjieff and the Buddhist Mind-Body*........................................ 319
*To Know Yourself Is to Be Enlightened* by Bhante Dharmawara........ 325
The Metaphysical Psychoanalyst ................................................. 329
*Huang Po* by Hubert Benoit....................................................... 333
Dr A. ........................................................................................ 341
*The Lama* by Rolf Alexander...................................................... 345
The Queen of the Dakinis ........................................................... 349
*I Do Not Know* by Jeanne de Salzmann ...................................... 359
*Determining the Nature of the Inner Perceiving Mind* by
    Dudjom Rinpoche................................................................. 363
Pamela Poppins ........................................................................ 367
*One with the Tao* by P. L. Travers .............................................. 373
*The Fourfold Universe* by Ruth Fuller Sasaki .............................. 375
Quart-de-sommeil ...................................................................... 383
*On Tibetan Soil* by Robert Godet ............................................... 393

*The Abrupt Way* by Robert Godet ............................................................ 407
*Spontaneously Written Song of Experience* by Jamyang Khyentse
    Chökyi Lodrö.................................................................................... 409
Babette ...................................................................................................... 413
*Awakening the Mind, Opening the Heart* by Sogyal Rinpoche ........... 417
Leader of the Washington Group........................................................... 427
*Stillness Is Always Here* by Hugh Ripman...................................... 433
*An Introduction to Zen* by Sogen Asahina........................................ 437
The Electric Lord .................................................................................... 443
*Ventures with Buddhism* by John Pentland.................................... 455
*Talk to the Nyland Group* by Chögyam Trungpa Rincoche................. 459

## Part Three: Ponderings of a Grandchild

Introduction to Part Three ................................................................... 465
The Sly Buddha....................................................................................... 467
Haida!  ..................................................................................................... 471
The Scientific Path................................................................................. 475
Recollection ............................................................................................ 477
Sleep Is Ignorance ................................................................................. 479
Empty and Endless................................................................................. 481
The Embryo ............................................................................................. 483
Triamazikamno or Trikaya.................................................................... 489
A New Organ........................................................................................... 491
The Gurdjieffian Book of the Dead....................................................... 493
Memory.................................................................................................... 497
Animate and Inanimate Phenomena .................................................... 499
Devils and Demons................................................................................. 501
The Subconsciousness............................................................................ 505
The Intelligence of Negativity .............................................................. 509
The Three Jewels .................................................................................... 513
Sectarianism ........................................................................................... 515
Idiotism.................................................................................................... 517
Animal Sacrifice...................................................................................... 523
Atlantis? .................................................................................................. 525

## Appendices

Interview with Sophie Perks ................................................................. 531
Appreciation ........................................................................................... 553

## Meetings with Remarkable Beings
### A Foreword

This adventure-filled book of research, spiritual journeys and meetings with remarkable encounters by Layne Negrin is a major achievement. I have known many of both the Buddhist and Gurdjieffian figures presented here and studied with a number of them.

On a personal level I find it deeply helpful and illuminating, and I aspire for all its readers to benefit from what is offered here. My spiritual search began more than 50 years ago and found me entering these two realms at once, that of Tibetan Buddhism and of the Gurdjieffian path. My first teacher in the Gurdjieff Work was Lord Pentland, a major figure in the development of the Work in the U.S.A., appointed by Gurdjieff himself to guide it, as head of the Gurdjieff Foundation in New York and later also in San Francisco. When I met Lord Pentland he was working with a team led by the renowned translator Lobsang Lhalungpa on a new translation of the extraordinary text, *The Life of Milarepa*, one of Tibet's greatest saints. That text and the compendium of his *Hundred Thousand Songs* are revered to this day as treasures of spiritual advice. Lotsawa (Venerable Translator) Lhalungpa helped orient me in my explorations of Tibetan Buddhist chant and mantra, and spiritual song (doha) as essential dimensions of the path. These and subsequent inspirations have evolved over the years into many opportunities to contribute musical offerings in these realms and others, for the benefit of all beings—opportunities for which I feel deeply grateful.

The journey into vast realms of authentic teachings can evolve over time into ever-greater appreciation and respect for the ultimate nonduality from which they emanate. The theme of nonduality arises and becomes more and more present here, like a slowly-woven tapestry whose many threads, patterns and connections come together and arise into a mandala of meaning. This weaving together of so much history and adventure, so many discoveries and meetings with remarkable beings, shines new light on these paths and beyond.

*David Hykes*

## PREFACE

There are several theories regarding the source of the Gurdjieff teaching. Besides the Tibetan Buddhist theory I present here, others I am aware of include a Sufi origin theory, a Christian origin theory, an Advaita origin theory, and a Gnostic origin theory. In addition, traces of other teachings such as Taoism can be found. Although as a Buddhist I am inclined towards the Buddhist origin theory, out of respect for these other paths I will avoid critiquing the other theories, as I would not want this to be misconstrued as a critique of the tradition itself, for I strive to support everyone I encounter on their path, regardless of the specific tradition they practice.

Also, to consider is the idea that Gurdjieff's source is the source of all traditions, which is something he himself alluded to. While this may be difficult to fathom, there is quite a bit of merit to the idea. But to understand this it is necessary to understand the concept of "source" in *essential* terms rather than *temporal*. As Gurdjieff says:

> [Man's] eyes are dazzled by the bright play of the colors of multiformity, and under the glittering surface he does not see the hidden kernel of the oneness of all that exists. This multiformity is so real that its single modes approach him from all sides—some by way of logical deduction and philosophy, others by way of faith and feeling. From the most ancient times down to our own epoch, throughout the

ages of its life, humanity as a whole has been yearning for a knowledge of this oneness and seeking for it, pouring itself out into various philosophies and religions which remain, as it were, monuments on the path of these searches for the Path, leading to the knowledge of unity. These searches radiate to the Path just as the radii of a circle join at the center, getting closer into contact with each other the nearer they get to the center.[1]

Similarly, Tcheslaw Tchekhovitch quotes Gurdjieff as saying:

There are not three, not twenty, not even two, religions. There is simply Religion. As for the rest, you can call them what you like: the study of Holy Scriptures, the teaching of theological principles, ritual practices, the Church or community of believers—but don't call any of that religion. True religion is always and everywhere the same—it is one and unique... I cannot accept, or even imagine, that at the heart of religion there is any division or conflict whatsoever. The name of religion is given today to a sect that yesterday was regarded as heretical... The essence of all religions... is the same. Fundamentally, they are all concerned with only one thing—evolution. The teaching of each great master enables his pupils to follow a certain evolutionary path, and to arrive at a level where contact with the highest cosmic force becomes possible. At their root, all the teachings are one and the same, each having as its purpose to help us attain this possibility.[2]

As well, Irmis Popoff recalls Gurdjieff equating religion with conscience, which he explains elsewhere as being the same in all men.[3]

Perhaps this is why the more esoteric sects of various traditions have greater respect and appreciation for other traditions. There are esoteric Tibetan Buddhist sects that recognize *mahasiddhas* (masters of great accomplishment) from Hindu and Sufi traditions in addition to their own. Likewise, a Sufi sect known as the Yesevi are known to have had quite open relations with those of other traditions.

Similarly, although Sufism is considered a Muslim sect, it

appears to have its origins in Zoroastrianism. Likewise, much of Dzogchen, an esoteric subsect of the Nyingmapa, appears to have come from Bön, the aboriginal Tibetan religion. Still, it is only because these sects are more concerned with the hub of the wheel, where all spokes attach, than with its own particular spoke, that they are able to enter or take in aspects of other traditions. It is at the hub that these spokes make a connection. One predating the other is not the point.

Dr Reginald Ray, a student of Chögyam Trungpa (who will be discussed later in this book), approaches the subject this way:

> Mircea Eliade contended that Vajrayana, though nomi-
> nally "Buddhist", in fact represents a "survival" of the aborig-
> inal spirituality of humankind, in other words, the pre-agri-
> cultural, paleolithic religious orientation of our forebears of
> perhaps a million years. It is quite interesting that Chögyam
> Trungpa in his Shambhala teachings said more or less the
> same thing: there is within each person, irrespective of his
> or her historical period, culture, tradition, or orientation, an
> inherent human spirituality that lies at the very heart of the
> human being as such.[4]

Gurdjieff himself alludes to this prehistoric aboriginal spirituality in his discussions of Atlantis. On the one hand, in a later chapter I will ponder a plausible relationship between the Bön and Atlantis. On the other hand, what is more essential is arriving at this spirituality innate to all humankind by going ever deeper with one's sincere, authentic practice.

Likewise, this book is only valuable in as much as it is an expression of my own search for truth. It is the searching, wonder and openness therein where its value lies, not the suggestions I draw as a result. This is yet another reason I avoid critiquing the other theories. While I strive to be as objective as possible, I have to consider that my Buddhist leanings color my perspective to some degree. I have to remain open. Although there is an abundance of evidence showing that Gurdjieff spent time in Tibet, it is impossible to prove definitively that Tibetan Buddhism was the primary inspiration for his teaching given all of the other spiritual traditions he explored.

Also, the strength of the evidence I present varies greatly. While much of the evidence leaves little doubt, there are also some subjects that remain inconclusive. Thus it is my hope that this book may inspire someone to pick up where I left off in the same way I was inspired to pick up where James Webb left off. Perhaps by building upon each other's work this way we will one day have more conclusive information. This particular search is but an expression of a greater search all humanity shares. As such, it may only be as a whole rather than through individual effort that a discovery may be made. Perhaps it is some communal self manifesting in us as individuals that engages in these searches. But it is only through the realization of no-self (or what Gurdjieff refers to as the realization of one's nothingness)—that is, a temporary knocking out of one's ego resulting in the identification of the All as one's Self—that a true sense of a communal self may be understood.

Thus, it is only after seeing myself that the wish to identify the source of the Gurdjieff teaching—be it Francis Role's wish to show it to be Advaita, Boris Mouravieff's wish to show it to be Russian Orthodox Christianity, J.G. Bennett's wish to show it to be Sufism, or my own to show it to be Tibetan Buddhism—is actually some communal self wishing to show the unity and source of all traditions, and after expressing this insight here, that I feel able to proceed with the specifics of my own findings.

I feel that showing the influence of Tibetan Buddhism upon Gurdjieff's teaching is important, because doing so makes its nondual essence more clear. The single essence of all spiritual teachings discussed earlier *is* nonduality. All these teachings are nondual although in some teachings this is concealed for one reason or another.

Yet this is not to suggest that the common dualistic interpretation of his teaching is invalid. Gurdjieff formulated his teaching such that it could be received by people with a multitude of backgrounds. I certainly needed that perspective at the start. My hope is only that those of us who have come

4

to a nondual understanding will be better supported in the Work. The dualistic interpretation is not the only valid interpretation. In fact, *All and Everything*, the title Gurdjieff gave to the series of his writings, suggests that he intended both of these interpretations to be understood. While the title is generally interpreted to mean something like "every teaching under the sun," it can also be interpreted to mean "unity and multiplicity." "All" appears to allude to *The* All (or oneness), and "Everything" appears to allude to multiplicity. Similarly, Gurdjieff's enneagram is regarded as a symbol of *All and Everything* (or unity and multiplicity).

In Part Three I will explain how Gurdjieff buried nonduality in his writings. But he actually was not always so cryptic about it. When he first began teaching he spoke openly about nonduality. In transcripts of his early talks, Gurdjieff often spoke of nonduality using terms such as "oneness" and "unity". The nondual interpretation cannot be denied.

And Part Two will discuss the direct pupils of Gurdjieff who were interested in Buddhism to one extent or another, and the Buddhist teachers with whom they engaged.

But let us begin with Part One, which looks at the evidence of Gurdjieff's presence in Tibet.

---

[1] G. I. Gurdjieff, *Lecture on Symbolism* (McMinnville: Stopinder Books, 2002), 1.

[2] Tcheslaw Tchekhovitch, *Gurdjieff: A Master in Life* (Toronto: Dolmen Meadow Editions, 2020), 42–43.

[3] Irmis B. Popoff, *Gurdjieff and His Work: On Myself, with Others, for the Work* (New York: Vantage Press, 1969), 152.

[4] Reginald A. Ray, *Touching Enlightenment: Finding Realization in the Body* (Boulder: Sounds True, 2008), 50.

# PART ONE

# THE QUEST OF URGYEN TAG

## Introduction to Part One

Gurdjieff's mythical Sarmung monastery is the one monastery of the many he encountered during his spiritual quest which he acknowledges as having the wisdom for which he truly sought and whose teaching is the basis of his teaching. His description of the monastery is embedded within the chapter "Prince Yuri Lubovedsky" in his second series of writings, *Meetings with Remarkable Men*. Although many of his students were privy to bits and pieces of the manuscript, knowledge of the Sarmung monastery was not brought to the attention of the public until the book's publication in 1963.

Three years later Chögyam Trungpa's *Born in Tibet* was published. It is in this work that the Surmang monastery of eastern Tibet was first brought to the attention of the English-speaking world. Trungpa Rinpoche was recognized as a *tulku*, an incarnation of a great lama, at a young age and subsequently taken to Surmang to undergo training to become its abbot, as which he served until forced to flee from the Chinese invasion in 1959.

Exactly who was the first to connect the two monastery names is difficult to say. Many readers who are familiar with one author are also familiar with the other. Several of Trungpa's students were previously involved in the Gurdjieff Work, and several leaders in the Work had attended Trungpa's public talks and seminars. Perhaps at the time it was not given much thought because of the difficulties involved in researching the subject—particularly Tibet having been closed off to foreigners.

James George and his first wife, Caroline, appear to have been the first Gurdjieffians to meet Trungpa Rinpoche. His wife had met him in London in the summer of 1967 and then and there invited him to their home in Delhi during his forthcoming trip to India. Trungpa subsequently stayed with them from October through December 1968. George was the Canadian High Commissioner to India and stationed at the Canadian Embassy in Delhi at the time. As Trungpa recounts in the epilog of *Born in Tibet*, "Returning from Bhutan through India, I was delighted to meet again with His Holiness Karmapa and also His Holiness the Dalai Lama. I also made the acquaintance at this time of Mr James George, the Canadian High Commissioner to India, and his wonderful family. Mr George is a wise and benevolent man, an ideal statesman, who holds great respect and faith for the teachings of Buddhism."

George had also been in the Work since 1951. With the approval of Madame de Salzmann, who was Gurdjieff's closest student and entrusted by him to continue his teaching, George and his wife were exploring the various traditions which influenced Gurdjieff since they were situated relatively near many of the places Gurdjieff had visited himself. Clearly George has a unique perspective by both having been in the Work for so many years and having been a good friend of Chögyam Trungpa. Yet as he related in private correspondence, the possibility of a connection between Sarmung and Surmang did not occur to him until some ten years later.

There is, however, some possibility that the thought occurred to Mme de Salzmann. George had arranged a meeting between her and Trungpa Rinpoche in Paris in the summer of 1968. Something about this meeting led Madame de Salzmann to believe that Trungpa might be able to "understand" Gurdjieff, which is something she expressed to Yahne Le Toumelin.[1] She also wrote to George saying, "I like him very much—he is clean and true."[2]

Also possible is that a connection between the names occurred to Lord Pentland—an English noble who Gurdjieff had entrusted with continuing his teaching in the U.S.A. under Madame de Salzmann's guidance. Pentland had attended The Battle of the Ego seminar with Trungpa Rinpoche during Christmas 1970 and met with him on other occasions as well. Although Pentland was a friend of Trungpa, very little is known about his thoughts of some possible relationship between their teachings.

Another possibility is that the connection between the monastery names occurred to Pema Chödrön, who was a member of Basil Tilley's Gurdjieff group before becoming a student of Trungpa. However, this could not be confirmed one way or the other.

Jeremy Hayward and Sherab Kohn are two other early devotees of Trungpa who were previously in the Work, but an association between the two monastery names is not mentioned in any of their writings.

The first on record to entertain the idea appears to be William Patrick Patterson. As he relates in *Eating the I*, he had read a flyer in the spring of 1970 announcing the imminent arrival of Trungpa Rinoche, when the similarity of names struck him.

The identity of Sarmung is central to the scope of this study. But this scope will also include the identity of some of Gurdjieff's fellow seekers (particularly the two others who Gurdjieff says were with him at Sarmung), some likely teachers of his, the identities of his two Tibetan sons, a look at an earlier journey to Tibet, his journey to the Hindu Kush, as well as Gurdjieff's acquaintance with various aspects of Tibetan culture.

---

[1] Private correspondence.
[2] "Interview with James George," The Chronicles of Chögyam Trungpa Rinpoche, www.chronicleproject.com/interview-with-james-george/.

## A SEEKER OF TRUTH

Gurdjieff tells us that the band of truth-seekers he co-founded began with his chance meeting with Lubovedsky and Skridlov at the foot of the Pyramids in 1895. Although for many years there was greater uncertainty as to the year of his birth, civil records recently discovered in Georgia indicate that with all likelihood Gurdjieff was born in 1877. A paper by Manana Khomeriki in *Gurdjieff in Tiflis* describes having found the family list of "Ivan Ivanovich Gurdjieff the carpenter" which places the birth of his son Georgi at 1880. But as Khomeriki relates, "...the years are shown not according to [documentation], but according to the appearance of the person. By this reason we can conclude that Gurdjieff might have been born earlier, as the year shown in his passport was 1877."[1] This means that he would have been 18 years of age when the Seekers of Truth began.

But it is not as if we did not have information indicating his youth earlier. It is more that people of our time and culture find it so difficult to believe. His passport indicated he was born in 1877. Clifford Sharpe, in an article about Gurdjieff's Institute from 1923, had stated, "The movement originated some thirty years ago in an expedition organized by Mr Gurdjieff—*then very young*—and two Russian savants..."[2] After the first edition of *All and Everything* was published citing 1872 as Gurdjieff's year of birth, it was changed to 1877 in the following edition at the insistence of his sister.[3] Similarly, J.G. Bennett states, "He told me later that he was born in 1866, but his own sister disputed this and affirmed that he was born in 1877."[4]

That he was only 18 at the time is particularly difficult to believe because by that point he had supposedly already made earlier explorations. And this is precisely why Gurdjieff's biographers tend to place his birth at or closer to 1866. But it seems necessary to consider the possibility that he truly did begin his quest so young.

Our difficulty in considering Gurdjieff beginning his various quests at such an early age is the tendency to judge a person based upon one's own nature and experience without considering the nature and experience of the individual. We all have this tendency to some degree—even those of us following a spiritual path who have a desire to overcome such weaknesses. To walk a mile in another's shoes is an ancient idea which Gurdjieff himself advocated, so it seems worth touching on this subject in relation to better understanding who Gurdjieff was as an individual. We must try to understand him not from our contemporary western culture in which such youthful quests would be virtually impossible, but from the perspective of his own culture and his own nature. If we could do this I think we would find such a thing to be possible, perhaps even probable.

The first thing to understand about ancient cultures such as that which Gurdjieff came from is that the age in which men became responsible and began their independence was much younger than ours. A clear indication of this in Gurdjieff's case is the fact that although still only a boy attending school, by the age of 11 he had begun working in his father's woodshop in all his spare time, and became such a good craftsman that in a short time he began attracting his own clients.

The next thing to understand is that unlike our society in which a child's desire for understanding and constant questioning is often stifled by well-meaning but preoccupied parents, Gurdjieff's father actually encouraged such questioning. His father was quite the philosopher and enjoyed pondering various subjects (mostly of a spiritual nature), preferably by

14

engaging in discussion with those of contrary views. The dialog was engaging and challenging, and Gurdjieff longed for the day when he would have sharpened his mind enough to be able to partake in such dialog himself.

Another wonderful trait that Gurdjieff acquired from his father was an indifference towards obstacles, both external and internal. This indifference coupled with his determination allowed him to accomplish an incredible amount in a relatively short period of time.

Yet another factor that needs to be considered is Gurdjieff's intelligence. He might even be considered a genius. What suggests this is his early teaching which was quite elaborate and revealed only a fraction of his knowledge.

According to Gurdjieff himself, the dean of the military academy he was attending was so impressed with his aptitude that he advised Gurdjieff's father to withdraw him from school and to allow him to arrange for private tutors to educate him.

In his youth he had a voracious appetite for knowledge and was constantly reading. Solita Solano records Gurdjieff as saying he used to read five or six books a day.[5] Although this may sound like another one of his exaggerations, this could easily be achieved with a photographic memory, which he evidently had. She also records Gurdjieff saying, "...can remember a page of writing, such specific have my memory, even where on page come a certain thought, even I can remember mistakes in printing—exact where on page they come."[6]

But he did not gain his knowledge from reading alone. He never missed an opportunity to question people he met who had information of interest. He was constantly asking people of different faiths and nationalities about their culture. He was constantly traveling to get information that could not be found locally. And in the process he picked up some 18 languages. This may sound like another exaggeration but there is really no reason to negate this. Many people have such a capacity and Gurdjieff certainly had the opportunity. Also, many of the languages he knew were likely from only a few language families. So having learned one would have made it easier to learn the next.

And considering Gurdjieff's father again, his genius was likely received hereditarily from his father.

To be clear, however, this is not to say that a great intellect is a necessity for spiritual work. The arrogance that often accompanies such a trait can just as easily be an obstacle. The specific characteristics of one's individual mind have no bearing whatsoever on the ability to be present to that mind and the world about. It is not the mind that is aware; it is consciousness that is aware. The mind certainly generates impressions which fall upon consciousness, but in no way, shape or form does it possess consciousness. Rather, consciousness possesses the mind and is the same in everyone.[7]

The only purpose in discussing intellect here is as one of the factors that enabled Gurdjieff to begin his quest at such a young age. He had ripened for life at an earlier age than most, even by the standards of his own time. By not denying this we will be better able to ascertain various aspects of his life and companions.

More important than Gurdjieff's intelligence, however, is his practicality and insight. He knew how to get things done, and this enabled him to accomplish a great deal. P.D. Ouspensky speaks of this when remembering his time with Gurdjieff in Essentuki:

> I always have a very strange feeling when I remember this period. On this occasion we spent about six weeks in Essentuki. But this now seems to be altogether incredible. Whenever I chance to speak with any one of those who were there they can hardly believe that it lasted only six weeks. It would be difficult even in six years to find room for everything that was connected with this time, to such an extent was it filled.[8]

This, by the way, is exactly why biographers such as James Webb and James Moore worked with an earlier date of birth for Gurdjieff. It is difficult to place everything he achieved in a shorter timespan.

Now let us look at Gurdjieff's own telling of some of his history. In the text of his that follows, there are hints regarding

16

his early years not provided in the series *All and Everything*.

_____

[1] Manana Khomeriki, "About the Origins of Gurdjieff and His Activities in Georgia," in *Gurdjieff in Tiflis*, eds. Constance A. Jones & Levan Khetaguri (Tbilisi: Shota Rustaveli Theatre and Film University, 2008), 30–31.

[2] Clifford Sharp, "The 'Forest Philosophers,'" *Gurdjieff International Review* 1, no. 4 (Summer 1998), 44. Reprinted from the March 3, 1923 issue of *The New Statesman*. My italics.

[3] Thomas & Olga de Hartmann, *Our Life with Mr Gurdjieff* (Sandpoint: Sandpoint Press, 2008), 256.

[4] J.G. Bennett, *Witness: The Story of a Search* (London: Hodder and Stoughton, 1962), 64.

[5] Solita Solano, et al., *Gurdjieff and the Women of the Rope* (London: Book Studio, 2012), 173.

[6] Ibid., 117.

[7] Here I speak of the "mind" in terms of what Gurdjieff called the lower centers and equate consciousness to what he calls the higher centers. In Buddhist thought the mind is said to include consciousness.

[8] P.D. Ouspensky, *In Search of the Miraculous:Fragments of an Unknown Teaching* (New York: Harcourt, Brace & Co., 1949), 346.

## THE HISTORY OF THE INSTITUTE

The very beginning of the Institute can be considered to have been in 1895 when three tourists met by chance in Egypt by the pyramids. Discovering that all three were Russians they became close friends and decided to continue their tour of Egypt together. Their conversations while wandering up and down the Nile and exploring the ruins of ancient Thebes enabled each of them to realize that the questions they touched upon had, as proved later, interested all the three for quite some time already.

All three had traveled a great deal before that meeting.

The first, Prince L., had already been in India, Tibet and Balochistan. Since he was wealthy and an ardent seeker, he had managed to visit places where no European had previously penetrated. He had begun his travels ten years prior, immediately after a misfortune that had befallen him—the loss of a loved one—which made him take up spiritualism. Since he was a man of inquiring mind, his initial enthusiasm had soon given way to a serious search into these matters. Finding nothing satisfactory in his surroundings and the available literature, and influenced by the opinion current in Europe that India was the land of miracles where answers to these questions could be found, he decided to go there. India disappointed him, but he did not lose hope in finding what he sought. From that moment his travels began, during which he only rarely came back to Russia on short visits.

The second was from his youth, attracted to archeology. Since he was an energetic man, immediately on finishing his university studies he was appointed the assistant curator of a well known museum and was often sent on archeological expeditions. Before our meeting he had visited excavated sites in Delhi, the Hindu Kush valley, Ani (Armenia), Babylon and others. At that moment he was on an archeological excavation in Old Thebes. Personally, however, he was chiefly interested in dolmens, about which he was collecting as much information as possible, sparing neither time nor money.

The third and youngest of them, Gurdjieff, was chiefly interested in magic. Having chanced to spend his youth among such peoples as the Yezidis, the Aisors, and the Annicles,[1] he constantly came face to face with phenomena and traditions which no enquiring mind could ever pass by without innumerable questions.

The following may serve as illustrations of such phenomena. A circle traced around a Yezidi does not allow him to step over it, not because of religious superstition, but in actual fact. Among the Annicles a girl to be married is subjected to certain manipulations, after which she is thrown into the water, which results in a phenomenon inexplicable to European science—the girl's weight proves lighter than water and she does not sink. If she sinks it is proof that she does not belong to the tribe. Aisors have a phenomenon of clairvoyance (*egungashah*). Investigations have shown that not a single case of such clairvoyance proved false. And so on.

The critical, incredulous and, at the same time, inquiring mind of Gurdjieff could not pass by such phenomena without determining its explanation. With this purpose in mind, he devoted himself to studies which would explain them—physics, chemistry, mechanics, psychology, etc. But the study of all available literature brought him no desired result, for from the point of view of these sciences the phenomena which interested him defied natural laws. But this did not make the fact of their existence any the less real, and so Gurdjieff never abandoned his original desire. Giving up books, he began to look for people who could satisfy his thirst. This was the beginning of his wanderings, which led him, before that meeting, to Persia, Afghanistan and Turkey. The same purpose brought him to Egypt.

Exchanging their impressions and the material acquired in the course of their travels, the three disagreed on many points but were unanimous in their conviction, based on their observations and studies, that there had existed another civilisation which, in the domain of science and art, had been much more advanced than that of the present, and that of the majority of phenomena which modern science is unable to explain had been known in ancient times. Having no date for the study of that civilization, and the constant obstacle of lack of information in general, clearly proved to them the necessity of some all-embracing philosophy. However, three people could not master the study of all religions, histories and special sciences in the course of a short life. So this brought them to the necessity of collective work—that is, the necessity of recruiting people of different professions and perspectives.

But since the knowledge of numerous specialists lacking interest in the above-mentioned search would have been of no use, a new plan suggested itself—to find suitable people open to our direction and advisory and material assistance.

For this purpose they separated and went in different directions, as a result of which fifteen other people joined them, among whom were people of Greco-Russian Orthodox, Catholic, Armenian Orthodox, Jewish and Buddhist faiths, and representatives of medicine, mechanics, chemistry, natural history, astronomy, archeology and philology. Moreover, each of them was obliged to study some craft. Among them were also women.

A few years later they all met by prearrangement in Persia and from there, armed with all the necessary knowledge, they left in 1899 partly for India, through the Pamirs, Tibet and Siam, and partly for Palestine through Turkey and Arabia.

For certain reasons, the meeting place was to be in Cabul in Afghanistan where, a few years later, twelve people arrived instead of eighteen. (Six had perished on the way.)

They decided to go to Chitral. Just before their departure the prince died, and soon after they set out on their journey seven of them were captured by the savage nomad tribe of Afridi.[2] So they never reached their goal and rejoined the others only much later. Thus only four people reached Chitral and, having fulfilled the task they had set themselves, returned three years later to Cabul.

Here they again began to collect suitable people, set up house together, and thereby laid the foundation of the Institute. The number of people around them increased rapidly and they passed on to these new people the results of their long and arduous search.

In 1910 they began their activity in Russia, where three of them met in Petersburg: Gurdjieff, a Persian named Tachtamiroff, and Dr Ornitopulo. Groups were formed in Petersburg and in Moscow where Gurdjieff later settled.

The war and the revolution that followed tore many people away from groups, and in 1916 those who remained met in the Caucasus where Gurdjieff had himself relocated.

Here was the formative founding of The International Fellowship of Ideas and Labor for the purpose of carrying on with the same problems and investigations. Along with this fellowship, a school was founded under the name of the Institute for the Harmonious Development of Man.

The curriculum of the Institute and the aims and on which it was founded are appended.[3]

From there the members of the International Fellowship organized a scientific expedition. Owing to political upheavals the school was disbanded and only a small group of people remained.

The members of the expedition settled in Tiflis and again formed a branch of the Institute for the Harmonious Development of Man. The number of pupils soon swelled to 500, but here too political events forced the founders of the Institute to move, this time to Constantinople. Here members of the Essentuki and Tiflis branches gradually began to assemble and a new branch of the Institute was opened.

Turkish authorities showed great interest in the Institute

and urged the founders to open the Institute in Kadikoy (the Asiatic part of the town) where several demonstrations were staged at their request.

The defeat of Wrangel's army, the flood of refugees from Russia, and the economic crisis in Constantinople, then forced the founders to accept an offer to open the Institute in Germany.

But in view of the economic situation and other political considerations, they abandoned the idea of opening the Institute in accordance with the full curriculum, as was originally intended. Instead they contented themselves with opening a home for those members and pupils who were unable to follow the main body of the Institute which received at the time an offer to come to England. A year before, an English group of about a hundred people had been formed to study the materials and principles of the Institute under the guidance of one of the older pupils of the Institute—Mr Ouspensky, a writer and professor of psychology.

But in view of the fact that the Institute bears an international character and has members of all nationalities, and owing to geographical and other considerations, Paris, as the world's center, was considered the only place where the central branch of the Institute could be opened.

*G. Gurdjieff*

---

[1] There is no known people who call themselves Annicles. One possibility, however, is that it is a word of Gurdjieff's creation to describe the descendants of the people of Ani, most of whom represent Turkey's Christian minority, as distinct from Armenian nationals.

[2] An Afghan tribe.

[3] These are not reprinted here.

Most of Gurdjieff's early typescripts, such as this one dated 1922, were translated by Olga de Hartmann, whose English was good but far from fluent. As such, I took the liberty of editing the text to make it more readable. The original, unedited text can be found in *Gurdjieff's Early Talks 1914–1931* (London: Book Studio, 2014).

*W.M. Flinders Petrie*

## SKRIDLOV

In *Meetings with Remarkable Men,* as well as in "The History of the Institute," it is said that Professor Skridlov, another of Gurdjieff's essence friends, was Russian. He was one of the three (the other two being Prince Lubovedsky and Gurdjieff himself) who founded The Seekers of Truth upon their meeting in Giza.

Although, according to Gurdjieff, he was not one of the seekers who journeyed to "Sarmung", and therefore his identification is less important to research into Gurdjieff's time in Tibet, if his identity could be established, and evidence of some sort of relationship eventually found to those who were on that journey, it would lend greater credence to the identifications of Lubovedsky and Soloviev later proposed here. As well, later on we will explore a possible link between the ancient Egyptian and Tibetan civilizations. So, his identity is not entirely out of scope.

A useful hint regarding the professor's identity can be found in Olga de Hartmann's unpublished autobiography, *What For?* Of particular interest is an essay she wrote on the Institute's history as an assignment Gurdjieff had given to his troupe while in Essentuki (probably early 1918). This essay also appeared in *Our Life with Mr Gurdjieff,* but in a severely edited form. In the original version of the essay, Skridlov is said to be English. In the published version, Skridlov's nationality is completely edited out, apparently not to conflict with other texts in which he is said to be Russian. As we will see later, Gurdjieff frequently changed certain details of his life events in order to conceal information and/or to adjust them so that they would metaphorically convey some idea he had in mind. Back in 1918, Gurdjieff apparently spoke of Skridlov as an Englishman.

It actually makes a lot more sense that Skridlov was English. Egypt was under British rule at the time and there were many more English archeologists engaging in excavations there than Russian. One notable exception, however, is Vladimir Golenishchev, who made over sixty journeys to Egypt. But he does not appear to have held any sort of faculty post until 1915 when he became the founding head of the Department of Egyptology at Cairo University—a post offered him in recognition of his earlier achievements. The sixty-some journeys accomplished before then were all self-funded; they were not funded by any institution. Golenishchev was more of a collector/merchant and self-taught scholar of Egyptology.

Of the many British Egyptologists of the time there is one in particular that stands out—W. M. Flinders Petrie. For one thing, his age was about right. Gurdjieff says that Skridlov was much older than he was. Petrie was born in 1853, which makes him 24 years older.

For another, Petrie was a professor of archeology as Gurdjieff states of Skridlov. Not every Egyptologist was. Some, like Golenishchev, were archeologists but not professors. Others were professors, or perhaps museum curators or researchers, but never attended an excavation. Petrie held the post of Professor of Egyptology at University College London from 1892 until he retired in 1933.

Also significant is that Petrie performed his first excavation when but a child, as Gurdjieff states in "The History of the Institute" that the unnamed professor of archeology that he met "was *from his youth* attracted to archeology." This is not the case for every archeology professor.

Petrie's travels correlate with Gurdjieff's account too. Gurdjieff says that soon after their initial meeting outside of

Cairo in 1895, he met Skridlov in Thebes for an excavation. According to Petrie's journal, on his journey to Thebes, he made a stop in Cairo December 3–9, 1895. The Thebes excavation began on December 16 and went on for about three months.[1] It seems as though Petrie invited Gurdjieff along but Gurdjieff was not able to accompany Petrie on his train for one reason or another. He may have had other matters to attend to before being able to join, or simply could not afford the fare and opted to journey to Thebes by other means.

Also suggestive that Skridlov was English is the name. Unlike the apparent nicknames Lubovedsky and Soloviev, the name Skridlov does not give an immediate impression of the person's character. The origin of the name, which means a stack of hay, does not appear to say anything either. However, Gurdjieff may have adopted the name Skridlov to suggest the English word *screed*. In "The History of the Institute," Gurdjieff refers to Lubovedsky as Prince L. but gives no name whatsoever for the professor of archeology. This suggests that Lubovedsky was a name actually used amongst the party, but Skridlov was not, as it was adopted only during the writing of *Meetings with Remarkable Men*. It is therefore possible that Gurdjieff consulted A. R. Orage (who was the editor) for English words of interest to come up with a name. It is quite possible that he wanted to use an English word to formulate the name in order to bury a suggestion that the professor was actually English when he says otherwise. Furthermore, the word *screed* does in fact seem to say something about Petrie. It suggests a person who gave long talks or wrote rather long works. There are three Egyptologists in particular who can be noted for their prolific output. The first of the three, E. A. Wallis Budge, can be ruled out as a candidate for Skridlov because he never journeyed to Egypt. The second, Gaston Maspero, can also be ruled out as he was French. The third is Petrie. Regarding Petrie's output, Eric Uphill's bibliography of his work contains 1024 citations, 102 of which are books.[2]

Also quite interesting is that Gurdjieff and Petrie had similar upbringings and mental capacities. It can easily be imagined that Petrie saw something of his younger self in

Gurdjieff, who was still but a teen at the time, and wanted to take him under his wing. Like Gurdjieff, Petrie too was tutored at home, learned several languages, appears to have had a photographic memory, and began excavating at a young age. These experiences and traits of Gurdjieff were discussed previously. Let us now look at Petrie's.

Firstly, Petrie's father taught him Christian theology himself. Besides having a similar acquaintance with the subject, this also suggests a similar admiration for their fathers. These studies began for Petrie at the age of six. Also significant is that Petrie's father would later teach him to survey.

At that age his great-aunt began tutoring him too. She taught him reading, writing, grammar, arithmetic, Hebrew, Greek, and hieroglyphics. As well, she taught the young boy Christian theology when his father was not available. At the age of eight, another tutor provided instruction in Latin and French, and continued his education in Greek. Apparently, like Gurdjieff, Petrie too was a polyglot.

At the age of ten Petrie visited a local geological museum and also went on a family trip to see the Acropolis of Athens. At the age of 13 he acquired an interest in antiques and numismatics. He was particularly interested in Greek coins.

At the age of 14 Petrie began surveying earthworks sites near his home. The following year he found himself interested in Euclid and read all he could of the ancient mathematician's work.

When he was 21, Petrie surveyed Stonehenge with his father. He was disappointed to have learned that the map room at the British Museum lacked up-to-date plans of Britain's best-known sites and set out to make one himself. He was unable to complete the task then but returned to the site three years later to do so. Between 1875 and 1880 he made ten expeditions to survey other English dolmen and earthworks sites. This is significant because in "The History of the Institute" Gurdjieff says that Skridlov "was chiefly interested in dolmens."[3]

After completing the plans of Stonehenge in 1877, that same year, Petrie donated the plans made thus far as a result of his expeditions to the map room of the British Museum. The

28

portfolio included the plans of about 40 earthworks and dolmens. As a result, he was invited by the Royal Archaeological Institute to present a paper on metrology (the study of measurement). Thus was the beginning of his career.

As to what gives the impression that Petrie had a photographic memory, Francis Galton notes that Petrie "habitually works out sums by aid of an imaginary sliding rule, which he sets in the desired way and reads off mentally."[4]

It is necessary to deviate for a moment because Gurdjieff says that he and Skridlov spoke in Italian to one another and there is no indication that Petrie spoke the language. However, there is reason to believe that the two seekers actually communicated in French, and Gurdjieff wanted to conceal that fact to make it more difficult to determine Skridlov's identity. It is odd that also in *Meetings with Remarkable Men,* the only European country he mentions visiting in his travels is Italy (Rome specifically), but the only time Italy is mentioned in *Beelzebub's Tales* is a brief visit he supposedly made between his institute's existence in Germany and France (which would be 1922). But in the "France" chapter of *Beelzebub's Tales,* Gurdjieff's alter ego says, "Although earlier... I had sometimes been in just that community of France...,"[5] suggesting that he was there in his seeking years, before relocating his institute to Fontainebleau in 1922. In fact, in *Life Is Real Only Then When "I Am,"* Gurdjieff mentions that in his early years he had spent time in Paris. He mentions the Montmartre district specifically.

And he says nothing whatsoever about speaking Italian in *Beelzebub's Tales.* The only place he mentions Italian is in *Meetings with Remarkable Men.* Besides saying that it was the language in which he and Skridlov spoke to one another, in that same chapter he explains, "I knew Arabic and Greek well, and also Italian, which was indispensable then for speaking to Europeans." But Italian is not widely spoken amongst Europeans. At the time, French was considered the lingua franca. All educated European travelers learned French to enable their travels.

There is also something peculiar about Gurdjieff's account of his time in Rome. This is where he became reacquainted with Vitvitskaia while working as a shoe-shiner. He attracted customers by having devised tubular headphones for his phonograph that enabled his customers to enjoy some music while being serviced. The one piece of music he mentions playing for his customers is "La Marseillaise"—the French national anthem. It seems more likely that he would have been playing "La Marseillaise" somewhere in France. This is not to suggest, however, that he was not in Rome as he states, since he mentions having been to Italy and Switzerland those early years in the third series. Only that he may be blurring together his trips to Italy and France in his account as a shoe-shiner in Rome. At the very least it shows that he obtained the recording while in France. Regarding Switzerland, he could have communicated in any of the nation's languages, including French.

Certainly growing up in the Caucasus there would have been much more literature available in French than Italian, and particularly in the subjects that interested Gurdjieff. It seems that at the very least Gurdjieff would have been able to read French well. How well he spoke French is another matter. But it seems likely enough that he spoke French well enough to be a tour guide who knew his subject well. Italian is a language he probably learned from the Italians he mentions having met during his travels. It is unlikely Italian was a scholastic study as French and German likely were for him.

Returning to Petrie, regarding his literary work, there is one book in particular that is quite interesting in connection to Gurdjieff—*Religion and Conscience in Ancient Egypt*. In it he offers a view of conscience that is similar to Gurdjieff's. It is not exactly the same, but it is easy to see how Petrie may have planted the seed for Gurdjieff's understanding of the subject. In particular, Petrie explains how conscience is something innate in us that needs to bloom, rather than something learned from the culture one lives in. A relevant excerpt follows.

30

[1] Egyptophiles may be interested in reading Petrie's book on his finds from this excavation—*Six Temples at Thebes.*

[2] Eric P. Uphill, "A Bibliography of Sir William Matthew Flinders Petrie (1853–1942)," *Journal of Near Eastern Studies* 31, no. 4 (1972), 356–79.

[3] Those interested in dolmens may wish to read Petrie's *Stonehenge: Plans, Description and Theories.*

[4] Francis Galton, *Inquiries into Human Facility and Its Development* (London: J.M. Dent & Sons, 1919), 66.

[5] G. Gurdjieff, *All and Everything: First Series: Beelzebub's Tales to His Grandson* (New York: Harcourt, Brace & Co., 1950), 664.

Photograph of Petrie sourced from Wikimedia.

## Conscience

Conscience is that mass of the intuitions of right and wrong, which are born in the structure of the thoughts, though they may often need development before the latent structure becomes active. A plant does not put out its leaves and flowers all at once; yet they are latent, and are inevitable if any development of growth takes place. And thus, perhaps, some can look back to a time when only one or two elements of conscience were yet active in their minds, just as a sense of justice and injustice, and they reflected then that no act would seem wrong or shocking if it was not unjust. Yet later on, as the mind grew (and growth or death is the choice to the mind, though the body may continue an animal existence), the various other elements of conscience unfolded gradually from some central stem (such as that of justice) which had first sprung up.

It is needful to remember thus that conscience is an inherited development, as much an inheritance in the structure of the brain as any other special modification is in the body— needful because in the consideration of the springs of action it has been generally the habit to deal with the individual as if he had a perfectly blank mind, and was only impressed by the facts of life around him in a perfectly calculating and unbiassed manner. On the contrary the untrained mind teems with prospects of every kind, possible and impossible, at every change of surrounding, and acts far more by impulse and intuition than by precise calculations of theoretical right or utility. This is seen most plainly in the waywardness of children and savages; the ideas of all kinds of possibilities are present, and the growth of conscience and of habit is not yet strong enough to determine uniformly which opening shall be followed. Thus we may look on each person as only a fragment of the common life of mankind, inheriting in his brain-structure a tendency to certain lines of action and certain choices between opposing claims. He is the heir of all his ancestors, and specially of those nearest to him; for, as Galton has shown by physical tests, inheritance of special characters rapidly diminishes in each succeeding generation, and there is a constant tendency thus to revert to an average type.

*W.M. Flinders Petrie*

"Conscience" is an excerpt taken from *Religion and Conscience in Ancient Egypt* by W.M. Flinders Petrie (London: Methuen & Co., 1898).

## MAGICAL TIBET

Gurdjieff was fascinated by the mysterious and by magic in particular. Magic was the subject of his particular *magnetic center*—his formative entranceway leading towards a true spiritual path. He wanted to be able to realize real magic himself. He also studied sensational tricks, but this appears to have been more a consequence of a search for true magic than any genuine interest itself. He needed to be able to distinguish the real from the false in order to eliminate the frauds while seeking out those who had authentic abilities he could learn from.

Perhaps he also took advantage of his knowledge of various tricks in order to earn the money needed for his expeditions. He certainly used his cunning to earn great sums without having to work endlessly. Still, such a practice would only have been secondary. As soon as he had enough money he would quit. He was far from a greedy man interested in mere wealth. He had grander ways in which he wanted to engage his time.

In the preceding "History of the Institute," he cites a few examples of what he considers to be genuine magic. One is the Yezidi unable to escape a circle drawn round him on the ground. Another is the Annicle bride who is unable to sink when thrown in water. Yet another is Aysorian clairvoyance.

P.D. Ouspensky relates some miraculous things he witnessed Gurdjieff perform, particularly the episode when

Gurdjieff transferred thought to him. C.S. Nott suggests that Gurdjieff had foresight of his automobile accident.[1] Nott was also convinced that he had witnessed real magic intermingled with the tricks performed during the movements demonstration he attended. Then there is Gurdjieff's knowledge of hypnotism and its application towards healing. This is how he healed his friend Soloviev of alcoholism. Some of these abilities he may have learned while in Baku. In *Meetings with Remarkable Men* he mentions studying an ancient Persian form of magic there.

Certainly with his interest in magic, Gurdjieff would have been keenly attracted to the magical side of Tibetan Buddhism with all its stories of lamas and yogis with great powers. But before we can discuss this subject, it seems necessary to convey something of the ordinariness of magic so as not to sensationalize it. To a large extent, real magic only seems sensational to us Westerners who have dulled to the magic of life. To Tibetans who see magic in everything, who see magic regularly, thought transference, prophesy and finding *termas* is not much more spectacular. These things are still spectacular to them, but no more so than the sunset or a snowfall or a smile. They have not lost that youthful wonder which perceives magic in the ordinary. Related to this, in explaining the concept of *yeshen,* which he says literally means the "supreme divine" principle, Chögyam Trungpa said:

> Bön, unlike the religious outgrowths of the Aryan culture—especially Hinduism, Buddhism, and Jainism in their quasi-popular forms—gives little heed to the pursuit of salvation through the practice of austerities. Bön philosophy speaks of Yeshen as being reflected in the interplay between heaven and earth. Thus the Bön aspirant seeks magical power through union with the Yeshen nature as manifested in mountains, trees, lakes, and rivers—all of which are impressively present in Tibet. There is a strong orientation toward waterfalls, falling snow, clouds, and mist arising from the deep valleys, since all these are regarded as activities of Yeshen. Belief in the magic of these natural features is paramount.[2]

Certainly there are many advanced spiritual teachers who are known to have attained various *siddhis*, but these powers are only viewed as extraordinary from the perspective of delusion. To these individuals who have seen through delusion and know reality, parapsychological abilities are merely an aspect of perceiving that reality, of perceiving the interdependence of all things. From this perspective the lack of these abilities is actually something of an illness. Somewhat related to the ordinariness of magic, C. S. Nott records Gurdjieff having said, "A man must be able to *do*. Magic, real magic, is rooted in *doing*."[3]

But because our Western culture sensationalizes magic, Tibetans have become sensitive about the subject and hesitate conveying this aspect of their culture to us. As Thubten Jigme Norbu says, "Tibet is not a land of saints or miracles. It is a land of people committed to the path of religion, who follow that path not as a mournful duty but with enthusiasm and great happiness. It is also a land where we can always expect the help of our protector, Chenresig, so long as we deserve it. If that is a miracle, then Tibet is a land of miracles, for Chenresig is always revealing himself, guiding and helping."[4]

Similarly, Chögyam Trungpa said, "From the point of view of vajrayana, real magic, or *siddhi* in Sanskrit, is the ability to work with and tame one's mind."[5]

Gurdjieff also seems to have shunned his magical abilities. They simply were not the point. He used them as seemed necessary for a particular purpose, but magic was never a purpose itself (that is, in his adult life, after his youthful pursuit of it).

I too do not want to make a big deal of the subject. The only intention here is to recognize magic as an aspect of Gurdjieff's search and see what forms he may have acquired while in Tibet. And much more important than the acquisition of such powers is being able to perceive the magic that continually surrounds us.

First let us look at one instance that Gurdjieff describes having witnessed in Tibet. The telling that is about to be related is what Tibetans call self-arising phenomena, which is when a scene suddenly takes on a miraculous appearance. Frequent examples are a rainbow appearing at an auspicious moment or clouds appearing in the form of a *yidam*. These phenomena often occur during the cremation ceremony of a great master. Gurdjieff's account is reproduced later in its entirety in the chapter "A Tibetan Ritual." In it he describes a sonic form of self-arising phenomena. As he describes there, "One arrives in the foothills and hears the music. But beautiful like that, never. Truly it was celestial music. Well, one heard the music but saw nothing. Everywhere, all around, there were mountains and that was all. How and from where could this music come? How was it possible?"

Regarding magical abilities that Gurdjieff may have acquired while in Tibet, thought transference is one. Although not exactly the same, Jeremy Hayward, a close student of Trungpa Rinpoche, describes an instance of Trungpa transferring thought to him which is somewhat similar to an instance with Gurdjieff that Ouspensky relates. In Ouspensky's account, he hears Gurdjieff's voice in his mind posing him various questions to which he responds aloud.[6] In Hayward's account, Trungpa transfers a thought to him which he believes to be his own.[7]

Mipham the Great was a Tibetan *tulku* who was a big influence on those who will later be suggested to have been Gurdjieff's teachers, and as such Gurdjieff may also have met. One of his many accomplishments was the discovery of various magical practices. One of these, the use of a mirror for divination, was transmitted to Trungpa Rinpoche through his teacher Karsey Kongtrül. Trungpa speaks about using it while escaping from Tibet during the Chinese invasion. He would consult his mirror to determine what locality to head to next to and when. Although it is unknown if Gurdjieff used the same technique, all accounts indicate that he somehow had a keen sense of imminent danger and an insight as to where would be best to go next while leading his entourage out of Russia during the revolution. Also indicative of his foresight abilities is that towards the end of his life he predicted that his student Yahne Le Toumelin would go to Tibet in 21 years time. Although Tibet was then closed to Westerners and she actually went to Darjeeling where there was a large Tibetan refugee community, the timeframe was entirely accurate.

While Tibetan Medicine is largely scientific, there are also treatments that might be considered more magical. As explained in more detail in the chapter on Tibetan Medicine, Gurdjieff seems to have had the ability to practice such a treatment known as *Tsa-rLung*. Really, *Tsa-rLung* is a yoga practice that enables the utilization of certain energies. Such yoga practices are often regarded as "real" magic because they have no apparent explanation.

Yet another Tibetan yoga that Gurdjieff apparently learned is *tummo*—a practice that enables the body to generate enough heat to melt ice and stay warm in the coldest of climates (a valuable skill to have living in the Himalayas). *Tummo* is one of the practices that Kagyu founder Marpa brought from India to Tibet and, as will be shown later, Gurdjieff was familiar with other teachings of Marpa. According to Mavis McIntosh, Alfred Orage pulled him up to the open deck of a bus on a bitter cold night and not only spoke to him of *tummo*, but through his calm suggested he was practicing it himself.[8] Who besides Gurdjieff could have acquainted Orage with this yoga?

It is very likely that Gurdjieff learned many more practices such as these while in Tibet. As was said earlier, he was very discreet about his abilities. Although the contents here are all that could be discerned, they are sufficient enough to demonstrate Gurdjieff's interest. So, let us continue on to the next subject of our exploration of Gurdjieff's searches.

¹ C.S. Nott, *Teachings of Gurdjieff: The Journal of a Pupil* (New York: Samuel Weiser, 1974), 80–81.

² Chögyam Trungpa, *The Collected Works of Chögyam Trungpa: Volume 3* (Boston: Shambhala Publications, 2003), 485–86. (*The Heart of the Buddha,* Appendix 1.)

³ C.S. Nott, *Teachings of Gurdjieff: The Journal of a Pupil* (New York: Samuel Weiser, 1974), 223.

⁴ Thubten Jigme Norbu & Colin M. Turnbull, *Tibet: An Account of the History, the Religion and the People of Tibet* (New York: Simon and Schuster, 1968), 36–37.

⁵ Chögyam Trungpa, *The Collected Works of Chögyam Trungpa: Volume 3* (Boston: Shambhala Publications, 2003), 432. (*The Heart of the Buddha,* Chapter 7.)

⁶ P.D. Ouspensky, *In Search of the Miraculous:Fragments of an Unknown Teaching* (New York: Harcourt, Brace & Co., 1949), 262.

⁷ Jeremy Hayward, *Warrior King of Shambhala: Remembering Chögyam Trungpa* (Boston: Wisdom Publications, 2008), 34.

⁸ Louise Welch, *Orage with Gurdjieff in America* (Boston: Routledge & Kegan Paul, 1982), 33.

## In Search of Shambhala

Shambhala, according to Tibetan myth, is an ancient kingdom whose entire population was enlightened. It was a utopian city where all its citizens worked together to achieve its ideals. It was an aristocracy with a hierarchical structure, but the king and his nobles worked in the best interest of the commoner and the kingdom as a whole, and the commoners in turn were happy to do their part. Everyone accepted his burden and responsibility with no sense of inferiority or superiority—in short, without any form of self-preoccupation that ego typically expresses. No role in society was considered better or worse than any other. The various roles citizens found themselves in were accepted as their fate, and citizens understood and perceived their roles in the context of the society as a whole. In this sense the society was something of a democracy—not in the sense of decision-making, but in the sense of the perception of equal worth its citizens had of one another.

Tibetans seem to understand the Shambhala story as allegory, as a factual kingdom, and as a kingdom existing on some etheric realm, all at the same time and differing amongst each other only as regards emphasis.

No doubt Gurdjieff would have been keenly interested in the spiritual teaching of a society in which everyone was enlightened—in a teaching adaptable to any role or psychological makeup, in a teaching so effective. He obviously appreciated the truths to be found in any religion, but he was especially intent on awakening himself, and it seems that to him, discovering some remnant of Shambhala would provide the best guarantee. Any clue regarding Shambhala would have been impossible for him to leave unexplored.

In fact, there is evidence that suggests that finding Shambhala was one of the intentions of the Seekers of Truth —perhaps their chief intention. As Alfred Orage relates in his commentary on *Beelzebub's Tales*, Gurdjieff wasted years hunting down leads fabricated by Madame Blavatsky.[1] One such wild goose chase appears to be a search for the historic Shambhala in the middle of the Gobi. The idea that Shambhala lies somewhere beneath the Gobi was first put forth by Blavatsky, and as Gurdjieff relates in *Meetings with Remarkable Men*, the Seekers once made an expedition in search of an ancient city beneath the Gobi which had to be abandoned. Blavatsky may have formulated the idea based on the discovery of the Mogao Caves located near the western edge of the Gobi desert. The caves are a complex of 500 Buddhist temples occupied between the fourth and eleventh centuries, and under Tibetan occupation part of the time. Although the Seekers abandoned that expedition, Gurdjieff evidently later found evidence of a much older site in the Gobi, as in *Beelzebub's Tales* he speaks of an ancient Gobi city he calls Gob and the surrounding country as Goblandia. In recent times archeologists have in fact found such a city.

Another attempt at finding Shambhala may have been the Seekers' expedition to Siberia. Another belief about the location of Shambhala is that it lies in the Altai mountains. Best known for a search of Shambhala in the Altai mountains is Nicholas Roerich. But it seems as though Gurdjieff may have sought for Shambhala in the Altai before Roerich. In the "Professor Skridlov" chapter he mentions an expedition through Siberia which began from Orenburg but gives no more detail than that. Yet if Skridlov was involved, it can be assumed the expedition had an archeological purpose. And in nomadic Siberia there is little to be found archaeologically.

Yet another theory equates Shambhala with the ancient

kingdom of Uddiyana, which was located in what is today called the Swat Valley—part of the northwestern region of Pakistan. Both Swat and Chitral are part of the greater Hindu Kush region that Gurdjieff journeyed through. Quite interestingly, J.G. Bennett relates that Gurdjieff "asserted that there was a special concentration of spiritual power in a certain place between Tibet and Afghanistan."[2] This is roughly where Uddiyana lies. By speaking of a *special concentration of spiritual power* there, Gurdjieff seems to be saying not only that he *believed* that an enlightened society once occupied the region, but that he was able to *perceive* the energy that remains from their collective spiritual practice.

When Buddha Shakyamuni passed through the kingdom, the king at the time, **Indrabhuti**, took the opportunity to beseech him for a spiritual practice which would not require the abandonment of worldly pursuits. His wish was granted and the kingdom thrived thereafter as a Buddhist Mecca.

Buddhism is thought of today primarily as a monastic teaching which requires the taking of vows to be strictly practiced. Yet the form of Buddhism practiced in Uddiyana was such that anyone could practice it seriously in pursuit of enlightenment. The teaching did not have the air of secrecy and exclusivity which the monastic forms have. It was available to everyone. So, from the perspective of the Tibetan Buddhist, it is somewhat plausible that all of Uddiyana was enlightened as is said of Shambhala. The other reason which many Tibetans have for believing Uddiyana to be Shambhala is that Buddhism is known to have entered Tibet from there.

Although Gurdjieff never mentions the Swat Valley or Uddiyana by name, it lies in the general region of the expedition described in the "Piotr Karpenko" chapter where the Seekers lose a member as well as their guide in an avalanche. The archeologist Skridlov was on that journey too.

Also very significant is that Uddiyanan Buddhism is entirely suggestive of Gurdjieff's insistence on practice while engaging in the varied situations of a normal life as opposed to practice in seclusion, as well as Gurdjieff's understanding that Buddha taught his disciples to practice in life, and the idea of practice in isolation was a later distortion of his teaching—a view which he expresses in the chapter "The First Visit of Beelzebub to India."

To understand what Gurdjieff is trying to relate about his life it is necessary to look at what he is saying from a macroscopic perspective. For when looking with a focused microscopic attention, the blatantly obvious is usually entirely missed. By zooming out various things come into focus. This is probably yet another truth he wants us to see. It is certainly the purpose of the ray of creation: to get us to see how everything is interconnected; to enable us to perceive the whole, the unity of all existence. The details are less significant. Also relevant is that there are other instances of knowledge hidden in this fashion in Gurdjieff's writings. With this in mind, let us look again at what Gurdjieff says of the three expeditions I suggest were in quest of Shambhala.

Gurdjieff mentions virtually no details whatsoever regarding the Siberian expedition. On the Gobi expedition the only significant occurrence related is the highly unbelievable death of Soloviev. (Mauled by a camel!?) Why mention either of these expeditions at all? Could Gurdjieff's intention be only to leave some markers pointing at Shambhala?

The Hindu Kush expedition is quite an adventure, however. But the destination of this expedition is well concealed. It is still a Shambhala marker but unlike the other two this tale has additional purposes.

If Gurdjieff wanted he could easily have kept his past from us entirely. Clearly this is not what he wanted, and equally clearly the purpose of concealing his past was not because of any shame. As was Gurdjieff's style, he avoided spelling things out for his pupils; he preferred to say things in such a way that would allow pupils to discover what he thought they should know through their own devices. The information Gurdjieff provides in *Meetings with Remarkable Men* is entirely calculated for this purpose. It even seems that he calculated exactly how long it would take to figure out his elaborate riddle. To the best of my knowledge, the only people now alive who knew Gurdjieff are a handful who knew him as children. I would like to suggest that his puzzle was designed such that it would be solved as soon as all his direct pupils have died. He actually implies having the precision required to effectuate events with such accuracy. As Ouspensky recounts him saying, "...if one has studied thoroughly what happened yesterday, the day before yesterday, a week ago, a year, ten years ago, one can say unmistakably what will and what will not happen tomorrow."[3]

One thing for certain is that Gurdjieff knew that any teaching he brought or adapted for the West could not be monastic. It would have to be a one that could be practiced whilst in the ordinary situations of life. While he himself apparently assumed a monastic life at times, he understood that very few Westerners would be able to do so. We are simply too concerned about our careers and family.

Chögyam Trungpa Rinpoche, the former abbot of Surmang, had the same understanding. Although he came from a monastic tradition, and he initially taught his Western students at a monastery he cofounded in Scotland called Samye Ling, that all changed upon discovering a secular teaching he received as mind *terma*. *Terma* are teachings intended for future generations hidden in the past. Some *terma* are physically hidden. Mind *terma*, however, are hidden in the depths of universal consciousness (or what Jung calls the collective unconscious). Significantly, he called this teaching Shambhala Training.

Other similarities between Gurdjieff and Trungpa will be discussed later. Before continuing, let us look at the interview Bill Segal conducted with Chatral Rinpoche wherein Chatral seems to imply an understanding that Gurdjieff had spent time in the Swat Valley. This is something that Chatral evidently learned from his Tibetan peers.

[1] C.S. Nott, *Teachings of Gurdjieff: The Journal of a Pupil* (New York: Samuel Weiser, 1974), 153.
[2] J.G. Bennett, *Gurdjieff: Making a New World* (New York: Harper & Row, 1973), 96.
[3] P.D. Ouspensky, *In Search of the Miraculous:Fragments of an Unknown Teaching* (New York: Harcourt, Brace & Co., 1949), 100.

*Chatral Rinpoche*

# A Conversation with Chatral Rinpoche

*The meeting with Chatral Rinpoche, known as the "Tiger" Rinpoche, was held in a monastery located in a mountainous sector, near Darjeeling. One of Chatral's disciples took part in answering, as well as carrying the task of translating.*

Translator: Ah, you know, Rinpoche wants to know about your background, your spiritual practice that you have done so far. Particularly were you initiated by any other great teachers or were you self-developed or was the man who?... If he does not know your background, it is difficult for him to speak very frankly.

WS: I understand. *(Here, Segal speaks of his relationship to Ouspensky during the 1941–46 period in America, and to Gurdjieff in 1947–49. He also speaks about his friendship with Daisetz Suzuki, 1950–66.)** Can you tell about training or esoteric centers in Tibet?

CR: Your question is about the Swat Valley in Pakistan, which was a center of Tantra practice? Your question concerns complete solitude? Because we mentioned a Sufi monastery in Pakistan and there is a description of this Tibetan lama by the name of Dnujembe. The Swat Valley was the important spiritual center from which many teachers came.

WS: When did they visit it, in what period?

CR: In various periods... thirteenth... twelve, thirteenth century, I think.

WS: Do you think this monastery still exists?

CR: No. This monastery, this center was Tantric, for Tantric practice; most of the devotees attained enlightenment. And so you have only the ruins, nothing left. There is also a very great stupa which contained many of the favorite writings on esoteric teachings and also relics.

WS: I see.

CR: Because in some way, this is, according to some of our own writings... this center was part of India—in the old days, when they had certain territory extended far beyond present borders. And in the case of Tibet, Tibet had a very great, extensive territories under its, you know, domination. But then, due to historical developments and, ah, the decline in the power of central authority, Tibet was divided into many little principalities and each one ruled by chieftains. So maybe this was the case with India, because foreigners came and they ruled and divided the country and, you know, then the territory sort of started shrinking. So perhaps the Pakistan then was part of India.

WS: Were there descriptions of special methods, training or teaching methods, in this monastery?

CR: This Swat Valley was certainly an important esoteric center and, according to our literary sources, somewhere near there was a great teacher, Padmasambhava. And so there was a good deal of spiritual activities propagating teachings. Even earlier, this was an important center during the lifetime of
48

the Buddha. While in India, Buddha propagated the teachings conducive to the temperamental need of people. These were mainly exoteric teachings. And then, in this Swat Valley, there was a king called Indrabhuti[1] at the time of Buddha, and he wanted a very special teaching which he could practice without giving up any of his worldly ties, worldly pursuits. Therefore, our Buddha found that the king was now ripe for receiving esoteric teachings. Thereupon, Lord Buddha gave him one of the highest teachings, giving him the initiation, and also instructions, about the practice. And a number of others got initiations and, ah, they then followed the teachings, practiced, and most of them in their lifetime got enlightenment—the enlightenment not only of the spiritual but even the physical. All of them obtained their radiant forms, and all of them taking their radiant forms. The whole place was filled with great yogins.

WS: Yes.

CR: So this was important center. Once the devotees attained their enlightenment, they left no earthly remains. They were all attained, both physically and spiritually. And, ah, then there were a good many Tibetan masters who either physically visited this sacred place, or in their spiritual form, in meditative trance, they spiritually visited this place. Some of them had the power to visit spiritually; while still in their sleep they visited sacred places. These things indeed happened like that.

WS: Yes. Now the whole problem is to carry one's remembering into life. In other words, while doing everything that one does in the city, to be the same as if one were in a monastery; this is a question on which I would like your views.

CR: We have been receiving many letters from the West and all of them, young people or old people, they all are anxious to get the teachings for meditation. Now, in your own tradition, we have great many seers and teachers who had such tremendous power to read the minds of their disciples and potential disciples, that they could foresee the potential nature of each individual, each disciple. And accordingly, they could give each person teachings, maybe even just three sentences, and he would find his enlightenment. Because in such case, there was, you know, the quality of teacher, the standard of the teachers was very great.

Secondly, the requisite qualities of the disciples, the inner urge for spiritual practice, for spiritual attainment, their devotion, their determination, and, ah, all these were there. In addition, the teachings that were suitable were also readily available from these great teachers. When these factors were present, there was no problem that any individual would gain his enlightenment without difficulty. And this was the case because in each case, the disciple meets his teacher and the teacher would at once know that this was his disciple, that his destiny was to attain his spiritual perfection.

WS: ...and today?

CR: This does not exist at the present moment. We are living in the age of moral, mental, and spiritual crises—all kinds of conflicts and crises. Therefore, men like me cannot claim to have the spiritual power which would easily read the inner capacities of prospective individuals or disciples.

Therefore, for us, it is much safer to follow the path laid down by the great teachers. That is, to follow everything according to the various teachings. That is, that once a disciple is anxious to get teachings, he must find time to devote himself to his practice and to go to his teachers and get this, receive the teachings. And he must know how he should really proceed in this practice. This, with his teacher, the relationship between the two—both are very important. Therefore, once this is done, then he does not straight away meditate because the teaching given is according to his own capacity. And therefore, step by step, he is given teachings and, ah, teachings certainly are not just one simple thing. First of all, an ordinary man must first observe, he must study the nature of existence itself, which is all impermanent, undergoing always changes... tremendous changes... nothing remains stable, nothing remains constant. Therefore, including his own physical body, and even his thoughts, everything undergoing changes.

Therefore, realizing this nature of things, he must also realize the nature of existence itself, which is so full of sufferings. And, having realized this, he must find a way out of this existence. Therefore, he has to develop strong determination to work for this liberation. And, ah, therefore he goes and he receives teachings... how to carry this practice. And, after that, the guru decides when to give him initiation, which is the most important beginning of his esoteric practice, which introduces him to esoteric practice, which is not itself enough, he must have also teachings which explain the various aspects of the practice, and, ah, with which he can carry on his practice.

Now, concerning this esoteric practice, as you have probably heard, there are, in esoteric tradition, different levels of Tantra, which is exclusive to our teachings, and which is actually divided into three parts.

WS: What is common to all four sects?

CR: These are four divisions of Tantras which are common to all. In the fourth stage, according to Nyingmapa, there is one higher division and this division of Tantra can be divided into three parts, three stages. But this is just by way of explanation. But this is not part of the, part of the answer to your question, but this is what I want to explain. And in these three divisions of highest form of esoteric teachings, the one is called Mahayoga, the second one is Anuyoga, the third one is Atiyoga. And, ah, the Atiyoga deals with the highest form of esoteric teachings. Therefore it is not a question of how an individual can follow all these different stages.

Now, in order to follow and receive higher teachings, you must really, you must practice certain fundamental teachings which bring about necessary qualities within one's own mind. In other words, make himself ripe to receive high initiations, high teachings. Without preparation, practice, the teaching will not help.

WS: That's understandable. Yes.

CR: And so, in order to receive high initiations, higher esoteric practice, it is necessary to overcome the barriers—emotional, intellectual—he does certain preliminary exercises. Going through these various stages, he develops greater and greater urge and determination. And, at the same time, prepares himself for doing higher practice. So that when he completes this, he receives the higher initiation.

WS: That's the same in almost every teaching, isn't it?

CR: Well, in the Tibetan Buddhist tradition, when we talk about tradition, there is always emphasis on the need, first of all, to concentrate on the mind, the nature of mind. Whether one talks about philosophy, doctrine, either way ultimately, everything comes to this point: dealing with the mind. There are other schools like Mahamudra which also deal under various different terms with the same thing—all concerning the mind: how men should understand it, should handle it, tackle it, develop it. All this comes to the same thing, it is the same thing.

Therefore, as far as the West is concerned, especially America, which is very, very materially advanced country with all your science and technology, which has reached such a tremendous scale of development, that you can now send men and men can land on the moon, and even perhaps you could go higher and higher. But, spiritually speaking, all these are creation of mind. And you have done so much in the field of tackling... (*Conversation breaks.*)*

(*Translator speaks with admiration of American and Russian outer space achievements, but at the same time indicates that Tibet's achievements in 'going inward' were equally important. Later, he again refers to the moon landing.*)*

CR: ...but no matter what tradition, no one has ever attained awakening or enlightenment simply by reading scriptures.

We have so many great masters through the history who all received the teachings from their teachers, teachers who had attained their enlightenment. There are great maharishis, great teachers who displayed their miraculous powers.

But there are equally large number of teachers who did not display such miraculous powers. But it doesn't mean that those who displayed miraculous powers had greater awakening or greater spiritual power than those who did not. In all cases, they had almost equal understanding and had equal awakening.

Now, when you talk about many other religions, there is always the feeling among the followers that his religion is the best. And all others are not as good as their own. This applies to Christianity, because Christians perhaps believe theirs is the only way. So does Hindu or even the Muslim. And this is because he has faith in his own religion.

Now if you think that faith is the right thing, then faith has different categories or different kinds of faith. For instance, people who believe in the doctrine of Communism, they also have faith in Communism. Or people who believe in tenet that is totally opposed to Communism they also have faith in this. Even as we Buddhists, we believe that the teachings of Buddhism are the best for understanding and teaching the highest goal of man. And even in our own teachings, there are various methods expounded by different teachers whose particular interpretation of the teachings of Buddhism concerning truth become different schools of thought and tradition. But our ultimate goal is to reach enlightenment.

That does not mean that we should only concentrate on this highest aspect without going through various stages of practice. Because only in cases of very few individuals is it possible for him to receive teachings in terms of few words and reach awakened state within a matter of a very short time. We had one such as... there are many, many who actually had attained spiritual enlightenment in a matter of just short time, but, nowadays, it is very difficult to reach such a stage without much effort. For instance, we had one teacher who was very young, in fact, he was a child. And he lived only up to the thirteen years of his age. And from his fifth year, he started learning teachings, taking teachings, and within a matter of just short period, a few years, he not only mastered the teachings—understood, got initiated, practiced, and attained enlightenment—and not only he attained enlightenment, but he also started propagating the Dharma. Therefore, in a matter of just few years, he did everything... ah, but perhaps we have to spend so many years, maybe many lives.

Therefore, according to the individual potentialities and capacities, some can attain enlightenment within a matter of a very short time. Others may not attain it at all in this life. But, as we talk about teachings, the ultimate goal is certainly our understanding, our efforts to understand the ultimate nature of things, the nature of mind.

But there are various other methods... for some minds, there is the devotional way, so that they reach a certain level of understanding and, in the process, they cultivate certain qualities and, therefore, they become ripe for receiving the higher teachings.

In some cases, some of the masters say, whatever you do physically or mentally, all these are just means to deceive yourself if you cannot just devote yourself to what is the ultimate practice, the most essential practice. This does not mean that everybody should follow and do the same thing. Milarepa, whose life was translated into English, has become well-known among the Western people. But we have had great many teachers like him, whose lives, whose teachings, have not been translated and made known to others.

For us, now it is to concentrate on the teachings according to one's teachers and traditions and, in our case, it is a matter to be taken very carefully. For instance, no one can simply read a text and meditate and attain. He has to look for a teacher, a guru, with all the qualities necessary for leading the disciple. Not only learning, not only the mastery of the scriptures, but also human qualities, the understanding, the warmth, the feeling, the compassion. Not only this, but also the inner quality, capacity and power, spiritual attainment. All these are necessary.

And on the part of the disciple himself, he must have deep spiritual urge for receiving teachings, for carrying on this inner practice. One is given certain initiation in which he is introduced to the nature of things, the nature of mind, and with this understanding, he gets more and, ah, instructions and therefore, he carries on his practice. It is just like your American scientists who have developed technology which made it possible for your people to fly and land on the moon. The practice can be compared with this same thing, because it is a journey from this existence to the beyond.

The Buddhas and great teachers are like the ones who landed on the moon, who traveled through this, who had the experience, who knew the techniques, the methods, who knew the conditions and everything. And, therefore, when they came back, they told their disciples... *"if anyone wishes to visit the planets, this is the way."* There are always obstacles, barriers. How to overcome these barriers? And this is what actually the teachings are.

*(Conversation resumes after a short break.)*\*

CR: Everything depends on the man—if he knows, if he has practiced, if he has understood. If he has reached a certain stage of spiritual development, then there is no reason why he cannot propagate and make teachings available to others. Otherwise, he will be just like a blind leading another blind.

*(Here the conversation touches on the Gurdjieff teaching. Chatral Rinpoche indicates that Gurdjieff himself received training at a Tibetan monastery in the Swat Valley referred to earlier in the tape.)*\*

CR: In the teachings of the Buddha, one of the most important factors is the development of mind. Whatever practice one follows, ultimately the practice must produce its own results in terms of reducing mental deficiencies, and in eliminating the defilements, the ignorance, the hatred, the lust, and all the prejudices and mental deficiencies. And, at the same time, development of human qualities... the sympathy, the compassion. And also sharpening of understanding, enlarging the intelligence in comprehending higher and more profound teachings. If these things are the results of the practice of meditation, then one's meditation is really making progress. It's producing good results. If, on the other hand, these qualities or results are not achieved, then meditation has no meaning at all. It has not produced good result. Therefore, on the one hand, we think always in terms of the elimination of defects, deficiencies of the mind; on the other hand, the development of the qualities. And, if these two results are there, then the practice is all right, the practice is good.

WS: Our teaching is in accord with yours.

TRANSLATOR: We are in agreement with you. We can understand whether a disciple has the understanding of the transmission that was given to him. He is, for instance, given a particular instruction to carry on in his meditation, and he is told that, by doing this, he will go through stages of experiences. And, once he does this, he comes and gives us his experience. And if his experience tallies with what we have already described, then he has reached a definite understanding. But then there are others who carry on the practice, but still cannot reach that level of understanding. Because this we know by exchange of ideas, exchange of experiences. So it is not difficult at all.

CR: In the Vajrayana tradition, guru gives certain instructions concerning the meditation, designed to make one understand the true nature of mind. And then disciple goes away and does meditation in solitude. After certain time, he comes back and relates his experiences to his guru. And if guru finds that he has reached definite understanding, then he gets more instructions, so that he can carry on to stabilize the gain he has already made. But if he does not reach that stage, he is again asked to go back and repeat the same practice. And there are people who have more, sort of, inner capacity to reach and understand quickly. And others, in spite of their repeated

56

attempts, still cannot come to the same position.

WS: That's very understandable.

CR: Well, that is what I repeat in the very beginning. You know, all the traditions, there are various methods, various ways of making the disciple to reach the level of awakening and understanding. For instance, we had great masters like Tilopa who did not give teachings to his disciple Naropa so easily without making him go through twenty-four sacrifices, personal sacrifices—twelve major ones and twelve minor ones—each involving tremendous physical, mental hardship. And after all this, then Naropa was found ready. One day Tilopa beat him almost to death. And when Naropa fell unconscious, he woke up from that state of unconsciousness and, thereupon, he found himself in fully awakened state, which was no different from anything that was attained by Buddha or any great master.

In our own time, there are teachers who can see a disciple's mental qualities, mental capacities, potentialities. In each case, the teacher only gives him so much teachings, just enough for breaking open awakening. But we don't possess the great qualities of the great teachers. Therefore, our approach is, since we don't know the inner capacity of the man—capacity that is in a latent form, that has not been developed, that is lying hidden—therefore, we give them more or less complete teachings so that any aspect of these teachings will help bring about the desired result.

WS: (*laughs*) Good.

CR: And at the same time, if these complete teachings don't produce the desired result, then we will give them what is known as instantaneous teachings.

WS: Which are... what are instantaneous teachings?

TRANSLATOR: (interrupting) Ah, well, he has not explained, but this is something that needs to be explained. Anyway, there are various methods where the disciple gets teachings in an unusual way... in other words, he receives teachings direct from the teachers, the great teachers of the past, who appear to him and give him the teachings directly.

WS: And his idea about everything being a dream... that we live in a dream and take the dream for reality?

CR: All things convert in our Buddhist tradition to, for instance, mirage...

WS: Ah, yes.

CR: ...dream, illusion, and, ah, having no entity or nature of their own. Everything like a dream. For instance, when you dream at night a huge, vicious tiger approaching you and trying to attack you and, ah, eat you up. You experience this in your dream, that you had experience, sensation of seeing the tiger and also the fear that he might certainly attack and harm you. When you get up the next morning, it was just a bad dream... it had not existence of its own, no reality of its own. Similarly, the fact that you and I meet here... is a dream.

WS: (*laughs*) You would say that?

CR: ...not more than a dream. We take it to be real... neither I nor you, in our sleep, take the dream to be false, as having no reality of its own. But we don't take life to be false, to be illusory. We take it to be real. We always hold onto it as real. Because of this grasping or holding to the sensations, to cognizance, taking as real—which is illusion, which is not real—in actual life we are so overcome by delusions that we don't see the reality. Because we are incapable of seeing things as they truly are... which is nothing.

WS: (*laughs*) Very good. Very fine.

## BROTHER ASIMAN

The Seekers of Truth were interested in discovering truths both by archeological and other forms of research, and by practicing and studying the traditions of the peoples they encountered. We recently discussed the archeological research they attempted in the Hindu Kush. In this chapter we will take a brief look at one of the contemporary traditions they engaged with there.

In *Beelzebub's Tales*, Gudjieff's alter ego speaks of a certain Brother Asiman he met in the Hindu Kush. And in the interview William Segal conducted with Chatral Rinpoche, in response to Segal bringing up the subject of Gurdjieff, Chatral speaks about a monastery of tantricism in the Swat Valley (which is in the Hindu Kush). But it would not have been a Buddhist monastery (despite the transcriber of the interview including a note interpreting this as what Chatral was saying) as Buddhism was overthrown in the region centuries ago. Still, the tantric sects of Buddhism, Sufism and Shaivism all have great respect for one another and even imported each other's teachings and practices. The knowledge Chatral had of Gurdjieff's association with a monastery of a tantric sect of another religion is testimony to this mutual appreciation. In fact, it seems to suggest that Gurdjieff impressed the Tibetans he met with the tantric practices he picked up in Swat.

Gurdjieff was very likely in contact with both Sufi and

Shaivist tantric practitioners, and it is possible the monastery Chatral is referring to is Sufi rather than Shaivist, but evidence suggests that Brother Asiman was Shaivist. One thing that suggests this is that the name Asiman is an anagram for Isanam—one of the five faces of Shiva and thus used as a male name in Hindi. This would not be the only instance of Gurdjieff concealing an identity by use of an anagram in his writings. A couple of others will be discussed in the "Sarmung" chapter.

One other thing that suggests Brother Asiman was Shaivist is that Gurdjieff says that his cult was experimenting with a concoction that enabled them to eat minimally in order to spend more time practicing, and Kashmir Shaivites are known for their ascetic practices.

As Asiman is identified as a brother rather than any sort of master, it is unlikely that any record of the individual Gurdjieff met by the name Isanam exists. The name being common also makes discovering his identity impossible. In this case Gurdjieff seems to be concealing an identity solely to conceal the individual's ethnicity. Yet, as is the case with other instances of his use of anagrams, he clearly wanted the information to be revealed in due time. Moreover, a comparison between Kashmir Shaivism and Gurdjieff's teaching is out of scope of this current work. Still, Kashmir Shaivism seems to be a much overlooked influence upon Gurdjieff's teaching and it may be useful to say a few words about the school of thought and briefly mention a few comparative discoveries. It may not have been pure sensationalism when Gurdjieff referred to himself as a Hindu in the 1914 advertisement for his spectacle, *The Struggle of the Magicians* (which P. D. Ouspensky relates having read in his work, *In Search of the Miraculous*).

Shaivism is one of the many schools of the polytheistic Hindu religion. In the same way that Advaita Vedanta is a nondual interpretation of the Vedanta school, Kashmir Shaivism, or Trika Shaivism as it is also known, is a nondual interpretation of the Shaivite school. Both Advaita Vedanta and Kashmir Shaivism arose as a result of the influence of the then-new Mahayana Buddhist school. Although Kashmir Shaivism originated in Kashmir, from there it spread into the

Hindu Kush and eastward across the Himalayas.

The sect is called *Trika* (meaning "triadic") Shaivism because its philosophy abounds with threefold conceptions, similar to Gurdjieff's teaching. Another thing curious about Kashmir Shaivism is that realization is considered the recognizing or remembering of one's true nature or inner Self—an allusion to Gurdjieff's idea of "self-remembering". Also noteworthy is Ian MacFarlane's observation that Gurdjieffian sensing exercises are based upon the Hindu tantric practice of *nyasa*.[1] Perhaps this is enough to inspire others to further research the subject.

---

[1] Ian MacFarlane, "Sensing Exercises," Endless Search, www.endlesssearch.co.uk/exercises_sensing.htm.

## Turkestan Tiger

Those familiar with the association that Gurdjieff has with Agwan Dorjieff may wonder if Dorje (the Tibetan name which was Russified to Dordjieff) was part of Gurdjieff's Tibetan name. Briefly for those not familiar with this, in his book *God is my Adventure,* Rom Landau reproduced a letter from a certain Captain Achmed Abdullah, in which the writer relates how certain he was upon meeting Gurdjieff in the early 1930s that he was the same individual he knew as Agwan Dordjieff when they were both in Tibet. Adding to this association is detailed research that James Webb provides in his book *The Harmonious Circle* into the lives of Dordjieff and several of his associates. Yet as Webb points out, Alexandra David-Néel wrote an article disproving the identification of Gurdjieff with Dordjieff.[1] Even so, Webb is unable to let go of the misattribution, as he puts forth his theory that Gurdjieff was a disciple of Dordjieff known as Ovshé Norzunov. He even mentions an account where a student undetected by Gurdjieff heard him repeating over and over, "I am dorje."[2] (This actually sounds like Gurdjieff was doing some sort of mantra practice.)

What is curious, however, is that Yahne Le Toumelin told me that Gurdjieff had asked her to one day go to Tibet and search for his two sons by asking for the "sons of Dorje." Yet when Le Toumelin went to Darjeeling (where there is a large Tibetan community) in the 1970s and enquired for the whereabouts of "the sons of Dorje," she was embarrassed by all the puzzled looks she received. Dorje, which literally means lightning bolt, is a symbol for enlightenment and is often part of Tibetan dharma names. She was simply told, "We are all sons of Dorje."[3]

At any rate, this seems to have been yet another gag Gurdjieff played on his students to shake them up and keep them on their toes, even after his death. Another such stunt he pulled was to give his students too-small measurements for his coffin, requiring them to find a larger one fast in time for the funeral. He was well aware of the association with Dordjieff that Landau had publicly made, and apparently made use of it for Le Toumelin's benefit.

Besides Alexandra David-Néel's article, there is additional evidence that the letter from Achmed Abdullah associating Gurdjieff with Dordjieff was Rom Landau's fabrication. According to Dushka Howarth, she once met Landau and confronted him regarding fabrications in his chapter on Gurdjieff. He admitted to her that he had never met Gurdjieff, got his information from other sources, made various embellishments, and apologized to her. After the admission she asked if he would rectify the matter, but he said he was too old and the book written too long ago to do so.[4] Clearly Gurdjieff was not known as Dorje in Tibet. The misattribution associating Gurdjieff with Dordjieff needs to be put to rest. However, Gurdjieff himself may have actually told us his Tibetan name.

At the end of "The Arousing of Thought," the first chapter of *Beelzebub's Tales*, Gurdjieff mentions that as a young man he was known as Tiger of Turkestan. In the 1931 version of the tales, the epithet is rendered instead as Turkestan Tiger. The two variations have the same meaning of course, but perhaps the original, truer to the form of Gurdjieff's thinking not having been as edited, says something about the language or naming conventions of those who thus named him. And certainly those who gave him the name were from outside Turkestan. Place names are always added to the given or assumed name of a foreigner by the natives of the country in which he is living. Sometimes the place name is even used by itself, as in El

Greco, the beloved painter of Spain who originally came from Greece.

A tiger is called *tag* in Tibetan, and in Tibet, Tag is also used as a name. Chatral Rinpoche is also known as Tag Rinpoche. Trungpa Rinpoche named one of his sons Tag. In Tibet, as in many other places, a tiger is a symbol of fierceness. The symbol does seem to say something of Gurdjieff's character and stealth. A common phenomenon of immigration (Gurdjieff was an immigrant in Tibet) is rendering one's names in the form of the language of the welcoming country, or changing it completely when there is no equivalent. So it seems likely enough that Gurdjieff would have been given some Tibetan name by his acquaintances there. Tag (or Tiger) rather does fit Gurdjieff's character, and Gurdjieff himself says he was known by the name.

When a place name is used as an adjective in Tibetan, it is placed before the noun or name it is describing. So, whatever Tibetan place name Gurdjieff translated to Turkestan would be placed before the name Tag, just as the name Turkestan Tiger is given in the 1931 edition of *Beelzebub's Tales*.

In Tibetan, Turkestan is called *horlungpa*, meaning land of (*lung pa*) the *Hor* people. A person from Turkestan is known as a *horpa* (of the *Hor*), and to make *horpa* an adjective it would become *horpey*. So Gurdjieff may have been called *Horpey Tag*. Yet to Tibetan ears, the name sounds peculiar because the Turkestani are Muslim and Tag is a Buddhist name. It sounds like a contradiction. At the same time, it is somewhat possible that a crazy wisdom teacher as Gurdjieff evidently had would have intentionally used a form that makes an impression like a koan. But there are other possibilities:

A region of Turkestan more associated with Buddhism is Baltistan. Before Islam entered the country around the 15th century, the country was Buddhist. In fact, the country was Buddhist long before Tibet. An early form of Buddhism entered Baltistan from Swat in the third or fourth century, and when Swat ceased to be a center of Buddhism, Tibetan Buddhism entered Baltistan around the eighth century. Between Baltistan and Tibet lies Ladakh which, unlike Baltistan, has retained its

Buddhist heritage. Today Baltistan and Ladakh are part of the Indian state of Kashmir.

"Bön" not only refers to the pre-Buddhist religion of Tibet, it also refers to the principal aboriginal tribe of the Himalayas, and especially of Tibet. Another such tribe is the Mön (the Bhutanese). At any rate, the Mön call the Baltistani *Turuk*, which very much resembles Turk. From a Tibetan perspective, Baltistan and Turkestan are nearly synonymous. The Baltistani are actually a mix of Bön and Aryan stock whereas the Ladakhi have more Bön blood.

All this is just to say that it is possible Gurdjieff was actually known as *Baltiyi Tag* (Baltistan Tiger) and instead rendered *Baltiyi* as Turkestan when giving us his epithet. Yet, like *Horpa*, neither is *Baltiyi* a known Tibetan name.

A much more likely possibility is that Gurdjieff was known as *Urgyen Tag* (Uddiyanan Tiger). Urgyen is in fact a common Tibetan name. One example is Tulku Urgyen, whose autobiography is occasionally referenced here. The name refers to Uddiyana, the ancient Buddhist kingdom centered in the Swat Valley, which today is in northwestern Pakistan. Remember that Chatral Rinpoche identifies Gurdjieff with the Swat Valley in particular.

Also to consider is that it is more likely Gurdjieff would have rendered *Urgyen* as Turkestan instead of *Baltiyi* because Uddiyana was hardly written about, if at all, in the West in his time, and "Turkestan" may have been the closest equivalent. In addition, it seems likely that he would have wanted to obscure the Buddhist origin of the name in the same way he obscured the Buddhist identity of "Sarmung".

Padmasambhava, being from Uddiyana, is sometimes called Urgyen Rinpoche. And it is worth considering if Gurdjieff was called Urgyen to associate him with Padmasambhava in addition to associating him with Uddiyana. Yet another name Padmasambhava is known by is Guru Rinpoche. And as Louise March tells us, "Mr Gurdjieff once explained his name. 'Gur' from guru: teacher. 'Teacher of exactness.'"[5] As well, the significance Gurdjieff places upon remembering impermanence and the teachings on impermanence associated

68

with Padmasambhava may be another reason for associating Gurdjieff with Padmasambhava.

Although Gurdjieff was not actually from Uddiyana or Turkestan, it was evidently understood that he spent many years in the region, very likely on expeditions in search of Shambhala. With no trace of a living Buddhist tradition in his day in the region once known as Uddiyana, and with an Uddiyanan being responsible for bringing the dharma to Tibet (Padmasambhava), Gurdjieff's arrival in Tibet may have been considered very auspicious, and he thereby may have been given special treatment. Perhaps it was even understood that Gurdjieff, like Padmasambhava, would be responsible for planting the seed of dharma in some new land. Trungpa Rinpoche certainly seems to have thought so. He saw as his own role the flourishing of the dharma in the West, and openly expressed respect for two pioneers in particular who preceded him—one being Shunryu Suzuki, who brought Zen Buddhism Buddhism to the West in 1959, and the other being Gurdjieff, who founded a new spiritual movement in the West 46 years prior, who he understood had spent time at Surmang, and therefore may have understood to have taught a reinterpretation of Buddhism formulated especially for those he brought it to. In the early days of Trungpa Rinpoche's Vajradhatu organization, photos of both men were to be found on his altar.

One final factor in Gurdjieff receiving his Tibetan name is the phonetic similarity between Ur*gy*en and *Gy*orgi, as well as with *Gû*rdjieff.

And with all likelihood, Urgyen Tag (or whatever name Gurdjieff went by in Tibet) was a dharma name given to him by his root guru, which may have been the nameless individual he only refers to as the chief of the "group of seven" in *Beelzebub's Tales*.

[1] Alexandra David-Néel, "Gurdjieff-Dorjieff," *Nouvelles Littéraires* no. 1390 (22 Avril, 1954), 1, 6.

[2] Evidently given to Webb orally, as I am unable to locate a published or archival record.

[3] Private correspondence.

[4] Told orally to a mutual friend of Dushka and the author.

[5] Annabeth McCorkle, ed., *The Rochester Years: 1957–1987: The Work of Louise March* (Palmyra: Stillwood Study Center, 2007), 41.

*Dudjom Lingpa*

## THE CHIEF OF SEVEN

Many of Gurdjieff's biographers and researchers have attempted to look into his time in Tibet circa 1901–1904. However, from what can be discerned, this was but the first of two periods of time he spent there and the second is yet to be discussed until now. Both are significant in different ways, and the significance of this first trip appears to have been overlooked by others.

In *Beelzebub's Tales*, Gurdjieff tells us that when the chief of a group of seven high-ranking lamas was struck dead by a British bullet while on his way to inform the public of the council's decision not to oppose the enemy, all of Tibetan Buddhism perished as a result. Although this tale is historically inaccurate in some ways, it does indeed refer to an actual event. Moreover, there is something very personal about the tale. His telling makes one feel his loss.

What is clear is that Gurdjieff is alluding to the Young-husband Expedition's Massacre of Chumik Shenko, which took place March 31, 1904. At that massacre, the Tibetan resistance refused to fight, but neither would they retreat. Obviously all of Tibetan Buddhism did not perish at that time. One possibility, however, is that this chief was the head of a specific sect or lineage whose tradition perished as a result of his untimely death.

According to the Buddhist Digital Resource Center, there

were two teachers who died that year, both of whom were lineage heads. Yet neither died on the date of the Massacre of Chumik Shenko. One died before and the other after. If one of these two were indeed Gurdjieff's root teacher, it would appear that Gurdjieff was intentionally combining his loss with the tragedy of Chumik Shenko to make some allegorical point or perhaps to better emphasize the tragedy he personally experienced.

But there is something else that is unusual about Gurdjieff's tale. Also suggestive that this chief of seven was Gurdjieff's teacher is the difference in his account given in the published version of *Beelzebub's Tales* and the private 1931 edition. The published version concludes the story of the chief of seven with the fantastic telling of the remaining six heads perishing in an explosion that resulted from a dangerous ritual they performed with the hope of making contact with their deceased chief in order to complete their transmissions and prevent their faith from coming to an end. But the version in the private 1931 edition of the text does not have this conclusion. In fact, in this earlier version a "fraternity of 'those who are delivering themselves'" is mentioned instead of the group of seven, and it is some unnamed "being" who died on his way to notify the public of their leaders' decision. Why these changes, particularly the fantastical addition?

Could it be that Gurdjieff decided to instead say that it was some high-ranking lama who died in order to leave a clue about his root teacher? In Tibetan Buddhism, as well as other Buddhist lineages, one may study and practice with a number of teachers, but can only take vows with and be devoted to one teacher in particular. But, again, why the crazy ending? Perhaps this tale that Carl Zigrosser heard from A. R. Orage will provide an explanation:

> Ouspensky arranged a lecture on the Gobi Desert for Gurdjieff before the Geographical Society of Moscow. Gurdjieff discoursed long and authoritatively on the subject, and then toward the end he told of having discovered a small valley with precipitous sides which made the bottom impossible of access. The floor glittered with diamonds which the

natives gathered by a novel method. They threw down lumps of meat, and trained vultures to retrieve the diamond-studded morsels. Many suspicious glances were exchanged by the savants; many of them rose and left... Ouspensky afterwards asked Gurdjieff why he had introduced that story from the Arabian Nights... Gurdjieff replied that he had told the scholars many things and given them priceless information. When he saw that they did not appreciate what he had given, he deliberately took the priceless things away from them by introducing in them a doubt about all he had said.[1]

In the same way that Gurdjieff wanted the members of the Geographical Society to have doubts about the information previously given, he apparently wants his readers to doubt something about the chief of seven. The Massacre of Chumik Shenko is historical, so it must be something specifically about the chief of seven that he wants there to be doubt about. But he says virtually nothing about the chief of seven. These two facts seem to indicate that this is a buried clue regarding his root teacher. This explains both why very little is said about the chief of seven, and why the nonsensical ending. But he clearly does not want us to doubt the clue about his teacher entirely; it seems rather that his intention was to discourage us from learning too soon that the chief of seven was one of his teachers. After all, there was obviously some reason to add the chief of seven to the tale. Gurdjieff apparently wanted the significance of the chief of seven in the tale to be discovered at a later date. As Gurdjieff said, he buried many dogs in *Beelzebub's Tales* to be unearthed. This particular dog was just buried in a different fashion than most others.

Although, as shown previously, the idea that Gurdjieff and Dordjieff (whose Tibetan name was Sokpo Tsenshab Ngawang Lobsang) were the same individual was entirely a fabrication, it appears that Gurdjieff met him after all. While James Webb was clearly mistaken in believing that Gurdjieff was Dordjieff's student Ovshé Norzunov, and therefore that Gurdjieff was a student of Dordjieff, there are too many similarities between Gurdjieff and Norzunov to negate some relationship. It will later be suggested that Norzunov was one fellow Truth-Seeker in particular, and that Gurdjieff accompanied Norzunov and Dordjieff on one of their journeys. So, Gurdjieff and Dordjieff likely knew one another. But it is doubtful that Dordjieff was a teacher of Gurdjieff's, despite him being a teacher of one of his companions.

Some readers may be aware that Olgivanna Lloyd Wright reports that while she was working on a sculpting task that Gurdjieff had given her, he himself was sculpting the bust of his Mongolian teacher.[2] Knowing that Dordjieff was Mongolian, one may be tempted to use this as evidence that Dordjieff was Gurdjieff's teacher after all. However, Dordjieff did not die in 1904 as appears to be the case with the teacher Gurdjieff calls the chief of seven. He died in 1938. Furthermore, as will be shown later, Gurdjieff appears to have been involved in the Kagyupa and Nyingmapa sects. Dordjieff was Gelupga and there is no indication that Gurdjieff was involved in that sect. Also, it is doubtful that Gurdjieff told Olgivanna that his teacher was Mongolian. Probably this was her impression based on the bust's facial features. Perhaps she meant to say mongoloid rather than Mongolian. Mongoloid was the word used at the time to denote the Asian race. As English was not her first language, she could have easily obfuscated the difference in meaning between the two words. Considering that the word mongoloid is now considered offensive, it is also possible that the editor intentionally changed the word in Olgivanna's manuscript. Certainly Dordjieff was a powerful lama with his connection to the Dalai Lama, but not as great a lama as a lineage holder. This too rules him out in trying to identify the chief of seven.

If in fact Gurdjieff accompanied Norzunov on his third journey to Tibet (as will be suggested later), he arrived in Lhasa on February 28, 1901 to be exact. As well, a little more can be discerned regarding the timing of this journey from what Gurdjieff says in the third series of his writings. In that work he mentions Tibet in passing while talking about the three times he was struck by a bullet. He says that at the time of the second, which he specifies as sometime in 1902, took place in the mountains of Tibet. The third bullet strike he says occurred in Georgia in 1904. Clearly he left Tibet sometime in 1904, possibly in part because of the death of his teacher.

Let us now look at the two great Tibetan Buddhist teachers who died in 1904 and consider their possible attribution. While the evidence for Bamda Gelek is not quite as strong as the next teacher to be discussed, it is still presented for the reader to make their own determination.

If we are to believe that an entire sect of Tibetan Buddhism came to an end with the passing of the chief of seven, then Bamda Tubten Gelek Gyatso is the obvious choice. When Bamda Gelek died on December 2, 1904, the entire Jonangpa order he presided over was believed to have come to an end. The Jonangpa, a subsect of the Sarma school, is one of the lesser known sects of Tibetan Buddhism. Although the Jonangpa flourished in the 17<sup>th</sup> century, in the following century they would be suppressed for reasons both philosophical and political. But in the late 19<sup>th</sup> century the Jonangpa were experiencing the beginnings of a second flourishing through the intervention of Rimé (a nonsectarian movement to be discussed later), but when Bamda Tubten Gelek Gyatso (also known as Bamda Lama), the last great teacher of the Jonangpa, died in 1904, the entire sect was believed to have died with him.

However, relatively recently, at first one thriving Jonangpa monastery, and then others, were discovered in the remote Dzamthang region of Tibet. As a result, the Tibetan government in exile has registered the Jonangpa as an official religion of the land. But for virtually all of the 20<sup>th</sup> century even Tibetans themselves considered the Jonangpa an extinct sect. As far as Gurdjieff may have understood matters, when Bamda Tubten Gelek died, the Jonangpa sect died with him.

It is also useful to consider a specific tenet of the Jonangpa in relation to Gurdjieff. They had a unique view of the subject of *shunyata* (which is commonly referred to as emptiness). This view was largely the cause of their suppression, in particular by the dominant Gelugpa sect. What the Jonangpa call the *zhentong* view is also known as "other emptiness" in English. Gurdjieff's hiding of the subject of emptiness in *Beelzebub's Tales* will be discussed later, but briefly, emptiness is the view that all is impermanent, transient, and therefore lacking an intrinsic self. The Jonangpa refer to this traditional view of emptiness as *rangtong* to distinguish the *zhentong* view from it. According to the *zhentong* view, all is empty *except* absolute reality, of which buddha-nature is a part. This was controversial at the time because whereas Buddhism professes that as individuals we have no essential permanent self, the *zhentong* view's understanding of buddha-nature can be interpreted as akin to what other traditions regard as a soul.

This is significant in relation to Gurdjieff in two ways. Firstly, having previously immersed himself in Christianity, Sufism and Shaivism, all of which have some concept of soul, it may have been easier for Gurdjieff to embrace the Jonangpa tradition in comparison to other Buddhist traditions. Secondly, in the same way the Jonangpa view of buddha-nature was unclear regarding whether or not it was something of a soul, Gurdjieff's view of soul was also unclear. As Olga de Hartmann notes in *Our Life with Mr Gurdjieff*, "In general, in his discussions with us Mr Gurdjieff never used the word 'soul'. He referred only to a 'something'. However, in his discussion with these new people, it was necessary for him to use words that they would understand and for that reason he used the word 'soul'."[3] All this is to say that both Gurdieff's view of soul and the Jonangpa view of buddha-nature seem to attempt to convey the same paradox but in different ways.

There are other things about Bambda Tubten Gelek that are interesting in relation to Gurdjieff. One of his teachers was the great Jamgön Kongtrul, one of the founders of Rimé, which both enabled an outsider such as Gurdjieff to practice in Tibet and was such a big influence on him. (This influence will be discussed later in the chapter "Sectarianism".) His other teacher, Dzogchen Patrul Rinpoche, is no less significant. His work, *The Words of My Perfect Teacher*, is a Dzogchen classic and is cited elsewhere here as a likely influence upon Gurdjieff. Besides being a lineage holder of the Jonangpa, Bamda Tubten Gelek was also a lineage holder of Dzogchen, which both James George and Paul Anderson recognized as an important influence on Gurdjieff's teaching.

Also of note is that one of Bamda Gelek's teachers was the Fourth Dzogchen Rinpoche. It may be because of this relationship that Gurdjieff later became a student of the Fifth Dzogchen Rinpoche—a possibility discussed later.

There are some minor similarities between Bamda Gelek and Gurdjieff that are also interesting: Like Gurdjieff, Bamda Gelek was greatly interested in the sciences in addition to spirituality. Like Gurdjieff, Bamda Gelek had a reputation for being harsh with his disciples. Like Gurdjieff, Bamda Gelek could read his disciples' minds. And like Gurdjieff, Bamda Gelek demonstrated magical powers. Certainly it makes sense that Gurdjieff would have sought out a teacher known for their magical abilities with his youthful interest in magic.

Yet if Gurdjieff left Tibet in part because of the death of his teacher, and had supposedly returned to Georgia in 1904, then considering that Bamda Gelek died that December and Dudjom Lingpa that January, Dudjom Lingpa would be the more likely candidate for the individual Gurdjieff refers to as the chief of seven. Clearly Gurdjieff left Tibet before Bamda Gelek's death. It is still possible, however, that Gurdjieff learned about his teacher's death after his departure, but that he would have left because of his death seems more likely. It should also be mentioned that Gurdjieff could easily have learned *zhentong* teachings and practices from a Rimé master; he need not necessarily have had a Jonangpa teacher for that. Dudjom Lingpa was in fact a Rimé master, as were three other masters to be later considered as possible teachers of Gurdjieff.

Dudjom Lingpa, who died January 5, 1904, is a candidate for the identity of the chief of seven for other reasons. Like Gurdjieff, he was something of a rogue. Unlike most great Tibetan Buddhist masters, he was a layperson; he was non-monastic. Compared to monastics, Dudjom Lingpa began his path late in life. And although he later received some teachings from various teachers, his primary training was received from beings who spoke to him in visions. As well as giving him various practices, they also told him where to find earth *terma*—teaching treasures hidden by great teachers of the past. As well, his visions directly gave him mind *terma*—teaching treasures hidden in the ether. Both forms of *terma* are hidden by teachers of the past to be later revealed for the benefit of a future generation in their need. At first, the masters of his time did not take Dudjom Lingpa seriously. But after unearthing so many *terma,* and so clearly expounding his understanding, they could not deny his attainment, and he was recognized as the incarnation of Kyeuchung Lotsawa—one of Padmasambhava's disciples.

At any rate, being a lay practitioner and a teacher to lay people is another indication that Dudjom Lingpa could have been Gurdjieff's teacher. It seems unlikely that Gurdjieff would have been a monastic. Although it is possible Gurdjieff could have been a monastic on this first journey to Tibet, he clearly was not on his second journey. As will be shown later, it was on this second journey that he had his small family. Moreover, it seems as though he had his family in Golok, which is where Dudjom Lingpa is from. All this will be discussed in the chapter on Gurdjieff's two Tibetan sons. This is just to say that Gurdjieff may very well have decided to settle in Golok because of Dudjom Lingpa's connections there.

Although Dudjom Lingpa was recognized as a teacher of the Nyingmapa Dzogchen tradition, he is also considered the founder of his own lineage, the Dudjom Tersar. This is not the same as being the head of an entire sect like Bamda Gelek was, but like Bamda Gelek, his death was certainly considered a great loss. Unlike Bamda Gelek, however, Dudjom Lingpa's lineage proliferated via the nine children he passed it on to. Still, he was certainly a *very* important teacher as Gurdjieff suggests of the chief of seven.

Like Bamda Gelek, Dudjom Lingpa's profound understanding of Dzogchen should also be considered in relation to Gurdjieff. His three-volume set *Visions of the Great Perfection* ("Great Perfection" is a reference to Dzogchen) is regarded as a classic text.

But there is something much more significant than any of the above that suggests Dudjom Lingpa was the chief of seven. When William Segal brings up the subject of Gurdjieff in his interview with Chatral Rinpoche, Chatral responds in part with an apparent reference to Dudjom Lingpa. He seemingly knew something of Gurdjieff's time in Tibet. The lama that Chatral speaks of has to be considered an "apparent reference" to Dudjom Lingpa because the transcribers of the taped interview were unable to clearly decipher the name given. In the text the spelling of the name is rendered as "Dnujembe". But when consulting a Tibetan scholar and friend regarding the actual name, he responded "Dudjom" without any hesitation. And when consulting him again after learning that there were several teachers with the name Dudjom, without hesitation again he responded "Dudjom Lingpa." Considering that Chatral Rinpoche was a close student of the Second Dudjom Rinpoche, later recognized his rebirth, the Third Dudjom Rinpoche, and was one of the teachers of the latter, it makes sense that Dudjom Lingpa was the one he brought up in relation to Gurdjieff in his talk with Segal. Clearly he was well acquainted with their Dudjom Tersar lineage.

Also, it seems as though Chatral Rinpoche, later in the interview, may have intentionally brought up the subject of receiving teachings "direct from... great teachers of the past." No Tibetan guru is more renowned for having received this sort of teaching than Dudjom Lingpa. He may have been trying to throw Segal another hint. In this regard, it is also possible that Beelzebub's telling of the six remaining lamas's failure to make contact with their chief was intended by Gurdjieff to express his belief that Dudjom Lingpa's spiritual heirs had not attained the same level of skill receiving mind *terma* as their teacher.

What follows is first the 1931 version of Gurdjieff's telling of Beelzebub's experience in Tibet. And following that is the Dudjom Lingpa's introduction to his *Buddhahood Without Meditation*. What is interesting about his introduction is that like Gurdjieff's "Objectively Impartial Criticism of the Life of Man" (the subtitle of *Beelzebub's Tales*), Dudjom Lingpa also provides an impartial criticism, but specifically of the spiritual practitioner. Besides demonstrating a possible influence for

Gurdjieff, the text is highly valuable for showing some of the ways we spiritual practitioners deceive ourselves.

1 Carl Zigrosser, *My Own Shall Come to Me* (Haarlem: Casa Laura, 1971), 158–59.
2 Maxine Fawcett-Yeske & Bruce Brooks Pfeiffer, eds., *The Life of Olgivanna Lloyd Wright* (Novato: ORO Editions, 2017, 35.
3 Thomas & Olga de Hartmann, *Our Life with Mr Gurdjieff* (Sandpoint: Sandpoint Press, 2008), 183.

Image of Dudjom Lingpa created for the author by Felipe Oliveira.

### BEELZEBUB IN TIBET

"As regards the third doctrine, that of Saint Lama, it spread less widely than the rest, owing to the geographical conditions of its origin. For the same reason, however, it more or less entered into the essence of those beings resident there; and for some centuries, it began actually to be realized amongst them, and especially amongst a certain group who were isolated on account of the inaccessibility of their locality, and thus could work without disturbance. This group, and their descendants gradually assimilated the objective doctrine of their teacher and began to apply it to the purpose for which it was created, that deliverance from the consequences of the properties of the organ Kundabuffer. Some of them attained this deliverance and many were on the path to it. But when the environment necessary for productive work in this direction was arranged, that same singularity of theirs, that is war, again, it seems, completely destroyed what had already been adjusted; and the complete adjustment was delayed for many years owing to this war. I know very well about this war because I happened to be on that planet at that period, and amongst the beings of this very Thibet.

"This peculiarity, war, occurred in the following manner. A certain King from the continent Europe, taking advantage of the civil dissensions of the Indian princes, and owing to a method invented by one of his people gradually conquered

India and the neighboring lands.

"One fine day the thought entered his warlike head, why should he not conquer Thibet also. He thereupon assembled troops from his own state, and from the newly conquered lands and advanced towards that inaccessible place.

"The expedition over awkward routes was very difficult and cost the king a great deal; but eventually after considerable exertions and sacrifices, he succeeded in ascending with his troops.

"The Thibetans knew nothing of this march upon their country. They only learned of it when the king had already arrived with his troops. Having heard of the strange event, however, they became anxious, because they had become accustomed to the idea during centuries that their country was inaccessible to other beings, and they were so certain of this that they had never even been aware of the preparations made to reach their land. As this situation was very serious, since the result might be the destruction of all their preparations, the Thibetans became exceedingly anxious and the members of the fraternity of "those who are delivering themselves" became very sad. They were sad chiefly because they saw that their preparations were in danger. They therefore met to confer and many of those took part in the meeting who had almost delivered themselves from the consequences of the properties of Kundabuffer, and many of those who had just started on the right path of deliverance.

"Having met and deliberated amongst themselves, they became convinced that it would be impossible by ordinary means of persuasion to induce the king to return home; and they had seriously to consider how to prevent this uninvited entrance into a stranger's house. Many methods were suggested, but one method in particular was favored by the majority present at the meeting, namely, to destroy entirely the king with his troops. And this was in fact much the easiest method, the nature of the place where Thibet is situated being such, that one unarmed being could destroy hundreds of enemy beings by dropping stones on them.

"Among the beings present however, some were strongly

opposed to this plan, proving that such action would be a little displeasing to Our Creator, to whom all creatures are dear. They succeeded in convincing the meeting, and the proposal was rejected by the majority. It was decided not to hinder events but to let them take their course. The king, meeting with no resistance, then began to advance further. One of the beings who had opposed the suggestion to slaughter the king and his troops, set off to the places where they must pass to persuade the masses to follow the decision of their leaders. In a town through which these troops passed, an accidental or intentional bullet from one of the soldiers killed the being whose intervention had saved many thousands of lives.

"When the king heard of this murder, do you think he felt any remorse? No, he only became proud, that owing to his lofty mind and force of arms, no obstacles could stand in his way, and he could go wherever he wished. He reached the interior of Thibet without having met any resistance. How it all ended is not important; what is important is, that after the events I mentioned, the core of this doctrine became like all the rest."

*G. Gurdjieff*

With the exception of three minor errors that were corrected, this text is exactly what appears in the 1931 typescript edition of *Beelzebub's Tales to His Grandson*. The quotation marks are there because it is Beelzebub who is relating the tale. This version of Gurdjieff's work is currently available from several publishers.

## Advice

Nowadays, when the five kinds of degeneration are on the rise, due to the uncouth nature of sentient beings and their powerful, negative karma, every one of them clings to this life —which is no more than an episode in a dream—makes long-term plans for living indefinitely, and shows no concern for meaningful pursuits pertaining to future lifetimes, those who strive for the states of liberation and omniscience appear no more often than stars in the daytime.

Although some people bear death in mind and enthusiastically practice dharma, they let their lives pass while engaging in mere verbal and physical spiritual practices and striving for higher rebirths as gods and humans.

Some, while lacking even the faintest understanding of the view of emptiness, ascertain their own minds as empty, merely identify the nature of discursive thoughts or inactive consciousness, and then passively remain in that state. As a result, they are simply propelled into rebirths as gods in the desire and form realms, without coming even a hair's breath closer to the path to omniscience.

Therefore, if there are a few individuals who have accrued vast accumulations of merit over the course of countless eons, conjoined them with fine prayers, and established a karmic connection with the ultimate dharma, I have bestowed this as their inheritance. Those who have no karmic connection with me and who lack the particular fortune of mastering the dharma of the Great Perfection will engage in either projection or denial regarding this teaching and will thereby banish their own minds into the wilderness. You people who are not like that and whose fortune is equal to my own, attend to this advice—and by investigation, analysis, and familiarization, recognize samsara and nirvana as great emptiness, and realize its nature.

Among the three divisions—the division of the mind, the division of the expanse, and the division of pith instructions—of the nature of reality, the Great Perfection, this is called the category of secret pith instructions. In this regard there are three sections: view, meditation, and conduct. First, the view is determined and authentically realized by way of four themes: nonexistence, oneness, uniform pervasiveness, and spontaneous actualization. This is a sublime, essential point.

*Dudjom Lingpa*

## A Breeze of Grace

The individual that Gurdjieff calls Bogga-Eddin is of interest because in *Meetings with Remarkable Men* he says that it was Bogga-Eddin who introduced him to a "kaphir" from Sarmung who escorted him and Soloviev there. He also appears in *Beelzebub's Tales* where he is referred to as Hadji Zephir Bogga Eddin. This is not to be confused with the individual Gurdjieff calls Nasr Eddin—his name for the fabled Mullah Nasruddin.

Some researchers have suggested that Bogga-Eddin is Gurdjieff's spelling of Bahaudin—the founder of the Naqshbandi Sufi order. Like Bahaudin, Bogga-Eddin too is from the region of Bukhara. But Bahaudin lived during the 14th century. So, Bogga-Eddin clearly does not refer to Bahaudin. In *Beelzebub's Tales* too, Beelzebub meets Bogga-Eddin in Gurdjieff's lifetime, suggesting an autobiographical component to the tale. Likely Gurdjieff gave the character a name similar to Bahaudin, and said he was from the same region, to intentionally misdirect the reader, as he frequently did when discussing aspects of his life. However, there is another possible understanding of the name Bogga-Eddin.

*Bogga* is the diminutive of *Bog* which means God in Russian, and *edin* means "is one." It appears that *edin* was spelled with two 'd's in English for the sake of proper pronunciation. So, apparently Gurdjieff is saying it was the oneness of God, or the grace of God, that led him to Sarmung.

Regarding the full name given in *Beelzebub's Tales,* Hadji is merely an honorific, and Zephir (or zephyr) means a gentle breeze. The idea of a gentle breeze also lends to the allusion of grace or a guiding force.

The character appears to serve the same purpose in *Beelzebub's Tales* too. Here Bogga-Eddin (or grace) is responsible for meeting the dervish Hadji Asvatz Troov.

More significant with regards to the purpose here, however, is that Bogga-Eddin (or grace) was responsible for Gurdjieff's meeting with a certain "kaphir" (more commonly spelled "kafir") from Sarmung. The word kafir is used in general to refer to foreigners, but more specifically to non-Muslims, and especially to those who do not believe in God. Clearly this indicates that Sarmung is not a monastery of any Muslim sect. Less clear, but also possible, is that this suggests Sarmung is a monastery of a nontheistic religion such as Buddhism.

Gurdjieff then goes on to describe a journey to Sarmung that is clearly allegorical. That he and Soloviev were hooded so they could not see where they were going is just a metaphor for how blind or naïve one is at the onset of one's spiritual journey. This too supports the suggestion that Bogga-Eddin is pure metaphor. It is much more likely that Gurdjieff met whoever introduced him to Sarmung (a.k.a. Surmang) within Tibet.

*Surmang Namgyal Tse*

## SARMUNG

Students of Gurdjieff's teaching have long wondered about the true identity of the monastery he calls Sarmung in his semi-autobiographical, semi-allegorical *Meetings with Remarkable Men*, the second series of his writings. Although Gurdjieff discovered valuable wisdom in many spiritual societies he encountered throughout the East, he is quite clear that Sarmung was the one which had the wisdom for which he had been seeking.

Note that the English edition of *Meetings with Remarkable Men* renders Sarmung as "Sarmoung" (with an 'o'). However, it is spelled without the 'o' in the original Russian text. The reason the 'o' was added to the spelling is because in Gurdjieff's time the convention was to transliterate the long 'u' vowel of foreign words with 'ou', as is done in French, so the word would not be mispronounced with a short 'u'. This is how Ouspensky ended up with the spelling of his name—to better assure his name would be pronounced *oo*-spensky. At the time, this practice was needed because there were not all that many foreign words adopted into English. Today things are different. We have adopted many foreign words into English. So, we know how to correctly pronounce words like "babushka", for example, without having to add the 'o'. If *Meetings with Remarkable Men* was first being translated into English today, the practice would be not to modify the spelling to "Sarmoung". Thus, throughout this work the name is intentionally rendered as the more accurate "Sarmung" rather than "Sarmoung", to show that the name is an anagram for Surmang.

One may wonder if other monasteries which Gurdjieff mentions in his work had been similarly disguised by use of an anagram. If so, this would give even more credence to the suggestion that Sarmung is a reference to Surmang. Although there is some evidence to this effect, the one other instance found is not as clear. The only other monastery he mentions by name, which, significantly, he does at the conclusion of the "Prince Yuri Lubovedsky" chapter (the chapter which describes Sarmung) is the Olman monastery. This is the monastery to which Lubovedsky is sent to live out the remainder of his life, which, he is told, has only three years remaining. We are also told that this monastery is on the northern slopes of the Himalayas. Unfortunately, no monastery by any name which Olman would be an anagram of can currently be found. However, one name for which Olman is an anagram, Monla, may indicate something. One of the Himalayan ranges dividing Tibet with Bhutan, which lies to its south, is called Monla Karchung. Its northern face would therefore lie in Tibet. Connecting Tibet with Bhutan through this range is the ancient Monla pass. There is also a village called Monla in the region. So, it is very conceivable that at one time there was in fact a monastery named Monla on the northern slope of Monla Karchung as Gurdjieff may be indicating. It is not uncommon for a town and an inlying monastery to share the same name. Surmang is one such example. There are in fact ruins of monasteries and temples on the slopes of Monla Karchung. There were some 6000 monasteries in Tibet before China invaded and demolished all but a handful. Making a survey of all that existed before the invasion would prove difficult. Still, as was pointed out earlier, the individual named Asiman in *Beelzebub's Tales* appears to be an anagram for the name Isanam. So, it seems clear enough that Gurdjieff made use of this encryption method.

But the above study of the name does not in itself indicate much. Let us now study what indicates that Sarmung is a Tibetan monastery. While it may be more difficult to show that the Sarmung monastery is specifically the Surmang, there can be little doubt that Sarmung is Tibetan. For one thing, many of Gurdjieff's direct students considered him a teacher of Tibetan wisdom. As some examples:

While lunching in Fontainebleau in 1924 with Alfred Orage, Jessim Howarth and Doris Tyndall, Ian Black was told that Gurdjieff "had studied in Tibet and knew the Buddhists who safeguarded the secret wisdom of the ages."[1]

Talking about Gurdjieff's distant healing abilities, Kathryn Hulme said, "Was it telepathy, assistance from 'higher forces,' or simply something out of his own great powerhouse of inner strength earned through remorseless work on himself all those years in Tibet?"[2]

A. L. Staveley even thought, "It is a great tragedy that the Tibetans who have come to this country after their country was destroyed by the Chinese are almost completely unable to pass on the great knowledge because so few people are even close to their level of understanding. Some of the Gurdjieff people do have contact with them and perhaps not all the Tibetan wisdom will be lost."[3]

Also consider the strange case of Rolf Alexander, a New Zealander who was a student of Gurdjieff for perhaps six months in 1913 while attending school in Moscow. He wrote several books detailing many aspects of Gurdjieff's teaching, claiming to have received the knowledge therein while in Tibet that year. It was only after *In Search of the Miraculous* was published in 1949, and thereby Gurdjieff and his work was brought to the attention of the wider public, that he admitted to having studied with Gurdjieff in 1913 (though he never retracted his bogus story about being in Tibet).

The understanding which Gurdjieff's pupils had regarding the Tibetan origins of his teaching is also implied in various journalistic accounts. C. E. Bechhofer understood Gurdjieff to have acquired his knowledge during "long journeys in the interior of Asia, where he studied in mysterious monasteries, Mongolian and Tibetan, and other secret places of the east."[4]

95

In an article called "Romantic Search for Life's Secret: Salvation in Dancing," the author ponders, "Has this extraordinary man Gurdjieff the secret of perfect happiness? Has he wrested from those remote and fantastic priests of Thibet some knowledge long since forgotten by the Western world?"[5]

Journalist Raymond G. Carroll in his 1924 article on Gurdjieff's Institute for the *New York Evening Post*, which gives the impression he got his information from A. R. Orage, mentions that Tibet was Gurdjieff's last journey before he began teaching.[6] If Sarmung contained the teaching for which Gurdjieff long sought, it stands to reason that he would not have had need for further searches—that it would have been his last.

Orage himself makes this point more clear. In a 1923 exposé on the Institute, journalist E. C. Bowyer quotes him as saying, "Gurdjieff, who is of Greek origin, after years of studying in Persia, Afghanistan, and Baluchistan, *discovered in Thibet 15 years ago a school of thought which completed his own system*, and then went back to Russia to undertake his work for mankind."[7]

Long before Gurdjieff began writing *Meetings with Remarkable Men*, he was clearly conveying to his students that the core of his teaching was derived from some specific Tibetan school. In addition, we can also deduce exactly *when* Gurdjieff was in Tibet based on the above reference. Fifteen years prior to the time the statement was made would be 1908.

It is also interesting to note that Orage's book *On Love*, which is no more than an expansion of one of Gurdjieff's aphorisms, is subtitled *Freely Adapted from the Tibetan*. Clearly Orage understood the origin of Gurdjieff's knowledge to be Tibetan.

Then there is William Segal's interview with Chatral Rinpoche (reproduced earlier). Chatral must have been close with those with whom Gurdjieff was in contact, as he seems to understand something of Gurdjieff's time in Tibet, his practice of tranticism of some sort in the Swat Valley, and who his teacher was.

Moreover, at a dinner in 1944, Gurdjieff himself in no uncertain terms says that the Sarmung monastery is in Tibet. In the transcript of the dinner meeting of January 11, 1944, Gurdjieff presents an engraving he had found of a Tibetan ritual and asks those present to guess what it is about. After someone finally guesses that it is some Tibetan spectacle, Gurdjieff goes on to describe it. In the process of his incredulous telling he says, "We have read in a chapter of the Second Series about Prince Lubovedsky some details about the temples of Tibet where the priestesses have studied such movements from infancy before the branched instrument which expressed the law of seven."[8] It is the chapter "Prince Yuri Lubovedsky" in which Gurdjieff describes the Sarmung, and it is the Sarmung in which the "branched instrument" is described. Clearly Gurdjieff is saying here that Sarmung is a Tibetan monastery.

Elsewhere in the discussion, Gurdjieff says that the Tibetan ritual he was describing was witnessed by him 35 years earlier. This takes us to the beginning of 1909, just about the same time derived from the Orage quote above. So, there are two references pointing to the same time period.

Another interesting point is that Gurdjieff seems to be describing an example of what is known as self-arising phenomena—the sort of ordinary magic described earlier—and the Surmang valley is known for manifesting such phenomena. He simply says, "It is a unique thing; a divine music that I heard in the mountains of Tibet. And at the same time, there was no music. And yet down in the foothills below one heard music." It is only after a student presses him for more detail that he adds some nonsense about the music being produced by the aid of a radio-like device held by one of the monk performers in the print he had shown them. This is yet another example of Gurdjieff adding something ridiculous to a story to create doubt about some truth. It appears that he too was sensitive about the sensationalization of this sort of phenomena.

Also significant is that before the talk begins, an exercise is given to those present which is an adaptation of various Tibetan yoga practices. The steps pertaining to breathing are clearly borrowed from Tibetan forms. Considering the exercise, the print shown, and Gurdjieff's recollection, he seems to have been particularly nostalgic for Tibet that evening. Just a few days earlier (January 5th) was the 40th anniversary of Dudjom Lingpa's *parinirvana* (transition from life). Could that have been the reason for his nostalgia?

Recall what Gurdjieff says about the chief of the group of seven Tibetan masters and the British invasion of Tibet in *Beelzebub Tales*. The horror he expresses in his recollection implies an intimate association he had with Tibetan Buddhism. Although Gurdjieff discusses most subjects with a certain neutrality, this is one subject where the grief he experienced in recalling it can easily be sensed. Clearly what he received from Tibetan Buddhism was particularly profound. That he returned to Tibet about four years after his first trip there also suggests this.

There is also evidence in Gurdjieff's telling in *Meetings with Remarkable Men* that Sarmung is in Tibet. Clearly the details he provides are conflicting—perhaps in order to obscure the author's past, perhaps in order to force its readers not to take his word for granted and to labor themselves for the knowledge they seek, perhaps both. Yet a careful reading may provide some clarity.

One such indication is that Gurdjieff describes having passed snow capped peaks en route to Sarmung and later describes his first day at Sarmung as a summer day. There are few places on Earth where mountain tops are covered with snow even in summer. Indeed the only such place in Central Asia where the altitude is high enough to allow this condition is the Himalayas.

Another indication from *Meetings with Remarkable Men* is that upon arriving at Sarmung after an arduous journey, Gurdjeff and Soloviev are given three days rest before entering the rigors of monastic life. What do they decide to do during their rest? Brush up on their Tibetan. In fact, he mentions this twice. Certainly we must be cautious about taking anything in this book literally. But it is typically the more extravagant statements we must question. What makes this detail particularly believable is precisely that it is so ordinary that it can easily be overlooked. Why would they be practicing Tibetan unless they were expecting to communicate in Tibetan? This detail is so natural that it is unlikely it was contrived.

Now that we have established with little doubt that the Sarmung is in Tibet, let us see what indicates that it is specifically the Surmang, or at least what increases the likelihood that it is the Surmang.

For one thing, the way in which Gurdjieff worked with many of his students is very reminiscent of how Marpa worked with Milarepa, the founders of the Kagyupa sect of which Surmang is a primary branch. Like Marpa, who repeatedly had Milarepa build a tower only to tear it down and rebuild it with a different design or in a different location, Gurdjieff had Orage and other male students dig enormous ditches only to fill them in and redig them somewhere else the next day.

Also increasing the likelihood that the Sarmung is the Surmang as opposed to other Tibetan monasteries is that it was one of the primary monasteries promoting the Rimé movement. Today most Tibetan monasteries support Rimé, but in Gurdjieff's time it was still relatively new. Rimé is a nonsectarian movement founded at the time in response to the rigidity and exclusivity of the dominant Gelugpa sect. Rimé literally means all-embracing and unlimited. Although it arose in response to sectarianism, Rimé is actually more of a universalism movement as its name implies. Not only were the Kagyupa, Nyingmapa and Sakyapa sects sharing their teachings with one another, but they also welcomed the Bönpa (the indigenous non-Buddhist religion of Tibet) and other traditions to partake in the exchange to some degree. Even before Rimé there were great Tibetan teachers who traveled to India and returned with non-Buddhist tantric teachings.

All this is to say that having practiced other traditions before taking his Buddhist vows, whatever Tibetan monastery Gurdjieff was at would likely have been a Rimé supporter. Gurdjieff may even have impressed his Tibetan teachers with the Shaivist and Sufi practices he knew. Chatral Rinpoche's awareness of Gurdjieff having previously studied and practiced some form of tantra in the Swat Valley indeed suggests this. And Surmang was one of the early supporters of Rimé.

Jamgön Kongtrul Lodro Thaye, who was one of the co-founders of Rimé, was the teacher of the tenth Trungpa tulku of Surmang.

Returning briefly to the subject of dance, it is worthwhile mentioning that the Surmang monastery collective included a school of dance. Chögyam Trungpa discusses his brief enrollment in the monastery's dance school in his autobiography, *Born in Tibet*. It is also significant that the dance Trungpa practiced utilizes such an alphabet of postures as the dances Gurdjieff describes having observed at Sarmung.

Another suggestion from *Meetings with Remarkable Men* that Sarmung is more likely the Surmang monastery rather than other Tibetan monasteries is that Gurdjieff says the Sarmung monastery he stayed at was the *chief* monastery, implying a network of monasteries with the name. Likewise, Surmang is a collective of monasteries rather than the more typical individual isolated monastery. The collective included about eleven.

He also describes the design of Sarmung as a concentric one with courts within courts. This is indeed a design feature of many Tibetan Buddhist monasteries as is in fact a design of Surmang's "chief" monastery.

But there is more that tells us that the monastery Gurdjieff speaks of in his Lubovedsky chapter, with all probability, had to have been Surmang. When asked about what Chogyam Tungpa may have had to say about the subject, James George replied:

> When I met Trungpa in 1967, he confirmed that he knew Gurdjieff had spent a few years in Tibet and had heard that Gurdjieff had visited the Surmang monastery, but it was not until about ten years later that I began to wonder if "Sarmoung" was a play on words hinting at Surmang origins which he of course wished to conceal and had perhaps sworn to conceal...[9]

James George is not the only one Trungpa had made such a comment to either. He also told his attendant John Perks essentially the same thing in the mid 1970s.[10]

Those who know something of the prankster Trungpa could be may doubt that he was sincere when he spoke of Gurdjieff having visited Surmang. Discerning the truth from the absurd is not so clear-cut when dealing with a crazy wisdom teacher such as Trungpa (or Gurdjieff for that matter). What may also raise doubts is the fact that Trungpa was born thirty years after Gurdjieff was there. How could he possibly have heard about Gurdjieff's presence there some forty-five years later? Both are valid doubts which need to be looked at.

In answer to the first, the fact that Trungpa recognized the child of a couple in his sangha as the tulku (or incarnation) of Gurdjieff also needs to be considered. As much as a prankster as Trungpa was, the recognition of a tulku is no joking matter. When it came to matters regarding his spiritual heritage and its continuation he was quite serious. And by recognizing the tulku of Gurdjieff in particular, Trungpa is very clearly indicating the certainty he had that Gurdjieff was part of that heritage. He once told the tulku's mother, a former Gurdjieff practitioner, that he felt Gurdjieff "was one of the best dharmic teachers to come to America."[11] And when a Buddhist master such as Trungpa refers to a *dharmic* teacher, he is no doubt referring specifically to a teacher of the buddhadharma. (The epilogue is an interview with Gurdjieff's tulku.)

In answer to the second, Trungpa evidently knew Gurdjieff's son. If I am correct, Gurdjieff's son was one of his teachers. This subject will be discussed in detail in a chapter of its own.

In addition, Shechen Kongtrul, who was Trungpa's root teacher (and also the incarnation of Jamgön Kongtrul Lodro Thaye), was a student of the Surmang abbot that Gurdjieff likely met. So, Trungpa could have heard something of Gurdjieff's presence at Surmang from Shechen Kongtrul as well.

So, if Surmang is actually a Kagyupa subsect containing some eleven monasteries, is it possible to know at which one Gurdjieff was? Well, if he says he was at its *chief* monastery, there can be little doubt he is referring to Surmang Namgyal Tse.

Moreover, the *shedra* (college) at Namgyal Tse was well-known for teaching Tibetan medicine. This is significant since

Gurdjieff implies that Soloviev studied Tibetan medicine at Sarmung, and that he picked up something of Tibetan medicine there himself.

Before we try to identify Soloviev and Lubovedsky, let us first take a look at the text of the meeting transcript mentioned above in which Gurdjieff says Sarmung is in Tibet.

---

[1] Ian E. Black, *Friend of France* (London: Jonathan Cape, 1941), 13.

[2] Kathryn Hulme, *Undiscovered Country: A Spiritual Adventure* (Boston: Little, Brown & Co.), 159.

[3] Kenneth Salls, *Talks with A. L. Staveley* (electronic manuscript), last note of 10/30/73.

[4] C. E. Bechhofer, "The Forest Philosophers," *The Century Magazine* 108, no. 1 (May 1924), 70.

[5] Unable to cite newspaper article clipping found. However, in *Gurdjieff in the Public Eye*, Paul Beekman Taylor provides the year 1923.

[6] January 26, 1924.

[7] E. C. Bowyer; "New Cult: Forest Temple of Hard Work and Rough Food," *Gurdjieff International Review* 1, no. 4 (Summer 1998), 14. My italics.

[8] G. Gurdjieff, *Transcripts of Gurdjieff's Meetings 1941–1946* (London: Book Studio, 2008), 100–102.

[9] Private correspondence.

[10] Private correspondence.

[11] Private correspondence.

*Engravings similar to the one Gurdjieff showed his dinner guests.*

## A Tibetan Ritual

[Mr. Gurdjieff has given an exercise and afterward he shows the group an engraving representing seven Oriental dancers, with headdresses like gigantic spherical hats surmounted by antennas; they are striking in cadence their tambourines and blowing into pipes like fifes under the direction of their chief who holds in his hand a sort of pennant. Mr Gurdjieff asks each pupil to give an opinion as to what this picture represents. No one knows. One woman thinks it is a Tibetan dance.]

Gurdjieff: That is it, the scene is in Tibet. It is a unique thing; a divine music that I heard in the mountains of Tibet. And at the same time, there was no music. And yet down in the foothills below one heard music.

[The group goes to the table and dines. After dinner a student speaks to Mr. Gurdjieff.]

Questioner: Sir, what does that picture represent that you showed us a while ago?

Gurdjieff: I have told you. I was very astonished when I saw that for the first time. It is a ceremony that takes place in Tibet. There in a valley is a place where special ceremonies are held, not for everyone, not for just anybody. They are reserved for a certain category of initiates. One receives there this initiation and I received it. There is simply a smallish, or rather a large house in a valley. Nothing more. It is there that this ceremony is held. One arrives in the foothills and hears the music. But beautiful like that, never. Truly it was celestial music. Well, one heard the music but saw nothing. Everywhere, all around, there were mountains and that was all. How and from where could this music come? How was it possible? There was not a house near by. One could see far off and there was no one to be seen. Who could be playing this music?

You can imagine what an impression it made and how I was astonished. It was only two years afterward that I knew the secret and that musicians were playing in the mountains. He that walked at the head of the seven musicians you see in this picture held in his hand an instrument that was a kind of radio. Due to it, he hears what goes on in the valley. And he directs. There is no music, only vibrations that are made by the movements of the body. In his hand is a special instrument. A radio. The radio was discovered only twenty years ago and I saw this instrument thirty-five years ago; the radio did not yet exist. You understand; it is with special movements that these vibrations are produced. These vibrations are gathered into the globe that they have on their heads and sent out through the antennas. There is in the valley a thing—something like the instrument that the leader has in his hand with which he establishes the contact. This instrument collects everything and the vibrations come forth in the form of music. But there isn't any music, no instrument. It is the totality of their interior experiences which produces the transmitted result.

QUESTIONER: But they have tambourines and fifes.

GURDJIEFF: That helps. It is everything together that gives that, but they don't play music with that. The interesting thing is that the movements and the interior exercises are what give the music. Very interesting thing. What you have all done just a while ago is child's play beside that. And what must be done is much more difficult. But it is well understood that interior experiences can give vibrations and that a strong experience of that kind can give vibrations capable of producing divine music. One can arrive at such results thanks to an exact effort in the work. If everything is not absolutely harmonious, there is cacophony. You must have the exact attitude necessary for this in order to produce celestial music. We have read in a chapter of the Second Series [*Meetings with Remarkable Men*] about Prince Lubovedsky some details about the temples of Tibet where the priestesses have studied such movements from infancy before the branched instrument which expressed the law of seven. They were able to perform their dances effectively only after years of study. It is the same for these dancers. They have studied these movements from childhood and only when they are old they may participate in the ceremony. You can imagine how they have had to work in order to be specialists.

You see my astonishment? I have seen a thousand astonishing things. But I remember still my stupefaction at this. Afterward I understood. But during two or three days I could not sleep; I wanted to know. I had heard the music and I hadn't seen anywhere a man or a house or a movement. Nothing but mountains and snow. Nothing more. And I was hearing that music. I was like a madman. Afterward, in studying this, I quieted myself and learned what it was about. But you understand now why I repeat always among other things—do not, for example, make a movement with the leg which should be made only with the foot. Perhaps you will need that leg for something else. You must do everything exactly from the beginning. But you must respect each detail. We will not play music. It isn't a question of music but a real feeling of the "I am." There are seven exercises for that. This present exercise is one of them. You can repeat for a thousand years "I am" with your mind; it will give you nothing real. This exercise can, however. That is why you must do it with exactitude from the beginning. Only an exactness in your work can give exact results. It's like what I heard in those mountains. One movement not exactly executed among seven persons and the result would be a cacophony. Everything depends on the totality.

And our Mr. District Attorney writes and writes. How can he understand all this when I myself do not very well understand all that I have been saying.

*G. Gurdjieff*

Engravings of costumed Tibetan dancers reproduced from *Mythologie du Buddhisme au Tibet et en Mongolie Basée sur la Collection Lamaïque du Prince Oukhtomsky* by Albert Grünwedel (Leipzig: F. A. Brockhaus, 1900).

*Ovshé Norzunov*

## PRINCE LUBOVEDSKY

As mentioned earlier, the first research into Gurdjieff's time in Tibet followed up on what turned out to be a false rumor. The letter Rom Landau claimed to receive from Achmed Abdullah stating that Gurdjieff was in fact Agwan Dordjieff was a complete fabrication. Despite having read Alexandra David-Néel's article discrediting the claim, James Webb continued his research along these lines, and for good reason. Webb discovered much in common between Dordjieff's student Ovshé Norzunov and Gurdjieff. So much so that he believed Gurdjieff was actually Norzunov. Also influencing Webb's belief was that he was unable to find any information on Norzunov after Gurdjieff began teaching, but more recently information on Norzunov's later life has come to light. Photographic evidence also makes it clear that Norzunov and Gurdjieff were not one and the same. Yet it seems as though Webb had stumbled onto something.

Norzunov was a wealthy Kalmyk—a group of four Mongol tribes who immigrated to the Russian Steppes between the 17th and 19th centuries. Norzunov himself belonged to the Dörbet tribe. As Mongols, they practiced Tibetan Buddhism and regarded the Dalai Lama as their spiritual leader. Although they ruled themselves originally, eventually they became a protectorate of Russia, known today as the Republic of Kalmykia. Norzunov was raised somewhere in Stavropol Province, where he also made a home with his wife and two children.

What is interesting is that he is known to have journeyed to many of the same places as Gurdjieff. He specifically mentions Siberia, the Caucasus, China, Chinese Turkestan, Tibet, India and Paris in his journeys of 1898–1901, and he certainly visited others before and after.

It is too bad that Webb did not consider that Norzunov could have been another of Gurdjieff's band, particularly Prince Yuri Lubovedsky. He likely omitted the possibility of Norzunov being Lubovedsky because he was working with an earlier date of birth for Gurdjieff which would have put the two at the same age when Gurdjieff relates that Lubovedsky was older. Because Prince Esper Ukhtomsky was one of Narzunov's sponsors, Webb suggests that Ukhtomsky was Lubovedsky instead. But there are many problems with the suggestion of this identification. For the purposes of the present study, however, only the greatest need be mentioned here —the date of Ukhtomsky's journeys. His travels with then-Tzarevitch Nicholas II embarked in 1889. Gurdjieff's date of birth was long in doubt, but generally considered to have been somewhere between 1866 and 1877. If Gurdjieff was born at the lower end of that range it might have been possible for him to have met Ukhtomsky on that journey. But as mentioned earlier, recent research has resulted in the discovery of civil records that strongly suggest he was born in 1877. Gurdjieff would only have been about thirteen years old at the time Nicholas' entourage was in Egypt. (Gurdjieff places his first meeting with Lubovedsky at the pyramids.) Also, the year that Gurdjieff cites in the "History of the Institute" as the time in which he met Lubovedsky, 1895, appears to be factual. Certainly Flinders Petrie, who we assume to be Professor Skidlov—the third founder of the Seekers of Truth—was in Egypt at the time. And this is long after the Tzarevitch's grand tour of the Orient which Ukhtomsky joined.

But let us return to the subject of Norzunov. One thing in particular that suggests Norzunov was Gurdjieff's friend Lubovedsky is that he was in fact a prince and had the wealth that Gurdjieff describes Lubovedsky having had. Like his father, Norzunov was a *zaisan* (a Kalmyk noble)—a title which is often translated to "prince". Supporting the suggestion that Lubovedsky was a tribal prince rather than a prince of the imperial Russian court is that in Olga de Hartmann's essay on the beginnings of Gurdjieff's Institute the prince is said to be "from an ancient lineage," implying that he was a prince of one of Russia's indigenous cultures. She also says that amongst the 15 seekers were representatives of various religions, including Buddhism to which Norzunov belonged.

In *Meetings with Remarkable Men,* Gurdjieff also says that Lubovedsky was acquainted with the Ceylonese monk "A." Norzunov says he made a stop in Colombo on his return from his third journey to Tibet. Quite possibly the monk he is referring to is Anagarika Dharmapala who was from Colombo. Regardless, it was at this stop in Colombo that Norzunov probably met this monk. It does make sense, however, that Gurdjieff would have wanted to conceal the identity of Anagarika Dharmapala due to his association with the Theosophical Society, of which he had spoken disparagingly.

Another thing that Gurdjieff says about Lubovedsky in *Meetings with Remarkable Men* is that he began his spiritual search after his wife died. Considering that this is also said in "The History of the Institute" and Olga de Hartman's essay, it is likely true. Certainly Norzunov said that he departed on his first journey to Tibet in 1898 "to strengthen my faith," but it is not entirely clear if Norzunov's wife had died. Still, it seems likely enough. Regarding his thoughts upon having finished his studies, Norzunov said, "Unlike my companions, I did not want to engage myself as an interpreter or as a Russian official, preferring instead the nomadic way of life of my native steppe for my dear family.... So I stayed in my steppe and took care of raising cattle, got married, and I was already the father of a one-year-old child..." This implies that his wife would also have been a Kalmyk. But the woman in the 1908 photo of Norzunov with his wife (provided in James Webb's book) is Chinese. This appears to be a second wife, perhaps met on his travels. Also supporting this suggestion is that Stavropol hardly has a Chinese population, if at all. However, Ulan-Ude, where the photo was taken, being in Siberia, is much closer to China and likey has more Chinese. Stavropol is in the Caucasus. Besides, a Chinawoman would not have been able to offer Norzunov the nomadic Kalmyk way of life that he says he made for himself.

There is another thing to consider related to this subject: Gurdjieff specifically says that Lubovedsky's wife died while giving birth to her first child. When you think about it, the formulation is very odd. By specifying a *first* child there is an implication that there are others, but if she died at the time that could not be possible. Why not specify her *only* child instead? Clarification can be found, however, in the original Russian text. There it specifies *the* first child, not *her* first, suggesting that Lubovedsky later had other children. Norzunov had two sons. The first was born around 1891, and the second four years later. So, it is conceivable that he had his first son with a Kalmyk wife and his second with his Chinese wife.

If the places where the various photos of Norzunov and his family were taken indicate where they lived, there is another photo that is significant. James Webb did not reproduce it in his book, but he mentions a photo found in the Joseph Deniker collection of Norzunov's first son that was taken in Moscow. This is significant because Gurdjieff said Lubovedsky had a house in Moscow.

Other things that Gurdjieff says of Lubovedsky cannot be ascertained regarding Norzunov. Some of these statements may be additional alterations of the truth. They are that Lubovedsky was in Egypt in 1895, had a sister, had a dog, and had a house in Pera.

We know about three expeditions that Norzunov made to Tibet between 1898 and 1901 thanks to an article that his associate Joseph Deniker wrote for him on the subject. It appears that Gurdjieff accompanied him on the third, made in 1901. Before discussing this, however, let us discuss what is known about this nobleman's life after these journeys.

In 1905, along with other *zaisans*, Norzunov advocated for greater rights and freedom for their fellow Russian Buddhists and the elimination of terms such as "idolater" and "pagan" when referring to them in official documents. In 1911 he was in the company of Dordjieff along with other attendants of the religious leader to oversee the construction of a Buddhist temple in Saint Petersburg. In 1913 he began working as a traveling salesman for a Petersburg firm. When the revolution broke out in 1917, Norzunov returned his family to his native steppes to run his farm. In 1921 he was appointed head of the Transport and Materials Department of the newly proclaimed Kalmyk Autonomous Region. Soon after he was assigned regional financial inspector. But then, in 1923, he acquired land in the Bolshederbetovsky ulus (district) and returned to farming. In January 1927 Norzunov attended the First All-Union Spiritual Buddhist Council, which was held in Moscow. In November 1929 Norzunov and seven other important *zaisans* were declared "harmful elements," their properties were confiscated, and Norzunov himself was expelled to the city of Kamyshin. In April 1930 Norzunov was expelled for the second time, this time to a specially designated plot of land with no resources. Faced with starvation, he escaped and disappeared without trace.

In *Meetings with Remarkable Men*, Gurdjieff says that when he arrived at Sarmung (a.k.a. Surmang), which was likely in 1908, he discovered that Prince Lubovedsky was there. Interestingly, there is no record of Norzunov's whereabouts between 1906 and 1910. Thus it's conceivable that he could have been at Surmang at the time. Yet this seems rather unlikely. In Norzunov's account of his trips to Lhasa, all of the many sites he mentions visiting are associated with the Gelugpa sect, of which he and Dordjieff were members, and Surmang is Kagyupa. Given the devotion he expresses to his sect, it seems doubtful that Norzunov would have been interested in Surmang. Also supporting this is the contradictory information that Gurdjieff gives about Lubovedsky's later life. Although while speaking about Sarmung in the chapter "Prince Yuri Lubovedsky" we are told that Lubovedsky left there for the Olman monastery to live out his few remaining years, earlier in the chapter, while speaking of their initial meeting in 1895, we are told that he and Gurdjieff maintained correspondence for nearly 35 years. This seems more factual. Thirty-five years from 1895 takes us to 1930, which is the time of Norzunov's disappearance.

Besides, Gurdjieff is clearly trying to say something metaphorically regarding the three centers in the Sarmung tale and he very likely had to alter the facts in order to do so in such instances. Lubovedsky represents the emotional center, Soloviev the intellectual center, and Gurdjieff the moving-instinctive center. He may have had other reasons for writing Lubovedsky into that tale as well. He probably genuinely wished that Lubovedsky could have been there with him. Gurdjieff may even have felt indebted to Lubovedsky for helping him acquire documentation on that first journey that enabled him to return without Lubovedsky's accompaniment.

Having said that Lubovedsky represents the emotional center, it would be good to say a little more about that. The name Lubovedsky is based on the Russian word for love. An equivalent formulation in English may be Prince Lovey-dovey. Looking at the photos of Norzunov from a physionomical perspective, his features do seem to indicate an emotionally centered individual; he has a very sweet, kind expression. Possibly hinting at this as well is that Joseph Deniker describes Norzunov as a "humble" man, and Norzunov's exploits reveal a certain naïveté.

The names that Gurdjieff gives his fellow seekers may not be entirely fabricated as is generally supposed. There is reason to believe that some of the names he provides in *Meetings with Remarkable Men* were nicknames. What particularly suggests this is that Gurdjieff spoke of Prince Lubovedsky long before writing the second series. In "The History of the Institute," Gurdjieff identifies him as "Prince L." So, it appears that Norzunov was actually called Lubovedsky by his companions.

The name of the other seeker who made it to Sarmung, Soloviev, also appears to be a nickname. It appears to be an allusion to Vladimir Soloviev (1853–1900), a renowned Russian philosopher. Calling someone Soloviev would have been the equivalent of calling someone Einstein today.

116

Before moving on to the subject of Soloviev's identity, let us read Norzunov's account of his third journey to Lhasa. Particularly interesting is that Norzunov says that his group crossed the Gobi Desert in record-breaking time, which seemingly corresponds to Gurdjieff's telling of his group navigating sand storms with ease by the aid of stilts when traversing the Gobi. Also interesting is his description of the Tibetan ritual which Gurdjieff taught as a movement he called "Measuring the Way by One's Length." Although it is unlikely that Gurdjieff found Norzunov at Surmang when he arrived there, it seems clear enough that Gurdjieff accompanied Norzunov on his third journey to Lhasa, which was made at a time corresponding to Gurdjieff's first journey to Tibet.

Photograph of Norzunov enhanced by the author. Original photographer unknown.

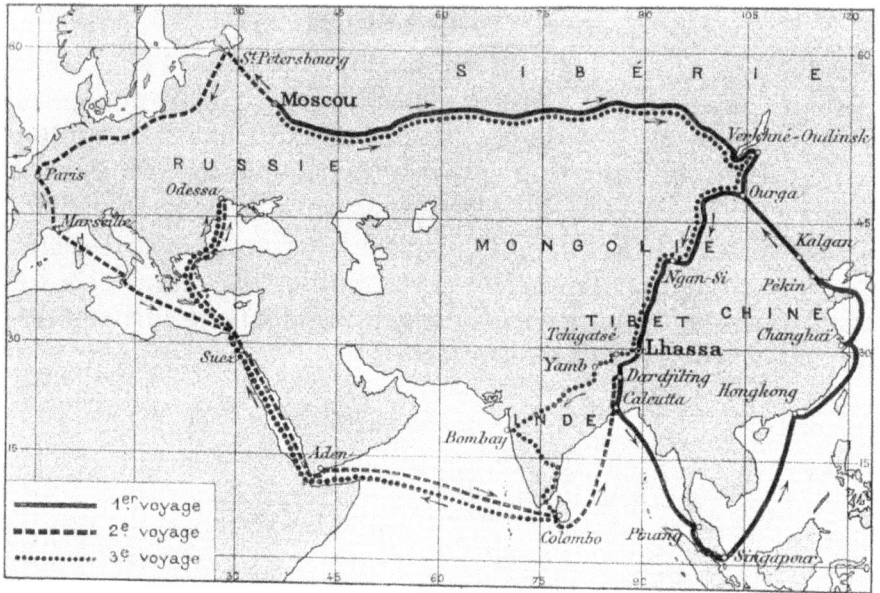

*Map of Norzunov's three journeys to Lhasa.*

*Engraving of the Tibetan ambulatory prostration practice that Gurdjieff calls "Measuring the Way by One's Length." The caption in the original article reads, "Pilgrims making the sacred circuit by measuring the circumference of Lhasa by the length of their bodies."*

# THIRD VOYAGE TO LHASA

*This text is the third part of the article "Trois Voyages à Lhassa," written for Ovshé Norzunov by Joseph Deniker, who pieced it together from letters sent to him and accounts told to him orally. Each part is devoted to one of the three expeditions Norzunov made to Lhasa and the account included here is that of his third voyage. As it is unlikely that Gurdjieff accompanied him on the first two journeys, only the third is presented here.*

*The article incorporates the Mongolian and Kalmyk names that Norzunov himself frequently used for various places, people, titles and objects of Tibet. Because Tibetan culture is better known today, I had wanted to replace these Mongolian and Kalmyk names with the Tibetan names with which readers would be more familiar. However, as I was unable to discover the Tibetan names of all of them, I elected instead to retain the original names used and include the Tibetan for the ones found in square brackets. Adding to the difficulty of translating the names of these Asian languages is that Deniker appears to have made some transliteration errors, and the probability that some of the places referred to no longer exist. Deniker's errors may be the reason that the Tibetan equivalents of some names could not be found. Where other sorts of errors of his were detected (i.e. obvious misunderstandings), I took the liberty to correct them. But beware that I may have introduced my own errors in editing this difficult text. (LN)*

Despite the mishaps of my second trip, as soon as I arrived in my camps, I had no other thought than to return to Tibet again. By a happy combination of circumstances, the Tsanit [Tib. Geshe] (doctor of theology) Khenpo (superior of the monastery) Agwan Dordjieff was in his homeland of Transbaikalia, Siberia, and on the verge of leaving for Lhasa. A few dispatches exchanged were enough to persuade my guru to wait for me in Urga. I arrived there by the express train and with hardy relay horses. We left Urga with six other traveling companions on December 5, 1900, and on February 28, 1901, we reached the sacred walls of Lhasa.

So we made the crossing of the Gobi desert in two months and twenty-four days. No one has made this journey as fast as us; usually it takes five to six months.

In Lhasa, I had the honor of being introduced to the Dalai Lama again. Through an interpreter, His Holiness the Dalai Lama deigned to caressingly ask me how I was treated by the English in captivity, and how I returned to my homeland. I told His Holiness the Dalai Lama everything in detail. For all my services, I received from him a gift of the highest order—a sort of carpet made of tiger skin. It is a seat of honor in all the solemn ceremonies of Tibetan Buddhists. Once having sat on a tiger skin in the presence of the Dalai Lama, the fact is entered into a register, and thenceforth the individual will always have the right to sit in his presence on such a carpet.

I spent more than a month in Lhasa and was able to take a large number of photographs with a new camera given to me by the Geographical Society of Saint Petersburg, whose secretary, Mr Grigoriev, received me very well and gave me valuable advice during my short stay in the Russian capital.

During this stay I visited all that was worth seeing in Lhasa. It was very easy for me to experience the peculiarities of the different buildings, but it was difficult taking photographs. I always had to hide because it is completely forbidden, even for Buddhists, to capture the figures, objects or people in a small black box to be transported to the West. Nevertheless, I took a lot of pictures.

The first temple I visited was Grand Ju, which is called

Jokhang in Tibetan. It is at the center of a large group of houses and shops. This temple has three floors. Its main entrance faces west. It is covered with four golden roofs, and it contains a large number of statues of Buddhist deities,[1] in the center of which is seen the figure of Shakyamuni, Lord Buddha, represented as he was at twenty years old, in the aspect of a young prince and of natural size. It is said that this statue was especially made in Magadha, India. It is claimed that it was Vishwakarma who made it under the auspices of the god Indra. Buddhist books say this statue was cast with five precious metals: gold, silver, zinc, copper, and iron, and five rarer substances, which some commentators equate to different gemstones. This figure is under a canopy supported by four golden columns.

To the left and right of Shakyamuni Buddha are larger-than-life statues, including that of Maitreya—the successor of Buddha Shakyamuni. Among the other statues, I especially noticed that of the deity that we Kalmyks call Niduber Uzukchi and is called Avalokiteshvara by the Tibetans, which has eleven heads and hundreds of arms. This bodhisattva is the heart disciple of Amitabha, the personification of charity, and of whom the Dalai Lama is the incarnation on earth.

On the second floor is the statue of Palden Lhamo, protector goddess of Tibet. Pilgrims throw handfuls of rice at her, and this rice accumulates in the folds of her clothes, attracting large numbers of rats in the temple. It is forbidden under punishment of death to kill these rats.

Pilgrims make processions around the temple at fixed times. A zone of four meters wide has therefore been created around the Grand Ju and its outbuildings so that pilgrims can circumambulate there freely. There can be seen a rising poplar, grown from a Buddha's hair planted in the ground. It is this area that we call the "internal circuit."

Beyond this line stretches the most commercial district of Lhasa, called Banakcho [Tib. Chengguan]; also, it is on the main street which passes by there (way of the average circuit), that is, the site of the market.

The temple of Little Ju [Tib. Ramoche] is further north. The houses surrounding it are more scattered and not grouped together like the Grand Ju complex. The Little Ju is surmounted by a gilded dome, and all its doors open towards the east.

I also did not fail to visit the sacred home of the protective genius of Lhasa, the temple of Choijin Tsangan [Tib. unknown]. It is both a temple and a monastery where two hundred monks live. Then I gradually visited all the monasteries that are grouped inside the largest circular path of Lhasa, the path of the outer circuit.

Towards the north of venerated Lhasa I saw the monasteries of Baldan Majud [Tib. unknown] and Bodjud [Tib. unknown] (each one contains two hundred monks) and the monastery of Muri [Tib. unknown] (three hundred monks). Towards the west of the holy city I visited the monastery of Tsemolin [Tib. unknown] (more than one hundred monks), then the monastery of Chidda [Tib. unknown], and finally that of Danjailin [Tib. unknown] (two hundred monks)—the old residence of the Khutuktu [Tib. Tulku] (an incarnated lama) Demo—the regent who assumes the legislative duties of the Dalai Lama during his childhood. Finally, I was able to still see and photograph the ancient palace of the kings of Tibet, which the people refer to as Gadan Kansar, and which is very close to the temple of Ramoche.

This palace, which has five floors, is still inhabited, although it is falling into ruins due to poor pilgrims who could not find accommodation elsewhere. I would have liked to photograph the west façade which is the most interesting. It is the highest and also the most remarkable. But it was unfortunately impossible with the Tibetans watching me so closely.

This palace differs from other buildings in Lhasa because it is not whitewashed, and here is why: King Gyurme Namgyal, the inhabitant of this palace, is famous for having fought the Dalai Lama, who then wanted to unite in his person spiritual power and temporal power like now. With the help of the Chinese, the Dalai Lama was victorious and the Chinese had the secular king of Tibet assassinated (1750). The seventh Dalai Lama, Kelzang Gyatso (1708–1757) was then proclaimed and inaugurated by the Chinese. To commemorate this event,

122

the Chinese left the old palace of the kings of Tibet as it was, and whitewashed the other houses in Lhasa.

I also walked around Lhasa before making my long excursions to the surrounding monasteries. Shortly after leaving the outer circuit and heading west of the Potala, I saw the Jagpori Hill. The Chogori Baydor [Tib. unknown] temple can be seen there rising to its summit, along with a monastery where the incarnation of Bodhisattva Vajrapani lives and where medicine is taught to three hundred student monks in its *manba* [Tib. *menpa*] (medical) *datsan* [Tib. *dratsang*] (college).

At the western foot of this hill is the Kundulin [Tib. unknown] monastery, where there is a chapel frequented largely by Chinese merchants. One kilometer further to the west rises the palace of Norbulingka. This is where the Dalai Lama lives during the summer. It is a charming and peaceful residence in the middle of the greenery of a large park. In front of this palace but on the side opposite the external circuit is seen the small residence of the *amban* (a high official representing the emperor of China), to whom Tibet is nominally submitted, as is known.

This house is surrounded by walls—the remains of the old enclosure of Lhasa—and the door is quite dilapidated. However, on both sides of this ruined entrance, there are poles decorated with banners, as in front of the various *yamen* (offices of civil servants in China). The wall which surrounds the residence of the *amban* was destroyed by the Chinese in 1721, at the beginning of the internal wars between the kings of Tibet and the Dalai Lamas, as a result of which China was able to establish its protectorate in Tibet.

I was not only in the immediate vicinity of Lhasa, I also wanted to visit the monasteries which are a little further from the Holy City.

I first went to Braipung [Tib. Drepung] monastery, because it is said to be the biggest and the most important.

On the way there I passed near a gigantic *obo* [Tib. *dobong*].² It was four meters high and six meters in diameter. It is said that the spirit of the locality inhabits this *obo*. After walking seven kilometers (which is a lot for a Kalmyk rider), I finally reached Braipung monastery.

This monastery is located northwest of Lhasa, on the slope of Mount Gephel. It is made up of four colleges and a great hall called Tsokchen (Prayer Hall) Lhakhang whose roof is gilded and is so enormous that it can accommodate all ten thousand monks of Braipung. So they meet there every day to observe religious services. The colleges each have their own chapel. The first three *datsans* are overseen by the *tsanit*, while the *gakbo* [Tib. *ngakpa*] (tantric) *datsan* is overseen by the *chödpa*. Among the buildings of this great monastery is also a small printing press.

I had the joy of meeting two of my compatriots in this monastery. One of them belongs to the Dörbet tribe like me, but he usually lives in the steppes of Astrakhan province. The other is a Kalmyk from the vicinity of Karachar in Chinese Turkestan. He is a descendant of the Kalmyks who followed Khan Ubucha who organized the famous exodus of the Kalmyks from Russia, in the 18th century. Both study at Braipung and already have the rank of *ghelung* (priest). I had a long conversation with them in Kalmyk which took my mind back to my native country.

I regretfully took leave of my two compatriots, and having visited all the buildings of Braipung I climbed the mountain on its side even higher. Four kilometers away I reached its summit, where among the wild rocks there rises a small chapel where remains the anchorite ascetic of Mount Gephel (Gephel Ritode). Nearby is one of the Dalai Lama's summer residences.

I also took advantage of my visit to Braipung to go and see the monastery of Nechung Kuten. It is a very small monastery, next to the immense monastery that I had just visited. Barely a hundred monks are there, but it is the stay of the principal *choiden* [Tib. *kuten*] (oracle and guardian of the religion, charged to defend it against its enemies). It is located southeast of Braipung and in the middle of shady gardens. The Dalai Lama himself sometimes honors the monastery with his presence when he comes to consult the great *choiden*.

The second excursion I made took me to the Sera monastery.

I left early and my first encounter on the way was a flat stone on which the dead are cut. It is known in fact that according to Tibetan Buddhist rites only high priests are buried or cremated after their death. All other Tibetan Buddhists are cut up and left on this flat stone for the birds of prey to devour. This funeral work is performed in a particular district of Lhasa by beggars whose houses are made of ox horns and goats, and smell very bad. These strange morticians are very insolent. Sometimes they throw their dirty hats at strangers they encounter, and if the stranger complains they will reply, "We do not insult you, lord, we salute you." It is on the road to Sera Monastery, two kilometers from Lhasa, where arises the Chinese fort of Chaxitan, which is composed of barracks, a Chinese chapel, and a Tibetan chapel. The position of Chaxitan, outside the enclosure of Lhasa, too easily makes Europeans conclude that the Chinese garrison is not installed in Lhasa. China was represented there by a troop of people, who, though they wouldn't confess so, are not very sympathetic to the Tibetan population.

Seraïnkit Monastery (the Mongolian name of Sera), located four kilometers from Lhasa, is very picturesque. It rises at the base of a bare mountain called Tatipu Hill, which is only occasionally adorned with holly and cypress. This mountain also contains silver mines. Sera is inhabited by six thousand monks.

There are also a large number of practice cells there, called *ritodes*. (*Ritode* can also refer to a cenobite occupying one.) These cells, at first very small, were transformed and enlarged until they took the proportions of real palaces. On the other hand, the current ascetics living in these *ritodes* have many servants and large estates. *Ritodes* are venerated not only during their lifetime but also after death, and there is no greater honor to be given to the deceased than to have them dismembered on the gravestone of a *ritode*. And one of the most sought-after among these stones is northeast of Sera, near the chapel of the cenobite Pabongkha.

There is no *khubilgan* [Tib. *tulku*] who regularly reincarnates at Sera, however, there are two theological faculties—

one where the *tsanit* teaches and another where the *chödpa* teaches.

After this visit, as in Braipung, I wanted to reach a small monastery nearby. This one, located at the top of the mountain, is called Chupzang.[3] From there can be seen the great mountains which rise above Sera. Also located there are the chapels generally called Sera Ritode, and where prior to the founding of the monastery resided the great cenobite Tsongkhapa—founder of our Gelugpa sect, which is currently the most popular in Tibet and Mongolia. It was he who laid the first stone of Sera in 1417.

A final excursion took me to Galdan [Tib. Ganden], which is the furthest of the three great temples surrounding Lhasa (40 kilometers northeast).

To get to this monastery we first had to cross very high mountains on horseback before arriving at the pass between Brogri and Wangori Mountains, which is on the banks of the Kichu and where the monastery of Galdan stands. I was told that the main temple is made of marble and malachite but could not verify this. It is one of the temples that contains the largest number of relics of Tsongkhapa, our great reformer who founded this monastery five centuries ago (in 1409).

Also, after bowing to the holy figures, reciting my prayers, and circumambulating the temple, I next visited the temple of the gilded *stupa*[4] of the great Tsongkhapa. This *stupa* is in gold and contains the remains of the great saint, wrapped in the most precious fabrics. Then we were shown the neighboring cell that Tsongkhapa lived in. It was in Galdan that I was told several stories relating to this holy man. Here is one of them:

I was told that when the mother of the founder of our doctrine died, Tsongkhapa cried out: "Ah!;" and then, on the wall, near the place where he was sitting, the letter *ah* (ཨ) appeared. (I was shown this letter.) I also saw the trace of the seat of Tsongkhapa, the mark that remained at the place where he left his *mala* (rosary), and the indentation in the place where he leaned. Where he was lying can still very distinctly be seen the imprint of his ear.

This story was retold to me: Long ago, when Buddha lived on earth, a *naga* spirit offered Shakyamuni a white conch shell, like those used by our lamas to call the faithful to prayer. Shakyamuni handed it to his disciple Mahamaudgalyayana and sent him to hide it in the rocks of the high mountains covered with snow, saying that one day a man called Losang Drakpa (another name of Tsongkhapa) would come to propagate the doctrine of Buddha, and this conch would be very useful to him. And it is in fact Tsongkhapa who accidentally found this precious object while building Galdan. It is shown today at the monastery; it is one of Galdan's most precious relics where it is on display enclosed in a precious casket of sandalwood and gold.

In this temple there are still many other holy relics, as well as the remains of two disciples of Tsongkhapa! But the most recent and the most beautiful relic is that which the current Dalai Lama discovered buried in the ground: the ceremonial headdress and certain ritual objects, which have been collected and put on display in a reliquary near the sacred burial place.

There are two schools in Galdan Monastery where the *tsanit* teaches. The superior of the two or three thousand monks who live there is Tsongkhapa's representative on earth, but he is not a *khubilgan*. He bears the name of Galdan Sertibat [Tib. Ganden Tripa], that is to say "the one who occupies the golden throne of Galdan."

Not far from Galdan, on the north side of the Kichu River, are great mountains. One of these mountains is crowned by the Dechen fortress,[5] and on the other stands an enormous statue of Maitreya (the bodhisattva who is to succeed Shakyamuni). Near this figure is a smooth black stone, bearing in huge white letters the sacred words *om mani padme hum.*

It was on my return from this excursion that I first saw the pious pilgrims who make the tour of Lhasa three or seven times, not walking like the rest of us, but making genuflections, salutations and bows in a special way. This is called making the *lingkhor* of the Holy City. This is done by measuring the perimeter of the city with their bodies. They all dropped to their full length, got up and fell again, having placed their feet where their heads had previously touched. They go around the city in two or three days.

I had just photographed them, when I saw other pilgrims who were also doing the same exercise of devotion, but measuring the way with their faces instead. They go around the city seven times, which takes them nearly a month; but they don't risk hurting themselves like the first ones. Moreover, they train for several days in this very difficult exercise. Often, to begin with, small boards are placed on the palms of the hands to absorb the blows. Then you learn to put your arms on the ground in a specific way that avoids strains and breaking one's wrist.

On March 28th I left for Tashi Lhunpo, where I arrived after six days of travel.

I spent two days at Tashi Lhunpo and I had the good fortune to be introduced to Panchen Rinpoche.[6]

The great monasteries of Tashi Lunpo, where more than three thousand monks live, are located on the banks of the Tsangpo River (the upper stream of the Brahmaputra), opposite the town of Shigatse. It has three faculties of theology and a faculty of mysticism. There is also a large temple where large paintings of holy figures are displayed for certain festivals. The town of Shigatse has seven thousand inhabitants and includes Chinese and Tibetan soldiers.

From Tashi Lhunpo I journeyed to the southern border of Tibet, crossing very high mountains where horses could not be used. Under such conditions it took more than seven days to make our descent to Nepal.

I went on foot, not without difficulty; but we hired a man to carry the Tsanit Kambo Agwan Dordjieff on his back. Our luggage was carried by fifteen Tibetans who we paid 15 rupees each.

On April 17th we arrived in Kathmandu—the capital of Nepal—where we spent five days disguised as pilgrims. There we were able to obtain a permit from the King of Nepal to enter India in order to venerate the holy places where Buddha spent his last days. Had he not given us the permit it would not have been possible to enter India.

Between Kathmandu and the British border we had planned on three customs stops. So, I put my photographic film in a small box, which I sewed into a cloth and tied around my thigh under my pants. Another portion of my photographs was put in a pot containing Tibetan toasted flour. As for my Russian passport, I put it in the sole of my boots. Thanks to these ingenious precautions I succeeded in overcoming the usually perceptive vigilance of the customs officers I was to meet.

On May 10th, we arrived at Raxaul Junction. We had gone sixteen days on foot from the Tibetan border to arrive at Raxaul (400 kilometers). There we were told that direct tickets to Bombay were unavailable—that they can only be obtained at the next station in Sikkim. Before issuing us tickets the station master questioned us in detail about the purpose of our trip to Bombay. He told us, moreover, that these questions are made following the trip of a Russian Mongolian subject who attempted to enter Tibet from Darjeeling last year and was deported by the district head. This official said that the Russians were not well-intentioned, and should not be allowed to go to Lhasa.

We did not contradict him and, on the contrary agreed: "Yes, yes, we ourselves carry out active surveillance so that no one enters our home in Tibet." But while giving this answer I was making a secret prayer asking the Buddhas to save my life which was hanging on very fine threads. And when my prayer was finished, I said to myself: "There! Now my soul is saved!" Indeed, we were issued tickets for Bombay.

From Bombay we went to Colombo by way of Thoothukudi. In Colombo we embarked on the boat of the Russian volunteer fleet Tambov, and on June 12th we arrived in Odessa having happily finished our long and perilous journey.

Agwan Dordjieff, who had accompanied me on this last trip, parted from me heading straight for Saint Petersburg as the head of the embassy that His Holiness the Dalai Lama sent (unofficially) to the Tsar the Russian Empire.[7]

*Ovshé Norzunov*

¹ There is some disagreement as to whether or not Buddhists believe in deities as such. Buddhism is generally regarded as a nontheistic religion. *Yidams* are primarily regarded as anthropomorphically symbolic representations of some aspect of enlightened mind. Meditating on them is a method of realizing that aspect oneself. However, these visualization practices also lead some practitioners to conclude that they exist in reality. It was Deniker who chose the word "dieu" (deity) to interpret Norzunov's thought. Although I disagree with it, retaining it is one of the decisions I made to make the article more readable. (LN)

² *Obo*, as they are called, are heaps of stones, often several meters high, crowned by stakes, between which are stretched strings lined with prayer flags. In the eyes of Buddhists, the wind stirring these flags carries their inscribed prayers towards the deities. (JD)

³ Chupzang is now a nunnery. (LN)

⁴ A *stupa* is a sort of elaborate mausoleum which holds the cremated remains of a revered guru, and where devotees make offerings. (LN)

⁵ More commonly called Dagtse Dzong. (*Dzong* means fortress.) (LN)

⁶ Panchen Rinpoche is the incarnation of Amitabha (that is to say of the bodhisattva Shakyamuni himself), while the Dalai Lama is only the incarnation of Avalokiteshvara, the heart disciple of Amitabha. Panchen Rinpoche is therefore theoretically superior, but in practice his power is much less. Moreover, many Tibetan Buddhist of the Gelugpa sect, including Agwan Dordjieff and Norzunov, believe that the Dalai Lama is the embodiment of Amitabha himself. (JD)

⁷ It is the famous embassy which the newspapers spoke about two years ago [1902]. It was perhaps the starting point of the more active policy of the English in Tibet, which has just ended the present war. (JD)

"Third Voyage to Lhasa" is an excerpt taken from the second installment of "Trois Voyages à Lhassa," published in *Le Tour du monde: Journal des voyages: nouvelle série* no. 20 (14 mai 1904), and translated for the author from the French by Sara Elliot. The map and engraving reproduced are from the same source.

*Gurdjieff posing for a photo with two close friends in Berlin.*

*The same individual to the far right in the top photo seen welcoming Gurdjieff upon his arrival at the Berlin train station.*

## SOLOVIEV

As Gurdjieff said that his friend Soloviev was an authority on Tibetan Medicine, one way to approach trying to identify him is by seeing which Tibetan Medicine practitioners of his era might have other attributes that Gurdjieff ascribes to his friend. This is the approach that James Webb took. A problem with this, however, is that there were at least two doctors of Tibetan Medicine that accompanied him on his journeys.[1] Specifically, he says that there were three European doctors and two of Tibetan Medicine (on his 1902 Tibetan expedition, anyway). It is possible there were more than two, however, because he specifically says that Soloviev was an "authority" of Tibetan Medicine, which is not the same as saying the person is a doctor of Tibetan Medicine. It may indicate a European doctor who was able to learn enough of Tibetan Medicine to be considered an authority. So, even if we were to find a specialist of Tibetan Medicine who may have known Gurdjieff, how would we know for certain that the doctor in question is Soloviev and not one of the others in Gurdjieff's party?

Let us start with this approach anyway. Even if it turns out that a particular candidate being discussed is not Soloviev, he may still have been another in Gurdjieff's troupe at some point. So, it would be useful to discuss all the possibilities. But in this work, we are particularly interested in Soloviev because Gurdjieff tells us he was one of the three seekers who made it to Sarmung (a.k.a Surmang).

James Webb suggests that Soloviev was Pëtr Alexandrovich Badmayev, a Buryat doctor of Tibetan Medicine who was probably the most acclaimed in his field in Russia in his time. The problem with this association is that Badmayev was about 27 years older than Gurdjieff, and the rapport Gurdjieff describes having had with Soloviev sounds like that between two about the same age. Even going by the earlier date of birth Webb gives Gurdjieff this seems unlikely. Actually, Gurdjieff seemingly suggests that Soloviev was younger than him.

A more likely candidate for Soloviev is Badmayev's nephew, Nikolai Nikolayevich Badmayev, also known by the Buryat name Ossor. He was born in 1879 and like his uncle also practiced Tibetan Medicine. What also makes him a candidate for Soloviev is that two of his supporters were very early associates of Gurdjieff.

The first is Gleb Boky who gave a coerced "confession" to Soviet authorities in which he says he was a member of Gurdjieff's United Work Brotherhood in the early 1910s. In reality, the United Work Brotherhood was an offshoot or imitation Gurdjieff school founded by Dr Alexander Barchenko circa 1920. Probably Boky said that this brotherhood was Gurdjieff's so as not to incriminate Barchenko, and said it was founded in pre-Soviet Russia when such institutions were permitted. Barchenko probably modeled the name off of the name of Gurdjieff's Essentuki Institute (The Essentuki Home of the International Fellowship for Realization through Work), which he would have known about from P.V. Shandarovsky, who was involved in both groups.

The second supporter of Badmayev is author Maxim Gorky, who likely knew Gurdjieff as a young man in Georgia where they both worked in the same railway yard. Boky and Gorky certainly knew one another.

Another candidate for Soloviev is the above-mentioned Dr Alexander Barchenko. He was interested in many aspects of the occult, as well as occult-inspired, Eastern and experimental sciences, including Tibetan Medicine and hypnosis. Generally speaking, he seems to have come from the same egg as Gurdjieff. Richard Spence describes Barchenko as "part occultist, part scientist, part explorer, and maybe just a bit of a charlatan."[2] The same could very much be said of Gurdjieff. Also like Gurdjieff, he was keenly interested in Shambhala. Another thing about him that is interesting is that during the 1909–1911 timeframe he does not appear to have held any office or been enrolled in any school. All he says about that period is that he was studying chiromancy and traveling. So, it seems feasible that he could very well have been in Tibet with Gurdjieff at the time.

Although Boky's confession has its inaccuracies, saying that Barchenko was Gurdjieff's successor may indicate that the two actually knew each other rather well. As Richard Spence states, "[Barchenko] was well-versed in Gurdjieff's teachings."[3] Also suggesting that they knew one another is that Barchenko's first teacher was Joseph Alexandre Saint-Yves d'Alveydre, who is known for putting forth the theory that the Sphinx is 14,000 years old. Although Gurdjieff does not give an exact age for the Sphinx, he asserted that it was built during pre-sand Egypt, which is roughly the same era given by Saint-Yves d'Alveydre. So, it may be that Gurdjieff formed his own ideas on the subject based on Saint-Yves d'Alveydre's thoughts heard by way of Barchenko.

Yet one wonders if Barchenko and Gurdjieff had some sort of falling out—if Barchenko left Gurdjieff to start his own school based entirely on his ideas. This seems much more likely than him being a successor. He did apparently give his school a very similar name to Gurdjieff's. This would also explain some of the things Gurdjieff says of Soloviev. Specifically, Gurdjieff's telling of Soloviev's involvement in counterfeiting which may be indicating that Gurdjieff felt he had stolen his ideas and began a counterfeit fourth way school. As well, this would explain Soloviev's absurd death (mauled by a camel) which is obviously not factual. Could it mean that Soloviev had simply died in Gurdjieff's heart so to speak—if Gurdjieff had written him off?

The name Soloviev itself may also have been intended to indicate something of this criminal aspect. Although the most obvious association of the name is to philosopher Vladimir Soloviev and implies an intelligent nature, it may also be an allusion to a Siberian prison called Solovky.

Yet it seems unlikely that someone who actually journeyed to Tibet would later have anything to do with a charlatan who called himself Lama Naga Naven and claimed to be a representative of Shambhala as Barchenko did. (Neither Naga nor Naven are Tibetan names.) Barchenko may have been one of the other authorities of Tibetan Medicine acquainted with Gurdjieff, but it does not make sense that someone who spent time at Surmang would continue naïvely searching for Shambhala.

Another doctor who Boky mentions in his confession as having been a member of the United Work Brotherhood is Dr Konstantin Nikolayevich Riabinin. It turns out that he too knew something of Tibetan Medicine. Besides this, he too was interested in Shambhala. His diary as a member of Nicholas Roerich's 1927–28 Himalayan expedition in search of Shambhala was recently published in Russian. What is particularly interesting is that he was raised in a merchant family as Gurdjieff says of Soloviev. Also interesting is that he attended secondary school in Tbilisi at a time Gurdjieff was likely there. Curiously, Riabinin was actually sentenced to the Solovky prison in 1930, at which time Gurdjieff was still revising his manuscript for *Meetings with Remarkable Men*.

Although the above research is inclusive, there is another way to research Soloviev's identity other than looking for a Tibetan Medicine practitioner with possible ties to Gurdjieff. And as mentioned at the outset, it may turn out that one or more of the Tibetan Medicine practitioners discussed were fellow Truth-Seekers other than Soloviev. So, that initial approach may yet be useful although this second approach comes closer to identifying Soloviev.

As it turns out, there's an anonymous German author who published a short story about Surmang in 1913, which is shortly after Gurdjieff was evidently there. Although the story is a work of fiction, there are elements of it that suggest the author had first-hand knowledge of the place. As well, it must be considered that outside of Tibet, Surmang was virtually unknown. Prior to Trungpa Rinpoche writing about Surmang in his 1966 autobiography, only its location was known as a result of the Jesuits' 17th and 18th century missions to Tibet. Consider too how difficult it was for Westerners to enter Kham. A few were able to sneak into Tibet proper, but hardly any explorers were able to enter Kham because of how dangerous it was. The author of the short story is apparently the only Westerner other than Gurdjieff to have visited Surmang at the time and therefore must have been Soloviev. He certainly could not have been Lubovedsky given everything discussed about him earlier.

The short story in question, published in pamphlet form, is a sensational goona-goona tale of false bravery killing primitives in the wilds of Tibet called *Surmang: die Felsenfestung* (*Surmang: the Stone Fortress*). This sort of publication, popular at the time, was known as a groschenhefte in German, or a penny dreadful in English. *Surmang* was one of a series called *Durch* Länder und *Meere* (*By Land and Sea*) published by A. Eichler, a publisher of children's stories. *By Land and Sea* contained 170 titles, all published between 1913 and 1915. Gurdjieff said he was in Tibet in 1908 or 1909, and as we will see a little later, he likely departed in early 1911. *Surmang* was published just two years after that.

All of the titles in this particular series feature the adventures of Clemens Rubbn and his young sidekick, Fritz Hagen. This may indicate that all the tales were written by one individual, but it was also common to have multiple contributers to this sort of series. Either way, there are a couple of other titles of *By Land and Sea* that may also have been written by the author of the *Surmang* tale, and therefore of interest here— *Die Schrecken des Himalaja* (*The Terrors of the Himalayas*) and *Im Heiligtum des Dalai Lama* (*In the Shrine of the Dalai Lama*).

Returning to the subject of Surmang, although all of these penny dreadfuls are sensational nonsense, it must be considered that Kham (the region in which Surmang is located), was a lawless land notorious for its tribes, ruled by independent chieftains, who robbed passing travelers and recognized the authority neither of the Dalai Lama nor the Emperor of China. Even today their rebellious reputation persists. Note also the subtitle of the pamphlet (*The Stone Fortress*). In the "Prince Yuri Lubovedsky" chapter Gurdjieff says, "As we came nearer [to Sarmung] we were able to make out something like a fortress..." As well, many of the Surmang monasteries are known to have a fortress (*dzong*) on the property's perimeter somewhere. So it seems to have been written by someone who was actually there rather than an author who got the details for their work solely from other written sources.

The same appears to be true of *In the Shrine of the Dalai Lama* and *The Terrors of the Himalayas*. The names that the author gives to the two guides in *In the Shrine of the Dalai Lama* (Depa and Ngaki) are actual Tibetan names. At the time, common Tibetan names were virtually unknown in Europe. Somewhat less indicative, though worth mentioning, is that in *The Terrors of the Himalayas* the author speaks of the beauty of the rhododendrons and there are in fact rhododendron forests in Darjeeling where the tale takes place. Although it seems that the author had to have been in Darjeeling to have written of the rhododendrons, there may have been English accounts of Darjeeling that the author had access to.

There is something else that is very curious about *In the Shrine of the Dalai Lama* as well. The character Clemens Rubbn appears to be based on Gurdjieff to some degree in this tale. Rubbn says he wants to penetrate Tibet and "the Dalai Lama's monastery" in order to learn the Tibetan Buddhist method of hypnosis. Gurdjieff, of course, is known for having had a hypnotherapy practice. Also like Gurdjieff is the hero's interest in magic—both genuine magic and trickery, and both of which Rubbn displays in the tale. The hero also keeps a keen eye on others performing magic to figure out how they do it, and Gurdjieff describes in *Meetings with Remarkable Men* having seriously studied various forms of magic. Also as Gurdjieff describes having done in *Meetings with Remarkable Men*, Rubbn travels in disguise to accomplish his mission. At

138

one point Rubbn even says something that Gurdjieff may actually have told his traveling buddy. When in a predicament that his companion expresses concern about, he tells him, "You will see that in every need there is a way out if you don't lose your presence of mind."

But who could this anonymous author have been? One may think to see if he may have been one of the handful of German explorers of Tibet, but none of them journeyed there at the right time. No Germans are mentioned as being in the party of other explorers either.

There is one possibility, however, when considering the various German travelog authors of the time. Walther von Waldberg, who wrote many travelogs and plays under the pseudonym Johannes Mayrhofer, wrote one particular travelog called *Durch Länder und Meer*—the same title as that of the penny dreadful series—and published at about the same time (1915).

Von Waldberg was born the same year as Gurdjieff (1877), and like Gurdjieff also had a religious education and traveled widely. He was born in Hamburg and attended a Catholic elementary school there until 1889 when his family moved to Oelde where he attended another Catholic school. Between 1892 and 1896 von Wandberg attended the Josephinum Gymnasium in Hildesheim. Upon graduating there von Waldberg joined the Jesuit order in Bleijenbeek, Holland where he spent a year as a novitiate. After completing his novitiate he remained in Holland studying philosophy at Exaten and Valkenburg until 1901. The following year his first writings were published. Altogether some 50 titles of his were published under the Johannes Mayrhofer pseudonym.

But does the fact that one of the Mayrhofer travelogs has the same title as the penny dreadful series actually make von Waldberg less likely to have been the anonymous author we are looking for because it suggests that he would have written all 170 of the series' tales, all published within its two- or three-year existence? Perhaps, but not necessarily. The tales are not very long and the low-grade writing quality would not have required much time. A prolific author such as von

139

Waldberg probably could have accomplished this. But can it be believed that a respected author (and Gurdjieff's friend) would have resorted to writing such racist trash?

Possibly after returning from a costly journey to Tibet, von Waldberg needed to earn money, devoted some time to writing better-selling penny dreadfuls, and published them anonymously so as not to tarnish the more serious reputation that the Mayrhofer name had acquired. Supporting this suggestion is that fewer titles were published under the Maryhofer name during the penny dreadful's existence than earlier output.

It may also be significant that von Waldberg was a Jesuit. The Jesuits were the first to put Surmang on the map. Their first Tibetan mission lasted from 1625 to 1721, and the geographical data they collected was compiled to create the first map of Tibet that included Surmang on it (published in 1708). It is possible that von Waldberg would have been able to obtain information on Surmang and Tibet in general from one or more of the Jesuit's archives.

Returning to von Waldberg's timeline, between 1901 and 1905 he taught at Saint Andreas College in Charlottenlund, between 1905 and 1906 he taught at Ignatius College in Valkenburg, and between 1907 and 1908 he served as editor at both *Germania* and *Die Welt*. After that he apparently held no position until his engagement in World War I. He could easily have been in Tibet with Gurdjieff circa 1908–1911.

After the war von Waldberg taught at Luisenstadt Gymnasium in Berlin for a year before moving to Regensburg in 1919. The remainder of his life he apparently only worked on his writing for income. Curiously, he died less than two weeks before Gurdjieff himself passed on in 1949.

There are photos taken of Gurdjieff's arrival in Berlin that may be helpful in determining whether or not von Waldberg was Soloviev and identifying Soloviev in general. One shows Gurdjieff seated next to two friends on a park bench and is obviously posed. Gurdjieff rarely posed for photographs. The only photos he ever posed for were the few publicity photos and family photos he had taken. Surely Gurdjieff considered the two men accompanying him in the photo quite close.

According to the de Hartmanns, Gurdjieff stayed with old Russian friends when he first arrived in Berlin. Although looks can be deceiving, the man seated center seems to have the despondent disposition a Russian might have, while the man on the right, with long hair for the period and an alert expression, looks like he might be a German adventurer. The same man can be seen in the photo of Gurdjieff's group arriving at Berlin Station. That photo was posed for too and the individual in question was positioned next to Gurdjieff, again implying a closeness. If that man is in fact von Waldberg, he was living in Regensburg and would have been staying with Berliner friends himself, and thus likely unable to accommodate Gurdjieff. It was probably the person seated center on the park bench with whom Gurdjieff stayed. Unfortunately, a photo of von Waldberg could not be located for comparison.

Although Gurdjieff had begun groups in Germany during the one year his Institute existed there, it is odd that none of the members of those groups ever visited him at the Prieuré. There are no accounts of the Prieuré period whatsoever that mention any German nationals visiting. One wonders if the German Soloviev (whether von Waldberg or not) was leader of the German groups and separated from Gurdjieff upon his departure to France. This too would explain Gurdjieff calling Soloviev a counterfeiter.

Now that we have explored who some of Gurdjieff's companions may have been, let us see what other teachers he possibly had. Remember that Dudjom Lingpa died in 1904. So Gurdjieff would have worked with other teachers during his second stay in Tibet.

---

[1] G. Gurdjieff, *Life Is Real Only Then When "I Am:" Third Series of All and Everything* (New York: Triangle Editions, 1975), 9.

[2] Richard Spence, "Red Star Over Shambhala: Soviet, British and American Intelligence & the Search for Lost Civilisation in Central Asia," New Dawn Magazine, www.newdawnmagazine.com/articles/secret-history/red-star-over-shambhala-soviet-british-and-american-intelligence-the-search-for-lost-civilisation-in-central-asia.

[3] Ibid.

Photographs of Gurdjieff in Berlin from the Howarth Gurdjieff Archive provided by New York Public Library who owns the collection. Photographer unknown.

*The Tenth Surmang Gharwang, Yondu Ningpo*

## THE ABBOT

The discussion of Sarmung concluded that the specific monastery Gurdjieff was alluding to by that name is Surmang Namgyal Tse. In *Meetings with Remarkable Men,* Gurdjieff says that two weeks after his arrival, he and Soloviev were introduced to the abbot. (Actually, he uses the word "sheikh" to mislead the reader regarding the monastery's identity.) The abbot of Surmang Namgyal Tse is the Surmang Gharwang.[1] In Gurdjieff's time, this would have been the Tenth Surmang Gharwang, Yondu Ningpo. Very little is known about him. Only that he was a teacher of the Second Jamgon Kongtrul.

Interestingly, the Second Jamgon Kongtrul was Chögyam Trungpa's root teacher. Besides having learned of Gurdjieff's stay at Surmang from Gurdjieff's son, he may have also heard something from Jamgon Kongtrul.

At any rate, it seems likely enough that the Tenth Gharwang Surmang was one of Gurdjieff's teachers. Presently, knowing hardly anything at all about him, it is difficult to say how significant a teacher he would have been. Still, it is useful to mention him in case more information about him is someday unearthed which can be assessed in this light. In fact, the current Surmang Gharwang is working on a history of Surmang Namgyal Tse. So, additional information may very well turn up.

Meanwhile, there are other likely teachers of Gurdjieff to consider.

*Tersey Tsewang Norbu*

## Dying Like a Dog

Tersey Tsewang Norbu (1856–1915) was the son of Chokgyur Lingpa—a great *tertön* (treasure revealer) of the nineteenth century—who was recognized as an incarnation of Yudra Nyingpo, and the teaching holder of the Dzogchen Desum lineage founded by his father. His first teacher was Jamyang Khyentse Wangpo, who was his mother's uncle. He also later studied with Patrul Rinpoche and Mipham Rinpoche—two other great Nyingmapa teachers—and Jamgön Kongtrul, a great Kagyupa teacher.

At first Tsewang Norbu was a monastic, but after Jamyang Khyentse rescinded his vows he became a *ngakpa*. He once joked about this saying, "Darn! I totally missed out in this life; I didn't get to keep my monk's vows nor did I get any children by giving up my vows. I've been a total failure."[1] But when a teacher says something like this, it is really not so much a joke; it is not an expression of false humility like an ordinary person might make. When such a teacher puts themselves down it is a way of telling their students not to worship them so slavishly. Likely his vows were rescinded due to similar irreverent antics—something he is well known for as the crazy wisdom teacher he later became.

Tsewang Norbu was also known for his yoga skills and clairvoyant abilities, but belittled and even denied them. This too was an act to dissuade students from overly revering him.

There is very little historically that suggests Tsewang Norbu could have been a teacher of Gurdjieff's other than being a contemporary. The only thing worth mentioning in this regard is that the Surmang monasteries is known for practicing a *terma* of Chokgyur Lingpa's called Lhakhang. Therefore it is possible that it was Tsewang Norbu who brought the practice there, and this is how Gurdjieff came to know him.

Yet there is much more than the above that suggests a relationship. In particular, it appears that Gurdjieff borrowed a couple of his unique antics.

On his deathbed Tsewang Norbu instructed his attendant to deliver a complete collection of his *New Treasures* to the reincarnations of his father and brother at Tsikey Monastery, and then circulate the tale that he died like a dog. More significant than being another example of intentionally debasing himself, is that he uses an unusual expression that Gurdjieff himself used. Not that the expression "die like a dog" itself is so unusual—it is a common expression in many languages— but what other spiritual teachers use the expression? They both used it for the shock value too. Creating shocks was a tool they both regularly employed.

Here is another device that Gurdjieff may have borrowed from Tsewang Norbu: There was an occasion when Tsewang Norbu was giving empowerments at Riwoche Monastery. Many high ranking lamas were there. As on other nights, there was an evening after the day's teachings and practices that lamas gathered informally in his private room for a meal and conversation. Only the highest ranking lamas and those closest to Tsewang Norbu were there. This particular night he raised his voice and bulged his eyes praising his young humble nephew, Samten Gyatso, who was hiding in a corner, as his spiritual heir, while deriding the important lamas in their fancy garb for their pride by questioning their recognition. One by one they were assaulted. Samten Gyatso himself was aghast.

Fritz Peters records an evening when Gurdjieff did something very similar. There was a gathering at Gurdjieff's flat towards the end of his life where Gurdjieff suddenly raised his voice to make an announcement. Before continuing, he looked at each person present intently. The gist of the announcement was that now that his final book has been finished, his work was done and he could now die. But not only because he completed his writings; more significantly because he had found his spiritual heir. Then he raised his arm with his index finger extended and slowly moved it around the room as if to tease his self-important guests. Finally, his finger landed on young Fritz Peters. Then Gurdjieff simply walked out of the room. The only differences between the two stories is that Fritz Peters was not quite as humiliated as Samten Gyatso. Peters was uncomfortable, but also considered that his recognition by Gurdjieff might not have entirely been a stunt.

There is one other story worth sharing. Although not something that Gurdjieff seems to have borrowed like the previous two, it demonstrates Tsewang Norbu's complete disregard for social conventions, which is certainly something that Gurdjieff exhibited in his own way. It is the story of the occasion that a lama named Tendzin Dorje went to meet Tsewang Norbu for the first time. He was in the waiting room of Tsewang Norbu's chamber along with many others who were there to see him. Suddenly a tall naked man burst through the door and stomped across the room with his genitals swaying, heading for the toilet. Many women ran out of the room in fright. A short while later the naked man stomped back across the waiting room and returned to the chamber. With few people remaining, it was not too long before Tendzin Dorje was able to enter the chamber to meet the teacher. Of course, when he entered, he discovered that the naked man was none other than Tsewang Norbu himself.

Another point worth considering is the fact that Chokgyur Lingpa is known to have found choreographic mind *terma*. So, it is reasonable to think that Tsewang Norbu may have studied this and other dance forms from his father, and transmitted these forms to Gurdjieff. Dance may very well have been another thing that attracted him to Tsewang Norbu.

One final point is that like Gurdjieff, Tsewang Norbu also abhorred money. As Gurdjieff states, "Coming from a poor family and not being materially secure, I had to resort rather often to earning this indeed despicable and maleficent money for unavoidable needs. However, the process itself of earning money never took much of my time..."[2] As for Tsewang Norbu's relationship with money, see the tale that follows.

---

[1] Tulku Urgyen Rinpoche, Erik Pema Kunsang & Marcia Binder Schmidt, *Blazing Splendor: The Memoirs of the Dzogchen Yogi Tulku Urgyen Rinpoche* (Boudhanath: Rangjung Yeshe Publications, 2007), 74.

[2] G. Gurdjieff, *Meetings with Remarkable Men* (New York: E. P. Dutton & Co., 1963), 252.

## Silver Is Poison

Once Patrul stayed in a valley where people were exceedingly devoted to him. One day a few learned khenpos (abbots), along with the treasure master Chögyur Lingpa's son Tsewang Norbu, came to his solitary retreat in order to receive teaching; all sat around Patrul in a meadow bedecked with wildflowers.

In the valley there was an old man who fervently desired to offer Patrul a hoof-shaped piece of silver the size of a stone. But he knew that Patrul rarely accepted offerings.

The old man arrived suddenly on horseback, dismounted, prostrated himself three times, and placed the silver at Patrul's feet. He cried, "Here is an offering. Please save me from being reborn in the infernal realms!" Then he jumped on his horse and galloped off, aware that if he stayed, Patrul would reject his offering.

Tsewang Norbu thought to himself, "Patrul will probably use this offering for some meritorious purpose." Patrul, however, never picked up the silver ingot. When he had completed his teaching, he simply stood up and left. One by one the disciples returned to their homes and monasteries, and the ingot was left, round and bright, lying like a full moon in the grass. Tsewang Norbu could not help thinking that it would have been better to use it for some virtuous deed, rather than just abandon it there, but he kept these thoughts to himself.

As he walked away, he looked back again and again: the

silver was still there, a sparkling dot in the green meadow. This image stayed with him as he descended the hill, and a tremendously powerful feeling of world-weariness and genuine renunciation arose in him.

Tsewang Norbu thought to himself, "When I think of my gracious guru and those around him who have totally renounced the illusory attachments of this fleeting life, it makes me think that it must have been just the same during the life of the Buddha and the liberated arhats."

Then he recalled a story:

Once Lord Buddha and his disciples—including Ananda, Kasyapa, and others—were walking along where they came across a large piece of gold lying on the ground. As they passed it, one after the other would exclaim, "Poison!"

A little girl who was collecting firewood nearby heard this. After they had gone, she saw the nugget of gold, without knowing exactly what it was. She thought, "How strange—here is a beautiful, bright yellow piece of stone, and all the esteemed arhats stepped aside and avoided touching it, exclaiming, 'Poison!' That must be something I also should not touch."

The child rushed home to tell her mother. "Today I saw a curious kind of poison," she began, relating what had transpired. Her mother went immediately to see for herself. She found the gold, brought it home, and used it to sponsor religious offerings.

The news spread like wildfire that the Buddha and his renounced followers had intentionally bypassed a piece of gold, leaving it in the grass, and had called it poison.

Tsewang Norbu was greatly edified, inspired to see how—even in modern times—his teacher Patrul Rinpoche naturally followed in their footsteps.

*Tsewang Norbu*
as retold by Lama Surya Das

*The Fifth Dzogchen Rinpoche, Thupten Chökyi Dorje*

## The Fifth Dzogchen Rinpoche

Like Tsewang Norbu, the Fifth Dzogchen Rinpoche, Thupten Chökyi Dorje (1872–1935), was both recognized by Jamyang Khyentse Wangpo and a young student of his. Also like Tsewang Norbu, teachers he later studied with include Jamgon Kongtrul the Great, Patrul Rinpoche, and Mipham Rinpoche. As the reincarnation of the Fourth Dzogchen Drubwang, Mingyur Namkhai Dorje, he was enthroned at Dzogchen Monastery—a very important Nyingmapa seat.

Besides caring for and developing Dzogchen Monastery, Dzogchen Rinpoche traveled far and wide, primarily in Kham and Amdo, but also as far as Sichuan and Mongolia. In these travels he taught to the laity as well as the monastics of his lineage, and recognized over 100 important Nyingmapa tulkus in the process.

Besides these recognitions he is known to have demonstrated his clairvoyant abilities in other ways as well. Shortly before his death he asked one of his disciples to check if there was enough timber in the forest to build a monastery. The disciple thought it strange knowing there were no such plans but did as he was told and reported back to his teacher that there indeed was enough timber. When Dzogchen Monastery burned to the ground about a year after Dzogchen Rinpoche died the disciple understood why he was asked to see how much tinder was available.

Dzogchen Rinpoche also demonstrated other powers such as leaving his footprint in rock. He was well-known for his magical abilities.

No doubt these abilities would have interested Gurdjieff. But neither these abilities nor having the same teachers as Tsewang Norbu proves anything. The only real reason for believing that the Fifth Dzogchen Rinpoche could have been one of Gurdjieff's teachers is that he recognized the rinpoche who was very likely one of Gurdjieff's two Tibetan sons. Before discussing this subject in detail, however, let us read this excerpt from Dzogchen Rinpoche's only known work, *The Excellent Path of Liberation: On Practice*. There is one thing in particular about the excerpt that is reminiscent of Gurdjieff's teaching—where he says to outwardly behave as expected of a monastic while inwardly maintaining the freedom afforded by Dzogchen practice. This statement is very similar to Gurdjieff's advice about externally playing the roles expected of one while being internally free from them.

For those unfamiliar with Dzogchen, it may be helpful to first read the chapter "Haida!" which correlates the teaching to Gurdjieff's.

# FREEDOM

When an undistracted state of non-meditation[1] is maintained continuously, however many different appearances may show up, their cause fades away naturally, of its own accord. All mental constructs of the eight assemblages of consciousness[2] are inherently free, right where and as they are. Let this be the cause for finally experiencing decisively the Great Equality of samsara and nirvana! When abiding in Original Purity and Great Emptiness, the very cause of all conceptuality of the mind and its emergent states is free, of its own accord.

This is taught according to five categories: primordial-freedom, freedom-from-extremes, freedom-upon-directly-seeing, self-freedom and single-freedom. Each of these categories have their own modes of freedom, their reasons for freedom, their vital points of practice, and the results which reasonably follow from these. Although each is explained individually, primordial-freedom has no fundamental basis on which it can be split up or divided. All apparent phenomena and the mind that perceives them are in actuality already perfectly free without having to do or not do anything. Maintaining self-freedom means that there is no need for any other antidote. With freedom-upon-directly-seeing, things vanish upon being seen, which is profound for those who are karmically attached to material possessions. Freedom-from-extremes means being free from the extremes of eternalism and nihilism existing throughout samsara-nirvana. Single-freedom means that *rigpa* is free solely through its own nature, in and of itself—that it has no other cause.

Apprehending unobstructed *rigpa* nakedly, immediately and directly, is like quicksilver falling onto the ground—uncontaminated by objects to be rejected or their antidotes. The two obscurations [viz. emotional and cognitive] are completely cleared away along with all karmic imprints; nothing is left behind. The result of the two purities [viz. freedoms from the two obscurations] becomes directly apparent, and from the primordial expanse of the *dharmakaya*—the originally pure space of the basis, present from the beginning—the music of the spontaneously present *rupakaya*[3] shines forth in many different forms. May benefit for beings actualized through the Four Activities[4] spread everywhere!

Now listen! Pure *tsultrim* (ethical discipline) is the basis of all spiritual qualities. Whoever trains in non-conceptualized *samadhi* free from any conceptual object, and in the cultivation of *prajna* which severs self-grasping—the very root of samsaric existence—must understand that these three (*tsultrim*, *samadhi*, and *prajna*) arise interdependently, in the manner of support-and-things-supported. Ethical discipline is the basis of all spiritual qualities or attainments. As such, any person shameless enough to presume to practice Ati Dzogchen without pure ethical discipline is no different than a person who tries to grow a lotus in the sky: they will certainly not perceive the truth directly and without error, just as it is. In sum: outwardly maintain your monastic vows, inwardly train in the Secret Mantra Vajrayana, and, on the most secret level, be in accordance with Ati Dzogpa Chenpo.[5] May this be the cause for your practices to be done diligently, with single-pointed, undistracted focus!

This is wonderful! So, listen well, fortunate ones! I have absorbed the kind Guru's stainless, oral-lineage instructions into my mind and have cut through the stain of doubt. Even so, ignorant as I am, I have not realized the natural, basic state just as it is. My explanations about principles of practice are like a thousand empty platitudes. Still, as laughable as this may be, may masses of other fortunate individuals, I and all other sentient beings like me, see the own-face of their basic nature and be freed within the primordial space of Reality!

Even though I don't have any direct experience myself, students with faith and dedication have encouraged and requested me to teach them again and again. Thus this attempt to point karmically fortunate beginners in the direction of the profound meaning. This Great Perfection, this Ati Dzogpa Chenpo, is the Supreme King of all vehicles. It is beyond the conception of all those types of people who hold wrong views associated with the lower vehicles. Looking to respond to the requests of karmically fortunate individuals, I have written a little down that clarifies the meaning [of the teachings] and which is easy to understand. Though my words may lack poetry, I believe that they do not contradict this meaning, presumptuous as it may be of me.

*The Fifth Dzogchen Rinpoche,*
*Thupten Chökyi Dorje*

---

¹ Effortless meditation, also known as *vipassana*.
² Viz. sight, sound, smell, taste, touch, thought, emotion and memory.
³ *Rupakaya* refers to the two form *kayas* (bodies)—*nirmanakaya* and *sambhogakaya*.
⁴ Refers to the four tantric ritual activity categories—pacifying, increasing, controlling and destroying.
⁵ Like "The Great Perfection," "Ati Dzogpa Chenpo" is another way of referring to Dzogchen with esteem.

Translated for the author from the Tibetan by Jigme Dorje (Dr Ben Joffe).

*The Sixth Shechen Rabjam, Gyurme Kunzang Tenpé Nyima*

# Two Sons

In *Gurdjieff: Making a New World*, J. G. Bennett mentions a casual remark made by Gurdjieff about having left behind a wife and children in Tibet. In his own words, "Gurdjieff told one of his characteristic stories, which might be literal fact or pure fantasy, about his Tibetan marriage. He said that his eldest son had become a lama and had made such spiritual progress that at a relatively early age he had been appointed the abbot of an important lamasery."[1]

Bennett questions the amount of truth in Gurdjieff's telling, but there is really no reason to doubt this. While it is true that Gurdjieff would often embellish facts, and even fabricate events outright, he primarily did so in order to make a point allegorically, although at times it was in order to show a particular pupil their naïveté. Here neither seems to be the case. He seems to speak of his son as any proud parent would. Also, Bennett was evidently unaware that most Tibetan Buddhist abbots begin preparing for their role at a very early age. And considering that Bennett heard this tale secondhand, it is very possible that Gurdjieff was actually speaking about his son's recognition and that this was misunderstood by Bennett's source or Bennett himself to mean his young son was so spiritually advanced.

Bennett was not the only one to hear such things either. Gurdjieff once told Irmis Popoff, "I have many sons away in monasteries."[2] John Shirley evidently acquired a text of C.S. Nott's mentioning something similar.[3] Moreover, in 1947 Gurdjieff asked Yahne Le Toumelin, a young French pupil who very much wished to go Tibet, "When you will go to Tibet ask for my two sons..."[4]

Although Gurdjieff covered his tracks well, having had a son with such a high status may have left some trace of his presence in Tibet. But where to look? And with all the destruction inflicted by the Chinese would such a record remain?

A logical thought would be to identify all the Surmang monasteries and search for an abbot of one born at the time Gurdjieff was there. But data currently available only includes the identity of two of about eleven monasteries, and the abbots of these were not born at the right time.

A meticulous reading of Chögyam Trungpa's *Born in Tibet*, however, reveals something quite interesting—specifically his description of the Sixth Shechen Rabjam, Gyurme Kunzang Tenpé Nyima. He explains that Shechen Rabjam was one of two abbots of Shechen Monastery where he had gone to study under his teacher, Shechen Jamgön Kongtrul. As Trungpa relates, "Tulku Rabjam Rinpoche was a great personality both spiritually and because of his wide vision in regard to practical affairs; I owe much to his teaching. He had a striking appearance because of his very large moustache, not common among our people."[5]

Most Tibetan men have little facial hair; their mustaches are usually narrow with sparse, thin hair. To have had such a full mustache seems to imply that one parent would necessarily have been a foreigner.

Besides his mustache, there is another western feature that can be observed in the photos of the Sixth Shechen Rabjam. His eyes are obviously more round than most Tibetans. In fact, his eyes look quite a bit like Gurdjieff's. Also much like Gurdjieff is the skull shape and the broad chin. In addition, the charisma and vision which Trungpa observed in Shechen Rabjam might well be psychological traits acquired by heredity from Gurdjieff.

So, what is known of Shechen Rabjam's birth? One thing

that Tibetans pride are the stories explaining how a great tulku is discovered, usually as an infant. Sometimes an old tulku will leave some indication he somehow perceived about the circumstances under which he will be reborn. Sometimes a higher-ranking tulku will receive a premonition in the form of a dream about the dead tulku's rebirth. Sometimes the details of these premonitions are vague, but often they are quite specific, indicating the town, the names of the parents, and other characteristics of the household.

According to the Sixth Shechen Rabjam's recognition story, "He was born in Golok in the Iron Pig year, to the chieftain Akhyung Khangsar, and recognized by the Fifth Dzogchen Rinpoche."[6] Let us look at these facts one by one.

The first thing that is curious about this is that he was born in Golok. Golok is not all that far from Surmang, and it makes much more sense that an entrepreneur such as Gurdjieff would have settled in a large city such as Golok instead of rural Surmang. Gurdjieff was clearly not a monk if he had a family while in Tibet. Obviously, he was a lay practitioner (a *ngakpa*) who commuted to Surmang (and perhaps other monasteries as well) for teachings. Another thing that is significant about Golok is that Dudjom Lingpa, who was likely Gurdjieff's root teacher, was born in Golok. So, Gurdjieff could easily have had contacts in Golok which would have enabled him to settle there.

The Iron Pig year corresponds to 1910, which is within our estimate of time of Gurdjieff's second stay in Tibet. But what about Akhyung Khangsar? The recognition story says he was Shechen Rabjam's father.

To start with, the name Akhyung Khangsar is a title. Akhyung means chieftain and Khangsar is a tribal name. And there is a biography of the Akhyung Khangsar line that exists. According to the text, it appears that Norzin Nyima Dhundup would have been the Akhyung Khangsar circa 1910. It says that he had a wife by the name of Dorje Dolma, and a son by the name of Panchen Norbu Sonam who succeeded him as Akhyung Khangsar in 1927. What is highly unusual is that Shechen Rabjam is not mentioned as a son of Norzin Nyima

Dhundup. Surely if a chieftain such as Akhyung Khangsar had a son who was recognized as a great master such as Shechen Rabjam it would be mentioned in his biography. Other Tibetan scholars consulted agree with this. So, it appears that Norzin Nyima Dhundup is not Shechen Rabjam's father as his recognition story states.

But why would Urgyen Tag (a.k.a. Gyorgi Gurdjieff) not be identified as Shechen Rabjam's father in his recognition story? Really, we should not expect him to be named as the father, for the fact that the father was not Tibetan would likely have prevented the acceptance of the child's recognition. Today, after the Tibetan diaspora, there are a number of foreigners who have been recognized as tulkus, but before then it would have been most unusual even for a half-Tibetan to be recognized. So, this fact would necessarily have been concealed.

It is difficult to guess how Akhyung Khangsar came to be identified as Shechen Rabjam's father. Perhaps he adopted Shechen Rabjam, perhaps Gurdjieff's wife remarried and he is actually the stepfather, perhaps he was the maternal grandfather, or perhaps Gurdjieff had an affair with his wife. Most likely, however, is that Gurdjieff was a wealthy patron of Dzogchen Rinpoche, as is common, rinpoches include the children of their patrons in the recognitions they make, and Dzogchen Rinpoche took care of the details, be it with or without Akhyung Khangsar's knowledge, so that the recognition would not be questioned.

Also important is that identifying Shechen Rabjam as Gurdjieff's son would explain how Trungpa had heard about Gurdjieff's presence at Surmang. Of course, Shechen Rabjam likely had no memory of Gurdjieff being that Gurdjieff left Tibet when he was only an infant, but he certainly would have inquired about his father from both his mother and Dzogchen Rinpoche. Dzogchen Rinpoche not only recognized Shechen Rabjam, he was also one of his teachers, and certainly knew Gurdjieff if in fact Gurdjieff was his patron. It actually implies they would have known one another rather well. Not only could Trungpa have learned about Gurdjieff from Shechen Rabjam, he could also have learned about him from his primary teacher, Shechen Jamgon Kongtrul, who, as Gurdjieff also appears to have been, was a student of the Tenth Surmang Gharwang. Jamyang Khyentse Chökyi Lodro is another who Trungpa Rinpoche could have learned about Gurdjieff from. He was a teacher for both Trungpa Rinpoche and Shechen Rabjam.

Chatral Rinpoche was also a student of Chökyi Lodro. So, it is reasonable to conclude that he and Shechen Rabjam knew one another. They were only three years apart in age. So, Chatral could have learned about Gurdjieff's time in Tibet from either Shechen Rabjam or Chökyi Lodro.

What is certain is that both Trungpa Rinpoche and Chatral Rinpoche heard something of Gurdjieff's presence in Tibet. It is possible that they heard about this from some other source, but that they would have heard about it from Gurdjieff's son, supposedly another great teacher, is the most logical. That both Trungpa Rinpoche and Chatral Rinpoche were very discreet about what they knew is very likely because of a wish not to disgrace Shechen Rabjam.

Whatever the case may be, the photographic evidence is quite compelling. Clearly Shechen Rabjam had non-oriental physical features and very much resembles Gurdjieff.

At the time of the Chinese invasion of Tibet, Shechen Rabjam successfully evaded capture for a while, but was eventually caught and imprisoned in Derge sometime in early March of 1959. The Chinese military was rounding up all the high-ranking lamas. In prison he was kept separate from his dharma brothers, but during a brief encounter Jamyang Chödrön was able to deliver a secret message to him from Chökyi Wangchug which simply said, "Existence arises from the symbol."[7] He died in prison later that year.

Another significant fact is that Shechen Rabjam had a brother known as Tertön Tulku Dönkho, also an important tulku. Remember that Gurdjieff explicitly asked Le Toumelin to look for his *two* sons. Although not as specific, the comments from Bennett and Popoff reproduced above also support the idea of him having had two Tibetan sons. This thus gives further credence to identifying Shechen Rabjam as the son that Gurdjieff said became an abbot.

It would be nice to have more evidence but I have exhausted all lines of research I can think of. Akong Rinpoche replied to my query about Gurdjieff's presence in Tibet saying he did not know anything about it, but never replied to my follow-up question about Shechen Rabjam. He has since died. Similarly, Namkhai Norbu replied to my queries regarding Shechen Rabjam only to say that I was misinformed about him being Shechen Rabjam's nephew, but did not reply to my follow-up message. He has also since died. Chatral Rinpoche's daughter forwarded a letter of my questions to her father for me, but he never replied and also is no longer with us. Perhaps they too did not wish to disgrace Shechen Rabjam. Chime Rinpoche, who immigrated to the U.K. together with Trungpa Rinpoche and Akong Rinpoche, never replied to my queries. Pewar Tulku is another old tulku who knew Shechen Rabjam but was very difficult to contact and has now died. An attempt to see what records may exist in the Golok civil offices turned up with naught. One remaining possibility, however, is that more information will eventually turn up at the archives of Shechen Tennyi Dargyeling in Nepal, which maintains the extant artifacts of the original Shechen Gompa. More information on Tertön Tulku Dönkho would also be helpful, particularly his recognition story. If he perchance had children, contacting their family may reveal more information.

What follows is a *terma* discovered by Shechen Rabjam. There is nothing about the text that corresponds to Gurdjieff in any way, but it is still quite interesting. It reads like a typical description of a sacred site, but contains much symbolism. It also includes examples of spontaneously arisen phenomena—the way Tibetans perceive deities in the formations of nature, magical and rich in meaning for them. Interesting too is the Rimé influence. Although Shechen Rabjam was Nyingmapa there are references or allusions to other Tibetan sects as well as to Hinduism.

1 J.G. Bennett, *Gurdjieff: Making a New World* (New York: Harper & Row, 1973), 95–96.

2 Irmis B. Popoff, *Gurdjieff and His Work: On Myself, with Others, for the Work* (New York: Vantage Press, 1969), 152.

3 John Shirley, *Gurdjieff: An Introduction to His Life and Teachings* (New York: Jeremy P. Tarcher, 2004), 98. When asked for his source Shirley was unable to recall. The statement is not in either of Nott's two books on Gurdjieff.

4 Private correspondence.

5 Chögyam Trungpa, *The Collected Works of Chögyam Trungpa: Volume 1* (Boston: Shambhala Publications, 2003), 76. (*Born in Tibet*, Chapter 6.)

6 "Gyurme Kunzang Tenpé Nyima," Rigpa Shreda, www.rigpawiki.org/index.php?title=Gyurme_Kunzang_Tenpé_Nyima

7 Chögyal Namkhai Norbu, *The Lamp That Enlightens Narrow Minds: The Life and Times of a Realized Tibetan Master, Khyentse Chökyi Wangchug* (Berkeley: North Atlantic Books, 2012), 97.

Photograph of Shechen Rabjam, copyright © Shechen Monastery, a copy of an original print made for their archives by Matthieu Ricard, is reproduced here with their permission.

## The Sacred Site Known as Halashiri

On the mountain is a sacred site which looks like a crack in its peak.

Over it the cloudbanks of the gurus of the Instruction Lineage[1] congregate.

In the center the assemblies of *istadevas*[2] mingle together like rainbows.

To the right and left the *dakas* and *dakinis* amass like clouds.

From below surges forth the ocean of oath-bound ones[3] assuming intimidating poses.

At the fore you will come to an offering goddess in dancing posture.

Near this sacred site, to the west, there are some foothills on which lies a *dakini* shrine known as Sangphuk [or "Secret Cave"].

Continuing on a short distance from there you will arrive at the misty cave of Guru Rinpoche.[4]

It is said that along the way of the secret path (if you are able to reach it) is where he spoke his promise that no one will need to experience an eighteenth instance of rebirth in the *bardo*.

Inside the misty cave is a shrine to the fifteen hundred arhats.

Upon the mountain range there is a ground which is the

field for the display of the eight classes [of gods and demons].

It is situated at the upper section and has the form of flags and victory banners.

In front of that is the form of the attendants of the Four Great Kings.[5]

Proceeding upwards from there, to the right side ascends a staircase for those fortunate enough [to be destined] for liberation; above this there is a spontaneously manifested image of a jewel, which is imbued with the Siddhi of Children and Wealth; and there is also a spontaneously manifested image of a longevity vase, arisen through the Siddhi of Longevity.

There is indeed no other sacred site which surpasses this one!

These are just a few remarks; the extensive account is clearly recorded in the treasure revelations regarding Sikkim.

Good fortune!

*Khutuktu Shechen Rabjam*

---

[1] The founders of the Kagyupa lineage.
[2] *Istadeva* is a Sanskrit word meaning the favorite deity that one regularly prays to.
[3] Dharma protectors.
[4] One of the names of Padmasambhava.
[5] The Four Great Heavenly Kings of Buddhism include Vessavana (King of the North), Virulhaka (King of the South), Dhatarattha (King of the East), and Virupakkha (King of the West).

The original Tibetan text of "The Sacred Site Known as Halashiri," provided by The State Library of Berlin, was translated for the author by Erick Tsiknopoulos. The full title given by its author is actually *A Note with a Few Remarks on the Contents of the Sacred Site Known as Halashiri, a Meditation Spot of Guru Rinpoche Which is Inseparable from Khecara.* (Halashiri is a Sanskrit name that literally means "sacred place," Guru Rinpoche is one of the names of Padmasambhava, the founder of Tibetan Buddhism, and the Sanskrit word *khecara*, which literally means "free-floating," here is a reference to the pure realm of Vajrayogini.)

*Kumbum Monastery 1936*

## THE SELF-TAMERS

In the chapter "Beelzebub for the First Time in Tibet," Gurdjieff talks about a rest stop made at the monastery of sectarians called the Self-Tamers, who belong to Tibet's orthodox Buddhist sect. His alter ego, Beelzebub, describes his horror at witnessing the inhabitants who spend their entire lives in practice cells that only have enough room to sit. There they eat and sleep, and are cared for by other monastics who revere their devotion to practice. Also mentioned is that it is the only monastery of its kind.

The only monastery meeting this description is one called Kumbum. It is the only monastery with such practice cells as Beelzebub says of the Self-Tamer's monastery. As well, the Kumbum complex is entirely surrounded by a protective wall as Beelzebub says of the Self-Tamer's monastery. No doubt the description given is based on personal experience.

Kumbum also has ties to the Mongolian peoples and, according to Ovshé Norzunov's compatriot Gombozhab T. Tsybikov, most of its residents are Mongolian. (Both Norzunov and Tsybikov were Kalmyk, who are Mongol descendants.) Tsybikov has a chapter devoted to Kumbum in his travelog, *A Buddhist Pilgrim at the Shrines of Tibet*. The two were both hired by the Russian Geographic Society to surreptitiously photograph their pilgrimages, and theirs were the first photos of Tibet ever to be published. Tsybikov was at Kumbum from

January 22 to April 25, 1900, and again for a shorter stay from February 5–12, 1902. Although an important Gelugpa monastery, Norzunov does not mention having visited it. Whether or not Norzunov and Tsybikov knew one another is uncertain, and therefore also uncertain if Gurdjieff and Tsybikov knew one another, yet there is still some small possibility that Gurdjieff would have accompanied Tsybikov to Kumbum during his 1902 visit. Then again, considering that Gurdjieff appears to have been involved with the Kagyupa and Nyingmapa sects, and therefore that while traveling about with his Kagyupa and Nyingmapa companions he would have been more likely to make stops at monasteries of those sects, it does seem more likely that he would have stopped at Kumbum while traveling into or out of Tibet with a Mongolian Gelugpa companion. So, perhaps having accompanied Tsybikov to Kumbum in 1902 is not so unlikely.

Although Beelzebub's description of the Self-Tamers is obviously a criticism of religious extremism, some Gurdjieffians consider it a dismissal of all of Tibetan Buddhism. Hopefully showing that Gurdjieff is speaking of only one particular Tibetan Buddhist monastery will make this more clear.

*The Twelfth Trungpa Tulku leading the Chakrasambhava dance.*

## DANCE

Now let us look at Gurdjieff's familiarity with Tibetan dance. In doing so we find ourselves confronted with four issues. The first is that there are dances attributed to the Tibetan tradition by eye witnesses that are apparently amongst the lost movements. The second is that there are movements that, while not authentic Tibetan dances, are clearly influenced by Tibetan culture. Some of these include the word "Tibetan" in the title while others do not. The third is that the authentic Tibetan movements which remain are not attributed as such. And the fourth is that any Vajrayana dances that Gurdjieff was initiated in would have been protected by a vow of *samaya*. As with verbal Vajrayana teachings, Vajrayana dances also require a vow not to share anything of the practice with those who have not received the proper initiation.

This appears to be the case with the dance Gurdjieff describes having witnessed at Sarmung. He relates that the dances he observed (and evidently learned) there employed a posture-based alphabet by which specific knowledge was conveyed. Here he is clearly speaking of *mudras*. The word *mudra* means gesture. Most people are familiar with the various hand *mudras* depicted in images of the Buddha. However, there are also *mudras* created with the entire body that are employed in Hindu and Buddhist sacred dance. As Trungpa explains, "The Lord Buddha is portrayed in sculpture and painting making different gestures (*mudra*), each of which has its own special significance. And so it is with our dancing; each step and each movement of the hands, arms and head has its own symbolic meaning and brings an increase of understanding both to dancers and spectators."[1]

Surmang is especially known for its annual Chakrasamvara dance which goes through a multitude of these full-body *mudras*. The dance takes place just before Losar (the Tibetan New Year) and lasts for three days. Ideally 64 dancers are required, but it has also been performed with fewer. *Samaya* does not prohibit people from gathering to watch the performance. Watching it is considered a blessing. But it does prohibit explaining any of the particulars about the practice. However, in his autobiography *Born in Tibet*, Trungpa provides some of the general symbolism while recounting how rigorous training for this dance was:

> The course went on for three and a half months without interruption, for there was a great deal to learn. The dancing had 360 different themes symbolic of the number of days in the year, and of the same number of worldly thoughts that must be transformed into the 360 forms of wisdom.[2]

As Lama Surya Das notes, this aspect of Chakrasamvara practice is associated with the Crazy Wisdom tradition.[3] It also relates to Gurdjieff's teaching of befriending one's demons and transforming them through the care of impartial observation. This is what true Crazy Wisdom is about—applying unconventional wisdom to address one's own conditioning rather than using it on some power trip thinking one can address the conditioning of others.

Also interesting about the dance in relation to Gurdjieff is Trungpa's description of how difficult the accompanying drumwork was. The technique involved holding in one's outstretched arm two cords from which suspended weights that served as beaters. This position had to be maintained for over an hour at a time. It is very feasible that this was the inspiration for the exercise Gurdjieff gave of standing with arms outstretched for a long period.

180

At any rate, it seems fairly clear that the postures Gurdjieff said he observed being taught at Sarmung were actually the *mudras* of Surmang's Chakrasamvara dance. Although he was unable to teach this dance, his description, along with the evidence that Sarmung is a reference to Surmang, appears to indicate the Chakrasamvara dance specifically.

Meanwhile, there are two authentic Tibetan movements that Gurdjieff taught (despite not being specified as such), and were not lost, that were not restricted by *samaya*. The first is called "Measuring the Way by One's Length." While Gurdjieff attributes its origin to Caucasia and Turkestan, this movement is clearly the Tibetan style of doing full-length prostrations. Anyone is able to do this practice. Besides doing these prostrations in place, it is also a practice to do them as a method of ambulation while on pilgrimage to a sacred site, or while circumambulating a sacred site. This is the way Gurdjieff taught it. Recall that Ovshé Norzunov describes having witnessed this circumambulation practice in the article on his third trip to Lhasa. Significantly, he described the pilgrims measuring the way with their bodies.

Similarly, there is apparently a women's movement which is an authentic Tibetan dance. According to Roger Lipsey, a dance he once witnessed in the mountains outside of Kathmandu was nearly identical to one of the women's dances he was familiar with.[4] Although Nepal is multicultural, as the community that performed the dance was Buddhist, it can be said that the movement belongs to Tibetan Buddhist culture. As a folk dance, this one too is free of *samaya* and can be taught to anyone. As with all the women's movements, the one Lipsey witnessed in the mountains of Nepal has no tradition attributed to it.

The lost movements are a result of Gurdjieff having stopped teaching them after his automobile accident the summer of 1924, and not resuming them until the beginning of World War II. Although Ouspensky's and Nicoll's groups practiced them during the 1930s, too much time had passed even before Madame Ouspensky initiated movements practice at Lyne Place—the Ouspensky group residence established in 1931. Among the lost movements are virtually all which were intended for Gurdjieff's ballet, *The Struggle of the Magicians*. One of two accounts which cite Tibetan origins of the movements explicitly indicates Gurdjieff's ballet. In his book *In Denikin's Russia*, C. E. Bechhofer Roberts makes an interesting comment about the movements he witnessed at Gurdjieff's Tbilisi Institute:

> In the evenings, I used to call at Georgiy Ivanovich's "Institute for Harmonic Human Development" and watch him rehearsing a ballet which he had himself invented, composed, and set to music. The story was a Manichaean theme—the strife of white and black magicians. The dances, he declared, were based on movements and gestures which had been handed down by tradition and paintings in Thibetan monasteries where he had been.[5]

While Gurdjieff's attributions cannot be trusted in general, in this case *mudra* is being described. So, the movements for *The Struggle of the Magicians* likely included a few authentic Tibetan dances. What also suggests this is that the music for one of the Tibetan dances from the ballet sounds like it could be Tibetan. The melody is obviously more Far Eastern sounding than the Near Eastern melodies of the majority of his music. It is the music for "The Struggle of the Magicians No. 6: Tibetan Dance," which is specified for Act III of the ballet. This is the act where the women of Gafar's harem, who come from a variety of cultures, come one by one to entertain him with one of their native dances. The first is specified as a Tibetan dance. This is obviously the dance for which the music "Tibetan Dance" was intended. Considering that this would have been a folk dance, there is no reason it would have been restricted and was therefore very likely authentic. (On the subject of music, it is also interesting that as René de Nebesky-Wojkowitz mentions, "...some Tibetan [musical] signs and some of their names are analogous to Armenian neumes."[6] Gurdjieff may well have been able to read Tibetan musical notation.)

The other account of having witnessed Tibetan dances performed by Gurdjieff's Institute comes from Alfons Paquet,

182

a German who was invited by his old friend Alexander von Salzmann to attend some of the Institute's activities when they met unexpectedly in Constantinople. Although he does not relate anything concerning *mudra*, he says the dances he saw were essentially replicas of those he had seen previously in the Tibetan Buddhist monasteries of Khovd and Uliastai, Mongolia. At the Constantinople Institute too, the movements for *The Struggle of the Magicians* were being rehearsed.

Note that Gurdjieff told Roberts that the "gestures" his sacred exercises employed were "handed down by tradition and paintings in Thibetan monasteries," whereas Gurdjieff says that the dances he saw being taught at Sarmung made use of an elaborate posture-teaching device. The device is purely metaphoric. Its seven limbs are clearly meant to convey the law of seven and could not possibly be used to teach human form. In the case of the Chakrasamvara dance, according to Zurmang Gharwang Rinpoche, "...the dances are passed down from teacher to student. There is a text that is memorized and explains how to perform the ritual dance, including visualization, mantra, and mudra."[7] Although Zurmang Gharwang did not explicitly mention painting, most Tibetan visualization practices are taught aided by thangka paintings that depict all the intricate details of what is to be visualized. What Gurdjieff told Roberts, which was long before *Meetings with Remarkable Men* was written, is much more accurate.

Also note that Roberts was told that the movements he was witnessing were *based on* Tibetan dances, not necessarily authentic Tibetan dances. Dorothy Caruso was also told that the movements were "*based on* the sacred temple dances [Gurdjieff] had seen in Thibet."[8] This is not to deny that *The Struggle of the Magicians* included some authentic Tibetan dances. Paquet apparently affirms this. But it might be good to discuss the existing movements based on Tibetan dance. Margit Martinu, an instructor of both the Gurdjieff movements and Namkhai Norbu's vajra dances, noticed that there still exist some movements in this category. As she details:

> I do not claim to know all of the movements which bear the name "Tibetan" but perhaps one resembling Tibetan

dancing is the Tibetan March. What to me could be close to Tibetan influence would be "Little Tibetan Standing" and "Little Tibetan Sitting." Especially "Tibetan Sitting" [which] has very clear *mudras* and is one of the few movements done sitting down and obviously is related to sitting meditation. "Tibetan Standing" [also] has a very real proof of the Tibetan influence because there is this sticking out of the tongue as one of the gestures, and that is a typical Tibetan traditional way of greeting.[9]

Similarly, the movement "Thirty Gestures" may have been inspired by the *mudra* concept. More clearly inspired by *mudra* is "March Forward" (also known as the "Third Obligatory"), which consists of a series of "Buddha positions." Note also that the first three obligatories, including "March Forward," are attributed to the Temple of Medicine in Sari, Tibet. This might sound unusual, but the study of Tibetan Medicine does include various yoga practices which may be regarded as sacred movement. In fact, Paquet mentions that "sacred physical exercises" was part of the Tibetan Medicine curriculum that Gurdjieff was giving to Dr Leonid Stjernvall. Sari is an actual place in Tibet too. It is located in northeastern Kham. The only monastery there is called Nyenthog, but it could not be ascertained if Nyenthog has a *shedra* where Tibetan Medicine is taught. But it is also somewhat plausible that Gurdjieff is referring instead to Tsari (also spelled Zari), a region of southern Kham renowned for its wild medicinal herbs. Being that Tsari is home to many monasteries it seems very likely that at least one has a *shedra* where Tibetan Medicine is taught. It is difficult to tell from the scale of the map showing Ovshé Norzunov's travel route in his original article, but it appears that he (and therefore Gurdjieff) passed through northeastern Kham on the way to Lhasa, suggesting Sari to be more likely. Still, it is possible that Gurdjieff visited Tsari at another time.

There are also some movements that, although not based on Tibetan dance, are practiced while reciting Tibetan words. One such movement is No. 15 of the 39 Series which is called "Tibetan Days of the Week." As the name implies, the Tibetan names of the days of the week are recited while executing the movement.

Although not a proof in any way, it may be useful to mention here that both Namkhai Norbu and Chögyam Trungpa had great appreciation for the Gurdjieff movements. Norbu once participated in one of Margit Martinu's movements classes and commented that they "directly bring one to [the] primordial state."[10] Both also developed their own movement practices. Norbu's vajra dances are a *terma* teaching he received while on retreat long after he witnessed the Gurdjieff movements, but Trungpa's mudra space awareness practice appears to have been developed as a direct result of the Gurdjieff Foundation having denied his request to have the movements taught at Naropa Institute (now Naropa University)—the college he founded with contemplative and mindfulness practices at the core of its curriculum. Considering that mudra space awareness is based upon the Chakrasamvara dance, Trungpa may have understood that the Gurdjieff movements were inspired by the Chakrasamvara dance to some degree. Besides having seen the Gurdjieff movements himself, Trungpa was also well-read on Gurdjieff's teaching and undoubtedly read his description of dance at "Sarmung". As well, those practicing mudra space awareness who had previous experience with the Gurdjieff movements noticed definite similarities between some of the exercises.[11]

Also interesting is that one of the movements films produced by Madame de Salzmann and René Zuber depicts the movement "Tibetan Masks" performed in traditional Tibetan costume.

Before continuing with these explorations of Gurdjieff's Tibetan influences, let us read Alfons Paquet's encounter with Gurdjieff's Institute and the movements he saw practiced there.

1 Chögyam Trungpa, *The Collected Works of Chögyam Trungpa: Volume 1* (Boston: Shambhala Publications, 2003), 92. (*Born in Tibet*, Chapter 8.)

2 Ibid., 93.

3 Lama Surya Das, *The Snow Lion's Turquoise Mane* (New York: HarperOne, 1992), 133.

4 Conveyed to the author orally.

5 Carl Bechhofer Roberts, *In Denikin's Russia and the Caucasus 1919–1920* (London: W. Collins Sons & Co, 1921), 67.

6 René de Nebesky-Wojkowitz, *Tibetan Religious Dances: Tibetan Text and Annotated Translation of the "Chams Yig,"* (Delhi: Pilgrims Publishing, 1997), 277.

7 As relayed to the author by his assistant, Daniel Aitken.

8 Dorothy Caruso, *A Personal History* (New York: Hermitage House, 1952), 152.

9 Private correspondence.

10 Ibid.

11 Private correspondence with David Stone.

## An Encounter with Gurdjieff's Institute

I had the most unusual encounter on the last day in Constantinople. It took place on the twisting road in Pera, leading up the hill. I stood on the corner of one of the many side streets, in order to examine the inexpertly written sign on an institute, the name of which interested me. Just at that moment I received a nudge, I turned around and saw the deeply furrowed face of a tall, gray-haired man. Like all Russians here he was dressed in a threadbare suit with a gray scarf and a flattened cap. The man said to me with a Munich inflection; "Well, what are you doing here?" It was Mr v. S.,[1] a painter who had lived in Munich many years before the war. I had not seen him since the spring of 1914. Exactly seven years had passed. I had heard that v. S., who was Russian, and his Swiss wife[2] had left Germany at the beginning of the war. I then came to understand from prisoners of war who had returned home that they had received much help from this man in Tiflis. The stream of refugees had also carried him to Constantinople. He was stuck here, and he was working, together with a few friends, in this very institute, the sign of which I stood before.

We met again late that evening and visited the institute. It was called the Institute for the Harmonious Development of Man. Nothing less. It was on the ground floor of a labyrinthine house which was teeming with Russians. I met the director[3] of the school, a Caucasian who for years had wandered through the mountainous regions of inner Asia, visiting the cloisters and coming to know the cults, dances and sciences of the monks. He contended that India is not the origin of the miraculous. He spoke of the highlands of Pamir, the names of which are hardly known in the West, and of their peculiarities (of which researchers never tire of telling). I saw the dances which were practiced by his students (of which there were barely a couple of dozen) in the exiguous hall with its black and white stone slab floors. At the piano sat a professor[4] of the Petersburg music academy whose name was known in Germany. He played oriental measures to the dances, unusual in their melodies and rhythms. Among the students was a physician[5] from Petersburg who was about to give up his whole knowledge of school medicine in order to undertake the study of Tibetan medicine with its knowledge of juices, medicinal toxins and the influence of special, sacred physical exercises. These were all things which I had once seen baffling examples of in the cloisters of Kobdo and Uliastay. In those places I saw dances, as are commonly performed in esoteric schools by the monks of Mazar in Afghanistan and in the Keri oasis—gymnastic exercises, intended to awaken will power, sense of hearing and memory, and to steel the muscles, exercises which were nothing other than a form of yoga. What are the famous exercises of the Jesuit Order or the Prussian Exercise Regulations but Yoga exercises that turn cloddish humans into the finest and strongest tools of great thoughts? Among the areas of study of this institute were lectures from the tradition of Asian schools on religious myths, on rhythm, the law of octaves, the science of numbers and all the rest that is related to the Cabbala and the magical arts. Here one learned an interpretation of the megaliths or stone monuments, those dolmen that seem to form a giant belt stretching from inner Asia, through the Caucasus, southern Russia and Poland, over the northern German heath land to Scandinavia and England, through Brittany, in the Pyrenees, and that can be found in northern Africa, the circle closing in Egypt. These mystical symbols stemming from long-forgotten peoples of the Bactrian and Atlantan antiquity who were highly skilled

188

in astronomy and geology. What's more, I saw myself here, standing as it were before the answer to a question that had been nagging me since Olympia and Delphi: The thought that there was something that conjoined those connections between worship of the gods and the study of nature, between the guidance of nations and banking, between gymnastics, healing and oracles and between sculpture, painting and tragedy at the sacred sites in Greece. There was a lost, deeper unity that determined the lives of men, and this unity, this creative equilibrium, was nothing less than the origin of all matters and laws of harmony. These people who joined together under this teacher have been uprooted and rerooted. Every single one of them must fight daily for their existence, not one of them has the means to enjoy the luxury of a study that requires all of their efforts. They are far removed from the excessive enthusiasm and pompousness that accompanies certain esoteric schools in the countries of the west. In comparison to the powerful language of their dances, all rhythmic gymnastics are simply the frisking of lambs. These people are performing active mysticism that feels superior to some others, that wishes to strengthen itself in order to one day take possession of the vacant cults, the theater, the churches, the great soul-shaping schools. Behind this mysticism threaten the magical flames, the witches powers, the diabolical grimaces of daemons. At the same time, however, it is illuminated by the gently resplendent sway of the gods, approached by orphic singing riding on the back of dolphins in the sea. Long into the night I walked with my friend through the lonely streets of Shishli, until dawn began to break on the Asiatic coast on the other side of the Bosporus. We spoke of Germany, with its subterranean currents of increasing skepticism of the moribund undertakings of the university faculties, with their searches for the expression of deeper insights, to this day still preliminary and disconnected, things that possibly do not occur anywhere else in the world. I had left Germany to recover from the atmosphere of pessimism and occultism that threatened to choke those who work intellectually, dragging them into an unknown maelstrom. In Greece I thought I had found traces that reconnect us with the myth and direct us to the meaning of the forgotten mysteries, the complete loss of which is threatening to tear modern Europe to shreds. Here I once again felt the Delphic breeze. A return of the East to the North would once again appear to be taking place. It is as if all that was dispersed is now searching for its origins. Without the last inner unity of all religions and cultures, all thoughts of internationality are preposterous.

*Alfons Paquet*

---

[1] Alexander [Alexandre] von [de] Salzmann.
[2] Jeanne von [de] Salzmann (ne Allemand).
[3] G. Gurdjieff.
[4] Thomas von [de] Hartmann.
[5] Leonid Stjernvall.

"An Encounter with Gurdjieff's Institute," an excerpt from *Delphische Wanderung* by Alfons Paquet (München: Drei Masken Verlag, 1922), was translated for the author from the German by Dr C. Bruce Boschek.

## CUISINE

Gurdjieff loved preparing dishes of the many cultures he encountered for his guests. In the same way he enjoyed figuring out how mechanical devices worked, he also evidently enjoyed figuring out how to recreate the traditional dishes he consumed during his wanderings through Asia. Although in the case of Tibetan cuisine, considering that he had a family there and was there for long periods, he likely received instruction in proper preparation. Generally speaking, Tibetan cuisine is fairly simple as well.

Solita Solano's notes of March 26, 1937 mentions a couple of things of interest. That day they consumed "small tinned lamb tongues from Tibet."[1] It is unlikely the lamb tongues they ate were from Tibet. Canned lamb tongues can be found in Paris, it is unlikely Tibet had much of a canning industry at the time if at all, and it is well-known that Gurdjieff often lied about the origin of the foods he obtained to create a special atmosphere. Yet lamb tongues are indeed eaten in Tibet. Cold lamb tongues is one of the foods enjoyed by the upper class. Given Solano's description, it sounds like they ate them cold with little preparation as Tibetans do.

Then, while serving his guests "Dalai Lama's tea" (likely another fabrication given Solano describes drinking the tea with sugar which Tibetans do not do), Gurdjieff says, "Too bad I not have time make Tibetan tea with butter—boiled, and small amount of flour of roasted wheat—such a drink have *all*."[2] Tibetan butter tea is in fact sometimes consumed with roasted barley flour as a means of sustenance. Probably Gurdjieff said it is drunk with roasted wheat not knowing the word for barley, or Solano did not remember what he said accurately. Yet also possible is that Gurdjieff learned, or got in the habit of, preparing butter tea with roasted wheat flour instead of barley flour. While roasted barley flour (*tsampa*) is a staple and the most commonly-used grain in Tibet, other grains are also used there. Either way, the only cultures which drink butter tea are Himalayan. Gurdjieff then adds, "You see, not such idiot there in Tibet. You can find everything, if you know how; Tibet direct communication with Karatas has."[3] (According to Gurdjieff's tales, Karatas is the planet that Beelzebub is from.)

For those who wish to try making butter tea, the best tea to use is puerh. Puerh is virtually identical to Tibetan brick tea. Yak butter is the most common butter in Tibet, and you may be able to find yak butter in an Indian grocer, but cow butter will suffice. Similarly, you can find himalayan salt to use for authenticity's sake, but using kosher salt will not make any difference.

A month later, on April 21st, Gurdjieff is found serving his guests a traditional Tibetan bone broth. He calls it "tea", apparently not knowing the word for broth and using a near equivalent, but his description is clearly that of a broth: "Tibet tea very wise creation. From centrum come and little by little through the ages man learn about this. Two days boil bones of yak, put in grains of wheat and butter. All is here what man needs."[4] Actually, it would be more accurate to call this dish tsampa soup, which is made by adding some tsampa and butter to a bone broth.

Similarly, Donald Whitcomb's notes for July 2, 1947 says that Gurdjieff "gave us Tibetan tea, from Dalai Lama's secretary, made in bouillon from yak bones and butter,"[5] that is, bone broth with butter but without roasted grains. Whitcomb was probably unaware of the roasted grain in it.

A good substitute for yak bone—which is what is most

frequently used for broth in Tibet—is ox bone, but cow bone works very well too. It is very simple to make; there are not many ingredients. But it does have to boil for hours. For tsampa soup, as with butter tea, cow butter works just as well as yak butter. And barley flour is easy to find nowadays but wheat flour is fine if more convenient.

Gurdjieff may have enjoyed serving bone broth in part because of its medicinal benefits. He frequently talked about the health benefits of the foods he served at his meals, and did in fact introduce the soup served on April 21st by saying, "All is here what man needs." In Tibetan Medicine, bone broth is actually prescribed for certain disorders, and it seems likely that Gurdjieff would have learned various ways in which bone broth might be prepared as a remedy.

With that said, let us now look at some additional evidence of Gurdjieff's acquaintance with Tibetan Medicine.

---

[1] Solita Solano, et al., *Gurdjieff and the Women of the Rope* (London: Book Studio, 2012), 138.

[2] Ibid., 138.

[3] Ibid., 138.

[4] Ibid., 151.

[5] "Donald Whitcomb's Notes of his Paris visit 23 June to 28 July 1947," an unpublished manuscript.

*Thangka painting depicting the branches of medical science.*

## MEDICINE

Medicine seems to be an important subject in the Surmang Kagyu sect. The *shedra* (university) at both Surmang Namgyal Tse and Surmang Dutsi Til continue to teach Tibetan Medicine. Perhaps it has been taught at some of the other Surmang monasteries too. In Tibet, medicine is inseparable from the buddhadharma; it is considered a dharma practice. This is true amongst other Buddhist cultures too. The relationship is an intimate one given Buddhism's emphasis on the cessation of suffering. This is why Georgette Leblanc tells us, "In Tibet, where [Gurdjieff] spent so many years of his life, the priests are doctors and the doctors priests."[1] It also explains how one of the Gurdjieff movements is said to originate from a Tibetan temple of medicine. The movement in question is likely a Tibetan yoga practice. In Gurdjieff's culture too, it was common for medicine to be included in theological training. As a child he himself was tutored in both fields.

Although it was primarily Soloviev who studied Tibetan Medicine at Surmang Namgyal Tse, Gurdjieff evidently picked up something of the tradition while there too. Tibetan Medicine is one of the primary subjects taught at the *shedra* of Namgyal Tse. Having previously studied other forms of medicine, Gurdjieff no doubt would have engaged in discussing subjects of interest with the medicine teachers and students there. *Menpas* (doctors of Tibetan Medicine) have historically been curious about other modalities, and Gurdjieff himself was particularly interested in medicine and learning various treatment methods. What follows is some evidence of Gurdjieff's acquaintance with the subject.

For one thing, according to Alfons Paquet, Gurdjieff was teaching Tibetan Medicine to Leonid Stjernvall. This in itself suggests that Gurdjieff had quite a good understanding of the science. Unfortunately, Dr Stjernvall left us no record of his work with Gurdjieff.

Nonetheless, some evidence of Gurdjieff's understanding of Tibetan Medicine may be found in Rolf Alexander's works. Knowing that Alexander was studying medicine, Gurdjieff may have shared some of his knowledge with him, as he did with Stjernvall. In *The Doctor Alone Can't Cure You,* Alexander has a short chapter devoted to *prana,* which he defines as "nervous energy." *Prana* is a Sanskrit term, literally meaning breath, used in Ayurvedic Medicine to denote one of the three humors, or energies, that keep the body in balance. Tibetan Medicine, which is largely founded upon Ayurveda, contains the same idea. In Tibetan Medicine, *prana* was translated as *loong,* which literally means wind, and it is said that an excess of *loong* results in nervousness. Gurdjieff was undoubtedly familiar with the idea as he talks about *prana* in *Beelzebub's Tales.* In the chapter "The First Visit of Beelzebub to India," "Saint Buddha" is quoted talking about the subject.

Gurdjieff also expresses his acquaintance with a particular idea of Tibetan Medicine in one of his discussions with Solita Solano.[2] The idea is that it is unhealthy to force or suppress bodily functions such as defecation, urination, coughing, sneezing and yawning. In explaining the law of seven to Solano, he mentions how one should let one's stool pass naturally when defecating without forcing it.

Admittedly the above is not very much, but there is also a small amount of evidence that Gurdjieff was employing something of Tibetan Medicine in the treatments he was giving his patients. The difficulty in researching this area is twofold. Firstly, Gurdjieff practiced a mix of various modalities. Besides the occidental medicine of his time and Tibetan Medicine, he is known to have practiced an eastern form of hypnotherapy and an experimental German modality. As well, there is also evidence that he was familiar with Chinese medicine, as Gurdjieff's food diagram appears to be an adaptation of how the modality understands the flow and transformation of *qi* in the body. And, secondly, there is very little record of the treatments that Gurdjieff administered. Nonetheless, a couple of records of the treatments he employed exist which may indicate his usage of the Tibetan science specifically.

Generally speaking, Gurdjieff is known to have treated both his wife and his brother for cancer, and Tibetan Medicine is renowned for curing cancers of all sorts. It is unknown what kind of cancer his wife had, but his brother Dmitri was diagnosed with stomach and intestinal cancers. Although there is no record of Gurdjieff treating his mother for her liver cancer, it seems highly likely that he was treating her as well. Regarding his wife, Madame Ostrovsky, she only survived until June of 1926 because the treatments Gurdjieff was giving her were interrupted as a result of his convalescence following his automobile accident of 1924. His mother, who died in the summer of 1925, likely suffered the same fate.

But his brother Dmitri had better luck. Gurdjieff was able to keep his cancer in remission for twelve years. Had Dmitri not ceased getting treatments from his brother because of a squabble they were having, he would certainly have lived longer still.

Of these three individuals, the only one we know anything about the treatment Gurdjieff administered is Madame Ostrovsky. Fritz Peters tells us that for her illness, she was given "a diet which included a large amount of blood."[3] Although Tibetan Medicine would not prescribe blood for cancer in general, such a remedy would most definitely be prescribed for blood imbalances, and would likely be prescribed for leukemia in which the patient suffers from a deficiency of red blood cells. So, it is conceivable that Gurdjieff was treating his wife for leukemia specifically.

Another instance in which Gurdjieff appears to have utilized something of Tibetan Medicine comes from Solita Solano. Her notes for January 25, 1936 describe an experiment Gurdjieff made on her which appears to be an adaptation of *tsaloong*, a Tibetan yoga similar to *tummo* that can also be employed as a form of energy healing. These yoga practices involve the intentional balancing and manipulation of one's *loong* (known as *prana* or *qi* in other modalities) for self-healing and health maintenance. When used to heal others, visualization practices are used to emit these energies from one's hands in the form of heat and cold. As Solano describes:

> One day after luncheon, he led me into his room and told me to stand at the window with my back to him. He remained at the door. He said, "Relax all body. If head or any part wishes to move, let move. I wish make experiment and at same time give you something." In a few seconds, my head began to move from side to side and up and down, slowly. Then a wide heat ray or wave struck my neck with force and moved down, then up my spine. Startled, I said, "Oh, you're touching me!" "No," he replied from the door. A minute later he said, "Now enough."[4]

The part of the experiment which may be related to *tsaloong*, of course, is the bolt of heat. But *tsaloong* generally is not practiced at such a distance. Still, Gurdjieff did say he was making an experiment. The purpose of the experiment could conceivably have been to see if *tsaloong* could be combined with some other practice he was familiar with that enabled its administration from a distance.

One final instance of Gurdjieff's possible application of Tibetan Medicine might also be mentioned though the treatment he employed is unknown. As the previously-mentioned quote from Georgette Leblanc implies, Gurdjieff was also treating her for some illness. This was during June and July of 1936. According to his diagnosis she was suffering from some liver disorder.[5] All that is known is that she fully recovered despite having been on the verge of death. Besides Tibetan Medicine's approach to treating cancer, its efficacy in treating liver disease has also been recognized. So, it is somewhat possible he was applying Tibetan healing principles to treating her.

[1] Georgette Leblanc, *The Courage Machine: A New Life in a New World* (London: Book Studio, 2012), 97.

[2] Solita Solano, et al., *Gurdjieff and the Women of the Rope* (London: Book Studio, 2012), 54.

[3] Fritz Peters, *Boyhood with Gurdjieff* (New York: E. P. Dutton & Co.), 76.

[4] Solita Solano, et al., *Gurdjieff and the Women of the Rope* (London: Book Studio, 2012), 28.

[5] Georgette Leblanc, *The Courage Machine: A New Life in a New World* (London: Book Studio, 2012), 96.

Thangka painting of the branches of medical science sourced from Wikimedia.

*Marpa Lotsawa*

## A Modern Marpa

Gurdjieff is frequently compared to both Marpa and Milarepa, the beloved founders of the Kagyupa sect. Like Marpa, Gurdjieff had a reputation for his harsh teaching methods. And like Milarepa, Gurdjieff felt remorse for having used his powers for maleficent purposes and abandoned them. Also like Milarepa was Gurdjieff's passionate diligence and commitment to the path. If he was indeed at Surmang Monastery, surely he had been initiated into that tradition and learned the ways of its masters. The two legendary figures are models for both student and teacher.

Olga de Hartmann had such devotion for Gurdjieff that she found it difficult to say "no" to any request he may have made. Gurdjieff apparently saw this as a weakness and at times gave her tasks that went against her better judgment and thereby created an inner conflict so that she may better see this feature and acquire greater faith in her own conscience. Shortly after one such incident, while reading Milarepa, she "found out that the Tibetan masters often made such difficulties for people so that they understood not to believe everything."[1]

Robert Godet was convinced that Gurdjieff practiced and taught the way of conscious labor and intentional suffering as he received it from the Kagyupa lineage:

> The Kagyupas... extracted the necessity of "conscious labor and intentional suffering." It suffices to be convinced

of this to read the admirable "explanatory statement" by which Marpa, the great root guru of Milarepa, explains why he overwhelmed his disciple with so much work.

For me it is the complete unity of path and conduct of my teacher and friend Gurdjieff with that of the purest Kagyupa tradition that confirmed what I always knew instinctively: that it was by this "single way"... that he had attained liberation.[2]

Lord Pentland, who initiated Lobsang Lhalungpa's translation of *The Life of Milarepa*, referred to Marpa and Milarepa in a different way in one of his talks:

> Milarepa, even after all the trials imposed on him intentionally by his teacher, Marpa, said in his autobiography, "Compared to him, I have given nothing to religion." If Milarepa could say that, we can certainly say the same of our little efforts compared to those of Gurdjieff and our teachers.[3]

Bill Segal notes, "We could be helped by the study of Milarepa's transformation. How did that come about? At what cost? What eventually made Milarepa a master was the determination to follow, to obey the instructions of his master, Marpa."[4]

In the account that follows this chapter, Solange Claustres recounts how Gurdjieff told the story of Milarepa at one of his dinners in order to explain his harsh behavior with her earlier in the day. Although her account occurred after the first publication of the book in French and English, since there is indication that Gurdjieff was familiar with *The Tibetan Book of the Dead* before its publication in the West,[5] it might be inferred that Gurdjieff also became acquainted with *The Life of Milarepa* while in Tibet, especially considering that Surmang, like all Kagyupa monasteries, regard Marpa and Milarepa as their founders. Briefly, the story goes something like this:

Because Milarepa was but a boy when his father was dying, his father entrusted his land and possessions to his brother, Milarepa's uncle, to care for until Milarepa was of responsible age to take possession. The brother was also required to take good care of Milarepa, his sister, and his mother. Instead the brother kept everything for himself and maltreated Milarepa's family.

Milarepa's mother became very distraught over the injustice, and to ease his Mother of her pain, Milarepa agreed to her scheme to seek revenge. She asked him to find a powerful magician to teach him the ways of black magic so he could one day return to inflict great harm to his uncle and the uncle's family and servants.

So, Milarepa did just that. He found a great magician who took pity on him and taught him all his evil spells and the power to manipulate the forces of nature after years of study and service. When he eventually returned to his village he summoned a hail storm to devastate the season's harvest of his uncle's field (actually his own field by right), and cast a spell that made his home collapse.

But his mother's life was not much better as a result and Milarepa felt great remorse for his evil deeds, not only against his uncle, but also for the opportunities he found to use his powers during his apprenticeship. His suffering had actually increased because of the path he had taken. This is what made him decide to find a teacher of the buddhadharma and led him to Marpa.

Marpa was very harsh with Milarepa. He had him repeatedly build a tower only to have him tear it down and start anew in some different place or with a different design. Finally, after the eighth had been built, after much pain, both physical and mental, and after some interference from Marpa's wife who took pity in Milarepa, Marpa gave him the teachings he needed to attain enlightenment, and sent him off to meditate in seclusion practicing with his instructions.

One day, after years meditating in a cave according to Marpa's instructions, Milarepa had a dream telling him of the death of his mother, whereby he broke from his seclusion to tell his teacher that he needed to return home. Marpa agrees after discussing Milarepa's understanding with him to make sure he had certain insights during his retreat, but convinces Milarepa to remain a few more days together, telling him that they will never see one another again. So, they spent some quality time together, during which Marpa gave Milarepa transmission as his spiritual heir, before he set off.

After finding the bones of his mother, making statuettes from them and placing the statuettes in a stupa, Milarepa continued meditating in various caves for many years. During these years of extended retreat, Milarepa often encountered those who wished him harm. Not only did he remain unaffected by their ill intentions, he moreover expressed concern about their own well-being knowing the karma that such intentions would attract, and persuaded them to take up the dharma by awakening their consciences with his eloquent words which he sung in poignant melodies.

It might be noted that Gurdjieff too had the ability to awaken the conscience of others by the power of music. Several students have recorded being brought to tears by his harmonium playing.

Let us end with one of Milarepa's moving verses before continuing on to Solange Claustre's tender telling:

In horror of death, I took to the mountains.
Again and again I meditated on the uncertainty of
the hour of death,
Capturing the fortress of the deathless unending
nature of mind.
Now all fear of death is over and done.[6]

[1] Thomas & Olga de Hartmann, *Our Life with Mr Gurdjieff* (Sandpoint: Sandpoint Press, 2008), 251.
[2] See the chapter "On Tibetan Soil."
[3] John Pentland, *Introducing the Ideas of Gurdjieff: October 20, 1959 & March 26, 1983* (New York: J.P. Society, 2017), 21.
[4] William Segal & Marielle Bancou-Segal, *A Voice at the Borders of Silence: An Intimate View of the Gurdjieff Work, Zen Buddhism, and Art* (New York: Overlook Press, 2003), 76.
[5] See the chapter "Sausage" for more detail on this subject.
[6] Sogyal Rinpoche, *The Tibetan Book of Living and Dying* (New York: HarperCollins, 2002), 40.

Image of Marpa Lotsawa created for the author by Felipe Oliveira.

## MILAREPA

During a class in which we had just learnt a movement, suddenly, Gurdjieff, stopping in front of me, said, "You—make hand movements like them," pointing to the pupils on my left. As it happened there was a slight difference between the pupils to my left and the rest of the class! Although Mme de S. then corrected this, it was the first time that G. had corrected a position! And it was me he asked to "do it like the others!"

I was stupefied: how could he ask me to do something other than what he had shown, as if I had made a mistake!? It hurt my sense of dedication to do well, to do it correctly, because I loved the movements, and, as always, I had paid very close attention to the positions G. was showing. Facing the class there were long, tall mirrors along the wall in which I could see Monsieur Gurdjieff's positions both from the back and from the front. I was never mistaken.

On top of this, because of my position as Movements assistant, I was always alert to their accuracy, with the feeling of having to guard the gestures that G. gave in their integrity; I would have fought to defend them.

One day in class, G. Gurdjieff had pointed out that there was no one behind one pupil in the first row to my left, whereas behind others there were two or three people, and behind me there were six or seven people, demonstrating that I was doing the movements correctly and the pupils could follow me.

Full of all that, I replied very sharply, "No, Monsieur! I will do the positions as you showed them to us!"

Quietly and calmly, G. Gurdjieff told me again to do as the others were doing.

He had *never* behaved like that with me. I did not understand. I felt suffocated, I was reduced to nothing, emptied. I felt lost, worthless, no longer having any strength, not even to be able to do the movements any more. In despair I was overcome with tears. Tears clouding my view, as the hurt was clouding my heart, I walked unsteadily out of my row and went to sit at the back of the room.... The class continued.

After a while, Monsieur Gurdjieff gently, slowly called to me in a honeyed, singsong voice, "Mélanche!... Mélanche!..." But I was absolutely incapable of moving, completely annihilated. G. repeated his call with sweet gentleness and insistence in his voice. Then, very slowly and heavily, I got up and rejoined the class, at the back of my file, unable to put myself back in my place in the front row. I did it "like the others" as G. had asked, my tears still flowing.

As the class went on, each person in my file, one after another came and stood behind me, pushing me forward. And I found myself back in the front row.

The movements finished. After the class, as always, there was a meal at Monsieur Gurdjieff's flat. We all went to the Rue des Colonels Renard.

During the meal, G. Gurdjieff briefly told the story of the ascetic Milarepa, of the earthen cauldron in which he cooked his nettle soup, which broke through wear and tear, whilst the inside, made up of a thick layer of nettles which had built up during the years of cooking, remained whole.

And G. turned towards me and said gently, "Mélanche, you, this evening, the earthen vessel broke, but the inner vessel remains."

I knew the very beautiful story of Marpa and his disciple Milarepa, whose adventures were rich in teachings about work on oneself. The story of the broken earthen cauldron and the inside which remained intact happened when he was a hermit, living in a mountain cave, after finishing his appren-

206

ticeship with his Master, Marpa.

But I connected my experience to another of the many adventures that happened to Milarepa: building a tower, which he had to build alone, without any help, not even the slightest amount from anyone. Milarepa carried out honestly what his teacher Marpa had asked him to do. And the latter, insisting that it was not what he had said, made him destroy and rebuild the tower differently. And again, Marpa became angry with him, saying he was mistaken, yet again making him demolish and rebuild what he had done differently. And all this happened seven times. The tower took various geometric shapes—square, rectangle, round, triangular, and others. I saw my test in this: I was carrying out what G. had shown, and he made me change it as if he had shown me something else.

However, the story of Milarepa and G.'s comment touched on another idea: "the earthen vessel is broken, the inner vessel remains." Thus, this test was a provocation, touching my being deeply, disarming it, and, like the broken cauldron, there was only the depth of the being left, what remained within.

There was no point in visually going over the movements Gurdjieff had shown us; I was still sure of what I had done. G. Gurdjieff sometimes clarified a gesture, but *never, never, had he acted like this with anyone*. He did not correct our positions, we followed what he demonstrated. He left us to sort out for ourselves the movements that he gave us one after the other. And there was often a complete dance per class.

This incident involving injury to my being left me questioning what purpose had G. Gurdjieff intended in carrying out this test—suffering and passing beyond that?

Why had I not obeyed what G. had asked, in the way that Milarepa had done?

Then I remembered that before he told me to do as the others did, he had moved over to my left in such a way that only I saw him from behind, and not in the mirror in front of us. Without my being able to see it from his position, he could have changed the hand movement. And that could only have been done intentionally without anyone suspecting it.

It is the *only time* that G. put me in this situation, as if he had chosen this moment. As if, at that precise moment, I could only say, "no!" What I absolutely cannot bear, is to be accused of being wrong, and this coming from him plunged me into a state of sleep. But in this situation where I appeared to be in the wrong, I did not feel judged by him. That was what was important for me, but it did not stop me from suffering.

I reflected that this test was linked to the stage in Milarepa's life when the earthen vessel, in other words the *outer layer*, the *personality*, no longer had a role to play, whereas the inside made by the cooking of the nettles, the *substance obtained* by work on oneself, by asceticism, had found its place. 'Something' in me had to be moved aside, separated, so that the 'inner' could be brought into the light.

Strangely, this test, and what it entailed, gave me a deep impression of belonging to something which I did not know how to define other than as a direction, following a path, a way, as at my first meeting. Well before that day, I had made the connection between Gurdjieff and Marpa. An impression that was reinforced by this experience: that very special quality of a Master.

My reaction could have been partly due to my susceptibility, but there was clearly a deliberate *provocation* from Gurdjieff, who had wanted to touch on something precise. I saw that I responded to provocations, as I had quite clearly on this occasion, though without being conscious of it—this came later. And the quality of my tears made me feel that they didn't come from a reaction in personality, but from the depth of my being.

I had noticed Mme de S. observing the scene in a very particular way. I had seen her being very attentive to what was going to happen in G. Gurdjieff's other tests. She knew he was going to provoke me. I felt afterwards that G. knew how I would react, through the looks they exchanged, their expressions. It was afterwards that I also became conscious of that.

Later, my understanding of my experience was confirmed: a fellow pupil was put to the same test in a different set-up. She defended her position, affirming the correctness of her action, whilst also obeying what G. Gurdjieff had asked. And in

208

her absence, I heard G. express to Mme de S. his satisfaction that she had behaved well under attack. So I had understood.

And later still, I heard Mme de S. say with satisfaction that I defended the work like a tigress.

*Solange Claustres*

## PHOWA

The Six Dharmas of Naropa are a set of tantric practices collected by Indian masters Tilopa and Naropa, and passed on from Naropa to Marpa, the founder of the Kagyupa sect. Although they are practiced by various Tibetan sects today, originally they were unique to the Kagyupa sect. Considering that Solange Claustres indicated that Gurdjieff had familiarity with Marpa's teachings, and that (as mentioned in the chapter on magic) he seems to have been familiar with *tummo*, which is one of the six practices of this set, it seems likely that he would have been familiar with some of the others. Specifically, there is some evidence indicating that he may have been familiar with the practice known as *phowa*.

*Phowa* means "transference of consciousness" and is a yoga practice intended to do just that—to intentionally transfer one's consciousness shortly before death would occur naturally, and while in a profound state, so that one can avoid rebirth by bypassing the bardos, and instead merge with one of the "pure realms." In Vajrayana, *phowa* is considered a direct path to enlightenment. It is believed that anyone can obtain enlightenment this way, and besides practicing it oneself, sometimes a master will perform it *to* the dying or deceased.

Experienced practitioners regularly practice opening their crown chakra, but do not eject their consciousness from it until their final moments. Doing so prematurely would be considered killing and thus have karmic repercussions. One sign that the crown chakra has been opened is the appearance of a drop of blood or lymph on the posterior fontanelle. Sometimes a small hole even develops there.

Yet another sign of successful *phowa* practice is the occurrence of involuntary movements. This may explain Pierre Schaeffer's description of Gurdjieff's final moments:

> In death he made a difficult, undefinable movement with his extraordinarily contorted muscles. There was a force behind the mask, apparently so calm, a gaze behind those lids that would never open again. This gaze imprinted itself on our pupils. Every eye caught a gleam and we assimilated this food too.[1]

It is not entirely clear from Schaeffer's description alone, but the contortions that he describes Gurdjieff having made might well have been involuntary movements brought on by the successful opening of the crown chakra during *phowa* practice. Knowing that Gurdjieff was likely familiar with another of Naropa's Six Dharmas, however, gives more credence to the suggestion.

---

[1] Louis Pauwels, *Gurdjieff* (Douglas: Times Press, 1964), 447.

## Return to Tibet?

In addition to Gurdjieff's 1901 and 1908 journeys to Tibet, he may have tried to return on various occasions. As suggested earlier, as he says of his first journey, he likely also had to leave from his second stay in Tibet due to health issues. No doubt it was difficult for him to leave his wife and two sons. So, it should be no surprise that there is evidence he attempted to return, unsuccessfully, in 1911. Bryn Thring reports that during a casual conversation, Ethel Merston—an early student of Gurdjieff who had gone on to work with other teachers and was then visiting J.G. Bennett's Institute at Coombe Springs—made a comment about "when the British wouldn't allow [Gurdjieff] to go back." When prodded, "Where? When?" by the others, she responded matter-of-factly, "To Tibet in 1911."[1] Although Gurdjieff does not say so, his failure to reunite with his Tibetan family may very well be the reason that in September 1911 he vowed himself "to lead in some ways an artificial life,"[2] which he states in *The Herald of Coming Good*.

By September 1932 Gurdjieff had completed this 21-year vow he took upon himself. Probably he was thinking of making another attempt to return to Tibet as early as then. But there was still some hope of reestablishing his Institute at the time. After about a year and a half of failures, however, he gave up hope and disappeared without trace for a period of four months. He was gone essentially all of May, June, July and August of 1935. No one knows for certain where he went. But one possibility is that he returned to Tibet (or attempted to). John Bennett places him somewhere in Asia. He supposedly heard Gurdjieff say so "once or twice in 1949."[3] However, Bennett imagines that Gurdjieff went to Turkestan to consult certain teachers there regarding the next phase of his mission. Although also conjecture, it is at the same time reasonable to consider that he had gone to Tibet to reunite with his family. It had been about 25 years since he had last seen his wife and two sons. And perhaps Bennett was partially right about Gurdjieff wanting to consult his teachers, only he was mistaken regarding the whereabouts of the ones he wanted to meet.

One further occasion can be mentioned as well. According to Yahne Le Toumelin, Gurdjieff had seriously looked into voyaging to Tibet about two months before his death. Likely he knew the end was near and wanted to make one final attempt to reunite with his family, and possibly make Tibet his final resting place.

---

[1] Bryn Thring, "Postscript: Mr Gurdjieff's Life," *The Enneagram* no. 7 (September 1976), 18.

[2] G. Gurdjieff, *The Herald of Coming Good* (London: Book Studio, 2008), 12.

[3] J.G. Bennett, *Gurdjieff: Making a New World* (New York: Harper & Row, 1973), 216.

# PART TWO

## CHILDREN SEEKING THEIR ROOTS

## INTRODUCTION TO PART TWO

This section collects together the thoughts and related activities of prominent students of Gurdjieff who investigated the Buddhist sources of his teaching. Some of them were able to investigate Tibetan Buddhism in particular, but because Tibet was closed off to the West and Tibetan Buddhism did not have much of a presence in the West until the 1970s, many likely opted to instead investigate other Buddhist sects (in particular Zen, which is another branch of Mahayana Buddhism), though it may also be the case that the individual was simply more drawn to another sect. So, those who investigated other Buddhist sects are also represented.

The amount of interest that the students included in this section had in Buddhism varies greatly. For some it was a very serious pursuit, but others included here believed some other spiritual tradition to have held more importance and relevance in relation to Gurdjieff's teaching. In no way is it my intention to misrepresent them. I only wish to collect all knowledge on the similarities between Gurdjieff's teaching and Buddhism together in one place. Although later I will provide my own thoughts, I did not know Gurdjieff myself and feel it is important to include research of the subject made by those who worked with him.

Following my writings on each student are relevant texts by the individual themself and/or by the Buddhist teacher who influenced them so that the reader can make their own interpretations and correlations. Collecting these texts together in one place will be of great benefit to Gurdjieffians who also practice or are interested in Buddhism.

It must also be added that writing about the Buddhist teachers these individuals studied with in no way is intended to be an advocacy for them. While they all taught the dharma with clarity, some of them have displayed questionable ethics. I have intentionally omitted discussing these aberrations as they do not contribute to the subject. If serious about working with *any* teacher (or group leader), do your research. Find a teacher that resonates for *you*. Who else has worked with them is immaterial.

*Louise March flanked by Tibetan monks visiting the Rochester Folk Art Guild*

## SAUSAGE

Louise March was 26 years old when she departed Frankfurt for Massachusetts in September 1926 to begin post-graduate studies in art history at Smith College. The following summer, after completing her studies, she met Georgia O'Keeffe who helped her establish herself in New York City and secure a position at the Opportunity Gallery. Through a connection at Smith College, March also found work teaching art history at Hunter College. After two years living the lifestyle of New York's rich art scene, in 1929, she was introduced to Gurdjieff by A.R. Orage, who she had met at a cocktail party.

Gurdjieff took an instant liking to March who he nick-named Saucisse de Francfort, or simply Sausage. As a result, she worked closely with him until his death two decades later (although their relationship was interrupted by World War II). Before the war she served as his secretary (replacing Madame de Hartmann) and was also responsible for translating *Beelzebub's Tales* to German. And after the war, at Gurdjieff's request, she returned to Europe to work on the German translation of Ouspensky's *In Search of the Miraculous,* which had been begun by Arnold Keyserling. Both books were published by Keyserling's press, Verlag der Palme.

After Gurdjieff's death, March participated in and supported the growth of the newly formed Gurdjieff Foundation in New York City. In 1957 she was asked by Lord Pentland to lead a group in Rochester that had become interested in Gurdjieff's ideas and commuted there monthly to provide them with guidance. Initially Christopher Fremantle traveled with her to provide support. During the first ten years activities were held in various members' homes. The activities in which they engaged, and through which they learned to apply Gurdjieff's approach to mindfulness, were largely craft-oriented. Members learned pottery, printing and sewing to name a few skills. March seemingly returned to her career as an art professor of sorts. The group incorporated itself as the Rochester Folk Art Guild and began selling their wares.

The 1960s saw that group grow with the younger, energetic, counterculture generation, and it was decided to look for a place that would serve as a group residence where Gurdjieff's ideas could be put into practice together. They wanted to create something similar to Franklin Farms or Armonk where they occasionally had Work retreats. In 1967 the ideal place was found in rural Middlesex, about an hour's drive from Rochester. East Hill Farm had many outbuildings which needed improvement and could be adapted for various functions. Most importantly, it was affordable. March stopped commuting to Rochester and moved to the farm herself.

Besides the personal benefits that members received, the guild's output has received recognition from the art community with exhibits of their work displayed and articles about their work in various magazines and newspapers. The guild community continues to thrive despite March's death in 1987.

But let us return to her earlier years. After translating *Beelzebub's Tales*, in the 1930s March had also somehow found time to translate *The Tibetan Book of the Dead* to German, working from the English text which had been first published in 1927. She too, like many other early students of Gurdjieff, seems to have understood Tibetan Buddhism to be the foundation of his teaching. She describes her arrival to the prieuré as "a genuine Tibetan scene,"[1] and notes that "The [monks'] corridor was painted in what Mr Gurdjieff called the 'oldest' colors on earth, an ocher yellow and dark ox blood red." (The colors of Tibetan monks' robes and two of the predominant colors in Tibetan art.) And, "Over each door a skull and cross-bones was painted."[2] A skull without crossbones is a common Tibetan Buddhist motif. March may not have remembered the decor entirely accurately. Or perhaps Gurdjieff wanted to use a motif similar to the Tibetan skull that was Western.

Certainly Gurdjieff was familiar with the *Bardo Thödol* (the actual name of the text). He alludes to it in the transcript of the meeting of September 30, 1944, where he says, "The soul finds a place 7 × 48 days after death."[3] According to the Tibetan text, it actually takes 7 × 7 days to traverse the bardo. Gurdjieff's modification appears to have been made to include a reference to World 48 (or personality), which he says is subject to the law of cause and effect (or karma). It is a very interesting adjustment because according to Buddhist thought, karma is what determines the individual's next incarnation.

He was also clearly alluding to the *bardo* teachings when speaking about his wife as she was approaching death and said, "...this most important moment in life for her. She live many lives, is very old soul; she now have possibility ascend to other world. But sickness come and make more difficult, make impossible for her do this thing alone. If can keep alive few months more will not have to come back and live this life again."[4] The whole purpose of the *Bardo Thödol* is to know how to navigate the *bardo* so as to merge with a *buddhafield* instead of being reborn into another life of suffering. Moreover, Gurdjieff said this in 1926, which is before any European translation of *The Tibetan Book of the Dead* was available. So, he obviously received this teaching while in Tibet (or some other Tibetan Buddhist culture if not Tibet proper).

Also suggesting that Gurdjieff was familiar with the *Bardo Thödol* is a connection it has to the Surmang Kagyu. As Trungpa Rinpoche explains:

> According to Surmang tradition, when *The Tibetan Book of the Dead* was first discovered by the fourteenth-century tertön, or treasure discoverer, Karma Lingpa, he presented it to Gyurme Tenphel [the Eighth Trungpa] and asked him to take care of it. He said that Gyurme Tenphel should

help in promoting this particular teaching. And the Eighth Trungpa became a very powerful source in presenting the teachings of *The Tibetan Book of the Dead*. So Surmang people, we regard *The Tibetan Book of the Dead* as a part of our tradition, and as one of our contemplative disciplines.[5]

Unfortunately, it is not known how March had become involved in translating the Tibetan work. At the same time, however, it seems very unlikely that a disciple who had worked so closely with her teacher would have kept such a project hidden from him. Although it is not known how much Gurdjieff may have advised March about the project, there is something March says in her preface that sounds like something that had to have come from Gurdjieff—namely, the suggestion that the text may be far older than commonly believed, sharing a common source with *The Egyptian Book of the Dead*.

Like other incredulous things that Gurdjieff has said, this is something that evidence is now beginning to confirm. In his book *Eden in the East*, Stephen Oppenheimer has shown through genetic, linguistic and cultural evidence that when the great Southeast Asian continent was flooded over by rising sea levels 8,000–10,000 years ago, two of the direct migration destinations made were to Egypt and Tibet. With contemporary water erosion evidence of the Sphinx confirming Gurdjieff's suggestion that it dates to "pre-sand Egypt" (over 10,000 years ago), and with it having facial features very similar to Southeast Asians, it seems likely that the Southeast Asians had migrated to and established a great city in Egypt long before the flood. So Egypt would have been an obvious choice upon evacuating their flooded homeland. Tibet seems to have been a migration choice for a different reason. One could well imagine that people uncertain how high the sea level would rise would choose to relocate to the highest place on Earth. Significantly, the Bön date the founding of their religion some 18,000 years ago, and as March also points out in her preface, the text may have originated with the Bön.

Like most students of Gurdjieff's method, March seems to have been greatly moved by Beelzebub's conclusion that one's only hope is to continuously remember death—both one's own and of everyone that one encounters. "The Inevitable Result of Impartial Mentation," the chapter in which this idea appears, was the first reading of *Beelzebub's Tales* she had ever heard. Gurdjieff had selected this chapter especially for her to hear. As she herself relates, "I was overcome, overwhelmed. I felt the truth of it all."[6]

Her understanding of the importance of remembering death is also expressed in a talk she gave on the subject of vision in 1983:

> Vision is more than seeing. The two hang together. So we are like a tree standing in ourselves, and no one can help us except our own vision, our wishing to see. You can look backward to the beginning, from your birth on, through the different years of growing up and being in the middle of life. And you can turn to the other and now the second half, and know that it ends in death. The wish to make something with your life, to develop something that grows, that's alive, that's formed at the end is your goal. Your vision may see many mistakes you made, and that you're going to make again—or not, if you have learned from the uselessness of the mistakes. So there where you stand inside yourself, life goes on. You cannot turn back. But you can have a different view as to what you wish to do with the rest of your days.[7]

So, it is with little doubt that the subject of ever remembering death provided at least some of the motivation to work on *The Tibetan Book of the Dead*.

Additionally, the preface March provided to the German edition gives much the same advice as regards taking in the text that Gurdjieff gives to reading his works, namely to read it *absorbingly* at first without being concerned about the meanings of the strange words used. Also like Gurdjieff, she suggests seeking understanding of the teaching from within somehow.

Similarly, she had also come to understand through translating *Beelzebub's Tales* how translation can be a form of spiritual practice, and that only as a spiritual practice could a faithful translation of a sacred text be possible. As she relates in her booklet *G. Gurdjieff: A Call for Attention to His Life and*

*Work,* "For us the translation [of *Beelzebub's Tales*] wasn't done just for the sake of translation, but was our schooling, which freed us from our subjective conceptions and views..."[8] Working on her translation of *The Tibetan Book of the Dead* was likely a means for her to continue this form of work on oneself.

Also note that her interest in *The Tibetan Book of the Dead* was not merely intellectual; its practice was a form that her group applied at times. On at least two occasions of someone in or close to the group dying, she had the text read aloud in order to assist the deceased in their transition, as the text is traditionally used.

Her interest in Tibetan Buddhism was not limited to *The Tibetan Book of the Dead* either. Significantly enough, she initiated a visit made by two old lamas once part of the Dalai Lama's entourage to the Rochester Folk Art Guild in 1984. While there, the monks conducted a ceremony consecrating the space of the Guild's movement and meditation hall. Such ceremonies consecrate the space specifically for the practice of the Buddha's teaching. So it seems likely that March would have conveyed, and the monks had understood, that Gurdjieff's teaching had some relationship to Tibetan Buddhism.

Photos of the visit depict four thangkas hanging on the wall of the hall. These were taken from March's personal collection and moved there for the occasion, and they too express her interest in Tibetan Buddhism.

It is also known that she kept a photo of the Dalai Lama in her room. Her possession of the photo, along with the fact that the visiting monks were associated with the Dalai Lama, suggests that she may have attended a teaching he gave on one of his visits. A student of hers confided, "Mrs March had great respect and reverence for the Dalai Lama and his tradition."[9]

A final thought from March before reading her preface for yourself:

I hope you are carrying "the Buddha" with you daily.[10]

1 *Remembering Louise March,* (Middlesex: Jonathan James Books, 2010), 127.

2 Ibid., 129.

3 This is an automated translation of an excerpt from the recently published French edition of *Paris Meetings 1944.* The wording in the forthcoming English edition may vary somewhat.

4 Fritz Peters, *Boyhood with Gurdjieff* (New York: E. P. Dutton & Co., 1964), 78.

5 Chögyam Trungpa, *The Profound Treasury of the Ocean of Dharma: Volume Three: The Tantric Path Path of Indestructible Wakefulness* (Boston: Shambhala Publications, 2013), 160.

6 Beth McCorkle, ed., The *Gurdjieff Years: 1929–1949: Recollections of Louise March* (Walworth: Work Study Association, 1990), 14.

7 The Rochester Folk Art Guild, "Louise March;" *Gurdjieff International Review* 3, no. 2 (Spring 2000), 31.

8 Louise March, *"Gurdjieff: A Call for Attention to His Life and Work,"* *Gurdjieff International Review* 6, no. 1 (Spring 2003), 58.

9 Private correspondence.

10 Annabeth McCorkle, ed., *The Rochester Years: 1957–1987: The Work of Louise March* (Palmyra: Stillwood Study Center, 2007), 2.

## THE GERMAN TRANSLATION OF THE BARDO THÖDOL

In all of the various sects in Tibet, *The Tibetan Book of the Dead*, or *Bardo Thödol* is, with few exceptions, the text that to this day is read to those dying or dead. The first writing of this work is attributed to Padmasambhava, the great Buddhist scribe, the actual founder of Lamaism. Whether the text originated in this time period, the eighth century, or whether it was used previous to that time in the local Tibetan religion, the Bön, is still undecided. When compared with *The Egyptian Book of the Dead* one feels compelled to conclude that both of these books derive from a common source, reaching back to a time that is fully in the dark for us. The only thing we can be certain of is that *The Tibetan Book of the Dead* was primarily preserved and passed on in Tibet by oral tradition.

Of the few known written records of the text, one of them fell into the hands of Professor Evans-Wentz, an American anthropologist who had been living in Tibet for many years.[1] Professor Evans-Wentz prompted the Lama Kazi Dawa Samdup, one of the greatest authorities on both the Tibetan and English languages, to translate the text, the professor himself assisting, serving as a living dictionary. The main objective of this lama/translator was to render the meaning of the original text as accurately as possible in English. Since he was a philologist, the viewpoints of his school would have played a part in his personal understanding of this foreign language, influencing his choice of words and expressions. Prof. Evans-Wentz suggested that this translation might later require revision, much as did our early translations of the bible.[2] The translator of the English version of the *Bardo Thödol* into German has made the effort to translate as accurately as possible, without allowing any freedoms to be taken; freedoms which, if at all, should only be entitled to the Tibetan translator.

The English and German versions differ in regard to the framework around the text. In the English version the text constitutes roughly half of the book. Prof. Evans-Wentz added an extensive introduction with detailed explanations about Mahayana Buddhism and the bardo in particular. In addition, the lama appended the translation with abundant footnotes. For the sake of clarity, the German version incorporates an alphabetic list of the most important definitions at the end of the book. Thanks go to Prof. C.G. Jung for the addition of a psychological commentary to bolster courage of the many who do not feel they could tackle the strange forms and conceptual worlds of this Eastern text alone, courage to search for truth and strength in the place it is found in both east and west; within ourselves.

*The Method*

It is, so to speak, the specific character of this text, as it is of all so-called secret texts, that its science, or let us say its theory, can only be acquired and understood by its practice. This is comparable to a medication that only shows its effect after it has been taken. The same applies to the spirit of this work in which an introduction is limited to providing a view of the first instructions for its use.

The *Bardo Thödol* shall be spoken clearly and explicitly into the ear of the dying person, entering through the "Path of the Ear." For this reason it emphasizes that the dying one is spoken to by name, making certain, so to speak, that he listens well, and this is forcefully and emphatically repeated at least three and usually seven times.

The text acts at the point where flesh and spirit begin to

separate from one another, where everyone, including those whose center of gravity had previously always been the ephemeral physical body, must take the stage called in the *Bardo Thödol*, the "transference of consciousness." When the body *becomes silent* for the first time, not intervening with its habitual imagination and wishes, consciousness, also referred to as "the knower," has, in a flash, the great opportunity to see itself from above or from outside and to weigh itself and determine its own worth. This great shock is the first and the best opportunity to collect itself and achieve that which the text calls "liberation".

Since consciousness is in most cases so weak that it cannot look death in the eye, however, it "faints" and only recovers after three days, as if awakening from a dream.

Gods, individually and in droves, dazzle him with frightening figures, both peaceful and terrifying that impress and confuse his senses, blind him with dazzling light and still more often beset and terrify him with ever-new menacing impressions. The text, a faithful guide, accompanies him through all steps of the way, calls the pursuing forms by name, describes their attributes, arrests their speed by describing them and banishes them through prayer. In short, it plays the role of *interrupter*, in the sense that it whispers in the ear of the tormented one, describing the real identity of the figures—namely, kaleidoscopes deriving from his own thoughts and impulses. They do not exist outside of him as entities of which he needs to be afraid. Instead, they are simply reflexes of his own worlds of thoughts and emotions.

All of life, terminated by death, continues in the dream world of straying snatches of consciousness. The deceased sees friends and relations, calls to them, however is unheard by them and suffers terribly as a consequence. He sees his treasures and possessions being used and squandered by others and becomes upset because of it. He constantly returns to the lost body and finally longs for a new will. He is torn to and fro, falls again and again into new sorrows and can change nothing. He has the same reactions as he had while alive and nothing but *reactions,* whereby, as the text repeatedly advises, *actions* alone could guide him out, namely away from himself, away from the dominating sympathies and antipathies, away from the bonds of his habitual inclinations.

This first stage is "learning to listen," wishing to hear, shrugging off the chaos in oneself just as one drops the body upon the physical death. This stage means that one no longer wishes to interfere, no longer wishes to change anything (not even oneself at first), does not want to argue or express opinions, will not automatically translate into regular daily language (which would be the same as allowing it to go out the other ear). It means that one quietly dwells apart from the multitudinous army of intellectual, emotional and physical associations.

The ability to listen is difficult, even though most Westerners do not want to believe this. The Chinese sage Lü Buwei is even recorded as having said "All people need a certain training of the mind before they are able to listen properly. He who lacks this training must obtain it by learning. It has never occurred in the past or present that someone is capable of listening rightly without learning."[3]

The various systems of yoga all teach this, each in its own way and corresponding to the various human types. Although adapted accordingly, the teaching is based on laws that are as exact as mathematics: The ability to listen, to put aside one's own opinion, whether prefixed with a sign of affinity or aversion, to be able to *empty* oneself of the subjective world so that there may be room to take up another within us.

As is well known, no one really learns to understand or rather to practice yoga without a teacher, and the *Bardo Thödol* repeatedly reminds the dying one of his guru as a reminder of his teaching. Furthermore, it goes beyond that— and should therefore be especially valuable for the European (Westerner)—taking on the *role of a teacher* for those who did not have one beforehand. It can achieve this because it describes the common means underlying all five yoga disciplines;[4] the way (the narrow path) that alone leads to the goal. For this reason the *Bardo Thödol* calls itself the "essence of all teachings" and considers those who encounter it to be blessed.

232

The *Bardo Thödol* is an unprecedentedly patient, forbearing teacher that consistently tries, by one means or another or a third, to bring the poor subject who is wandering aimlessly in his own labyrinth of heaven, hell and earth to self-liberation in the intermediate state after death of the body (bardo).

In principle, liberation can take place as soon as the identification of consciousness with the illusory events and the illusory self becomes interrupted; or put more positively, the moment the observer arises in us, watching our thinking, feeling and sensing *automatism.*

In practice, liberation is possible at any stage, depending upon the inner circumstances and peculiarities of the individual. For this reason the admonitions throughout the text fall on the right soil in different times and places for different people. The right soil is that place where the person sits face-to-face with reality at each step, finally able to recognize it, namely himself, battling death with death whereby liberation becomes the liberator.

Liberation, true deliverance, is achieved where self-knowledge is gained on the path of *impartial* self-observation.

Bardo Thödol means "liberation through listening in the intermediate state" or "from the intermediate state." The "intermediate state" is the long, precarious duration between death and birth, the chain of self-deception, misdirection resulting from illusory, i.e. unrecognized conscious content, delusions of one's own nature. These are referred to by various religious systems as egoism, jealousy, hate, avarice, thirst for glory, etc., etc. Buddhism does not fail to include stupidity and obtuseness as Christ spoke of the blind, lame and deaf. Those, whose ears are not yet open, are blown "hither and thither by the wind of karma," remain, in a manner of speaking, endlessly in this state, not even recognizing it when they themselves are befallen by death. However, those who have ears to hear, whether living or the dead, abrogate the intermediate state. They draw the imaginary boundary points of death and birth, to themselves—the line becomes a point, time becomes eternity.

Still, it cannot be foreseen what the one who learns to listen will achieve. That which enters him along the "Path of the Ear" enters into the secret chamber from whence nothing goes out again, crystalizes therein into the master who then governs his further thoughts, words and actions.

In order to begin, which in itself is a difficult task, one should try to approach this text as a disciple approaches his guru—with an important question that has nothing to do with the "burning question of the day." It is better yet to approach it with a presentiment of one's own nothingness ("you believe that you are pushing, but in reality you are being pushed"),[5] that you nonetheless believe you can change, or are free of curiosity with a wish for real knowledge.

It remains to be said that right listening requires waiting and patience (exactly as with right questioning—remembering the legend of the Grail). For those who would make use of opportunities, this book offers many. For example, one can try to simply accept the unfamiliar names, some derived from Sanskrit, some from Tibetan, as one would an unknown in a mathematical equation, without immediately searching for a (literal) explanation in a glossary. Most importantly, acceptance is essential when reading this book—accepting the apparent digressions and repetitions or the seemingly weak philosophical expressions that have faded over time or through translation so that the bloodstream of the text is often imperceptible. Some seem to have been intentionally muted in order that the next inflection all the more surely and deeply hits the mark. One should avoid judging the book, instead using it as a supporter for oneself.

Perhaps one will then experience what it means when in *The Secret of the Golden Flower* it says, "The hen can hatch her eggs *because her heart always listens.*"[6]

*Louise Göpfert-March*

¹ Mrs March actually mistakenly refers to Evans-Wentz as an "English scholar of religion and philosophy." She was not completely wrong, however. Although actually American, he did study at Oxford. And he certainly was such a scholar. However, that was not his profession. So, I took the liberty of making the correction in her text. (LN)

² At this point in time several other translations have in fact appeared in English. One in particular that is recommended is the translation made by Francesca Fremantle, which includes an introduction by Chögyam Trungpa Rinpoche. (LN)

³ The published English translation of Lü Buwei's work differs considerably from the German edition that Mrs March made use of. In order to retain Mrs March's context, the quote as offered here is an English translation of the German that she utilized rather than what has been published in English. The German edition she cites is *"Frühling und Herbst" des Lü Bu We*, Germanized from the Chinese and explained by Richard Wilhelm, Eugen Diederichs Verlag 1928. (LM & LN)

⁴ The reader is referred to the best depiction there is of the various yoga systems—the chapter "What is Yoga" in P. D. Ouspensky's *A New Model of the Universe,* Alfred Knopf 1931. (LM)

⁵ Johann Wolfgang von Goethe. (LM)

⁶ The published English translation of *The Secret of the Golden Flower* differs considerably from the German edition that Mrs March made use of. In order to retain Mrs March's context, the quote as offered here is an English translation of the German that she utilized rather than what has been published in English. The German edition she cites is *Das Geheimnis der goldenen Blüte,* translated and explained by Richard Wilhelm, Dorn Verlag 1929. (LM & LN)

The original German text, "Zur Geschichte und Übersetzung des Bardo Thödol," copyright © Sylvia March, was translated for the author from the German by Dr C. Bruce Boschek for inclusion here with her permission. A revised version of the text, translated by Mrs March herself, was previously published in the revised edition of *The Gurdieff Years: 1929–1949* (Utrecht: Eureka Editions, 2012).

*Paul Anderson*

## A Special Secretary

At different stages, Paul Anderson worked under the leadership of A. R. Orage, P. D. Ouspensky, and Gurdjieff himself,
having even worked for a period of time at Gurdjieff's renowned
Institute. It was Anderson and his wife Naomi who arranged
the printing of the 1931 private edition of *Beelzebub's Tales*—
a limited edition of 102 copies. He also served as Gurdjieff's
secretary on his last trip to the U.S.A.

In the mid 1930s the Andersons were living in Washington,
D.C. and had started a group there. When Gurdjieff visited
the U.S.A. in those years, he would take the train from New
York to Washington to spend time with the group, bringing
his other writings with him for group readings.

In 1935 specifically, Anderson had convinced New Mexico Senator Bronson Cutting to repurchase the Prieuré for
Gurdjieff. Cutting, who also had an apartment in New York
and had been a member of Orage's writing group, evidently
became interested in Gurdjieff's teaching and met Anderson
through that connection. The chateau had been repossessed
by the banks when Gurdjieff defaulted on his loan, and he was
hopeful about the possibility of reestablishing his Institute.
Unfortunately, the senator died in a plane crash before he
could meet with Gurdjieff in Washington, and the purchase
did not materialize. Nonetheless, Anderson's recruitment of
Bronson, along with his group leadership and his undertaking

of the 1931 edition of *Beelzebub's Tales,* demonstrate his commitment to Gurdjieff and the trust Gurdjieff had in him.

Like other group leaders, the Andersons helped to establish the Gurdjieff Foundation in the early 1950s. However, they left after a few years to work independently, which was their understanding of Gurdjieff's wishes. Nonetheless, Anderson contributed to the spread of Gurdjieff's ideas to the greater public with reviews he wrote for Ouspensky's *In Search of the Miraculous* and Gurdjieff's *Beelzebub's Tales to His Grandson.*

Their Massachusetts group began in 1969 as a small independent study group at Clark University in Worcester. At a certain point the group asked the advice of J.G. Bennett, who wrote back suggesting that they reach out to Anderson, saying, "He is one of the very few who have attained the level of true teacher."[1] Bennett and Anderson were good friends and, having the same mission, supported one another in their Work endeavors. As an example of the support going the other way, it was Anderson and his Massachusetts group who organized Bennett's lecture tour of the Northeast U.S.A. in the early 1970s and provided transportation. Gurdjieff thought highly of Anderson too. Commenting on his ability to decipher the numerous hidden meanings within *Beelzebub's Tales,* Gurdjieff remarked, "He not only has eaten one dog, but swallowed whole packs of dogs… and I rest very contented when I leave because you are my special American Secretary."[2]

So it was that in July of that year that two of the group drove from Worcester to Brooklyn, New York to try to make contact with the Andersons. After finding a Brooklyn phone book, they actually called every Paul Anderson listed until they found the person they were looking for. They explained how Bennett had recommended him to them, and Anderson then invited them to the small apartment he shared with his wife where they asked them to be their guides.

Having found a teacher generated a bit of excitement in the group which subsequently grew to thirteen before their first meeting in October. They drove to Brooklyn every two weeks for talks the Andersons would give, and met the weeks between in Worcester for readings and practicing the exercises they were given. The Andersons called them their Massachusetts group.

Later that autumn one of the group rented a large old house out in the woods of Phillipston which served as a group home they called The 1800s House. That winter they began having work weekends, and after the house was fixed up sufficiently they invited the Andersons for a couple of extended work weekends. But the lease was coming to an end and they had to find another situation where they could work together.

They all scattered during their summer break, but remained in touch—both with each other and with the Andersons who had given them tasks to work with in the interim. When they resumed in the autumn, they met in an apartment two of them shared. Further temporary accommodation was found, including an apartment in Amherst and a house in West Townsend, before discovering and leasing an old B&B in Wendell in the fall of 1972. The Wendell House (as they called it) had plenty of space to accommodate movements practice, and enough land to create and maintain a garden—another opportunity for group work. A distinguishing feature of the house was the stained glass enneagram they made for its front door. It served as their home for two years.

About this time the group incorporated itself as the American Institute for Continuous Education—an organization loosely modeled after and affiliated with Bennett's International Academy for Continuous Education. Although they produced a prospectus utilizing the name, it was not used otherwise. The only purpose of the name was to register for nonprofit status.

When the lease for Wendell House was up, in 1974 the group purchased a former dairy farm in rural Conway, Massachusetts to serve as a communal work home. There they converted the garage into a movements space and renovated the milk house as accommodations for the Andersons. It was simply referred to as Conway House.

In the late 1970s the group began shifting its focus towards Buddhism. Anderson had begun taking classes in Tibetan

Buddhist Tantra with John Reynolds at the University of Massachusetts, and this was influencing his talks. Soon after, Anderson had a surprise for the group. One Saturday he escorted the entire group by caravan to Providence, Rhode Island with no explanation on the purpose of their journey. He led them to an apartment in a questionable neighborhood where they were greeted by an American nun of Tibetan Buddhism. They were all sitting on the floor of the living room when Rahor Khenpo Thupten entered and proceeded to give them their refuge vows with the nun translating. In the process they were provided with instructions for maintaining their vows and given dharma names. Although the ceremony was quite foreign to the group, and they were being thrown into it without warning, the effect was "magical" (as one group member put it). For a year or so following this, Thupten traveled to Conway every week or two on Saturday to guide them with their practice of the *longchen nyingthig ngöndro* (a Dzogchen initiation). He was their first Buddhist teacher.

The group also had regular contact with the Fourth Dodrupchen Rinpoche and Tulku Tundrup (who translated for Dodrupchen Rinpoche). Anderson and his group was involved in the building and dedication of a *chorten* at Dodrupchen's Maha Siddha Nyingmapa Center in Hawley, Massachusetts. They took this on as a Work project and completed the task one summer. Dodrupchen also dedicated his pamphlet *The Short Preliminary Practice of Longchen Nyingthig* to Anderson. Some of the group continue to maintain contact with this sangha.

Another teacher Anderson introduced the group to was Dudjom Rinpoche, a teacher with whom other Gurdjieffians had also made contact. Dudjom gave them a Dzogchen teaching which Anderson wanted them to receive. Although Dudjom Rinpoche was one of Khenpo Thupten's teachers, this was something that upset Thupten who felt they needed to complete their *ngöndro* before receiving actual Dzogchen instruction.

But none of these Dzogchen teachers was the teacher for whom Anderson was searching. His quest especially came to a climax when he had a stroke in 1981, and then a second one in

240

1982. As a result of his ill health the group experienced something of a crisis, and Anderson's need to find a true master to take over his group was becoming desperate.

That same year one of Anderson's students gave him a transcript of a talk by Dzogchen master Chögyal Namkhai Norbu to read and was immediately impressed. With the help of Reynolds, Anderson was able to make contact with Norbu and invite him to Conway. That summer Norbu arrived to lead a ten-day retreat, the first of what would be many for the community. There was a mutual recognition between the two teachers, thenceforth the group worked exclusively with the Dzogchen teachings, and their center was renamed Tsegyalgar, which means something like "victorious peak encampment"—a curiously unintentional allusion to Rene Daumal's novel, *Mount Analogue.*

Regarding this brief period when both teachers were guiding the group, John Foster recalls, "In a memorable moment... Rinpoche and Mr A. sat together for one of the last times as Rinpoche helped him to eat. Rinpoche came again in the Winter of 1983 and by this time Mr A. had to be moved into a local nursing home due to the degree of care he needed."[3]

Chögyal Namkhai Norbu was one of the great Dzogchen masters of our time. Like other great Tibetan masters, he was recognized as a tulku at a very young age and underwent rigorous religious training to realize his destiny. In 1955, at the age of 17, he met his root teacher, Rigdzin Changchub Dorje, from whom he received his Dzogchen transmissions.

At the time of the 1959 Chinese invasion he was on pilgrimage in Sikkim and remained in safety there for a while, working as an author and editor for the government. The following year he was invited by Professor Giuseppe Tucci to work at the ISMEO Institute in Rome, and in 1962 he joined the faculty of Istituto Universitario Orientale in Naples where he taught Tibetan language and literature—a post he remained in for thirty years.

In 1971 he began building his sangha, at first only teaching Tibetan yoga, and a few years later teaching Dzogchen to a small group. This group became Merigar, his first *gar*

241

(Dzogchen community). As his teaching spread, other *gars* were founded, including Tsegyalgar, which was the second *gar* instituted.

The transition from Gurdjieff to Dzogchen was easier for some group members than others. The vast majority deeply trusted Anderson's guidance and followed his lead although a few had left the group to find another Gurdjieff group to join. For Woody Paparazzo it was more smooth: "When Rinpoche came, after some hesitation and doubts, I went and listened to the teaching and I was very interested and by about the third day I was just amazed and I saw Rinpoche as an incredible teacher. I also saw how this teaching was very much in keeping with the real essence of the teachings which I had learned from the Andersons."[4] For Gerry Steinberg the transition was more rough: "Initially it seemed somewhat foreign and strange, passively going along with our teacher Mr Anderson and trusting in his understanding that this was the right path for us."[5]

John Foster affectionately recalls Rinpoche's intimacy during his first years guiding Tsegyalgar: "This was a very fortunate time with Rinpoche, he was readily accessible and engaging, singing, card playing, weddings, wine, protection cord making, more wine, astrology, stories, more wine and he was always teaching, not just formally, but always. It seemed that what he taught was just for you, if you could hear."[6]

Despite Anderson's death on February 24, 1983, and his wife's on August 13, 1984, the Tsegyalgar community continued to grow with Namkhai Norbu now leading the way. As part of this growth, Namkhai Norbu saw the purchase of a plot of land for the establishment of a private retreat center as essential. (The first retreats with Rinpoche were held on a parcel of land leased to the group by a community member. Conway House, situated on a busy street, was not suitable.) With the help of community members, a 220-acre parcel was found in the neighboring town of Buckland that he thought rather special, and the plot was eventually purchased in 1987 from funds acquired from the sale of Conway House which had been divided into two properties. The land was given the

242

name Khandroling.

The first structure built on Khandroling was a retreat cabin for Namkhai Norbu. During a personal retreat he held there in 1990 he identified spots for six additional cabins. But due to objections from the local community and subsequent litigation, work on them was delayed about 10 years. Also delaying the building of the cabins was prioritizing the building of a "Vajra Hall" on the land. The Vajra Hall is a huge gazebo-like structure where the vajra dances that Namkhai Norbu taught are practiced. At present only two additional cabins have been built.

The litigation mentioned necessitated finding other accommodations for retreatants and in the mid 1990s the old Conway Grammar School was purchased. Today the schoolhouse is the main center of activity.

Besides the Andersons, there are two other Gurdjieff group leaders who were interested in Namkhai Norbu's teaching. Madame de Salzmann is known to have had a personal meeting with him in Paris sometime. More significant, however, is that Henri Thomasson attended Merigar's inaugural retreat in 1981, during which he had a long practice discussion with Norbu. In their talk, Norbu was reluctant to compare teachings. However, there was another subject that interested Thomasson. He wanted to know how Norbu was able to teach so many people. His reply was, "We throw seeds scattering them in the space, and whoever is able collects them."[7] As they said farewell Norbu also told Thomasson that he was a bodhisattva. The significance of this comment would not strike him until later. When asked himself about the two teachings (Gurdjieff and Dzogchen), Thomasson said, "C'est la même chose." ("It's the same thing.")[8] He also said that Norbu reminded him of Gurdjieff very much.

Although there is significance to Thomasson attending the retreat at Merigar and the Anderson group falling under Norbu's guidance, there really is not very much connecting Gurdjieff and Norbu. As mentioned previously, Norbu did not have anything to offer in our correspondence. Still, there is evidence that Gurdjieff was acquainted with the Dzogchen tradition. As discussed earlier, there is evidence that the Fifth Dzogchen Rinpoche was one of his teachers. And the influence of Dzogchen upon Gurdjieff's teaching will be discussed somewhat in the next section. Here there are just a couple of other correlations that might be made:

Although Norbu's vajra dances differ stylistically from the Gurdjieff movements, Norbu clearly detected the benefit of such a practice. The group had performed Gurdjieff's movements for him on an early visit, and he reportedly commented on them saying, "Here you see the contemplation."[9] Sometime later, Norbu received the vajra dances as *terma* in a dream, and subsequently began teaching them.

Tsegyalgar member Ellen Ruth Topol asked Lopon Tenzin Namdak during his 1995 visit to the community, "In the Gurdjieff work, in a moment of presence, we say 'I AM!' In Dzogchen we dissolve the 'I AM'. However, I believe that the intention of both is the same." Lopon responded: "Many traditions, not just the Gurdjieff Work, try in this way; however, in Dzogchen we ask the question 'Who Am I?' In asking this question we begin to see the Nature of Mind."[10]

It is very interesting that both Namkhai Norbu and Dodrupchen Rinpoche were students of Jamyang Khyentse Chökyi Lodrö, a renowned Rimé master. As will be seen later, Chökyi Lodrö was a teacher for several others with connections to Gurdjieff. Also interesting is that it was the Fifth Dzogchen Rinpoche who recognized Dudrupchen Rinpoche, and the Sixth Shechen Rabjam was one of the three tulkus who recognized Namkhai Norbu. Anderson seems to have been on the right track.

What follows is a talk by Anderson, given before his group's transition to Dzogchen, that demonstrates his Buddhist influences. The subject is the Buddhist notion of taking refuge in the Buddha, dharma and sangha, but using Gurdjieff's terminology. And after the talk is an excerpt from *The Cycle of Day and Night,* a book by Norbu which was dedicated to Anderson.

1  Russell Huff, "Paul Anderson: 1897–1983," *Gurdjieff International Review* 6, no. 1 (Spring 2003), 43.
2  Ibid., 43.
3  John Foster, "Origins of Tsegyalgar East, U.S.A.," *The Mirror* no. 152 (June 2021), 46.
4  Mario Maglietti & Woody Paparazzo, "Director Meet Director," *The Mirror* no. 26 (April–May 1994), 9.
5  Gerry Steinberg, "Impermanence, the Preciousness of Human Birth and the Precious Master," *The Mirror* no. 90 (January–February 2008), 23.
6  John Foster, "Origins of Tsegyalgar East, U.S.A.," *The Mirror* no. 152 (June 2021), 47.
7  Conveyed in private correspondence by Roberto Cacciapaglia, a student of Namkhai Norbu who had previously been a member of Thomasson's group.
8  Ibid.
9  Heard secondhand by Roberto Cacciapaglia and conveyed in private correspondence.
10  Ellen Ruth Topol, "Lopon Tenzin Namdak Visits Tsegyalgar," *The Mirror* no. 32 (August-September 1995), 19.

## Taking Refuge in the Work

We wish to touch briefly upon this theme, from which—and from your experience of it—pondering about it actively (which means in all situations trying to understand by actual experience) we may be able to have a view as from a mountain top of this new Octave of the Work. This will be not so much verbal as from deep inner need, and the realization of the widening of meaningfulness in your life. In *All and Everything*,[1] if you have been creative and imaginative enough, you should be able to see the step-by-step process of renewal or revitalization for Hassein, as well as the transfiguration of Beelzebub himself! We bring in this allusion, so to speak, for those who have been intelligent and alert in their reading of *All and Everything*.

Why do we say that? Because the whole of the drama taking place in the reading of *All and Everything* is itself a true indication of what the expression "Refuge" means. *All and Everything* is an experience, not a reading and memorizing... so long as the experience itself does not become for you a mere mechanical listening, or something done out of a sense of "well, it has some importance, and we have to listen to it"— whereupon we miss the point of it all. It is for this reason that Mrs Anderson recently revived the readings—because it is the "Refuge" we have.

In fact, in truth and in conscience (objective conscience), it is implicit in all Work together, as well as individually on ourselves as members of this Group, that we always begin every task, every activity, every movement, almost every breath we take, with the acknowledgement of our taking refuge. There is a profound stage of understanding and experience here that, during this second octave, everyone who sincerely commits himself to this path may now begin to share in. When we work individually, either alone or in the world among others, deep inside us we acknowledge the man whose name is used to describe this Work—not so much as a man, but as an embodiment of the great aim and universality of his meaning to all and everything.

If you reflect on this, you can see very clearly that you are all members of the Seekers after Truth mentioned in the Second Series, committed to the same Great Aim. This aim is expressed in the Teachings, or the Work. And the Work is here and now, addressed to all three centers—body, mind, feelings—and to the eradication of all that is fictitious, negative emotional, and false. When we arrive at the point of being able to discuss the three sacred impulses, and to understand the active role of objective conscience in our lives and work, we had come to a very definite plateau. Hence the emphasis on the Five Being Obligolnian Strivings. This is because at this stage we begin to understand something about what we call "objective"—that is: objective morality, objective reason, the understanding of Time, and the beginning of and living quality of what Being really is.

Many times we have stressed the realization of the importance of working in a Group, and working together... Rereading the (reference to) the Seekers after Truth, this time, following from Working in a Group together, we can begin to perceive a living lineage of the Teaching. It goes back into very ancient times. From this we can begin to have another view of what the past means—a view that is not historical, nor political, nor even understandable to outsiders. Now it is possible to understand the statement that: "There are neither Russians nor English, Jews nor Christians, but only those who pursue one aim—to be able to be!"

Hence, we are connected with a great Source, a living

Source, and all those who have gone before us in terms of achieving real beingness, in the sense that they have either achieved or exemplified a meaningful life! We shall surely discover as we go along that this is not something vague, or even mystical—in the misused sense of that term. Not is it a body of doctrine, or an institutionalized, imposed set of beliefs. Rather it is open, always self-creating, ever revitalizing and meaningful. And as we go through the stages of the Work before us, we shall see how these stages are something like initiations, not formalized at all, only seeming to be that way because of language and misunderstanding.

Why do we need a refuge? Because we already have discovered that in the midst of the swiftly altering changes in value of ordinary life and culture, we see only uncertainty, only excesses, fears and disintegration. There is another saying of G.'s which is worth pondering. It is this: "One of the best means for arousing the wish to Work on yourself is to realize that you may die at any moment. But first you must learn to keep it in mind." There are many ways to do this, one of them being helpful to you now—namely this: If we continue to work on ourselves, we shall become aware of growth. If we grow, something dies—and so for us the process is a recognition of death in the sense of change of Being, and in this way we begin to see, and learn to live more intensely. All things must pass away; it is the nature of reality. And to constantly face this, we have a powerful refuge in the Work. This will enable us to develop equanimity and compassion, and in turn lead us to equanimity, joyfulness. It is in this way we go to real Being.

Doesn't G. point out in *All and Everything* that it is egoism which has taken over the place of objective conscience in Man? Does he not also point out that, being darkened and clouded by that unique particular impulse of egoism, we suffer needlessly and endlessly? Why? Because egoism may be undercut completely. Reflect a moment—you have read the chapter on "The Organization for Man's Existence Created by the Very Saintly Ashiata Shiemash." Doesn't G. mention also remorse of conscience? Also, organic shame? Doesn't it come through to you that if you are aware, for instance, you would recognize the particular negative emotion that stops you from externally considering? Let it be say aversion, or pre-conditioned response, antipathy, any of these or more—all mentioned by G. You, already being aware, know it for a negative emotion. Love, as was pointed out, real love, or conscience, real conscience, is already in your awareness, and mirrors your action. You, being aware, cognize this—and change to its opposite emotion. This is to say, the four great impulses are able to alter the pattern of your response... even if you are darkened at first, the fact that you are aware of external considering will be present, and enable you to change the pattern.

Now to pass to next week's center-of-gravity. Having glimpsed what REFUGE has meant to you and to us, it is imperative each day that when we are in life we should learn to practice being more conscious in our activities and relations with people not in the Group. Implicitly we should try to approach life activities aware of the Presence that exists behind the Work itself. Against that Presence we should also be aware of the "Teaching" itself as something quite vivid and living. This also means that we are members of a living and active Group.

Briefly this means that now we can always be in a different place in all we are active in, shall we say, in a place of refuge, of evaluation, and awareness of our own value and place. There is to be in this situation nothing of egoism, for we are not acting from our image, or aggrandizement. During this part of our activities we are aiming to transform our interactions by the playing of a conscious role. How? First we begin to change our ordinary mechanical roles, especially those filled with negative responses, preconceived judgments, and pettinesses. Instead of being dead, so to speak, we now choose to try to be alive, much more conscious of the worth of others, seen objectively, and generous in our praise or esteem.

So long as you remain aware, so long as you see things quietly, without the usual excitation and useless talking, you may try to maintain this level of relationship. Incidentally, it is one of the ways in which Ashiata Shiemash influenced his period of time. It is a challenge to you, we admit, but it is a stage of this Work, in which we value humanity, and, by being present, influence others who know naught of the Work, but for whom we are trying to learn to be compassionate, and to act with equanimity—or balance. Do, make the effort, let us hear from every one of you of what came about! For today, we wish sincerely that all of you actively participate in the reciprocal feeding of your impressions.

*Paul Anderson*

---

[1] *All and Everything*, the series title Gurdjieff gave to his three books, was used as the main title of the first edition of *Beelzebub's Tales to His Grandson*. When Anderson refers to *All and Everything* in his talk, he is referring specifically to *Beelzebub's Tales* rather than the entire series.

## Relaxing with Presence

The usual term for being relaxed is *glodpa* or *lhodpa*. However, we can be relaxed and yet drowsy. The term *lhugpa* means being relaxed, but alert and present. Thus, being relaxed (*lhugpa*), whenever appearances arise, in whatever fashion they may arise, then without the mind making any corrections or modifications of them, they are seen to exist as mere ornaments or embellishments of that state itself which is the real condition of existence. In the Dzogchen *upadesa*,[1] there is the practice of leaving what appears just as it is. We do not enter into reasoning or into altering it with judgments. Thus, whenever appearances arise, they are left just as they are, and they in turn in no way condition the individual. These appearances are like the ornaments of the individual's energy. The individual finds himself in the true condition of the mirror. Anything which arises as an appearance is like the rising of a reflection in a mirror. These reflections, whether beautiful or ugly, in no way condition the mirror. Therefore, whatever arises creates no problems for the individual. As the Master Phadampa said, "The individual is not conditioned by appearances but by his attachment to appearances; this attachment originates within the individual and not in the object." Internally, there exists a state of pure presence (*rigpa*) which is uncorrected, clear, vivid, and naked. It is uncorrected and unmodified because it is unconditioned by discursive thoughts or the working of the mind. "Naked" means that, in the instant when the thought arises, we are right there present and do not enter into any judgment or reasoning. Thus, while being alertly relaxed, when thoughts arise, we relax them into their own condition such as it is in itself.

"Relaxing with presence" means that when the senses have contact with an object, we do not enter into conceptualizing, reasoning or judging with respect to that object. Normally, when we see something, the mind makes a judgment with respect to it and as a reaction to this, a passion of attachment or aversion may arise. Then, by entering into action because of the passion, we come to accumulate more karma and so continue to transmigrate in Samsara. However, the phrase "not entering into reasoning or analysis" does not mean that we try to block thought. In Zen practice, for instance, one enters into a nondiscursive state where one experiences emptiness without any blocking of thoughts. For example, we may see a book on a table. We could take this book away or we could leave it where it is as if it were not something important. To block a thought means that we are taking something away and we are trying to eliminate it. But when we speak about not entering into reasoning and judgment, this means leaving something just where it is, as it is, without being disturbed or distracted by it. Nonetheless, even though we do not enter into reasoning and judgment, thoughts continue to arise in a state of clearly aware presence without interruption or obstruction. It is important to understand what is meant by "not being distracted" in the Dzogchen context. It means being aware. It does not mean that some mental policeman keeps popping up inside the mind saying "Now pay attention!"

When we find ourselves in a state of *rigpa*, then its inherent qualities manifest as whatever appears, so that there is nothing to be interrupted or constructed. The sun's rays are the inherent nature of the sun when it shines. In the same way, everything arises as an ornament of one's energy, and this presence is self-perfected (*lhun grub*) in this state. The idea of spontaneous self-perfection is a very important one in Dzogchen. If we were to speak of primordial purity, then

254

Dzogchen would be no different than Zen. But this understanding of *lhun grub* sets Dzogchen apart from Zen. When we are present in the state of *rigpa*, everything we see is a manifestation of our own individual energy, like a reflection in a mirror. The whole dimension around oneself is spontaneously self-perfected in the potency of pure presence. As it says in the text, "When appearances, which are objects of the six faculties, arise as mere ornaments of one's state in a lucid fashion without any obstruction and without any analyses, then they are entirely perfect and complete just as they are. They are experienced as the potency of pure presence without any grasping or entering into conceptions and judgments." So, we enter into this nondual state and continue in it present and relaxed. This is what is meant by *lhugpa*.

When we speak of a period of contemplation or *mnyamb-zhag*, this means being in a state of *rigpa*. The term *rjesthob* refers to the time after the period of contemplation has been concluded. "Great Contemplation" means that the practitioner has reached a level of development where his contemplation is no longer limited by formal periods of practice. But for the beginner, there are always these two moments of contemplation and non-contemplation. So, while continuing in the period of contemplation, without engaging in any analysis of or reasoning about the objects of the five gates of the senses, appearances are allowed to rise clearly and luminously in an alert, relaxed fashion without any distraction or grasping at conceptions and judgments. The *mi gyoba* means "unmoving" or "not distracted." When the state of *rigpa* is interrupted, this is *gyoba* or distraction. Shakyamuni Buddha is said to have been many times in a state of unmoving samadhi or undistracted concentration. But this did not mean that his physical body was necessarily immobile. Rather, it meant that he was in a state of pure presence and he did not move from that, becoming distracted by mental activity. He was neither distracted nor conditioned by thoughts, and yet he performed all actions perfectly—moving and speaking and reasoning. Then, after this period of contemplation is concluded, even when something concrete appears to the senses, it seems as if it has

255

no inherent reality in itself. The case is the same with the passions; they have no inherent reality or self-nature. In this way, whatever arises to the senses becomes a means for remaining in primal awareness.

Having considered external appearances, we now consider the subjective side of things, that is to say, the individual himself. The five poisons are the five passions of delusion, anger, desire, pride, and envy. Whenever discursive thoughts engendered by these five passions arise, we alertly relax (*lhugpa*) in the face of them without entering into conceptions or judgments. On the other hand, we should not try to block them by means of some antidote as we do in the Sutra system or transform them by means of some method as we do in the Tantra system. For example, in the Sutra system the antidote to desire or attachment is meditation on the repulsiveness of the flesh, the antidote to anger is meditation on loving-kindness, the antidote to envy is rejoicing at the merit of others, and so on. And again, in the Tantra system, we transform the passions into primal awareness, as for example, anger is transformed into the anger of Heruka. Since they are neither blocked nor transformed, the passions which arise during the practice of the path are self-liberated and a primal awareness is present.

When we are not in the state of rigpa, the passions become poisons; since they interrupt and hinder our realization, they are called demons. They compel us to continue in transmigration. If we chase after a discursive thought and enter into mental activity, this thought may become a poison for us. In this way, we become a slave to our passions. But if we remain present, we will not be conditioned by our thoughts in any way and whatever arises will be merely like a reflection in a mirror. Thus, we need not apply some antidote to block the passion because the passion will self-liberate of itself. We are not even speaking here of *gcergrol*, liberation through bare attention, that is to say, when we look into the face of a discursive thought which arises in the mind and it self-liberates. This procedure still involves some kind of effort. But this is not what we are speaking of here. The term *lhugpa* means to relax

256

with awareness. If we feel some passion arising, we then relax that passion without attempting to block it or trying to apply some antidote to it. We are not succumbing to the passion; it is simply that now the passion is governed by our awareness of presence (*rigpa*). With this relaxed presence, our passions themselves become merely the inherent qualities of our primordial state manifesting themselves. This is the method for self-liberating the passions.

Now we shall consider the experiences which arise during meditation practice. Manifesting as clarity and emptiness, they are found present in a state of vision and emptiness, or in a state of the continuing movement of thoughts and emptiness or in a state of pleasurable sensation and emptiness, etc. Thus, there may arise various different kinds of conscious experiences of the presence of pleasurable sensation, of clarity, and of nondiscursiveness. All of these experiences are linked to the individual.

The term *kaya* means the entire dimension of our existence. Having understood all phenomena as the *dharmakaya*, the entire dimension of existence, we enter into a state of knowledge or awareness of the real condition of things such as they are without any modifications made by the mind. This non-dual self-perfected awareness is present like a perfect sphere which is whole, uniform, and without duality. Such a sphere has neither angles nor limits. And around this center, our energy manifests spontaneously self-perfected. Thus, we may speak of attaining the whole dimension of primordial awareness or the *jnanakaya* and a primal awareness of clarity is present.

Objects and their contact with the senses are many, but here the individual is no longer conditioned by these objects. Now we have a vivid experience: whatever arises has no inherent reality, but is like a reflection in a mirror. Since the objects which we perceive are present as manifestations of the real condition of existence, our passions and obscurations become purified. In this way, we overcome the obstacle of the passions and are liberated. Because a primal awareness of pure presence is present within oneself, the individual can disentangle

257

himself from engaging in negative behavior. We are no longer limited by having to learn what to do and what not to do. We have overcome the limitations of the passions and have developed clarity. We are no longer slaves to external appearances, but govern ourselves autonomously with our own awareness. Negative attitudes and actions cannot arise. Why? Because all that arises in the individual which is negative arises through a lack of clarity and awareness. As the individual is liberated from his passions, karmic traces, and obscurations, he or she is now said to belong to the family of the noble bodhisattvas.

*Chögyal Namkhai Norbu*

---

[1] Upadesa is a Sanskrit word meaning the guidance and instruction given by a spiritual teacher.

*Saru Bill Segal*

## SARU-SAN

William C. Segal was a successful magazine publisher and artist. He and his first wife Cora first met the Ouspenskys soon after their arrival in the U.S.A. and the establishment of their Work residence, Franklin Farms, in Mendham, New Jersey. They attended Mr Ouspensky's meetings in Manhattan, regularly attended Work weekends at Franklin Farms, and occasionally attended longer Work periods there as well. After a while they purchased a home near Franklin Farms to be more part of the community. Segal was also part of a small group of men who regularly drank with Ouspensky late into the night. They frequented Longchamps and Ouspensky's favorite drink was apricot brandy. Segal said of his teacher, "...he was a regular fellow in many ways. We had a very good relationship."[1] Yet as a regular participant of the Work life at Franklin Farms, he was hardly like so many other students of Mr Ouspensky who primarily attended the lectures and had a more intellectual approach to the Work.

Segal first met Gurdjieff when Gurdjieff visited Franklin Farms during his last trip to the U.S.A. in 1948. He said of that initial encounter, "...there was something very different about Mr Gurdjieff. Absolutely no pretense. He was an authentic spiritual master."[2] Segal subsequently made a trip to Paris the following year for a while to be under Mr Gurdjieff's guidance.

In 1952 he made his first trip to Japan at the encouragement of poet and Zen practitioner Paul Reps. Reps had been contributing articles to Segal's magazine *Gentry* and proposed the trip with one of his submissions. Reps' book *Letters to a Friend* is a collection of letters written to Segal who wrote the preface for it. Coincidentally, shortly after Reps suggested going to Japan together, Segal met D.T. Suzuki. Suzuki was working at Columbia University and Segal approached him about contributing an article himself. Hearing that Segal was considering the trip, Suzuki offered him written introductions to three Rinzai and three Soto monasteries (the two major sects of Zen). As a result, Segal befriended all the abbots, who never failed to meet with him when visiting New York. He had a particularly strong bond with Soen Nakagawa, the abbot of Ryutakuji (a Rinzai temple) who was introduced to him by Reps and would later become his root teacher.

Yet it was at Eiheiji that Segal had some sort of epiphany. On this he said, "I had my own experience after three or four months in the headquarters of the Soto Zen monastery. I came out and said, 'My God, I've been in the Gurdjieff Work for seven or eight years, and here after three months, I made a leap.'"[3] (Eiheiji is the main monastery of the Soto sect.) He also felt that, "...it was after several weeks at Eiheiji that I came closer to what might be called a better understanding of what the meaning of Buddhism is."[4]

Back in New York, Segal returned to work with Madame Ouspensky at Franklin Farms, took part in activities at the formative Gurdjieff Foundation which now overlooked Franklin Farms, and sat zazen at New York Zendo (a Zen center in New York of which Soen Nakagawa was the guiding teacher) and the First Zen Institute. He also brought D.T. Suzuki to Franklin Farms where he gave a talk to the group, a private talk with Madame Ouspensky, and had an opportunity to view movements classes and a film on the movements. As a result Suzuki declared, "You know, Zen and Gurdjieff are very close."[5] Of this proximity between the two teachings, Segal himself said, "...the actual nuts and bolts practice is to be as present as one can at each moment. It's Gurdjieff's remembering one's self and Zen Buddhism's every minute Zen. They're not very far apart."[6] Elsewhere he notes, "...they both propose that only with tough disciplines and practice is it possible to relate to a 'changeless self.'"[7]

His 1952 journey to Japan was but the first of numerous ones made throughout his life. Although the next trip he discusses with any detail was his 1964 trip, he apparently made at least two between these. In the text that follows, Segal brings up a couple of memories of a trip made in 1956. It was that summer that Soen Roshi gave him the nickname Saru (meaning monkey) for his agility climbing a persimmon tree to get some of its fruit while out on a hike together. In addition, Segal's book *A Voice at the Borders of Silence* includes a photo of him with Kobori Roshi somewhere in Japan in 1960. Nanrei Kobori was the abbot of Ryokoin Temple at Daitokuji Monastery in Kyoto. Besides having Zen in common, Kobori too was a painter and poet. The two immediately struck up a friendship and visited one another whenever possible. One thing in particular that Kobori said at times that struck Segal is the idea that "...between zero and one a soul is born."[8] The Zen and Gurdjieff teachings both share the paradox that unity is realized through one's nonentityness, although Gurdjieff places greater emphasis on so-called Real 'I' (apparently to better appeal to the egoistic Westerner) and Zen emphasizes more the concept of no-self. (As a side note, Trungpa Rinpoche also talked about the subject in terms of the relationship between zero and one.)

His 1964 trip was more of a leisure trip with his family. He had also become something of a business celebrity and was treated lavishly by his Japanese business associates. But he still made time to visit his old friend D. T. Suzuki and practice with his new friend Ruth Sasaki. (Sasaki is discussed in more detail in the chapter "Pamela Poppins.") Suzuki was now 94 years old and had returned to Japan to retire. Regarding his meeting with Sasaki, Segal evidently learned of her work in Japan through his membership of the First Zen Institute. Whether he learned about First Zen through Suzuki or Reps is uncertain. It could have been either. Also during this trip,

Segal visited Asahina Roshi, the abbot of Engakuji, one of the priests he had met in 1952. (Asahina Roshi is discussed in more detail in the chapter "Leader of the Washington Group.")

The next trip to Japan that Segal discusses was made in 1966. On this trip he visited many of the same people, but this time taking Madame de Salzmann with him. He was hoping to convince her of the benefits of meditation, which he felt was something lacking in the Gurdjieff Foundation. Also accompanying them (besides Cora) were de Salzmann's son Michel and Jean Vaysse, author of *Toward Awakening*. Segal specifically mentions taking them to an informal visit with Suzuki, and a five-day visit to Ryutakuji to experience Zen practice firsthand and meet Soen Nakagawa. Evidently de Salzmann was impressed as she began giving guided "sittings" to Group One (the more advanced group) shortly after.

Madame de Salzmann also initiated trips to India in 1970 and '71 that included Segal and a friend from Franklin Farms, Canadian ambassador James George. In Darjeeling they met Dudjom Rinpoche, Kangyur Rinpoche (Yahne Le Toumelin's teacher), Chatral Rinpoche, Gyurtala Rinpoche, and others at the Canadian Embassy. They were also escorted by Lobsang Lhalungpa in Dharamsala to meet the Dalai Lama. Many of these talks were later reproduced in Segal's works as well as *Parabola Magazine*.

But 1970 and '71 were difficult years for Segal. In 1970 Cora suddenly died, and in 1971 Segal survived a near-fatal automobile accident. His injuries were so severe that Segal remembers a priest being called into his hospital room to perform his last rites. Then, as if to add insult to injury (literally), his daughter and sister-in-law were involved in a fatal collision on the way to visit him in the hospital. His daughter broke her neck and his sister-in-law died instantly. But this actually marked a turn for the better in Segal's recovery. Having his daughter's well-being to focus on motivated him to overcome his own troubles. All his doctors told him he would never walk again. Remarkably, after only two years he was completely on his feet. He had progressed slowly from using a wheelchair, to crutches, to a cane, to no support at all. Certainly Segal had a strong will. When told there was a danger of becoming addicted to the pain medication he was receiving he gave it up on the spot.

1971 was also eventful for taking his Buddhist vows. On September 15th, after sitting sesshin at New York Zendo, Soen Nakagawa gave him the dharma name Shi Katsu, which he also rendered in English as Birth and Death. (Actually, while *shi* means death, *katsu* is closer in meaning to life or vitality than birth. The name as a whole has the connotation of rebirth—of some new life emerging from the ashes of death.) The name is apparently an allusion to some realization that Segal had reached as a result of his accident. Visiting Segal after the accident, Nakagawa remarked, "Lucky man. One accident like yours worth ten thousand sittings in a monastery." He was speaking from experience too as he had suffered a near fatal accident himself in 1967.

Over the years, as a result of his many trips to Japan, Segal acquired a great appreciation for the culture and their arts, and had assembled a small collection of Buddhist artifacts. A Buddhist theme he often returned to in his own artwork is "The Ten Oxherding Pictures"—a series of ten images depicting the various stages of development along the spiritual path. Kobori Roshi seemed amused that the seeker Segal depicted had Western eyes. Segal's first rendering of the theme was published along with Suzuki's commentary in *Gentry*. The limited edition booklet *The Ten Oxherding Pictures*, published in 1988, includes Segal's own commentary with another set of his depictions.

Although more acquainted with Zen Buddhism, Segal had an appreciation for Tibetan Buddhism as well. Certainly the various rinpoches he met had also made an impression. Segal and his second wife Marielle frequently read from *The Hundred Thousand Songs of Milarepa* to one another and he kept a copy of Milarepa's biography on his nightstand. Considering that Segal had met Lobsang Lhalungpa in Dharamsala, and that Lord Pentland, who Segal knew since his time at Franklin Farms, through his Far West Institute had funded Lhalungpa's translation of the Milarepa story, it is likely this edition that

265

he owned. Like other direct pupils of Gurdjieff, the similarity between the teaching styles of Gurdjieff and Milarepa (as well as his teacher Marpa) likely did not evade him. On the story itself, Segal comments, "We could be helped by the study of Milarepa's transformation. How did that come about? At what cost? What eventually made Milarepa a master was the determination to follow, to obey the instructions of his master, Marpa."[9]

Segal also had an appreciation for *The Tibetan Book of the Dead*. No doubt his near-death experience provided some conviction of its truths.

Another Buddhist text he enjoyed reading is the "Heart Sutra" (which is common to both Zen and Tibetan Buddhism), sometimes aloud. The text is actually a chant and is often recited in services. Segal comments, "In the ultimate prayer there is no object... no thing as it says in the Heart Sutra. If we stop right now and are aware, without being aware of anything— that would be a very high state. As long as one objectifies, one hasn't reached the highest."[10]

Of the many Buddhist teachers that Segal befriended and worked with, it is clear that Soen Nakagawa was the most significant being that he took his vows with him. Part of Soen Roshi's appeal may have been that he was a poet and calligrapher. Segal himself was a painter, was very attracted to the arts and culture of Japan, and acquired quite a Japanese art collection from his repeated travels. Soen was a renowned poet too, having frequently been compared to Basho, the great haiku poet of the Edo period.

Although it is common for Zen priests to learn poetry and calligraphy as part of their dharma training, for Soen poetry came first. He was attracted to poetry as a child, and upon graduating high school he attended Tokyo Imperial University where he majored in Japanese literature. At university he further developed his youthful passion for poetry and was very involved in the campus' art scene. But he was also dorming at Pure Land temple Gangyoji, studying the Buddhist sutras as part of his curriculum, and started a sitting group on campus. The dharma was very much a part of his life although living

266

as an academic. Also part of his curriculum was Western philosophy and religion, which no doubt helped to develop a curiosity about the West and planted something of a seed in that regard.

Upon completing his university studies in 1931, Soen attended a dharma talk of Keigaku Katsube and decided to become a monk. Shortly after, Katsube Roshi gave Soen his monk ordination at Kogakuji, the monastery founded by Bassui Tokusho—Soen's favorite Zen master—and the head monastery of the Kogakuji subsect of Rinzai. It was Katsube Roshi who gave him the dharma name Soen. (He had previously gone by his given name, Motoi.)

Following in the footsteps of Bassui, Soen regularly alternated between attending to his duties at Kogakuji and taking solitary retreats at Dai Bosatsu Mountain. It was while on these retreats that he both composed his original mantra "Namu Dai Bosa" and conceived the idea of an International Dai Bosatsu Zendo.

In 1935 Soen first heard Gempo Yamamoto give a dharma talk and was greatly struck by his understanding. After attending a few of his talks Soen asked to become his student and began studying with him at Ryutakuji (the temple where Segal first met him).

It was also in 1935 that Soen began corresponding with Nyogen Senzaki, a roshi who had been living in San Francisco and serving its Japanese community since 1905. Senzaki, who was impressed by Soen's poetry, had initiated the correspondence. Soen was planning to visit Nyogen in 1941 but was inhibited by the political climate of World War II. However, he eventually made the trip in 1949 and found Nyogen's style of teaching refreshing compared to the traditional Japanese approach.

The following year Soen took over as abbot of Ryutakuji. Soon after, he began accepting Americans referred to him by Nyogen wishing to study Zen. Over the years he would receive many Americans visiting Japan and make thirteen trips to the U.S.A. all together to support various American sanghas. His American students include Robert Aitken, Paul Reps,

267

John Daido Loori and Joko Beck, as well as many others.

1967 was the year of his near fatal accident. He had fallen from a tree on the property of Ryutakuji that he had climbed, was rendered unconscious from the resulting head injury, and was not discovered until three days later by one of the temple's monks. Yet he recovered and continued his responsibilities despite the life-long effects of his injury.

The following year Soen helped establish New York Zendo, the Zen center that Segal frequented, and in 1971 he helped establish Kongoji—the zendo's affiliated retreat center in the Catskills.

After returning to Ryutakuji from his final trip to the U.S.A. in 1982, Soen retired from teaching. He died in 1984 just short of his 77th birthday.

In order to avoid acclaim, Soen only issued his poetry privately. The four titles he produced are *Shigan* (*Coffin of Poems*), *Meihan* (*Life Anthology*), *Henkairoku* (*Journal of a Wide World*) and *Koun-sho* (*Ancient Cloud Selection*).

Following are two excerpts of interest from *Soen Roku*, a collection of teachings and memories of Soen Nakagawa. The first is Segal's contribution which also provides Madame de Salzmann's impression of the roshi. And the second is an edited version of one of Soen Roshi's talks, chosen for its illustration of his playful application of providing shocks.

¹ William Segal & Marielle Bancou-Segal, *A Voice at the Borders of Silence: An Intimate View of the Gurdjieff Work, Zen Buddhism, and Art* (New York: Overlook Press, 2003), 202.
² Ibid., 191.
³ Ibid., 196–97.
⁴ Ibid., 105.
⁵ Ibid., 195.
⁶ Ibid., 194.
⁷ William Segal, "The Patriarch Goes West," in *Gurdjieff: Essays and Reflections on the Man and His Teaching*, eds. Jacob Needleman & George Baker (New York: Continuum Publishing, 1996), 425.
⁸ William Segal & Marielle Bancou-Segal, *A Voice at the Borders of Silence: An Intimate View of the Gurdjieff Work, Zen Buddhism, and Art* (New York: Overlook Press, 2003), 78.
⁹ Ibid., 76.
¹⁰ Ibid., 228.

## ENERGY FROM HIGH

Back in 1956, when I visited Ryutakuji, Soen suggested we meet for early (pre-dawn) walks. Two memories stand out:

1.  As we looked into the zendo with all the young monks still fast asleep, Soen waved his hand at the early dawn-darkened room and said, "Look at all the Sleeping Buddhas."

2.  Walking along the raised earth banks near the monastery, we would make a pre-breakfast meal by eating the pomegranates from the trees. Soen would tell me to go up the trees to pick the fruit. I was a good climber (in my youth), so Soen gave me the Japanese name, "Monkey" (Saru-san).

Another memory is of visiting Ryutakuji with Madame de Salzmann. Soen had been very ill—it was directly after he was found disabled in the mountains. Still, he appeared regularly to direct the morning ceremonies in the temple. I recall watching him, and Madame remarking, "Look, each movement he is making costs him great pain. But look how his inner life animates the smallest gesture."

Of course there are many anecdotes of the period when I would accompany Paul Reps to the monastery. Soen valued Reps as a poet and friend—we always had great laughs together.

I also recall Soen Roshi's visit, with Eido Roshi, after my auto accident. Soen gave me a silk scroll, inscribed with his calligraphy, "Energy from High," to help me in my recovery.

*Saru Bill Segal*

# THIS!

This is the first teisho[1] of the sesshin. Everything is scheduled, not only human beings. Everything, indeed. Mountain, running river, sound of wind, singing of birds—everything. Especially children, who are wonderful Zen teachers, of course.

Everything is our teacher. This! (Bang!) This is the real one point; very easy to understand. Too clear, too easy to get This! (Bang!) Everything is giving a teisho.

Please, don't miss this (Bang!), this most important point, okay? There are many sutras and shastras. Many, many teachings, not only about Buddhism and Christianity. There are many, many books. But when we meet (Bang!) this one point, all sutras and shastras and all philosophical and spiritual words become a mistake. Only one point. (Bang! Bang! Bang!) Only one. This is the true teaching of Bodhidharma, all patriarchs, Buddha Shakyamuni, This! Okay?

Each of you is a wonderful bodhisattva. I'm not saying this in praise, or for encouragement. Truly, you are living bodhisattvas. Living Dai Bosa.[2] There is a wonderful Buddha statue at the Metropolitan Museum. There are national-treasure bodhisattvas and many statues. They are wonderful, of course. But, you are *living* bodhisattvas, each of you, living! Not bronze, or wood. Sometime, something bad may happen. If something goes wrong, "Oh, I will pray to Buddha." No, no, no! There is no such Buddha. Realize this! (Bang!) and every human becomes wonderful.

So in the Bodhisattva's Vow, "Extend tender care even to such beings as birds and beasts." Not only beasts, not only birds. But to insects too, okay? Even one flower, one speck of dust. There is a Zen saying, "When I pick up one speck of dust, all nations are united."

Teisho is not always a talk about some great Zen master, or Buddha Shakyamuni's sutras, or Rinzai's lectures. Rinzai himself says, "Don't take my teisho"—don't hold to my teisho. OPEN YOUR OWN EYES! Everything is a living sutra. Every day you are (Bang!). Each deed is a living sutra. Picking up a cup, drinking water—nothing else. As the Bodhisattva's Vow says, "In any event, in any place, and in any moment"—now!—none can be other than *This!* This! THIS! There is no need for Buddha's teaching, or some brilliant exposition. *This* is best.

So, after Purification, we recited together, "Opening This Dharma. This Dharma, incomparably profound and minutely subtle, is hardly met with, even in hundreds of thousands of millions of eons." *Hardly* met with. During hundreds of thousands of millions of eons, we are always meeting with This! "Meet" is one "This", and one "meet", not thousands. Nothing else but This, okay? Nothing else but This. ANSWER!

[Students: Hai!]

OKAY?

[Students: Hai!]

Wonderful! *Congratulations.* This is true teisho. Only This.

In Dr Daitsu Suzuki's translation, "Opening 'The' Dharma. 'The' Dharma, incomparably profound and minutely subtle, is hardly met with, even in hundreds of thousands of millions of eons. Now we can see 'it', listen to 'it', accept and hold 'it'." It, it, it. No! So it takes us over thirty years to correct wonderful Dr Daitsu Suzuki's translation. Not "it". But "this". Now we can SEE! I can see your face. I cannot see my own face, of course. Now we can see (bang!). Now. *Now* we can see *This.* Listen to *This*—all the birds are chirping; not only you can get

274

This. Indeed, I'm not telling a lie. Everything is wonderful! So, we get these miserable karma relations—world war, all over—such miserable, cruel karma relations changed into wonderful dharma relations, with (bang!). Please, (bang!), nothing else but This. I'm explaining, talking too much. Excuse me.

"Now we can see This, listen to This, accept and hold This. May we *truly* understand...." There are many kinds of understanding: I understand you; I understand everything. But true insight, true understanding is with This. Not only understanding. True understanding becomes true realization, and true actualization. This is our training, not just our vow. We should *actualize* EVERY DAY, okay? *Every day*. Every day. Nothing else but This, is our training.

This is the true teaching of Buddha Shakyamuni and all the patriarchs. And this morning's teisho is a true teisho, true Buddha Dharma. There are many Zen centers and many Zen temples, Zen churches. But truly to get This is very difficult. I'm congratulating myself. Without your wonderful bodhisattva's response, I cannot talk like this. In my own room, I cannot talk like this. You are talking my talk. You are giving teisho. Thank you very much; thank *you*.

With this mind, everyday life becomes "every day is a good day." You know this saying. Even in fear, we can say, EVERY DAY IS A GOOD DAY. Even a miserable day. Even a cruel day. We must become every-day-is-sun-shining day. With This! This is the point. This is the wonderful key to open many things. Probably after my teisho, you will forget my This, of course. So, reciting Namu Dai Bosa, Namu Dai Bosa... is a very good help. Not only to you, to me too. I'm *always* losing This, forgetting This, and committing mistake after mistake. But mistakes and failures are very good lessons for us. Don't become sorry, "Oh, again I committed such a miserable mistake." Okay! With this one experience, we become more, more, more—"this mind." Every day is a wonderful training place. Training is not always joyful training, but every day becomes more and more joyful, more and more full of gratitude, and more, more, more, endless long wonderful.... So, Namu Dai Bosa.

There's no need for reciting Namu Dai Bosa of course, but

Namu Dai Bosa is very effective. As you know, "bosa" means bodhisattva. Bodhisattva's Vow. Probably you have memorized it already. "Okay," you say. "I understood the Bodhisattva's Vow." But *each* time I recite this Vow, or the Heart Sutra, *each* time, some part of it really touches me.

"Bodhi" and "sattva". "Bodhi" means so-called enlightenment. But don't think, "Oh, I am not yet enlightened. Some day I'll get enlightenment." From today, forget such! From the beginning, we are the Enlightened One. Believe this with definite faith. This is not only the Song of Zazen, "From the beginning, all sentient beings are Buddha...." You are not merely chanting. It means, from the beginning, you are the Enlightened One! Realize this. Realize this. And have definite faith in this. Not only the Song of Zazen, but also the Heart Sutra is saying so. "Bodhi" means "enlightenment"—"some day, I will get enlightenment," no! There's no need for more enlightenment; already we are full.

Some Zen master said, "When I hear the term Buddha, I want to close my ears." There's no need for the name of Buddha, or Zen, or such-and-such. After we realize This, and have understood This, there's no need to hear more. We chant sutras, we practice zazen together with mindfulness. We should be *mindful.*

Please recite from the Meal Sutra: "Thirdly, what is most essential is the practice of mindfulness, which helps us...." All together, please, "Thirdly...

[Students: "Thirdly, what is most essential is the practice of mindfulness, which helps us transcend greed, anger, and delusion."]

What is the English word? "Neurotic?" Neurotic mindfulness is no good. It must be with This. This is the teaching of the Tea Ceremony, and Flower Arranging. Tea master Rikkyu said, "The Way of Tea is nothing else but boiling cold water and making tea." Make tea and drink it. Nothing else. To become mindful is wonderful training. It is very good to become mindful. But Rikkyu said, the Way of Tea is nothing else but, with hot water, making tea and drinking it. Nothing else but this. So Rikkyu is giving us a teisho about This. Nothing else!

*What is Buddha?* What is Buddha? "Shit-wiping stick," Ummon said. "Shit-wiping"—the ancient Chinese didn't have paper; paper was very difficult to get. So they always brought a shit-wiping stick. It is as important as your spoon and knife.

[Laughter.]

So, Ummon, our great patriarch. When I think of Ummon, Cloud Gate Zen master, my tears are many. What is Buddha? Ummon answered, "Shit-wiping stick." So, for us, "What is Buddha? One piece of toilet paper." One piece of toilet paper. One drop of tea. One drop of coffee. Nothing else but that. Realize this. There's no need always to be thinking, "Oh, this is wonderful, this is Buddha." No *need*.

Some of you are nurses—wonderful. You are living Kanzeon[3] Bosatsu. I am only a lazy, mountain monk. But please, with this mind, take care of your many patients. Nursing is wonderful training.

I do not like to say "Zen", but as I need the name, so I am talking Zen, Zen, Zen.... Everyone—not only nurses—each of you is a wonderful bodhisattva. So, I am bowing, of course to the Buddha, bowing to you all. So with this mind, please, let us bow to each other. Wife and husband—please, I am not joking, okay?—bow with This Mind. Not only to Buddha, but to each other. To the living bodhisattva that is each of you. So, bow together, looking at me. So, without exception each of you is a living Buddha, Dai Bosatsu. Without exception, okay?

So, each one is best. Not only human beings, *each* is best. Nothing else. Each one is BEST! This is the teaching of Buddha Shakyamuni.

In the sutra about Buddha's birth, where he takes seven steps in each direction—this is not true of course; he cries the same cry we all do when we come out of our mother's sacred womb. What does that saying mean? "Under the heaven, on the Earth, tenjo tenga yuiga dokuson?"[4] The literal translation is, "I am the best one." No, this is wrong. Not myself only, but each one is best. Wonderful. This is not a conscious thought. Truly this is so. Tenjo tenga yuiga dokuson. Each one is best.

Almost all Zen students begin with the Mumonkan's first koan, "Mu." The serious student did not visit Joshu to talk to him about a dog, or a Buddha-dog, or whether a dog has Buddha-Nature. In front of such a wonderful, great Zen master, Joshu, the sincere, honest student really asked, "What is *true* enlightenment? Please show me and let me see true enlightenment. Enlighten!" To this, Joshu only responded, "Mu." This "one piece of toilet paper." This "mu". Nothing else but this. Mu-uu-uu-u! So, in Zen training, Mu is not just the first koan. *All* is Mu. Mu, mu, mu, mu. Namu dai bosa and mu are the same; nothing else but. But to continue practice with "one piece of toilet paper, one piece of toilet paper" is probably very difficult. Namu dai bosa, or Mu, is very good!

So, we have been thinking about birth. When your mother was giving birth, she was not speculating, What is birth? She was not thinking, Is it a boy or a girl? She was just making the birth-sound.

But some time, some day, we all leave this wonderful world. Some day. But looking at your faces, I see no "Some day I'll leave this wonderful world; I must die." There is a senryu, a short, witty verse: "When I look at your face, all faces, show 'now I live for ever.'" I thought this was a sarcastic comment. But Dr D. T. Suzuki told me, "This wonderful senryu—it is not sarcastic at all. We live forever! No need for 'some day I will die.' Do you understand?" That's what Dr Suzuki said to me. But *truly* (Knock! Knock!) our life is forever!

So, when some day we will say goodbye, let us not cry. Some crying is okay, but don't make others cry. My wonderful teacher, Gempo Roshi, was smiling. Many Zen masters know one week before. They know the day. My last day, I promise Eido Roshi, with smiling, okay? When it is our last breath, it is our last breath. "Is that so, doctor?" That is our last Mu. When we're born, there is our mother's birth-sound. And when we leave, just this Mu.

*Soen Nakagawa*

¹ A teisho is a dharma talk given by a roshi.
² "Namu [Homage] Dai [Boundless] Bosa [Bodhisattva]" is the title of a chant spontaneously composed by Soen Nakagawa while on solitary retreat.
³ Kanzeon is the Japanese name for Guanyin, which is the Chinese name of Avalokitechvara, the bodhisattva of compassion.
⁴ "Tenjo tenga yuiga dokuson" is the Japanese translation of Shakyamuni Buddha's words after attaining enlightenment. The English translation is "Above heaven and below heaven, I alone am the world-honored one."

*Yahne Le Toumelin and Kangyur Rinpoche*

## MADEMOISELLE POURQUOI

Yahne Le Toumelin met Gurdjieff in 1942 while studying art at the Académie de la Grande Chaumière. She was only 19 years old at the time. As she recounts:

> I was received in the twilight. Gurdjieff turned his back on me grumbling and invited me for a coffee. He played his curious button accordion for me, nostalgic tunes. I cried and said, "I am in prison." He replied, "I love you for saying that. Me take you on my shoulders."[1]

For constantly barraging him with questions, Gurdjieff christened her Mademoiselle Pourquoi (Miss Why). Under Gurdjieff's guidance she eventually became an instructor of his sacred movements.

One of her first commissions as an artist was offered to her by Pierre Schaeffer—the father of musique concrète and a fellow group member. Other friends of hers in the French groups included Robert and Babette Godet, René Daumal, Lanza del Vasto and Luc Dietrich.

In 1945 Le Toumelin married author Jean-François Revel and the following year their son Matthieu Ricard was born. The small family moved where Revel found work—Tlemcen (Algeria) in 1947 and Mexico City in 1950. While in Tlemcen their daughter Ève Ricard was born. In 1952 the couple separated and eventually they divorced.

Returning to France, Le Toumelin at first lived in Valmondois amongst some artist friends and began to give her career more attention. One of her friends there, the author André Breton, gave the first exhibition of Le Toumelin's work at his gallery in Paris in 1955. She moved back to Paris the following year and over the next decade had additional exhibitions and built her reputation as a surrealist artist. While in Paris Le Toumelin also renewed her friendships with many people she knew from the Gurdjieff groups, but remained separate from the groups themselves.

In the fall of 1967 Le Toumelin's son, photographer and author Mattheiu Ricard, went to India to seek out a Tibetan Buddhist master. Le Toumelin was seriously considering going to Tibet in 1943 but Gurdjieff dissuaded her at the time. Evidently something of this interest had rubbed off onto her son. Despite having dissuaded Le Toumelin from initially going to Tibet, Gurdjieff clearly understood that she would one day make the journey, as he asked her to seek out his two sons when she eventually goes. In fact, he told her that she would go in "3 × 7 years"[2]—a precise prediction according to her. Le Toumelin also knew that two months before his death Gurdjieff had seriously looked into making another journey to Tibet himself, and this likely reinforced her wish. But with having to raise two children she simply had not been able to go herself just yet. However, now having Ricard's encouragement, she finally made the trip herself six months later.

She went for three months, staying most of the time in Darjeeling, and it was there on April 1st that she met the man who would become her root teacher—Kangyur Rinpoche. She felt that he "was wisdom and love embodied."[3]

It is interesting that she met Kangyur Rinpoche on April Fools day as a prank that Gurdjieff played on her manifested that day. In the same conversation in which he predicted she would go to Tibet in 3 × 7 years time, he asked her, "When you will go to Tibet ask for my two sons, but tell my name Dordjieff."[4] Knowing that the name Dordjieff is the Russification of the name Dorje, Le Toumelin inquired of Kangyur Rinpoche about the "sons of Dorje." Kangyur Rinpoche must have first looked at her somewhat puzzled; Dorje is such a common name. Then he burst out laughing, saying, "Here in Darjeeling we are all sons of Dorje." The name Darjeeling means "land of the thunderbolt"—thunderbolt (*dorje*) being a symbol for enlightenment. Then he added, "Do not think about it anymore."[5]

Gurdjieff of course knew that the rumor associating him with Dordjieff was a fabrication and creatively came up with this prank to provide Le Toumelin with a shock after his death. He did something similar with other students of his by providing them with measurements for his coffin that were too small, requiring them to secure another with little time to spare. But Le Toumelin does not seem to have understood this. Her appreciation for Gurdjieff waned after the incident, though she still maintained appreciation for him as a first teacher.

Also note that Gurdjieff duped J.G. Bennett in a similar manner by telling him that in Tibet they pronounced his name as Dordjieff because there is no letter 'g' in Tibetan.[6] This is blatantly false. The Tibetan alphabet most definitely includes the letter 'g'.

It is a shame that she did not continue her search for Gurdjieff's sons. Although a prank meant to give Le Toumelin a shock, Gurdjieff apparently did have two sons in Tibet and likely wanted Le Toumelin to continue in this search. Then again, considering the accuracy of his prediction that Le Toumelin would go to Tibet in 21 years time, perhaps he even foresaw that her son would provide the author of this book with a photo of his son and complete her mission for her. After inquiring Shechen Monastery Archives about the photo of the Sixth Shechen Rabjam, it was Ricard who provided it. Regardless, she came to believe that Gurdjieff had never set foot in Tibet as a result. It reinforced her understanding of the way in which Gurdjieff liked to "play with reality" (as she put it). Also influencing her was her new teacher having told her to forget about it. In her view Gurdjieff paled compared to Kangyur Rinpoche and other great Tibetan masters she met. Afterall, Gurdjieff could not have disagreed. He himself is known to have said, "I am small man compared to those who sent me."[7]  So, she followed Kangyur Rinpoche's advice.

Another thing Gurdjieff asked of Le Toumelin is also worth mentioning. He also asked her to seek out someone named Yeshe Lama when she goes. But Yeshe, like Dorje, is also a common name. How could she possibly find the Yeshe who knew Gurdjieff? When you think about it, he could not possibly have expected her to find any such person. Remember that Gurdjieff foresaw her making her journey in 21 years time. Everyone in Tibet who Gurdjieff knew, except those he knew as children, would be long dead when Le Toumelin would eventually go. This appears to have been a part of the trick he played on her. Yet with Gurdjieff, there is always more to such tricks. In all likelihood, in his obtuse manner, Gurdjieff was asking Le Toumelin to become acquainted with the classic Dzogchen text by 18th century Nyingma master Jigme Lingpa titled *Yeshe Lama*. But Le Toumelin did not understand this; she was convinced Gurdjieff wanted her to find some lama he once knew. Even so, Le Toumelin never asked about Yeshe Lama. As far as she was concerned she had found the lama she was looking for. Still, it might be considered that she had found Yeshe Lama in the sense that Kangyur Rinpoche was very influenced by Patrul Rinpoche, an incarnation of Jigme Lingpa.

Kangyur Rinpoche was born in 1898, recognized as an emanation of Namkhai Nyingpo (who was one of Padmasambhava's close disciples), and given the name Longchen Yeshe Dorje. His root teacher was Jedrung Rinpoche of Riwoche monastery, which was one of the main proponents of the Rimé non-sectarian movement. Although he had a prominent post at Riwoche and contributed greatly to the life and practice there, he was inspired by the life of Patrul Rinpoche and felt the need to assume the life of a wandering hermit, to enable himself to do more humanitarian work. Having studied medicine at Riwoche, Kangyur Rinpoche was a skilled physician and sought ways to help the orphaned, the elderly, and the infirmed. (Le Toumelin's recommendation to the author that he read Patrul Rinpoche's book *The Words of My Perfect Teacher* no doubt came to her from Kangyur Rinpoche.)

Understanding the need to preserve their culture from Chinese devastation, the Dalai Lama asked Kangyur Rinoche to undertake an urgent mission—the safe transport to India of the Kangyur—a collection numbering over 100 of the foundational texts of the early schools of Buddhism, largely consisting of Shakyamuni Buddha's own words, in Tibetan language. The collection weighed over two tons, making the journey evermore time-consuming and arduous. Longchen Yeshe Dorje came to be known as Kangyur Rinpoche, not only because he accomplished this mission, but also because he gave transmission of this vast collection over two dozen times.

But teaching and assuring the safe delivery of the Kangyur is not the only way that Kangyur Rinpoche was interested in seeing the proliferation of the buddhadharma. He was also very interested in teaching Westerners, and a small group had already begun to meet with him by the time that Le Toumelin arrived.

In Darjeeling, Kangyur lived in a small two-room hut with his family. Le Toumelin found a place to stay near their hut but was soon invited to live with them. He had a practice routine that took up most the day and continued into the evening, and Le Toumelin joined him.

Only two weeks or so after they met, Le Toumelin left for Sikkim in order to renew her visa and take advantage of the trip to meet the Sixteenth Karmapa who was there at the time to conduct a retreat for a group of aspiring nuns at Rumtek Monastery. Le Toumelin evidently did not realize the purpose of the retreat she was joining. As she explains:

> At dawn a monk knocked on the door and said to me, "You will be ordained in an hour." I was very surprised but what to do? His Holiness Karmapa took me to his apartments where a thousand Buddhas were introduced to me: "Here is your family." This is how I returned to Paris with a shaved head, a Buddhist nun without knowing anything about Buddhism.[8]

The Karmapa gave her the name Karma Dolma Tsultrim, which loosely translates to "The Virtuous Action of the Mother of Liberation." Things were progressing rather quickly for Le Toumelin, as is often the case when working with such great masters.

Yet upon returning to France she found herself quite occupied with her art. So, she was not able to return to India to be under Kangyur's guidance for another two years. On her second trip Le Toumelin stayed in a hermitage, but was still able to practice with her teacher every day. At this point she had given up painting. This period of intensive practice lasted for four and a half years. Had Kangyur Rinpoche not died she would have remained longer. He passed away on January 23, 1975 and Le Toumelin returned to France shortly after the funeral ceremonies concluded 49 days later.

Later that year Kangyur Rinpoche's eldest son, Pema Wangyal Rinpoche, along with some of his father's French students, began creating a monastery in Dordogne—a department in the south of France—to continue his father's legacy and fulfill his wish to spread the buddhadharma in the West. Le Toumelin became a resident and Pema Wangyal settled there himself a few years later. In 1980 Dudjom Rinpoche and Dilgo Khyentse Rinpoche came at Pema Wangyal's invitation, and the Centre d'Études de Chanteloube was officially established by them. At this time Le Toumelin began serving as Dudjom Rinpoche's attendant. In addition to these rinpoches, Kangyur Rinpoche's other two sons, Rangdröl Rinpoche and Jigme Khyentse Rinpoche, were also teachers for her.

In working together, Dudjom Rinpoche encouraged Le Toumelin to return to painting. In doing so, however, she abandoned her earlier surrealist style, whose hellish themes seemed incongruent with her Buddhist path, and began painting abstract works with Buddhist themes.

Later, Dudjom Rinpoche also encouraged Le Toumelin to do a three-year retreat. After that retreat she spent a year in Bhutan at Dilgo Khyentse's invitation—another big practice commitment.

Returning from Bhutan, Le Toumelin lived primarily in Dordogne where she continued to paint. She passed away in 2023 just short of her 100<sup>th</sup> birthday, having been the last surviving direct student of Gurdjieff.

Although no suitable writings of Le Toumelin were found to include here, offered instead is an account of meeting Kangyur Rinpoche by her friend Arnaud Desjardins. In 1948 Desjardins met Madame de Salzmann who put him in a group led by Bernard Lemaitre in March of 1949, but he never had the opportunity to meet Gurdjieff before his death later that year. He remained in the group for 14 years before exploring other traditions. Although interested in a variety of teachings, Desjardins regarded Advaita master Swami Prajnanpad as his primary teacher, wrote many books on Advaita himself, and established an Advaita retreat center where he was head teacher. It was because of Kangyur Rinpoche's brief appearance in Desjardins' film *Message of the Tibetans* that Matthieu Ricard was inspired to meet the master. Yet the painting used for the dust jacket of this book, made by Le Toumelin, might also be considered a contribution of hers. And following Desjardins' account is a text from Kangyur Rinpoche himself on a subject so important to Gurdjieff and his followers—impermanence.

---

[1] Sophie Solère, "Yahne Le Toumelin: peindre l'unique lumière," Bouddha News, bouddhanews.fr/yahne-le-toumelin-peindre-lunique-lumiere.

[2] Private correspondence.

[3] Matthieu Ricard, *Yahne Le Toumelin: Lumière Rire du Ciel* (Paris: Éditions de La Martinière, 2016), 16.

[4] Private correspondence.

[5] Private correspondence.

[6] J.G. Bennett, *Gurdjieff: Making a New World* (New York: Harper & Row, 1973), 95.

[7] Solita Solano, et al., *Gurdjieff and the Women of the Rope* (London: Book Studio, 2012), 2.

[8] Sophie Solère, "Yahne Le Toumelin: peindre l'unique lumière," Bouddha News, bouddhanews.fr/yahne-le-toumelin-peindre-lunique-lumiere.

## MEDITATION WITH THE GURU

Regarding meeting with sages, and the shock which one can receive from it, I ought at once to state what one may expect from this shock or influence, and what are its limits. I think above all of my two meetings with Kangyur Rimpoche, a Nyingmapa whose young son speaks good English, and who lived at that time in the tiny *gompa* of Chhata Gong, at Lebong, near Darjeeling. It was the morning of the day of my departure from Darjeeling at the end of my second stay there, and Sonam and I were due to return to Kalimpong, where Dudjom Rinpoche was awaiting us. "There is still one great rinpoche whom we have not seen. Would you like to meet him before we leave?" Naturally I said that I would, and we went to find him, though that was no easy matter, in spite of the fact that Sonam speaks so many different languages and dialects.

What happened that morning and the next day went beyond even what one would expect or hope from the mysterious and fascinating legend which has always surrounded Tibetan lamas. We came, by way of a little wooden balcony which ran round all sides of a very modest house, to a room which was almost in darkness, and there took our seats before the couch, covered with rugs, which is to be found in all rinpoches' rooms. In the half-light I made out the shape of a man, sitting cross-legged, motionless, from whom came a kind of lucency, like an indefinable phosphorescence, and whose eyes appeared in the darkness to be luminous. I turned to Sonam, whose position near the little door on to the balcony illuminated him a little better. He was looking at the lama, but his eyes showed no particular brilliance. Then I turned again to Kangyur Rinpoche, and again I was aware of that same luminosity, and particularly of his eyes, which were as if lit up in the darkness. He was looking at me fixedly, and I was aware that an extraordinary and indescribable feeling was beginning to take hold of me. I was aware that Sonam was going out of the room, and after that it seemed to me that nothing existed in the world save that presence in the shadows and myself. The intensification and acceleration of the whole of my psychic existence, of all my thoughts and emotions, was beyond all description. All memories, mental images, possibilities, were present at once. I had ten, a hundred brains which were all working at the same time. Perhaps people who have believed they were drowning and afterwards claim to have re-lived their whole lives in a few seconds have a somewhat similar experience. I was able to follow ten lines of thought at once, at once live through ten remembered situations (remembered now, but at other times how totally forgotten!) Then all inward functioning came to a stop, but this was neither unconsciousness nor the blank associated with a fainting-fit. Indeed consciousness, wakefulness was absolute; this was to know the true silence "beyond the mind," which transcends thought and individuality, names and forms, time and space, and above all, duality.

Afterwards Sonam simply said, "I saw you were in deep meditation with the guru and I left the room;" and pointed out that what he called "meditation with the guru" lasted for nearly an hour. Wanting to confirm my opinion of Kangyur Rinpoche, I persuaded Sonam to put off our departure for a day. The next morning exactly the same thing happened, an experience as intense and of the same length, and one whose effect was to last for several days and leave me only gradually. To disappear completely? No; for the memory, the imprint of this experience (or others of the same order) are ineffaceable. But it is no less true that that exceptional state, that level of consciousness, does not last. Suddenly comes the thought, "I am living at this moment through a sublime, a miraculous, experience," and at once all is lost.

This glimpse of Realization owed nothing to me, and everything to the guru. Then why not drugs, LSD, or mescaline?

It was an experience which can never be forgotten. But the Tibetans know, and teach, that such exceptionally conscious moments, which their gurus have the power consciously to arouse in their disciples, have value only as a call, a sign, like the beam of a lighthouse on a foggy night. This experience is only a loan, something borrowed which has to be paid back, only the reaction of the individual to a combination of outside influences, not the manifestation of a freedom which he has conquered for himself. It is the teacher who is already free, not his pupil. The master is the virtuoso, the pupil the instrument on which he plays. The master is the Light, and the disciple reflects only as much of it as he is given. May he in turn become the source of Life, the conscious manifestation of Reality!

That no one else can become for him. It is true that many disciples, whether Hindus, Tibetans or Europeans, seek to live their disciplines at the expense of their teacher's Realization, to shine with their light, to be still with their stillness. But that will not take them one step forward on the way to the independence and autonomy whose aim is Liberation and Freedom itself. Are you awakening, you who sleep? What awakening? Why awaken? How awaken? To these three questions Tibetan tantrism can certainly help one to reply.

But whatever may be the powers of the great sages and the value of certain transcendent experiences, the serious study of Tibetan spirituality and esotericism is not a romantic and mysterious enterprise pursued, as so many European dreamers whom I have met try to persuade themselves, in a supernatural world of magic and of outlandish phenomena. On the contrary, it is a series of problems requiring to be solved day by day, and a discipline requiring to be observed every day and without flinching. These things demand feet well planted on the solid earth, the determination not to tell oneself lies, and the ability to keep in view what actually is, even if, indeed especially if, that is not what one expected, imagined or hoped.

*Arnaud Desjardins*

## IMPERMANENCE

It is written in the *Condensed Prajnaparamita-sutra:*

Wind arises grounded upon space.
On this the mass of water stands,
And thereupon, the earth, the ground of living beings.

Phenomenal existence, as this appears to deluded perception, consists of the three-thousandfold universe: an inanimate basis or vessel together with the beings that are its animate contents. This universe passes through a sequence of formation, duration, destruction, and voidness. Each of these phases lasts for twenty intermediate kalpas, and the eighty taken together make up one great kalpa. A single universe, which is the impermanent environment of living beings, comprises four continents situated around Mount Meru with its celestial abodes of the desire realm and the pure realm of form. A thousand of such universes make up a so-called thousandfold universe. A thousand of these form an intermediary universe, and these yet again multiplied by a thousand comprise what is known as the "great three-thousandfold universe." In Tibetan, the word for universe, *jigten,* is a pejorative term, since it means "basis of decay." It is so called because, from the moment it comes into being, decay and death are intrinsic to it. One could almost say that the world and its inhabitants are tormented and punished by these four phases of formation, duration, destruction, and voidness. Indeed, the root verse specifies that there will be seven destructions by fire and one by water. As the *Anityartha-parikatha* says:

> Then the earth will be destroyed,
> Then the mountains will collapse in dust,
> And all the waters of the seas run dry—
> No need to mention, then, the fate of living beings.

Because they see that ordinary beings entertain false views, imputing permanent existence to what is composite and fleeting, the Buddhas, foremost among the living, and teachers of gods and humankind, display their joyful passing into nirvana, even though they possess the supreme and adamantine form, the Dharmakaya, that is immune to decay. They relinquish their capacity to remain forever, untouched and unmarred by the passage of time. Therefore, if Buddhas themselves are impermanent, is there any need to doubt the transience of ordinary beings whose lives are as fragile as bubbles?

Some beings perfect the four worldly samadhis and the different levels of absorption. As a result, they can sustain the burden of a life span ranging from an intermediate kalpa in the heaven of the Pure, up to eighty thousand great kalpas at the Peak of Existence. But even this falls short of the goal of permanent happiness. Even beings like these must follow the effects of their white and black actions and without a doubt will come to die. Brahma, Ishvara, Shiva, Vishnu, and the other gods who possess supernatural knowledge and miraculous powers, together with all the Chakravartins—even they are disappointed in their bliss, for they know of no way to escape the demon Lord of Death. What need is there to speak of people like ourselves?

To enjoy perfect happiness and pleasure in the higher realms of samsara is to be like the deer roaming wild and free for the three months of summer in a landscape filled with wholesome plants and flowers. But just as the hunter lies in wait, hidden from sight in a gully on the mountainside, thinking constantly of how to kill them, the robber Lord of Death, with his deadly club in his hand, thinks of one thing only: how he might draw beings into the snare of death and steal away their lives. As Ashvaghosha has written:

Of all those born upon this earth
Or in the upper realms,
Did you see, or hear, or even doubt,
That some were born and have not died?

People are tormented by the heat of early summer and cannot bear to go out in the sun. They long for the cool light of the autumn moon, but they do not worry, in fact the thought never crosses their minds, that with the arrival of autumn, a hundred days of their lives will have passed and brought them nearer to their deaths.

People also mourn at the deaths of others, without reflecting that the Lord of Death is advancing upon them as well. They spend their time immersed in the hopes and fears of life as though they were going to live forever. This is so foolish!

As it is said in the *Anityartha-parikatha:*

To enter on the path of life
Adds nothing to your length of days,
And death is not a flaw within the scheme of things.
Why therefore do you sorrow at it so?

Imagine that four giants, tremendously strong, stand back to back and each shoots an arrow directly in front of him; it would be a quick man indeed who could run round and catch them all before they fell to earth! Yet even quicker are the pretas that move over the earth, propelled by the miraculous force that is the fruit of their karma. Faster than the earth-bound pretas are the pretas that move through the air, and even faster are the chariots of the sun and moon, while the swiftest of all are the divine beings who move miraculously through the strength of their merit. Yet quicker than all of these is the passing of this human life!

The body of a man or woman still growing to early adulthood is magnificent and strong. But in due course, their constitution begins to falter, and it is as if they are being punished by the scourge of old age. When the four elements[1] are bal-

295

anced, all is well, but then illness strikes and torments both body and mind. It may be that, for the moment, thanks to positive actions done in the past and the coincidental effect of favorable conditions, people experience great happiness and the pleasure of companions, wealth, fame, and so forth. But "since all that meets must separate, and all that is accumulated drains away," all of this will decline. When the momentum of this life is lost, or when certain untimely circumstances occur, death in all its dreadfulness will throw itself upon them without delay. This is described with many examples in the *Rajavavadaka-sutra*.

When the time of death comes, our much-cherished bodies are overthrown in the struggle with the Lord of Death. Even Vajrapani can give us no protection, and we plunge into the abyss of hopeless suffering. At that time, the provisions of this life mean nothing anymore, and the glow of youth fades and withers like a flower in the frost. The five sense faculties fail and cease to function, like a flame blown out by the wind. No medicine can soothe the pain of the cutting of the thread of life. Even if the universal remedy were to hand, it would be to no avail; and even doctors as skillful as Jivakakumara[2] must turn away from such patients who look at them with eyes wide and staring with terror. There is nothing to be done. When the energy that imparts movement to the body begins to decline, there comes complete exhaustion and paralysis, and as it begins to flow abnormally, the limbs shudder and twitch. Respiration is difficult, and the rattling of the breath is short and feeble. All around the family stands—father, mother, friends, and kin. Everyone is sobbing and lamenting, pleading with their loved one not to leave them. But the hook of their prayers can find no purchase. The dying person starts to gasp as respiration becomes increasingly shallow, fine like a strand of horsehair. And then the ruthless Lord of Death severs it with the edge of his sharp ax. In that instant, the bloom and beauty of life vanishes, the face becomes livid, the eyes fill with tears, and as the skin of the face is stretched toward the back of the skull, the mouth opens and the teeth become visible in the grinning rictus of death. The thick darkness of the bardo of becoming comes to meet the dying, and they are driven from behind by the cyclonic wind of karma. They must pass through many terrifying hallucinations. Six uncertainties will come about: those of location, resting place, behavior, sustenance, companions, and mental state. Then there will be the three dreadful abysses of hatred, desire, and confusion, white as ash, dark red, and black. Four dreadful sounds will occur. As the energy of the earth element reemerges, a roar will be heard as of collapsing mountains; as the energy of the fire element reemerges, there will be the sound of blazing forests; as the energy of the water element reemerges, there will be the crashing of tumultuous seas; and as the energy of the air element reemerges, there will be the shrieking of a gale like the winds of the end of time.[3]

From now on, may the thought of our impermanence spur us on!

*Kangyur Rinpoche*

---

[1] The body is said to be composed of the elements of earth, air, fire, and water, corresponding to the principles of solidity, movement, warmth, and liquidity. To these is added space, without which the others could not exist. When equilibrium between the elements is lost, a disease occurs.

[2] 'tsho byed gzhon nu, the most celebrated physician in the time of the Buddha.

[3] For a detailed description of the bardo state, see *The Mirror of Mindfulness* by Tsele Natsok Rangdrol.

*Paul Beidler making measurements on Meydum pyramid, 1930*

## Maverick

Paul Henry Beidler was introduced to the ideas of Gurdjieff while studying architecture at Frank Lloyd Wright's Taliesin Fellowship. He had enrolled in the fall of 1933 and began studying and practicing Gurdjieff's teaching under the guidance of the acclaimed architect's wife, Olgivanna. Before meeting Wright she had spent time at Gurdjieff's Institute, and the program developed at Taliesin was largely influenced by her experience there.

As a result, Beidler met Gurdjieff himself when he visited Taliesin the following summer. They developed something of a friendship and enjoyed going to the movies together. At this early stage Beidler was not entirely invested in the Work; it was more thrust upon him. But Gurdjieff evidently saw potential in him, gave him attention, and in doing so sowed some seeds that would sprout later.

Gurdjieff was particularly impressed that Beidler had been initiated into the Yezidi sect while studying the Kurds (of whom the Yezidis are an ethnic minority) of Iraq and Turkey as part of the archeology program he was enrolled in at the University of Pennsylvania, and had seriously studied and practiced that tradition during his two years there. The two men often discussed the Yezidis as well as other cultures of the East. Of particular note is Gurdjieff telling Beidler of a certain esoteric group situated somewhere in the Gobi desert, and encouraging him to make contact with them—a feat Beidler claims to have accomplished.

Perhaps it was because of his interest in the Yezidis—a little known tradition, especially at that time—that Gurdjieff gave him the name Maverick. Certainly Beidler was not your typical Quaker American and approached his pursuits in an unconventional manner.

In 1946 Beidler purchased Northeon Forest—a tree farm and nature reserve near Easton, Pennsylvania. There he made a home for his family and a base for his architecture practice. Sometime during the following year he began commuting to Mendham, New Jersey regularly on the weekends to work with Madame Ouspensky's group at Franklin Farms. By this point he was clearly more invested in Gurdjieff's teaching. Beidler continued to work with Madame Ouspensky's group until moving to Iraq in 1954.

Before moving to Iraq, however, he is known to have made a trip to Mexico to help Rodney Collin Smith establish his Work group there. Surely Beidler would have been interested in the surrounding archeology. He wrote an article about an expedition to Belize made in December 1950 to survey the Mayan sites,[1] and no doubt was also interested in the Aztec sites of Mexico.

He also helped establish the Gurdjieff Foundation in 1953 and served on its board of directors until his move overseas. But he would have left the Foundation despite the move, having been disillusioned by the direction in which the organization was heading.

The move to Iraq was the result of a position he accepted with the State Department. He was a diplomat whose role was offering engineering advice to the various countries in which he was stationed. Iraq was but the first of many.

The following year he was visited by his friend John Bennett to make a road trip to Persia to visit the Babylonian ruins and meet some highly regarded Dervishes. The Beidlers had made a stopover in London on their move to Iraq and likely visited the Bennetts then too. In the late 1950s Beidler participated in the Subud groups of Tokyo, Singapore and

Yogyakarta while stationed there. As he mentions in one of his letters, "John Bennett had found it about a year ago and has pursued it ever since, in preference to the G. system."[2] Beidler is also known to have visited Bennett's Coombe Springs estate sometime around 1962. Possibly they first met when Madame Ouspensky and Madame de Salzmann invited Bennett to give a series of lectures in New York in 1952 to launch the Gurdjieff Foundation. Whatever the case may be, Beidler and Bennett evidently were quite close, for Beidler was asked by Elizabeth Bennett to take over the leadership of the Claymont College for Continuous Education—Bennett's Gurdjieff school—after Mr Bennett died in 1974. Beidler, however, declined, feeling he was too occupied with his own Gurdjieff school to give it proper attention. In 1973 the school he called The Search at Northeon Forest was established on his land in Pennsylvania. Besides the Northeon Forest group, Beidler had several satellite groups under his directorship. He was already too overextended to accept Mrs Bennett's offer.

Before establishing The Search at Northeon Forest, Beidler spent some 25 years in Asia, having lived in several different countries there. No doubt he accepted the position with the State Department in good part to explore many of Asia's spiritual traditions. Besides Subud, he is also known to have studied Taoism and a contemporary indigenous religion of southwest Japan called Odoru Shukyo (meaning "Dancing Religion"), from whom he learned their "non-ego dance." However, he seems to have been drawn to the study and practice of Buddhism most of all. Writing home from Bangkok he once remarked, "I am feeling more and more rootless which is as you know so desired by Zen itinerant monks."[3] This may have been another intention of accepting a position that gave him the opportunity to travel.

While living in Japan he was ordained as a Zen monk. It is unclear who he was ordained by, but in a 1958 letter he mentions having worked with Ruth Sasaki for a month and possibly continuing work with her later on. A Zen text in particular that moved him was the Diamond Sutra, as he recommended the text to his own students. (As a side note, the

Diamond Sutra is common to Tibetan Buddhism.) He also sat in meditation with sanghas in other Buddhist countries such as Vietnam and Cambodia. Also significant is that in 1972, a year before returning to the U.S.A., he leased Northeon Forest to some disciples of Gosung Shin, a Zen master of the Korean Chogye sect. At the time Gosung Shin was teaching religion at Lehigh University, and it may have been through the university network that he made contact with Beidler, who taught architectural design there earlier in his career. For a few years the Zen sangha and the Gurdjieff group coexisted on the property, and while they were distinct groups, the two often practiced together.

In the late 1960s and early 1970s he was a resident at Wat Pa Pong—a monastery of the Forest Tradition of Theravada Buddhism in northern Thailand—where he was again ordained as a monk. Significantly, Ajahn Chah, the abbot of Wat Pa Pong, had a profound appreciation for Gurdjieff. In working with his students, Beidler often read from Ajahn Chah's writings, particularly *A Still Forest Pool*.

Also of note is that while in Hong Kong, Beidler studied with Charles Luk, the respected author and translator of many of the English language's first publications on Zen. But Luk also practiced and taught Taoism, and Beidler only mentions having learned some Taoist practices from him. He was probably introduced to Luk by Hugh Ripman who made contact with Luk himself, and who Beidler surely knew from his time at Franklin Farms.

Yet it seems appropriate to bring up another tradition that Luk was familiar with—Tibetan Buddhism. Luk's first teacher was actually a Tibetan Buddhist who he refers to as the Khutuktu of Xikang. "Khutuktu" is the Mongolian word for tulku—a word often adopted as a title by Tibetan Buddhist teachers—and Xikang is the province of the former Republic of China which occupied much of present day Kham. While western Kham is comprised primarily of ethnic Tibetans, eastern Kham is more ethnically diverse and includes an ethnic Mongolian population. Unfortunately, it is difficult to know exactly who Luk is referring to with such an ambiguous title.

302

Regardless, it is interesting that Luk specifically mentions having learned from him the practice of *phowa* , or "transference of consciousness."

Although primarily acquainted with the Forest Tradition and Zen, there was one work in particular of Tibetan Buddhism that Beidler greatly appreciated and recommended to his students—*The Way of the Bodhisattva* by Shantideva. A bodhisattva is one who vows to help others awaken before awakening oneself, and this text gives great insight into what Gurdjieff refers to as *the fifth striving,* which he formulates as, "the striving always to assist the most rapid perfecting of other beings, both those similar to oneself and those of other forms..."

Although only peripherally related to Tibetan Buddhism, there is another "trip" that Beidler went on which is of interest. It involved another excursion to Mexico, this one in May and June of 1963. He was the unnamed architect who took part in the first and only group of the Zihuatanejo Project—a psychedelic retreat center founded by Timothy Leary and Richard Alpert (later known as Ram Das) which was subsequently shut down by the authorities. It should be noted that the retreat was not for recreational psychedelic users. Most of the participants were involved in one or another spiritual tradition and interested in the potential that LSD had as a supplement to their practices. There is no indication that Beidler continued LSD usage after his participation in the project. The way in which the retreat relates to Tibetan Buddhism is that *The Tibetan Book of the Dead* was used as a model for the project's session manual. In this sense, Beidler not only studied the bardo teachings, but, more significantly, acquired an experiential understanding of them.[4]

What follows is a prose-poem of Beidler's that demonstrates some Buddhist influence. It was originally written as an untitled Northeon Forest program for April 12, 1992 and later included in his privately issued *Adventures in Awareness*. And after that is the chapter "Sangha Life" from Gosung Shin's book, *Zen Teaching of Emptiness*. What he says on sangha is very much in line with Gurdjieff's teachings on group work.

[1] Paul Beidler, "An Architect in Mayaland," *Natural History* 61, no. 10 (December 1952), 440–45, 473–74.

[2] From a collection of excerpts of letters Beidler sent to his first wife Margaret, shared with the author by his daughter.

[3] Ibid.

[4] Beidler's participation in the project was discovered in a letter to him from Margaret Beidler (his first wife) dated February 20, 1965. In it she tells him that she was reading a fascinating book called *Utopiates* when she was reminded of his participation, and "made me realize why you were so remote from all the family that summer." It is in Chapter 8 of *Utopiates* that the Zihuatanejo Project is discussed.

Also of note is that it may very well have been Beidler who introduced Leary and Alpert to the Gurdjieff teaching.

Press photo of Paul Beidler.

## STRIVING

An ascetic in a forest lamasery disclosed that transubstantiation for being what we are began with striving for celestial comprehension with interludes of deliberate mindfulness gained by draining the mind of lassitude and pointing a ray of illumination into the crevices of one's innermost core.

Striving became intensified in a hilly terrain pulsing with insight beyond plan or caprice.

Harmony in a wilderness of stillness was tuned by woodsmen who had heard the wind strumming thru trees like witches dancing in minuets and elegies.

Cacophonous undertones of discord, regret and tears precluded such fervent fugues of arrogance, conceit and curiosity.

A strummer of modern time defines petty laments as an assortment of negative views, jealous suspicions, unwarranted lies, specious reprisals and feigned sincerity.

Learned widows endure their thorny weeds when tormented by these tenants of their former jungles.

Earth plays the role of a lodestone attracting the interment of residue from worthless lives of appetites that curb natural I-am-ness.

On a dead-end excursion of no return, bards choraled an epic respect for death trimmed with awe, wariness and fear.

Dedicated to the raising of levels of awareness, seekers share the warmth of vertical relationships.

So as to ignite a spark of turbulence in their cage of somnolence, alert seekers often dramatized provocative gestures with tones of wit, empathy or memory despite symptoms of empty talk, malice and rancor.

But don't worry! Smile, bide your time!

Ways can be found to emulate those rare savants who in solitude quietly charted a path through a maze of anguish.

Fate may be swayed to favor those rangers who harken to a voice deep within urging penance for the tremors of transubstantiation in them for having been what they were.

A sachem in time to come will propose authentic ways to arrest the stealthy creep toward Erewhon.

Methods will be found for seekers to participate in more vital formulas for work on themselves and to conduct their lives in a search for the magic of mindfulness on changing from what they are to what they are striving to become.

*Paul Beidler*

## Sangha Life

Every form of relationship in this world is an expression of sangha, or community. Right now, at this very moment, we are intimately connected with all sentient beings, and we are friendly with everything around us—the cushions that we are sitting on, the lamp by which we see each other, the radiator that warms us, and so on, endlessly. Sangha life means to harmonize oneself, whether it be with one or with millions of beings, depending on one's individual karma. When people organize into small groups, these small sanghas or harmonious groupings may in turn be organized into a greater whole, such as, for example, exists in grouping together the Chogye sect of Korean Buddhism with the Rinzai and Soto sects of Buddhism in Japan, or of the American Buddhist sangha with that of the entire Asian continent.

In human life, it is almost impossible to make one's way without some form of interpersonal cooperation. It is very difficult for a single individual to provide all of his basic necessities by himself. When people form communities, the basic necessities of food, clothing, and shelter are easily provided for each individual by the principle of division of labor, thus allowing more time to practice meditation.

If someone wishes to ease his suffering mind by practicing meditation, then it will be of great advantage to him, especially at the beginning, to practice meditation with a group of people, in a sangha. Being alone, it would be very difficult for him to train his body and mind. But within a group, where everyone follows the same way of practice, it will be much easier for him to work on himself by practicing together with others, so that, for example, when everyone gets up early in the morning to sit zazen, he also has to get up, since otherwise people would be very upset with him. In this way, he will be able to develop his practice by keeping in step with the practice of others, thereby reducing the dangers of falling into laziness or arrogance, which can occur when one tries to practice by oneself. Also, he will be able to see when his mind is wandering, because it will be reflected in actions that are not in harmony with the mind of the sangha.

Sangha is more than just an expedient for strengthening one's practice; it is the source and the very expression of wisdom. There is a story about Buddha Shakyamuni asking one of his disciples, "How much of what you know did you learn from your friends?" One disciple answered, "One half." Buddha shook his head, "No." Another disciple answered, "Two thirds." Again, Buddha said, "Not correct." Then, a very bright disciple answered, "Everything I know I have learned from my friends." Buddha said, "Yes, that's right."

From the first moment of our lives on this earth, we are dependent on the aid of our friends, and we learn everything we know from our friends who are our parents, brothers and sisters, close friends and acquaintances. Family is included as friends, because mother is mother, but she is also, very deeply, your friend. The sangha carries forward this most basic human fact for the well-being of all who are its members. One little chopstick by itself is easy to break, but when it is in a bundle of chopsticks it cannot be so easily broken. It might be possible to break the practice of one person who has faith in the Buddhist life but does not have any help to carry it out; but when a group practices together, they are not so easy to disrupt.

It is not only, Buddhist communities that are sanghas; societies and countries are sanghas too. But when societies make war among themselves, and between other societies, then they are not sanghas, but asuras (packs of demons). When society lives in harmony with itself and others, then we call it a sangha, because its collective goal in life is to stay free from suffering. When the members of a society accumulate individual knowledge, which is based on ignorance of their true selves, then no matter how much technical progress that a society reaps as a result, the society as a whole will be very weak, and out of balance. But if there is one person in that society who is very bright and knows without any shadow of ignorance where he came from, and where he is going, then the whole society can grow because of him. In the same way, when one member of a sangha has good knowledge, then the whole sangha can grow with him, like ivy climbing up a tall tree. As tall as the tree is, the ivy can grow. Living alone in this world, without any help from others, can only lead to suffering. But if someone lives alone, and is able to meditate seriously, then we can say that though he is physically alone, he is actually part of the sangha, because he is working on the same thought, and has the same goal as other members of the sangha. Even if he never sees anyone else, he is really and truly united with all of his fellow meditators, and with the entire universe as well.

Bodhisattvas love to gather in places where the truth of existence is studied and practiced. That is why in each sangha dwelling or meditation hall, there is a special spiritual power that is a result of the efforts of the sangha to know and to testify to the truth of the dharma. Anyone who steps into this meditation hall, or zendo, will be able to feel this spiritual power which is the great blessing of the sangha. Though atmosphere is intangible, it is also a very real and solid thing. Even if one does not know how to practice the right way, should he step into such a place, he would feel somehow better for it, as if his cloudy mind were being penetrated by light.

During sesshin (periods of intensive meditation), when sangha members meditate together for eight, ten, fourteen, sometimes twenty-four hours a day, a tremendous momentum of spiritual energy carries everyone forward as one unit, making it possible for everyone to have great progress in their individual practice. This is because such practice is already the accomplishment of true dharma—the unification of one with the many, and many with the one. At this time, bodhisattvas come there to bless them, and they receive great spirits, directly and indirectly, into their being. It is very difficult for anyone to leave in the middle of a sesshin; it is almost like trying to jump out of a fast-moving truck, and the consequences may be equally as bad. At least he will feel bad for such an action. It is as if he were being kicked out by bodhisattva and dharma protectors for his bad attitude. So, anyone who joins a sesshin must do so with a serious attitude of mind to contribute as much as he can to the good practice of the entire group, which is no different from his true self.

*Gosung Shin*

"Sangha Life," taken from *Zen Teaching of Emptiness* by Gosung Shin (Washington: American Zen College Press, 1982, copyright © Gosung Shin, is reproduced here with his permission.

*John G. Bennett at Lyne Place*

## Mr Hazard

John G. Bennett met Ouspensky and then Gurdjieff while he was serving for the British Intelligence in Turkey in 1921. Later that year, after returning home, he joined the London group of Ouspensky, who had immigrated there. Bennett remained in the group until Ouspensky moved to the U.S.A. in January of 1941, and, significantly, also spent three months at Gurdjieff's Institute in 1923. After Ouspensky's death he learned that Gurdjieff was still alive and working with students in Paris, and commuted regularly to Paris to work with him from 1948 until his death in 1949.

Bennett first began leading groups of his own in 1930, at first sending reports to Ouspensky for review. The group was formalized in 1946 as a nonprofit called the Institute for the Comparative Study of History, Philosophy and the Sciences, and the Coombe Springs estate was purchased as a Work residence. When he began working with Gurdjieff again, he took a few prepared group members with him each trip.

Gurdjieff instructed Bennett to oversee the Work in all of England, and after Gurdjieff's death he did so under Madame de Salzmann's guidance. But because of disagreements with her he began to work independently of the international organization that de Salzmann was forming.

Over the years Bennett introduced a variety of traditions to supplement the teaching he had received from Gurdjieff and was passing on to his groups. Because he had somehow gotten the idea that Gurdjieff had initiated in the Yesevi sect of Sufism, there was something of a focus on Sufism and Islam in general. Yet it is impossible that Gurdjieff was involved with the Yesevi as that particular sect had died out centuries ago. Although Bennett was constantly revising his ideas and spoke of uncertainty in terms of what he referred to as "hazard", many of his followers have taken such implausible theories of his as fact. Another such theory he promoted was that of an impending ice age. Bennett knew well the value of retaining an element of uncertainty regarding any understanding one may have. Otherwise they just feed one's ego.

At any rate, in 1966 Bennett donated Coombe Springs to Sufi teacher Indries Shah with the understanding that their two schools would unite, but Shah sold the property instead and chaos ensued amongst Bennett's people. It was not until 1971 that Bennett decided to return to a Gurdjieffian focus, purchased Sherborne House, and established the International Academy for Continuous Education there for the purpose. An American branch, the Claymont Society for Continuous Education, was founded shortly before Bennett's death in 1974.

Another reason that Bennett likely had for focusing on the Sufi roots of Gurdjieff's teaching was that his ability to speak Turkish enabled him to travel in the Near East and meet with various masters there. Indries Shah was not the only Sufi master he worked with. Yet Buddhism was actually the first of Gurdjieff's influences that he explored, and quite seriously too.

Inspired by his studies with Ouspensky, in 1922 Bennett began studying Sanskrit and Pali at the School of Oriental Studies so that he would be able to understand Hindu and Buddhist texts in their original languages. He also studied these languages and particularly Buddhist scripture with Caroline Rhys Davids, a Buddhist nun who, together with her husband Thomas Rhys Davids, were among the first to translate Buddhist texts to English. He moreover became a member of the Central Asian Society to learn about other aspects of these Eastern cultures. As Bennett himself recounts:

Ouspensky's meetings occupied three or four evenings every week, and during the day I worked either at the School of Oriental Studies or the British Museum Library. I became one of those silent figures that wait for the library to open, collect an enormous pile of books that have been reserved overnight, and settle down for the day to read and make notes.[1]

Much later, in February of 1950, Bennett gave a talk at the Buddhist Society comparing the Theravada concept of mind body (also called the mental body) with Gurdjieff's understanding of the soul. However, it seems that the talk did not go very well. One reason for this was that Bennett's presentation was unnecessarily confrontational. Although the study presented had merit, instead of allowing the affinity discussed to evoke a sense of shared belief and brotherhood, he referred to Buddhism as a "dead system" and expressed his opinion that Gurdjieff's teaching was more appropriate for their culture.

The other reason may be that in the discussion that followed the talk, poet and senior society member Cyril Moore took the place of their bhikkhu who was ill. Had the bhikkhu been present he may have handled Bennett more diplomatically. However, Moore, evidently taking offense, decided to take Bennett to the task and negate the merits of his study.

Perhaps Bennett's disappointment with the outcome of his lecture is why he abandoned this Buddhist line of research and shifted to a focus on Sufism instead. Even if so, he frequently brought up Buddhist ideas in talks to his groups and gave exercises based on Buddhist concepts such as emptiness.

In the early 1970s, however, he was persuaded to give Buddhism another go when he was introduced to the teaching of Bhante Dharmawara—a Theravada monk from Cambodia. As his son Ben Bennett recounts:

> The way Bhante came into our lives was via Michael Sutton, who was a pupil of J. G. B. in the early '60s and was kicked out when he became a dysfunctional junkie. After several years of his destructive self-abuse, J. G. B. made a rescue bid and sent Michael to India to break his Jones. There after two years of wandering, Michael met Bhante at

the Mission[2] and formed a strong connection. He returned to the U.K. about six months before Sherborne started and told J.G.B. all about his life with Bhante. About halfway through the first Sherborne course, J.G.B. told Michael that he had received an occult message from Bhante. About six months later, in December 1972, J.G.B. was invited to India to speak at a Symposium to celebrate the 100th anniversary of Shri Aurobindo in Delhi.... He took this opportunity to go to Bhante's mission and it was love at first sight. Bhante accepted an invitation to come to Sherborne the following summer with Sam St. Clair Ford as his attendant.[3]

Before establishing his Asoka Mission, Bhante had practiced with and ordained in the Forest Tradition in Thailand. This is the same tradition that Bennett's good friend Paul Beidler had ordained in, and it is likely that Beidler had recommended Bhante to Bennett. After his monastic training, Bhante studied traditional medicine in Burma and India, and upon finishing his studies established the Asoka Mission to provide medical treatment to those in need. This is why Bennett sent Sutton there in particular. Also regarding his healing ability, Bhante himself expressed regret that Bennett did not ask him for treatment. Although he felt strongly that Bennett's condition was treatable using his methods, he knew Bennett was seeing a Western doctor and did not want to interfere. (Bennett died in December of 1974.) In 1975 Bhante emigrated to the U.S.A., the following year he established Vatt Buddhikarma in Silver Spring Maryland, and in 1979 Wat Dharawararama in Stockton, California.

Bhante was invited to give talks yearly at Sherborne between 1973 and 1976. He was also invited to give talks and lead retreats at Claymont and affiliated groups in later years. In his first talk at Sherborne, one of the subjects that Bhante brings up is how the idea of three forces is discussed in different traditions.

To give a feel for Bhante's style and understanding, presented here is an excerpt from one of his talks to the Claymont Society. But first is an account of Bennett's talk to the Buddhist

316

Society that was published in their journal, *The Middle Way.* Although it was not quite a success, his study remains an interesting one.

[1] J.G. Bennett, *Witness: The Story of a Search* (London: Hodder and Stoughton, 1962), 106.

[2] The Asoka Mission founded by Bhante in New Delhi.

[3] Personal correspondence.

## GURDJIEFF AND THE BUDDHIST MIND-BODY

Mr J.G. Bennett, in a public address sponsored by the Buddhist Society at Caxton Hall on February 22nd [1950], took the exposition of Gurdjieff's idea of "soul" where he had left it in his book,[1] relating that idea to the description of the way the "mind body" is acquired in the Samannaphala Sutra. The idea was further expounded by Mr Bennett in a discussion-meeting a week later when he related this "soul" or "mind body" to the "spirit body" of *The Secret of the Golden Flower*.

Cyril Moore, at the public meeting the following week, when he took the place of the Bhikkhu who was ill, went further into the question of "mind bodies," "formless bodies" and supernormal powers and explained why, in his opinion the Buddha rejected such bodies on the path to Enlightenment.

The Gurdjieff system, as Mr Bennett explained it, started from the idea that man consists only of physical components destined for obliteration at death, unless he had by his own exertions made for himself a "soul". The way to achieve this "soul" was similar to that described in the *Majjhima-Nikaya* and the *Digha-Nikaya* where the bhikkhus were told to become mindful and self-possessed; mindful by bringing into consciousness every operation of the body; self-possessed by following the method of the sutras for the attainment of the *jhanas*. By breathing and concentration the body and mind could be stilled and poised and the devotee, after purging the mind of the five hindrances as described in the *Samannaphala Sutra*, was prepared to embark upon the deeper meditations:

> The bhikkhu chooses some lonely spot to rest on his way—in the woods, at the foot of a tree, on a hillside, in a mountain glen, in a rocky cave, in a charnel place, or on a heap of straw in the open field. And returning thither after his round for alms he seats himself, when his meal is done, cross-legged, keeping his body erect, and his intelligence alert, intent. Putting away harkening after external things, he remains with a heart that hankers not, and purifies his mind of worldly thoughts. Putting away from him the corruption of the wish to injure, he remains with a heart free from ill-will and purifies his mind of malevolent thoughts. Putting away torpor of heart and mind, he awakens his heart and purifies his mind of lazy thoughts. Putting away uncertainty, he makes his heart steady and purifies his mind of doubting thoughts. Just so long as these five hindrances are not put away within him, the bhikkhu looks upon himself as in debt, diseased, in prison, in slavery, lost on a desert road. But when these five hindrances have been put away within him, he looks upon himself as freed from debt, rid of disease, out of jail, a free man, and secure.

In that condition the bhikkhu experienced in succession the bliss of the *first jhana*, and ecstacy of meditation, the bliss born of detachment; the *second jhana*, and the bliss of concentration; the *third jhana*, with its bliss that is apart from active joy; and finally the *fourth jhana*, a state of mind completely detached from pleasure or pain, joy or sorrow. It was in this calm and collected state that the devotee realized the perishable nature of the physical body and bent his mind to the creation of a mind-made body.

> With his heart thus serene, made pure, translucent, cultured, devoid of evil, supple, ready to act, firm and imperturbable, he applies and bends down his attention to the calling up from this body of another body, having form, made of mind, having all the physical body's limbs and parts, not deprived of any organ. Just, O king, as if a man were to pull out a reed from its sheath. He would know: This is the reed, this is the sheath. The reed is one thing, the sheath another.

It is from the sheath that the reed has been drawn forth.

This process corresponded exactly to that by which, in Gurdjieff's system, a second body was made. Such a body, Mr Bennett claimed, would be able to withstand death and would have the supernormal powers man needed.

Mr Bennett, at each meeting, laid stress on the fact that he was not interested in mere philosophical speculation, or the study of a dead system, but in a system practical to-day. It was because the terms and conditions of Gurdjieff's system were those of to-day that he followed Gurdjieff instead of Buddhism.

Cyril Moore said he was going to attempt to answer Mr Bennett's challenge, for challenge it was to the Schools and exponents of Buddhism today. Why, he asked, was it that although in the *Samannaphala Sutra* and in other parts of the *Digha-Nikaya*, from which that sutra was taken, the Buddha spoke of the way a man made his physical body, his mind-made body and even beyond that could make a formless body, and he also explained the acquirement of marvelous supernormal powers, yet these subjects and the way to realize those powers were neither practiced nor discussed among Buddhists today—at least as far as we could hear or read in the West?

For those who wished to develop all their powers there were many active schools available. The western methods of physical culture, as exemplified by the Swedish or rhythmical systems, were perhaps primitive in their objects and methods; the Theosophical analysis of man into physical, etheric, emotional (or astral) and mental bodies and Theosophical methods of cultivating these vehicles might be considered dilettante by the serious student; but for those who wished to go to the trouble and were prepared for years of rigorous discipline there were to-day schools of Hatha Yoga, Prana Yoga, Bhakti Yoga, Karma Yoga and Raja Yoga in which conscious control and development of every physical, etheric, emotional and mental operation possible to man might be gained. It might take a lifetime, it might take two, but one would get marvelous supernormal powers. All these were possible today. Many in the East and a few from the West had attained them.

It was clear from the sutras that Buddha had followed the systems of yoga to the end. In the *Samannaphala Sutra*, after describing the mind-made body, it goes on to describe how, in the *fourth jhana*, the Bhikkhu got the powers of making a number of formless bodies, of levitation, of clairvoyance, remembrance of his former lives, and penetrated into all the processes of life and the working of karma. All powers and all dominions were possible to him. But, like Christ, when he was led onto a high mountain from which he surveyed the world and the tempter offered him dominion and power if he would give up the path he had chosen, so the Buddha, with the power to become the world's greatest conqueror and most magnificent king, chose the path of a homeless one. This was the supreme choice which awaited every man on the threshold of ultimate Realization. Christ had said, "Except a man lose his soul he cannot find it." So the Buddha firmly rejected attachment to any of his bodies. As it was recounted later on in the *Digha-Nikhaya*:

> The Exalted One said: There are three ways of getting a self, Potthapada, namely: the getting of a physical body self, the getting of a mind-made self, and the getting of a formless self. [These selves are explained.] Now I, Potthapada, teach you a teaching for the rejection of the getting of any self: a way by practicing which impure conditions can be put away by you and pure conditions brought to increase, and by which one, even in this very life, may attain the fulfillment and perfect growth of wisdom, realizing it by his own abnormal powers, so as to abide therein.

This is why the *Samannaphala Sutra*, which had been the basis of these discussions, after the gaining of the three selves, and the acquisition of supernormal powers, the Bhikkhu is described, not as exercising those powers, but as going on to the final goal which is the realization of the Four Truths: suffering, the cause of suffering, the cessation of suffering and the path leading to the cessation of suffering.

It may be that on the path to this final realization there would be won the powers of making mind bodies and formless bodies, of gaining marvelous supernormal powers. It might

be that we should have to gain these powers in order to re-
nounce their use. But, following their Master, the Schools of
Buddhism, for the most part, warned their followers to turn
aside from the pursuit of those powers, as snares and delusions, and to direct their efforts straight at the final goal.

> As we go to press we have received from Mr Bennett some correc-
> tions to our report of his meetings. We apologize, and invite Mr
> Bennett to let us publish them, with his reply, in the next issue.—
> Editor [of *The Middle Way*].[2]

---

[1] *What Are We Living for*, J.G. Bennett, Hodder & Stoughton. (MW)
[2] Unfortunately, Bennett's corrections were never published. (LN)

"Gurdjieff and the Buddhist Mind-Body" originally appeared in the Summer 1950 issue of *The Middle Way*. Author unknown.

## To Know Yourself Is to Be Enlightened

The meditation by yourselves I think is the most important part. It is the part that you are left free to discover for yourself, not I to discover for you. That is not your discovery. Discovery consists of about three minutes only. You see things for yourselves. That is your discovery, and that is why some times are left free to you to try to discover for yourselves.

The importance of maintaining silence is that each and every action involves the expenses of energy—even in just thinking in your mind. And please remember that we are all talking, although we say we are keeping silent. We are silent only in terms of speaking through our mouth. But our mind is speaking all the time. And this is the difference, and you have to try to remember when "silent", it is silent from the mind. I have seen so many people, they keep silent and they have paper and they wrote on the paper. So they are speaking in their minds, not through the mouth. Now how is that possible?

I believe there is nothing impossible in the world and in life. When we are too learned we are not inclined to believe in anything much, because we are too learned. And I am not learned. That is why you know before coming here I went to the church, in spite of the fact that somebody came up to tell me that "You should not go to that church." Well a good friend wanted to advise me. But I told him that I had to go. I had already given my word, and moreover I do not mind that I would be badly treated by others in the church. I have been badly treated many times by other religious people who thought themselves to be very high and they thought that it was only their religions that are superior and that have the truth. The others do not have it. But I do not mind. Why? Because I want them to understand that they cannot preach, they cannot tell other people to love each other when they themselves do not love each other. I have been many times ill-treated. But I have no shame because it's not my shame. The shame should be with the man who ill-treats the other; the man who does not ill-treat others, he has no shame.

Now here is the crux of the matter. We never thought about all this; we thought in a different way. Now I request all of you to forget everything you left behind. You come here to be yourself. Now you have to realize that to know yourself is to be enlightened because no man or woman who is not enlightened can know himself or herself. It is not a small thing, when you know yourself, you know the whole universe. Each one of us is a universe in itself. We are not so small, so insignificant and powerless as we think. We are the most potential beings on earth. If there is any being living somewhere who is unknown to us and is being searched by scientists to find them. They have already gone to the moon and they did not find any life. Of course the occultists are dreaming of finding some form of life or beings on Mars. Let us see. So far we have not discovered any beings anywhere so far. We have to believe that human beings are the highest beings of all creation. There is no other being known to us, known to the world anywhere which is higher than human beings. And the Buddha says that to be born as human beings is the greatest gift, the most fortunate. If we compare ourselves with other beings, I think we will find that Buddha was correct. Now I am saying this to you so that you may know that we are occupying the highest place. As such, we have to behave ourselves according to our higher place.

*Bhante Dharmawara*

*Dr Hubert Benoit*

## The Metaphysical Psychoanalyst

In college, Hubert Benoit studied both music and medicine. He was a prize violinist at the Nancy Conservatory and began practicing surgery in 1935. During World War II he continued practicing surgery for the French Civil Defense, but his practice came to an abrupt end as a result of injuries sustained during the bombing of Saint Lô in July of 1944. Despite all the surgery and rehabilitation he underwent, his right hand remained partially paralyzed.

It was before his injury, however, that he acquired an interest in various spiritual traditions. As a result, he became a member of one of the French Gurdjieff groups sometime in the early 1940s. Possibly he was introduced to Gurdjieff by his friend Luc Deitrich, though the two may actually have met one another in the group. Dietrich had been a member of Mme de Salzmann's group since 1938. He was actually with Benoit at the time of the Saint Lô bombardment. Dietrich himself survived injuries only to die of a resulting infection about a month later.

During Benoit's convalescence he began studying psychiatry—a subject that had been interesting him. He also dove further into his spiritual studies and meditation. No doubt Benoit's survival of the bombing and the loss of his friend had awakened something in him.

Benoit began writing his first book on psychiatry, *Méta-*

*physique et Psychanalyse,* in 1948—while he was much involved in the Work; and it was published in 1949—three years before he began practicing psychotherapy. It is also his only book to touch on the Gurdjieff teaching. Although Gurdjieff is not mentioned in the work, it is primarily his teaching that is referred to by metaphysics.

When Gurdjieff died that same year, Benoit began pursuing Zen more seriously. It is likely that he perceived some relationship between the two teachings and viewed Zen as a continuation of the Gurdjieff Work. Benoit apparently never had a Zen teacher, though. In his view there should be no need for one. As he explains, "I have need of a master to learn some movements that I wish to make with my limbs, but I have no need to learn how to decontract my muscles. I have need of a professor of philosophy, or of poetry, in order to learn how to think in the truest or most beautiful way; I have no need of such a person if I wish to learn not to think."[1] Yet surely his work with Gurdjieff led him to this understanding. The whole point of any authentic teaching is to enable the student to eventually perceive life itself as one's teacher and discover an authority within.

The fact that Benoit was able to grasp the essence of Zen so well from its classic literature, without having had a Zen teacher, and based on his experience in the Gurdjieff Work, suggests some relationship between the two teachings. His formulation of Zen, although untraditional, not only affected the literary world, it is highly regarded by various Zen masters. I have not been able to confirm this, but according to a student of Joko Beck I know, Beck had been a student of Benoit for a period of time. Certainly she refers to him in her writing and talks, as do other great Zen teachers.

It should be noted, however, that Benoit had contact with D.T. Suzuki. No doubt they would have corresponded during work on Benoit's French translation of *The Zen Doctrine of No-Mind.* As well, Benoit briefly mentions a conversation he had with Suzuki in *The Interior Realization.* In some cases such a casual relationship is entirely sufficient. It is also known that although most of Suzuki's time in the West was teaching at Columbia University in New York, he went on a lecture tour of Europe in 1954, and spent time in Europe upon his return to Japan in 1958. It is likely Benoit would have spent time with him on those occasions.

Another work that Benoit translated to French is the Zen classic *The Huang Po Doctrine of Universal Mind*. Benoit's first work of his own on Zen, *The Supreme Doctrine,* was written about the same time. As a result, he quickly became regarded as a pioneer of Zen in the West. He is particularly known for taking a very occidental approach in expounding Zen teaching. His formulations are very erudite for Zen. In this regard, he seems to be following in Gurdjieff's footsteps. Gurdjieff too formulated the knowledge of the Eastern traditions he encountered (particularly Tibetan Buddhism) in a way that Westerners can grasp.

The reverse is true as well, as Benoit integrated Zen teaching into his psychotherapy practice. Although this sort of synthesis is common today, it was entirely new in his time. He may very well have been the first to have had such a practice. Certainly he is considered something of a proto transpersonal psychologist. Ken Wilber views him as such, occasionally quoting Benoit in his writings.

Closer to the main subject of this present work, G. Jay Jordan Jr. makes an interesting observation in the introduction to his English translation of *Métaphysique et Psychanalyse*.[2] He says, "At certain points it seems to be implied that the moment of man's highest realization, of his final liberation coincides with the moment of his physical death. In one sense this is true and among the writings of the metaphysical tradition there is considerable evidence indicating that the moment of death physically speaking is a rare opportunity for realization. Particularly striking in this connection is the *Bardo Thödol*." It is very likely that Benoit got this idea from Gurdjieff. Certainly Gurdjieff was familiar with the text, and it is conceivable that Gurdjieff would have said something of it to Benoit in connection to his near death experience.[3]

In all of Benoit's Zen works, hints of Gurdjieff can be detected. It seems as though he never left the Gurdjieff Work

331

entirely. In fact, although there is not much of Gurdjieff's teaching in his first two books on Zen (*The Supreme Doctrine* and *Let Go!*), in his final work, *The Interior Realization,* which he considers his best, he reviews the idea of man's three centers as presented by Gurdjieff, and elsewhere in the book paraphrases one of Gurdjieff's tales. Speaking from personal experience, when one seriously practices more than one tradition, they tend to merge into one for the individual.

An additional title of Benoit's not previously mentioned that the reader may wish to pursue is *The Many Faces of Love.* Following this brief introduction to Benoit is a work of his previously unavailable in English—his introduction to the French edition of *The Huang Po Doctrine of Universal Mind.* It is particularly useful for how it distinguishes between superficial and authentic inner work. We all begin with the superficial approach. The question is whether or not one is able admit its failure and discover a more holistic approach. When reading his introduction, I suggest regarding what Benoit says of Zen as being true of all of Mahayana Buddhism, for all Mahayana sects are the same in the ways he speaks of Zen. As well, if one considers Gurdjieff's teaching to be a reformulation of the buddhadharma, his teaching can be seen in the same light. Everything Benoit says of Zen is also true of *authentic* Gurdjieffian work, though they differ somewhat in their emphases.

---

[1] Hubert Benoit, *Let Go!* (London: George Allen & Unwin, 1962), 276.
[2] Written in 1952 as a thesis for his masters degree at The University of Southern California.
[3] Although it is unknown if Benoit actually had a near death experience, the severity of his injuries and his subsequent taking more seriously of spiritual practice leads me to believe so.

Photograph of Benoit enhanced by the author. Original photographer unknown.

## HUANG PO

Our human condition, as we experience it from our first glimpse of consciousness, is unsatisfactory. Confronting our I, the Non-I rises relentlessly, with its obstacles and threats. We want to exist—to exist forever—but we have an appointment with death, the date of which alone is uncertain. Our condition is unsatisfactory because our natural aspirations will eventually face, more or less quickly but inevitably, our physical mortal condition; for these aspirations are in themselves limitless. It is therefore insufficient to say that our condition is unsatisfactory. If we consider it exactly, stripped of the illusory compensations which lull us to sleep and console us, it is truly unbearable.

This is the fundamental fact of any philosophy—that man begins to question because he suffers. As he gains self-awareness, he is increasingly confronted with a contradiction, for he can only feel "being" in his distinct individual while he is surrounded by creatures who claim to be also. His entire psychological make-up is developing from an unresolved dualistic fashion. He always sees, inside as well as outside himself, two adversaries. His self-image as a unity is torn—torn between two poles. The specter of non-being is always there, at the bottom of his imagination and his sensitivity, with his anguish.

Since man's natural condition appears to him to be founded on this contradiction, it necessarily poses a problem for him. And this problem is actually one of anguish. The drive of a man's whole life, as he feels himself to be an individual person, is the fight against anguish. Whether or not man understands it consciously does not matter; each of us lives to overcome this anguish. And all philosophical doctrines, in the broadest sense of the term, tend toward reaching this one goal.

Innumerable doctrines have been born in the minds of men, intending to solve the problem of the human condition. And they are all based, consciously or not, on an understanding—whether faulty or luminous—of metaphysics. Beneath this plethora of doctrines resides the same singular Truth, though expressed with varying clarity. Doctrines are in opposition to one another only superficially—that is to say only due to the specious elements that they may contain—but never due to aspects of the underlying singular Reality.

If the various "teachings of life" differ, it is not, therefore, as is generally believed, by their doctrinal content. If the Zen teaching of which Huang Po lays out some essential ideas is, as is my opinion, quite unique in its kind and stands out from all the others, even if it would refute all the others, it would not be only by its doctrine, for its doctrine continued that of the Vedanta which is practically identical to it. So how is Zen unique?

Man, as we have said, engages in metaphysics because he is anxious and seeks the Truth in order to overcome his anguish. But this "overcoming of anguish" can use two different methods which are in a sense opposing. To illustrate these two methods we will use a parable: A man has a garden full of weeds that he despises, and dreams of having a beautiful garden instead of this sordid place. He imagines the beautiful garden for which he longs, and he works to bring his vision into reality. In order to hide the weeds, he makes artificial flowers, puts their stems into the ground, and spends a large part of his days dusting his artificial flowers and repainting them. Meanwhile, he contemplates the garden as it now appears. His grief is thus relieved and this relief gives him joy. He is able to completely quell his suffering, now firmly be-

334

lieves that he has a beautiful garden, and that it is real. This "belief" may thus make him happy. Now comes another man. He is in the same situation as the first and acts like him at first. But after a while his perspective changes. This unlucky man does not have the ability to make the artificial flowers beautiful and maintainable despite all his care. This man is then forced to change his method. He realizes that he only has one option left: to stop spending his time making his garden look pretty and instead use this time to patiently pull out the weeds while accepting his garden's ugliness while this work is being accomplished. He does so, and one day—the instant he pulls up the last weed (without him knowing that it is the last)—he realizes that his garden is a wondrous, real garden, and that it has always been that way. The first method was "palliative", the second is the "curative" method.

Man can destroy his anguish through the radical transformation of his condition. But he will only try this "curative" method if he is endowed with great lucidity or after having exhausted all other "palliative" possibilities (because he always and necessarily begins with the "palliative" method).

The artificial flowers of our parable are the various compensations that man can find in life to alleviate his anguish. These compensations are very diverse, but all involve the "belief" in the actual value of such and such a thing, external or internal, existing in the world. The more subtle the thing that is believed to be real (for, among the multiplicity of aspects of the created world, there is an immense hierarchy, from the grossest to the most subtle), the more effective the compensation which is based on this apparent value. Metaphysics, when man is intelligent enough to study himself via its concepts, offers such aspects of the Truth which, although not being this very Truth since Truth transcends all of its expressions, can describe the most subtle and beautiful views of the formal world. So when man turns to metaphysics to counter anguish, he will find marvelous "beliefs" and consolations, so marvelous in fact that he mistakenly takes this garden for his real garden, and nothing could convince him otherwise. In this case, metaphysics has been used against anguish, but to alleviate it, not to annihilate it.

This illusion, wherein the palliative method is undertaken in good faith and vigor as a form of annihilation, is so widespread (not in the teachings' theory, of course, but in their practice), that it is in fact the general rule. In my personal opinion, Zen teaching is the only one that succeeds, and only through some of its representatives, in making an exception to this rule and in refusing any palliative help offered indirectly by metaphysics.

This is where Zen is exceptional. Yet this is also what can make it appear "inhuman", because everyone considers it "human" to be sensitive to suffering and seek immediate relief from it. However, Zen refuses such immediate relief because it is not genuine. Originating from Chinese genius, which is practical and concrete at the same time as capable of the most subtle abstract conceptions, Zen has assimilated the Vedanta doctrine without being tempted by any of the marvelous opportunities for immediate consolation. Zen found faith, that is to say intuitive intellectual evidence, but by refusing all "belief"—embodiments of Truth which touch the emotions at the same time as the intellect. Zen does not adore any "God", it does not expect help from any intercessor, it does not rely on any moral rule. Among the many inner states that man can experience in his ordinary dualistic condition, he does not seek any "higher", "spiritual" state. His refusal of the word "spiritual" shows how firmly he refuses all consolation. At no time does he dwell on the ideas that metaphysics provides. He uses it as a craftsman uses his hammer—without attaching any value to the hammer in itself, attentive only to his real goal, to that "conversion" of the ordinary human condition in which the higher "spiritual" states, the most impressive supernatural powers, have no value. For Zen there are no partial measures, there are no degrees between the ordinary state of man and his "realized" state. There aren't different paths suited for different temperaments in Zen. The formal structure according to which the human condition presents itself is different in each man, but the human condition is one. To go from this condition, one in all of us, to the Absolute Principle, which is One, there aren't multiple paths but only one. The man who attains the goal of Zen is not an extraordinary or great man. He has not matured in order to provide support to those who approach him. A man after having attained satori, insofar as one can perceive him, is absolutely ordinary, absolutely simple, absolutely earthly. He is as imperceptible as the Timeless and Informal Principle with which he is definitively identified. This man is at the same time no longer among us and the only one who is really among us.

I don't want to get drawn into talking more about Zen in general here. I have tried to deal with certain aspects of this subject in a book called *The Supreme Doctrine*—a book to which those interested in this teaching can refer. I am currently limiting myself to showing how Zen differs and is even opposed to all other teachings.

When I say that Zen is opposed to all other teachings, this word should not evoke the slightest sectarian aggressiveness, nor the slightest desire to recruit new followers. The idea of actively "converting" anyone is the last idea that can come to anyone who understands Zen. A Zen master will only answer questions, and only if he feels they are sincere. But it is in his responses that the opposition we are talking about manifests. The one who questions reveals, through his question, that he "believes" or wants to "believe" in a specific discipline, or in some describable inner work having a "form". It thus always suggests, consciously or not, the usefulness of a formal system. But Zen aims at the informal, at "transformation" or a passage beyond form. So he refuses to stop at any form, denies all interest in actions, thoughts and feelings, endeavors neither to control, contain nor encourage anything in this plane of forms, and lets the formal life go as it goes. All that is usually called "inner work" is not really internal for Zen, since it relates to phenomena (even to suspend them)—on formal aspects of the created world. For Zen, only that which resides beyond the form is "internal"—this informal source of our life which it calls "true nature", or "buddha-nature", or "self-nature". Also, inner work according to Zen can only be expressed in the plane of forms in a negative way; it is a matter of gradually uprooting all beliefs and all opinions.

To carry out this negative work man leans on a positive but informal understanding that is developed surreptitiously in him beneath the concepts that he accumulates (without granting them any importance themselves) during patient and conscientious intellectual labor. Zen requires an acute intelligence and the minding of ideas capable of illuminating this intelligence.

The text of Huang Po is fundamental for the understanding of Zen. The idea he develops—the idea that the Cosmic Mind is the only reality—is truly "explosive". To the extent that we are able to receive it—to the extent that it "rings true" to our intellectual intuition—this idea pulverizes in our eyes the illusory value of the world of forms and thus puts us on the path to true inner work.

*Hubert Benoit*

"Huang Po," an edited version of Benoit's introduction to *Le mental cosmique selon la doctrine de Huang Po* by Yun Hsi (Paris: Éditions Adyar, 1951), was translated for the author from the French by Vaillant Gicqueau.

*Dr Rolf Alexander*

## Dr A.

Rolf Alexander was one of Gurdjieff's first students, having worked with him for a period of about six months in 1913, the year that Gurdjieff began teaching. In fact, he may very well be the student identified as "A." in "Glimpses of Truth," an introduction to Gurdjieff's teaching that he had another pupil write, which can be found in *Views from the Real World*. Alexander was probably studying in Moscow for a semester. He claims to have graduated from Charles University in Prague in 1912 where he was studying medicine, but the school has no record of him having matriculated. Probably he dropped out and spent some time in Moscow before continuing his education. Supposedly he subsequently attended a number of other European universities, but it is difficult to say given his reputation for lying. Similarly, he claims to have worked at the Mayo Clinic, but they too have no record of his employment. Nevertheless, Alexander was a renowned psychologist and a successful author.

Although his first books were greatly influenced by Gurdjieff's teaching, no credit whatsoever is given to Gurdjieff. Instead Alexander claims that the knowledge presented was acquired during his studies in Tibet in 1913. It is only in his works written after the publication of *Beelzebub's Tales* and *In Search of the Miraculous*, and Gurdjieff's teaching became more widely known to the general public, that he mentions having studied with Gurdjieff in 1913. Although he eventually admitted to having studied with Gurdjieff, Alexander never did credit Gurdjieff for the wisdom he was presenting. His only purpose in mentioning Gurdjieff seems to have been to exploit the attention the Gurdjieff teaching was then receiving. Alexander never retracted his claim to have gotten his knowledge from Tibet.

There are a few things which indicate that Alexander's claim to have been in Tibet was fabricated. For one, at that time it would have been extremely difficult to have spent so much time both in Moscow and in Tibet in the same year. The logistics of planning a Tibetan journey and the journey itself would have taken considerable time.

Another suspicious detail is that like Alexandra David-Neel, Alexander too says that he studied under an English-speaking lama at Shigatse Monastery. In all likelihood he borrowed that idea from her account, *Magic and Mystery in Tibet*.

Even more revealing is that he says the name of the Tibetan lama he studied with is Tsiang Samdup. In *The Voice of Talking Valley*, in which he has an entire chapter devoted to him, he is spoken of as "old Tsiang," and in *The Mind in Healing* he opens Chapter 9 with a quotation attributed to Tsiang Samdup. This name is clearly a fabrication. While the name Samdup is Tibetan, the name Tsiang is actually Chinese. And the name Samdup was apparently borrowed from one of the very few Tibetans known in the West at the time—Kazi Dawa Samdup, the lama who translated the first English edition of *The Tibetan Book of the Dead* together with Walter Evans-Wentz. But it was not Alexander who came up with the name. It turns out that he found the Tsiang Samdup quote in a novel by Theosophist Talbot Mundy. In his novels *Om: The Secret of Ahbor Valley* and *The Devil's Guard*, Mundy begins each chapter with a quotation from the fictional *Book of the Sayings of Tsiang Samdup*. Indeed the quotations sound more Theosophical than Buddhist. Alexander may have been a Theosophist himself. He in fact begins two other chapters of *The Mind in Healing* with a quote from Talbot Mundy. The quotes beginning every chapter of *The Doctor Alone Can't Cure You*, which he attributes to *The Tibetan Book of Right Feeling*, may well have been taken from Mundy's *Sayings of Tsiang Samdup*. Alexander's *The Voice of Talking Valley* is particularly influenced by Theosophy. So, it is with little doubt that he borrowed the name Tsiang Samdup for his own tale.

Interestingly, his telling of his journey to Shigatse, which follows this chapter, is clearly an account of a journey made with Gurdjieff which he resituated in Tibet. The entire purpose of the journey seems to have been a practical demonstration of Gurdjieff's teaching on tapping the main accumulator by making super-effort. Significantly, Olgivanna Lloyd Wright provides an account of her own being pushed to the extreme by Gurdjieff which is virtually identical to Alexander's.[1]

So, why mention any of this at all if Alexander never in fact journeyed to Tibet? Because it reveals how utterly convinced he must have been that Gurdjieff was a teacher of Tibetan wisdom. In fact, of all Gurdjieff's students, he seems to have been convinced of this most.

Another unusual aspect of the case of Rolf Alexander need also be mentioned. He cannot so easily be dismissed as a conniver and plagiarist. While this seems likely enough to be the case, we are at the same time indebted to him for preserving something of Gurdjieff's early teaching—a teaching which had greater emphasis on hypnosis as a means, not only of healing, but of work on oneself as well. These teachings would be lost were it not for Rolf Alexander.

Regarding hypnosis, it is worth mentioning here that Gurdjieff spoke of Eastern forms that were unknown in the West. This along with Rolf Alexander's apparent conviction of a Tibetan origin to Gurdjieff's teaching may indicate that Gurdjieff practiced Tibetan hypnosis (amongst other forms).

Another aspect of Gurdjieff's early teaching was the distinguishing between real magic and mere trickery. While Alexander never wrote about the practice of real magic per se, he received attention in the press as a "cloud-buster"—as having the ability to dissipate clouds with the power of the mind. Might this not be an ability he learned from Gurdjieff, or perhaps one he developed based on Gurdjieff's teaching? Might this even be a form of Tibetan magic? Tibet is certainly renowned for its shamanistic magic. While a definitive answer cannot be given here, it certainly seems a possibility given Alexander's preservation of Gurdjieff's early teachings on hypnosis.

---

[1] Maxine Fawcett-Yeske & Bruce Brooks Pfeiffer, eds., *The Life of Olgivanna Lloyd Wright* (Novato: ORO Editions, 2017, 42–43.

Photograph of Rolf Alexander taken from the June 30, 1956 issue of *Picture Post.*

## THE LAMA

Years ago a young Western student of psychology had journeyed to Tibet in order to study some of the lamaistic disciplines practiced there. His teacher, an aged English-speaking lama, had tried to explain that by detachment from the internal affairs of our own bodies, we automatically gained control over them. The young man was doubtful, for this philosophy was contrary to all the principles of Western psychology taught at that time. At last the old lama said: "Very well, tomorrow we shall go to Shigatse, and you shall demonstrate the principle to yourself."

At daybreak the following morning, the young man and his teacher set off on the narrow, slippery and winding trail to Shigatse, thirty-five kilometers distant. The path at times seemed to climb almost straight upward and, at others, to drop straight downward, and it was not long before the young man's lungs were laboring and his head spinning in the rarefied atmosphere of 17,000 feet altitude. The aged lama, however, was apparently quite unaffected... he strode along rapidly, breathing easily, and keeping up a continuous conversation.

When finally they came in sight of Shigatse, the young man felt as though his chest were constricted by a red-hot band of iron; he was gasping for breath, reeling from fatigue, and was sustained during the final two or three miles only by the visions of a long rest, then a hearty meal, and then more rest.

They had no sooner reached the outskirts of the town, however, than the teacher turned around and said blandly: "Now let us try to make better time on the journey back." And he commenced walking rapidly back over the trail they had just traversed. The young man expostulated that he could not do it, that his heart would give out, and so on, but the lama merely smiled and kept on walking. Finally he said: "It is not important that you die, since all men must die, but it is very important that you should learn to live."

After a time the emotional state of desperation in the young man seemed to change to one of mental numbness... He no longer protested even to himself; he was beyond protesting. He felt almost like a disembodied spirit observing in a disinterested way his physical body in action. Then a seeming miracle took place; his fatigue dropped away, the constriction loosened from his chest, and he moved forward almost without a sense of effort.

At last they rounded a bend and came within sight of the home lamasery about a mile distant, and, at the sight of it, all the fatigue and utter weariness seemed to rush back and take possession of the young man. He commenced to stagger and the old man looked back at him with concern: "You seem weary, my son; therefore let us hurry so that we may the sooner enjoy food and rest." And he led the way at a rapid jog-trot. Again the sense of fatigue dropped away from the young man, and he finished that last mile fresher than he had begun the first mile of the journey.

In discussing the phenomenon of second-wind afterwards, the teacher explained: "The body does not tire—it is a machine —and so long as a machine is in good repair and is plentifully supplied with fuel there is no reason why it should tire. Since it automatically eliminates its own waste products by sweating and breathing, the body can continue to work indefinitely if the mind is not entangled in its operations. The submerged mind is a monkey and cannot sustain its attention; it wants to hop about and look at this, and toy with that, and dally with some imaginary thing. The introverted mind may find freedom in which to enjoy introspection and daydreams only

346

when the body is idling. To bring about this desired situation, therefore, it halts a sustained effort by suggesting to the subconscious controller that the 'body is tired,' that its 'lungs are constricted,' that its 'heart will give out,' and so on."

The old lama continued: "The introverted mind may be forced to detach itself if the demand to sustain the physical effort comes from another, and is stronger than the effect of its autosuggestion. In such a case, we see the phenomenon called 'second-wind', but all great athletes learn this secret of detaching their minds from their physical mechanisms. They may learn this accidentally, and perhaps do not fully understand the nature of their power themselves, but look upon the face of a great marathon runner, for instance, and you will see the same expression as is observed in a Tibetan 'lung-gompa' runner... an expression of serene detachment."

*Rolf Alexander*

"The Lama" is an excerpt from *The Power of the Mind* by Rolf Alexander (London: Werner Laurie, 1956).

*Jeanne de Salzmann and Dudjom Rinpoche*

## The Queen of the Dakinis

Jeanne de Salzmann first met Gurdjieff while teaching Emile Jaques-Dalcroze's eurhythmics method in Tbilisi in 1919. At the time she was known by her stage name, Jeanne Matignon. Her meeting Gurdjieff came about as a result of her husband reuniting with his friend Thomas de Hartmann during rehearsals of a production of *Carmen* that was happening. Alexandre de Salzmann, an art nouveau painter and designer, and de Hartmann were involved in the same art circles in Munich the previous decade. De Salzmann was working on the stage design and de Hartmann, who was now a member of Gurdjieff's entourage, was employed as artistic director at the theater where the production was being held.

Gurdjieff soon took advantage of these new talents. With the dancer he began teaching a series of sacred movements and made her movements instructor, and the artist was tasked with painting the backdrops for his ballet.

The couple followed Gurdjieff to Constantinople (as Istanbul was then called), Dresden, and on to Fontainebleau where his Institute for the Harmonious Development of Man finally settled in 1922. When Gurdjieff's wife died in 1926, de Salzmann took her place as second in command, and remained at his side in this capacity until the end of his life. They were close in more ways than one as she had given birth to two of Gurdjieff's children and was thus regarded as part of his family. They were not legally married, nor did they live together, but Gurdjieff was sure to provide de Salzmann with the financial support needed to raise their children, and she was sure to give their children the sort of comprehensive education that Gurdjieff desired.

Later, during Gurdjieff's years teaching at his flat in Paris, de Salzmann served as a sort of intermediary between Gurdjieff and his students, providing Gurdjieff with more detail about some aspect of the student's situation or self-work, or providing the student with the details of a given exercise that Gurdjieff wanted them to work with. She also led satellite groups of her own and introduced new people to Gurdjieff.

De Salzmann was also Gurdjieff's primary movements instructor. She taught the movements for him from the time they met in Tbilisi, through the Institute's subsequent moves to Constantinople and Hellerau, and until the closing of the Institute's final location in Fontainebleau-Avon in 1929. (The property continued to house Gurdjieff's family and other Russian refugees he supported until 1933, but the Institute had effectively closed in 1929.) And in the 1940s when Gurdjieff revived the movements and began teaching a new series of these exercises, de Salzmann resumed this role and trained some newer students as instructors.

When Gurdjieff died in 1949, no one, including Madame de Salzmann, had yet attained the being of a nascent spiritual teacher (what he refers to as "man number five") able to assume his mantle. As well, Gurdjieff left no clear instructions on how one who has had the first major realization—what he refers to as "the realization of nothingness" and is the mark of what he calls a "man number four" (that is, an individual who is in limbo between the worlds of ordinary and enlightened individuals)—must proceed along their path and reach the level of an individual number five. (Although there are hints in Gurdjieff's incomplete third series of writings, *Life Is Real Only Then When "I Am,"* which he had intended to serve this purpose.) And yet de Salzmann was assigned the task of overseeing all the groups and continuing Gurdjieff's Work. In short, she was in an extremely difficult situation. Anyone in

350

that position would have faced criticism no matter their approach. There were group leaders such as J.G. Bennett and Willem Nyland who helped initially with the Foundation that de Salzmann was creating, but disagreed with her on some aspect or other of her leadership and decided to keep their groups independent of de Salzmann's umbrella organization. Fracture was inevitable.

She is criticized specifically for trying to fill in the gaps left by Gurdjieff's untimely death by adapting certain ideas and practices from other traditions (particularly meditation). Because of this her critics refer to her approach as "the New Work," implying a lack of authenticity. In contrast were groups such as the Nyland groups that only study Gurdjieff's writings and only work with exercises that Gurdjieff himself gave. Yet this is not to criticize the traditionalists; both approaches have their merits. The intention here is only to show how difficult a situation de Salzmann was contending with.

Encouragement to explore Zen Buddhism and see what aspects of that teaching might vitalize the Work came from William Segal. He had already made a few trips to Japan and was practicing Zen seriously. Thus, de Salzmann made her first trip to Japan with Segal in 1966. She reflects:

> I think of Japan with nostalgia. Our trip will have some consequences. It was an important thing to be done—Bill has been the best help and friend one could imagine. I have sent *In Search of the Miraculous* to Kobori with a letter and have written also and sent the book to Asahina and Myoko—To Mrs Sasaki I gave it when she was still in Paris—So, the relation with Japan is kept alive—I have asked Myoko to let me know when Dr Suzuki will go to Italy and I certainly will see him there. There is something precious in the relations which have been established there. It can lead to something important and I will remain quite open to it.—You see what you have done!—[1]

She also makes an interesting observation about the Zen rituals she observed in relation to group work:

> It is true that a participation to a rite has a very strong effect on one, also because of the feeling of togetherness, of

351

fulfilling a task beyond one's egoist subjectivity—I remember very well the dignified, religious way Soen Roshi led the ceremony in Japanese and it is true that he is an artist, a kind of poet.[2]

Segal explains how de Salzmann introduced sittings to the Foundation shortly after her Japan trip:

> My view is that Madame de Salzmann, in an effort to help the sittings become truly effective, took a most indirect approach. In first introducing sittings to Group One, for example, she refrained from announcing that any formal or structured sittings were taking place. We gathered together and she would speak of the importance of correct physical posture. She would make comments to the necessity of relaxing and so on. At no time, as I recall, were sittings as meditation labeled as such. So this was a very indirect introduction to the idea of sittings. After a while, we realized that sittings needed some guidance, especially for people unfamiliar with them. She provided the guidance in the form of taking our mind off the "self-conscious sitting." In other words, we find today that in many people who take up meditation, there's a self-conscious element that interferes with a true sitting.[3]

Lee van Laer makes another observation on de Salzmann's introduction of sittings to the Foundation:

> Her insights—though undeniably and inseparably in a direct line that evolved from her work with Gurdjieff—unmistakably echo Zen insight and Zen practice, and her introduction of Zen-type sittings to the everyday practice in the Gurdjieff Foundation's work must have followed directly on her discovery of the similarities between Zen understanding and objective understanding, as taught and practiced by Gurdjieff himself. De Salzmann, in other words, understood both aim and practice in Zen, and how closely related they were to Gurdjieff's own work and aims.[4]

According to William Segal, de Salzmann eventually did reach the level of a master. He says, "...there was a point where she came into touch with this spark within herself... She was in her early 60s. She suddenly emerged from being one of us and we began to look up to her."[5] This is also supported by the great respect the various Zen masters she met had for her. Ruth Sasaki told Hugh Ripman, "She is a wonderful woman—what I like about her particularly is that she has lots of guts. I like people who have guts."[6] And Kobori Roshi told Ravi Ravindra, "She is the most remarkable woman I have ever met."[7] The appreciation was mutual.

The following year James George arranged a meeting between de Salzmann and Trungpa Rinpoche that took place in Paris. She would later describe Trungpa as "clean and true,"[8] and told Yahne Le Toumelin that he might be able to "understand"[9] Gurdjieff. And her son Michel expressed appreciation for Trungpa's teachings on "meditation in action," which obviously relates to Gurdjieff's teachings on adapting one's activities in daily life as a form of spiritual Work. Perhaps this is what was behind de Salzmann's thinking. She evidently met Namkhai Norbu Rinpoche in Paris at some point too.

James George was tasked by de Salzmann to explore some of India's spiritual traditions, and she initiated trips in 1970 and 1971 with him and Segal to meet many of the rinpoches who had immigrated to India from Tibet. He says that in Darjeeling she met Dudjom Rinpoche, Duksey Rinpoche, Kangyur Rinpoche, Kalu Rinpoche and Chatral Rinpoche, and that they all began reverently calling her the "Queen of the Dakinis." Like the Zen masters that de Salzmann met, these rinpoches also regarded her as an equal. George adds, "She was very interested in both streams of teachings [Zen and Tibetan Buddhism], and I believe her interest has influenced how we, in the Gurdjieff Work, approach sittings."[10]

Yahne Le Toumelin, a student of Gurdjieff during the 1940s who was now under Kangyur Rinpoche's guidance, was also there when de Salzmann met with Kangyur Rinpoche. However, she was disappointed that de Salzmann asked to be alone with Kangyur Rinpoche during their half hour together. So, she was unable to witness their discussion.

Regarding how de Salzmann was influenced by Tibetan Buddhist teachings and practices, José Tirado makes an interesting observation:

One of the main Kagyu practices (also used by the Nyingma) is the visualization, above one's head of Vajrayogini, a female deity who is said to then receive teachings of the highest level into herself, all of which is then visualized as being absorbed into oneself. I recall a picture of Mme de Salzmann meeting with the late Nyingma teacher, H.H. Dudjom Rinpoche and hearing stories of her receiving teachings about opening the top of [the] head to receive guidance from above. We might assume an influence.[11]

Similarly, James George notes that Michel de Salzmann had occasionally used Tibetan cymbals when leading group sittings.

De Salzmann clearly understood that there was some relationship between Gurdjieff's teaching and Buddhism (as well as other traditions). Besides being evidenced by her meetings with all these different teachers, she told Ravi Ravindra, "You have to acknowledge that you do not know who you are, and that you need to know it. This opening is the most important step. You can read in Hinduism or Buddhism what this opening means; or you can read it in Mr Gurdjieff's books. It is the same thing."[12]

Of the many roshis and rinpoches that de Salzmann met, it is difficult to know who had more of an influence on her. Information on her contact with them is scant. But there are reasons for singling out Dudjom Rinpoche. He had opened Paris' first Tibetan Buddhist meditation center in 1978 and directed it until his death in 1987. So she would have been able to meet with Dudjom Rinpoche much more frequently than with others. Babette Bridault, who loaned Dudjom Rinpoche the apartment which became that meditation center and was a great supporter, was previously a student of Gurdjieff and likely maintained contact with de Salzmann as she did with others she knew through his groups. It makes sense that Bridault would have been the go-between for the two.

Also to consider is the possibility of a karmic link between de Salzmann and Dudjom Rinpoche. They may have been drawn towards one another without understanding exactly why. De Salzmann as we know was Gurdjieff's chief disciple,

354

and Dudjom Rinpoche was the incarnation of Dudjom Lingpa, who appears to have been Gurdjieff's root teacher. As well, he was one of Yahne Le Toumelin's secondary teachers, and one of the rinpoches that William Segal interviewed. So, let us look briefly at Dudjom Rinpoche's life.

Dudjom Jigdral Yeshe Dorje, the Second Dudjom Rinpoche, was born in 1904 in Pemakö—a forest in Southeastern Tibet that borders India. His parents, who were nobles, gave him the name Jnana—a Sanskrit name which means knowledge and translates to the name Yeshe in Tibetan. At the age of three he was visited by students of Dudjom Lingpa looking for their teacher's incarnation. His ability to greet them all by name immediately confirmed his recognition.

He first studied with Khenpo Aten before attending various *shedras* (monastic colleges). In Central Tibet he studied at Mindroling, Dorje Drak and Tarjé Tingpoling Monasteries, and in East Tibet he studied at Kathok and Dzogchen. However, it was at Mindroling, a chief monastery of the Nyingmapa sect, that he refined his understanding. Yet Dudjom Rinpoche never lived the life of a monk. Like his predecessor Dudjom Lingpa, he too was a *ngakpa*. Also like his predecessor, Dudjom Rinpoche had many visions. At only thirteen years of age he met Padmasambhava in a vision and received *terma* from him.

Dudjom studied with many high-ranking teachers. Perhaps the most significant was Phungong Tulku Gyurme Ngedön Wangpo, a holder of the teachings of his predecessor with whom he spent sixteen years. Some others include Jedrung Trinlé Jampa Jungné, Khenchen Jampal Dewé Nyima, and Minling Dordzin Namdrol Gyatso. In short, he accumulated a wide variety of teachings and practices from all schools of Tibetan Buddhism.

In 1956 Dudjom Rinpoche fled Tibet with the Dalai Lama's entourage and settled in Kalimpong. Four years later the Dalai Lama designated him the supreme head of the Nyingmapa sect. Previously the sect had no such head, but in exile the Dalai Lama found the need for one.

In 1973 he traveled the world, making stops in Europe, the

355

U.S.A. and Hong Kong, attracting his first Western students. It was on this trip while visiting the Dordogne countryside that Dudjom Rinpoche recognised the Vézère Valley landscape as the one he saw in a prophetic dream before emigrating from Tibet, and which he understood would be where the dharma would flourish. Later in the decade he established the Urgyen Samyé Chöling retreat center there, as well as the meditation center in Paris previously mentioned. Sogyal Rinpoche served as his translator when he taught Westerners.

Dudjom Rinpoche left this world on January 17, 1987. Like Dudjom Lingpa, he left us many teachings to guide us in our practice.

Following is an essay from Madame de Salzmann's book, *The Reality of Being*, and an excerpt from one of Dudjom Rinpoche's commentaries to illustrate how Dudjom Rinpoche's teaching may have influenced de Salzmann. They are both on the value of uncertainty. Gurdjieff himself did not talk about the subject explicitly, yet it is implied in his teaching on idiotism.[13] So, de Salzmann evidently saw the value of talking about the subject in a more direct way, as Buddhism and other teachings do. The same can be said of J. G. Bennett who spoke of "hazard" as he preferred to call the subject.

1 William Segal & Marielle Bancou-Segal, *A Voice at the Borders of Silence: An Intimate View of the Gurdjieff Work, Zen Buddhism, and Art* (New York: Overlook Press, 2003), 127. Note that "Myoko" appears to be de Salzmann's spelling of Mihoko [Okamura]—Dr D.T. Suzuki's attendant. Asahina Roshi was the abbot of Engakuji, and Ruth Sasaki was an American Zen priest teaching at a zendo for Westerners that she established in Kyoto.

2 Ibid., 131.

3 Ibid., 212.

4 Lee van Laer, *The Law of Three: Essays on the Gurdjieff Ideas* (Sparkill: Doremishock Publishing, 2012), 71–72, PDF.

5 William Segal & Marielle Bancou-Segal, *A Voice at the Borders of Silence: An Intimate View of the Gurdjieff Work, Zen Buddhism, and Art* (New York: Overlook Press, 2003), 75.

6 Hugh Brockwill Ripman, *Search for Truth* (Washington: Forthway Center Palisades Press, 1999), 224.

7 Ravi Ravindra, *Heart without Measure: Work with Madame de Salzmann* (Halifax: Shaila press, 1999), 39.

8 "Interview with James George," The Chronicles of Chögyam Trungpa Rinpoche, www.chronicleproject.com/interview-with-james-george/.

9 Private correspondence.

10 "Interview with James George," The Chronicles of Chögyam Trungpa Rinpoche, www.chronicleproject.com/interview-with-james-george/.

11 José Tirado, "Beelzebub's Buddhas: The Influence of Buddhism and Its Tibetan Variants in Gurdjieff's Fourth Way," *The Proceedings of the 12th International Humanities Conference: All & Everything 2007* (North Haven: All & Everything Conferences, 2007), 21.

12 Ravi Ravindra, *Heart without Measure: Work with Madame de Salzmann* (Halifax: Shaila press, 1999), 9.

13 This thought is elaborated upon in the chapter "Idiotism" in Part Three.

## I Do Not Know

In my search to see reality in myself, I may come to the door of perception. But it will not open, truth will not be revealed, so long as I cling to what I know. I need to have empty hands to approach the unknown.

At the outset I cannot affirm who I am. All I can do is begin to distinguish myself from my ordinary 'I', to see that I am not my associations, I am not my feelings, I am not my sensations. But the question then arises: Who am I? I need to listen, I become quiet to mobilize all my attention and come to a more balanced state. Am I this? No, but the direction is good. From dispersion, I go toward unity. My search can continue. Yet I see that the energy of my thinking, moved by all the thoughts that seize it, has neither force nor direction. In order to go toward the source of 'I', it must be gathered and concentrated on one question: "Who am I?" I learn not to turn away.

I do not know who I am, and all that I know cannot be an answer. The unknown, the mysterious, cannot be discerned by the known. On the contrary, what I know, what I have learned, prevents me from discovering what is. The whole process of my thinking, the conditioning of the known, encloses me in the field of my thought and prevents me from going further. I find pleasure in this conditioning and security, and unconsciously cling to it.

I am unable to face the unknown. I feel it empty, like a void that must be filled. I have a constant tendency to fill it with answers, projecting a false image on the screen of my mind. I am afraid I will not find myself. And in order to resolve this uncertainty, to avoid dissatisfaction, I constantly allow something false to be affirmed. Yet I need this uncertainty, this dissatisfaction, as an indication from my feeling that shows the way back toward myself. It shows the necessity of being more sensitive to the one thing I turn away from, to accept emptiness, the void.

To approach the unknown would mean to come to the door of perception and be able to open it, and to see. But I can see nothing as long as I am taken by words, always putting a name on something and recognizing the object by its name. Words create a limit, a barrier. To enter the unknown, my mind must see this limit as a fact, without judging it good or bad, or submitting to its influence. Can I see myself without putting a word on what I see? I am at the door of perception with an attention that does not turn away.

I learn to listen to the unknown in myself. I do not know, and I listen, constantly refusing each known response. From moment to moment, I recognize that I do not know, and I listen. The very act of listening is a liberation. It is an action that does not flee the present, and when I know the present as it is, there is transformation. I go toward the unknown until I come to a moment when no thought moves my mind, when there is nothing outside myself. I do not know who I am. I do not know whence I came. I do not know where I will go. I doubt all that I know, and have nothing to rely on. All I wish is to understand what I am. Without words, without form, the body and its density seem to disappear. I become as if transparent to myself. Now there is only room for purity, a quality as light as air. I feel that in the search for myself, and only in this search, lies my liberation.

*Jeanne de Salzmann*

## DETERMINING THE NATURE OF THE INNER PERCEIVING MIND

Turning your attention within, look directly into the very face of mind itself. When you look like this, you experience a state that is beyond any duality—beyond any separation between one who looks and something that is looked at, between an experiencer and experienced, between subject and object.

Instead, you experience a self-cognizing, objectless state of openness beyond any conceptual elaboration. Simply settle directly and evenly into that very experience, without spoiling it by trying to change or modify it in any way. This is how those of the highest capacity meditate—"settling into the immediacy of the universal awareness of *rigpa.*"

Still, for most people, whose minds are disturbed by the churning waves of thought, this is difficult to recognize, and so they should search for the mind using the path of *rigpa* and *rigpa* alone. This means that as soon as a flash or flicker of thought appears, you look directly into it and ask, "Where does this come from? Where does it remain right now? Where does it cease in the end?" You can also ask: "Who is the one to attain Buddhahood? Who is the one that wanders in samsara? Who creates happiness and suffering?"

If you think it is the mind, then ask yourself, "Does it have a beginning? Or an end? Or a middle? Is mind real or unreal? If it is real, what is its color or its shape?" If you think it is unreal, then ask yourself, "Is it completely nothing or what is it like?" Ask questions such as these again and again, without letting your attention slip, and look into the mind.

If you can't arrive at a clear decision, but think of mind as something concrete and real with certain characteristics, or if you consider that it is an empty void of nothing at all, or if you think that it has never existed because you can't find it, or if you think it clearly exists so how could anyone ever fail to find it, then continue to search and ask yourself more questions. You won't find one who looks or something that is looked at, neither a 'see-er' nor one who is seen.

Not finding anything at all by searching and analyzing, it is like looking into the sphere of space and not seeing anything at all. It is an experience of awareness, without any essence that could be identified. It is inexpressible, beyond thought and not something to be 'seen'. It is the union of emptiness and clarity, unchanging naked awareness beyond any object. When this arises as a stable experience then the instruction has truly penetrated your being.

*Kyabje Dudjom Jigdral Yeshe Dorje*

*Pamela Travers circa 1934*

## Pamela Poppins

Pamela Travers was introduced to A. R. Orage in October 1933. As a burgeoning writer she was keen to meet the editor, and Orage, short on funds, was interested in new raw talent he did not have to compensate well. Some of her early poetry can be found in Orage's *New English Weekly*.

It was probably easy for Orage to veer their private discussions in the direction of Gurdjieff given Travers' health and relationship issues. She was suffering and needed solace, and Orage was more than happy to help. Yet Orage was no longer leading Gurdjieff groups. At this point in time, he had returned to London to resume his career after Gurdjieff dismissed him as leader of the U.S.A. groups. So, Orage evidently provided Travers with private guidance on Gurdjieff's teaching. Orage was convinced that Gurdjieff had acquired his teaching in Tibet and this was likely conveyed to Travers. In her review of the film adaptation of *Meetings with Remarkable Men* published in *Search: Journey on the Inner Path*, she appended a different translation of the Gurdjieff transcript included here as "A Tibetan Ritual" as if to discreetly correct the impression the film gives that Sarmung belonged to some other tradition. Still, editor Jean Sulzberger, who was also in the Work, evidently saw fit to edit out the explicit reference to the "Prince Yuri Lubovedsky" chapter of Gurdjieff's work to prevent readers from getting that message.

Orage died in November 1934. He and Travers had only known one another for a year. Yet in that time his elaboration of Gurdjieff's teaching, including tales of the master himself, had made a strong impression on her. Earlier that year she had begun writing, and soon submitted for publication, her cherished *Mary Poppins,* a tale about a character apparently a female version of Gurdjieff—strict yet caring at the same time, and full of surprises. At a talk Travers gave in 1972, she actually appreciated the suggestion that the Mary Poppins character was modeled after a Zen master. But Travers began her Zen studies later in life. It is difficult to say how acquainted she may have been with Zen, if at all, when she wrote the first Mary Poppins novel. Gurdjieff seems to be the more likely influence, though also possible is that Mary Poppins is a mixture of the two.

After Orage's death Travers made her way to Ouspensky's London group and continued her Gurdjieffian studies there. Like others in Ouspensky's group who knew of Gurdjieff's existence, she would have been required never to talk about Gurdjieff to the others.

In early 1936 Travers and Orage's widow Jessie (who had become close friends) joined Jane Heap's newly-formed Gurdjieff group. In March of that year the two also visited Gurdjieff in Paris. As a dancer herself, Travers dove headlong into movements practice. She became close with movement instructors Rosemary Nott and Jessim Howarth, especially Nott who she regarded as a mentor. Travers also visited Gurdjieff regularly the last two years of his life as part J.G. Bennett's group.

Simultaneous with her lifelong involvement in the Work, Travers was exploring other traditions, and it actually was not until later in life that she is found exploring Tibetan Buddhism. Sometime in the late 1960s while writing *Friend Monkey* and living in an apartment in the Chelsea area of London, certain Gurdjieffian friends had convinced Travers to host a family of three Tibetans visiting for a few months. Perhaps she was inspired by Guanyin—the bodhisattva of compassion.

More significantly, early in 1983, Travers was desperately

trying to find a Tibetan teacher. At that particular time she was apparently in an interval in the Work. She felt that it was no longer feeding her, and at the suggestion of Jessmin Howarth was trying to make contact with Eve Galantzine, a mutual acquaintance from the Ouspensky groups who was apparently now involved in that tradition.[1] Even so, Travers never left the Work. It is uncertain, however, why she apparently had no luck finding a Tibetan master, or why she was not looking for a Zen master which she had had prior success with.

It was in the summer of 1964 that Travers went to Kyoto for intensive Zen practice with Ruth Sasaki, who was introduced to her by Gurdjieffian friends. Sasaki was an American who first studied Zen with D.T. Suzuki in Japan in 1930 and later became a member of the Buddhist Society of America in New York. In 1944 Sasaki married the Society's resident priest, Sokei-an Shigetsu Sasaki, who died less than a year later. After Sokei-an's death the Society changed its name to the First Zen Institute. In 1949 Sasaki went to Kyoto to find another resident priest for the Institute, and remained there much the rest of her life. In 1957 she founded the First Zen Institute of America in Japan to translate Zen texts to English, and the following year she became the priest of Daitoku-ji. First Zen was actually located on the Daitoku-ji complex in a subtemple called Ryosen-an. At Ryosen-an Sasaki also established a zendo for Westerners called Zuiun-ken. It was at Zuiun-ken that Travers studied and practiced Zen with Sasaki. Other Gurdjieffians who practiced at Zuiun-ken at one time or another include William Segal, Paul Beidler and Hugh Ripman.

While in Kyoto herself, Travers became greatly moved by the statues in the lecture hall and treasure house of Koryu-ji Temple, which dates to 622 AD, and studied them intently. William Segal's favorite statue is actually the lifesize wooden statue of Miroku Bosatsu at Koryu-ji. He loved to meditate before it. Travers must have meditated before these statues too. This experience may have planted the seed for later studies of Buddhist art she made. Also, their shared appreciation of Koryu-ji suggests that Segal was the one who introduced Travers to Sasaki.

Travers was also very influenced by the work of Karlfried Graf Dürckheim—particularly appreciating his way of synthesizing together something of Zen Buddhism, Christianity and Depth Psychology—and put herself under his care in Todtmoos, Germany in 1968.

In the early 1970s she was living in New York and a member of William and Louise Welch's group.

In 1976 Travers moved back to Chelsea and started her own Gurdjieff group there. Also that year, after being approached by Dorothea Dooling, Travers began contributing to *Parabola*, a magazine on myth established by Dooling and other Gurdjieffians. Her Zen contributions to the journal include "Zen Moments," "The Silk Drum," and a poem called "Nirvana Is Samsara."

Another text she wrote, found in her archives, is a 17-page document called "The Unfolding of Buddhism: Some Notes on the Sources of the Iconography of the Exhibition," which explains the symbolism of 48 objects of Buddhist Art. Considering that it was never published, and that it is unlikely a museum would have hired her to compile such notes, with all likelihood this is something she wrote for the benefit of one of her Gurdjieff groups. It suggests that she gave the group a private tour of a special exhibit happening at one of the New York or London museums.

Another reason for believing that "The Unfolding of Buddhism" was written for one of her Gurdjieff groups is that her archives also contains the transcript of a talk she gave to the Welch group which includes a Zen tale. The brief story follows this chapter. It was chosen because it illustrates how Gurdjieff and Zen agree that light cannot exist without darkness, and therefore darkness need be embraced rather than resisted. Unity cannot be achieved via dualism—by opposing darkness. Zen talks about the inseparability of nirvana and samsara. Gurdjieff talks about getting help from one's devils as well as from one's angels. Although expressed somewhat differently they are the same idea. Bill Segal once expressed the same idea in recalling the words of a roshi who said, "Sleeping beside the waterfall, I stopped the war."[2]

Following this tale is an excerpt from one of Ruth Sasaki's books. This piece is significant in that the four major realizations or views it discusses, encountered by the Zen practitioner along the way, seemingly correspond to the realizations of individuals number four, five, six, and seven in Gurdjieff's ideology. This is a subject that Gurdjieff never went into detail about. Practically speaking, one can only have glimpses of the view immediately ahead. So, he only saw fit to discuss the realization of nothingness—the view of an individual number four. However, individuals number four need to begin to let go of their realization and work toward the succeeding view. Trying to ever reproduce the experience of nothingness is a mistake. Although it may seem like it, nothingness is not an end in itself; it is but one step along the way. So it would be useful for the individual number four to have clearer instruction on how to proceed. As well, with so many delusionals professing to be teachers of Gurdjieff's ideas today, it might be useful to have some understanding of the views further ahead so one can better distinguish between such misguided "teachers", who mistake the realization of nothingness for enlightenment, and authentic guides.

---

[1] Letter from Travers to Howarth, dated 13 Feb. 1983, found in the Howarth Gurdjieff Archive.

[2] William Segal & Marielle Bancou-Segal, *A Voice at the Borders of Silence: An Intimate View of the Gurdjieff Work, Zen Buddhism, and Art* (New York: Overlook Press, 2003), 228.

Publicity photograph of Pamela Travers. Photographer unknown.

## ONE WITH THE TAO

There is a zen story of a little countryside that was parched for rain—none had fallen for so long that the crops failed and the people were hungry. So they sent to fetch the priest. "All of you," he advised, "must work together to build me a hut in which I can live alone." So they set to work to make a bamboo hut, the priest entered and sat himself down and in no time there was a cloud no bigger than a man's hand and very soon it was raining.

"But how did you do it?" they wanted to know, for it looked to them like magic.

"No magic at all," the priest replied. "I realized I was not in the way of the Tao, so I asked that together you build me a hut, sat there until I was one with the Tao, and since the Tao needs that all things work together for good, look, you have rain!"

If the myths and fairy tales have anything to tell us, it is that the shadow is as necessary to the sun as the sun is necessary to the shadow; that without the Wicked Fairy, as she is known in the fairy tales under many guises, how will the Good Fairy do her work, how will the story be thrown forward and brought to its necessary conclusion?

I was once told by a child something less than three, "I am two boys, Goodly and Badly." I was interested. Which of them was there at the moment? A seraphic smirk came over his face, really it was almost too good. "Goodly," he replied.

Then he closed the door behind him, immediately opening it again and looking as much like a demon as anyone so seraphic could. "This is Badly!" he declared and then with a dubious, anxious look, "Which do you like best?" "I like them both the same," I said, and with joy he threw himself upon me. He was he, whatever he was, and that was enough for me.

And I knew that he was unconsciously telling himself and me that the myth is no one-sided thing, you can't be good without being somehow dealing with the bad in you, a symbol of multiple facets. Indeed, if the myth were not one-sided, if it did not carry both sun and shadow, where would we human creatures be? How could we progress or move or carry on the process of life—inwardly or outwardly? If we force the myths to be all good, lop-sided, distorted things, they quickly take their revenge. What they are telling us perhaps—mind you, I'm not imposing it, not laying it down as an axiom—is that the interaction of dark and light, positive and negative, affirmation and denial, serves to renew the world—or perhaps teaches us to renew the world.

*Pamela Travers*

## THE FOURFOLD UNIVERSE

One of the last and greatest scriptures to be brought from India to China was that known, under its Sanskrit name, as the *Avataimsaka Sutra.* Upon the teachings of this sutra there developed in China a great school of Buddhism, known in Chinese as the *Hua-yen,* in Japanese as the *Kegon,* school.

The Kegon philosophy and doctrines formed a magnificent structure, immense in conception and intricate in detail. From them Zen has taken and made its own use of one concept, that of the Fourfold Universe. According to Kegon teaching, the universe in which we live is a fourfold universe and is to be observed or, better, realized under four aspects. The subject is somewhat technical, but I shall try to be as simple in my statement of it as my understanding permits.

The total universe—earth, sky, sun, moon, planets, stars. Infinite space—is known in Buddhist-Sanskrit terminology as the *Dharmadhatu,* in Japanese as the *hokkai.* The word *dhatu,* Japanese *kai,* means "field" or "realm", and the word *Dharma,* Japanese *ho,* has two meanings: the Absolute Truth and also the individual elements which constitute the universe. So the *Dharmadhatu,* the *hokkai,* is the "Realm of Absolute Truth" and also the "Realm of All Elements."

Kegon and Zen observe this *Dharmadhatu* or *hokkai* in four ways:

First it is observed as the actual world in which we live

everyday, the world of phenomena. The universe under this aspect is termed the *ji hokkai* in Japanese. *Ji* means "things", "phenomena". So this first way of observing the universe is as the world of things, the actual, factual world as such. Of this world as it appears to us ordinary men, Zen at first has nothing to say. Later, however, when we are prepared to understand its real nature we shall have to make a thorough investigation of its every phase.

The second way of viewing *hokkai*—and when I use the English words viewing or observing, it is always with the deeper meaning of realizing—is as the Absolute World, the world of Reality. The world under this aspect is termed *ri hokkai,* the Realm of the Absolute principle. This is the undifferentiated world, the world of complete Oneness, Emptiness, Shunyata. To enter this world, to realize this world, and to make this world our permanent abiding place, the place where we stand, this is the *sine qua non* for the Zen student. This is the world entered by many artists and mystics, and by people who go through some personal religious experience, the world of cosmic consciousness, as it is sometimes called. I was interested to read some time ago the following quotation from the famous European art critic Berenson: "It was a morning in early summer. A silver haze shimmered and trembled over the lime trees. The air was laden with a caress. I remember... that I climbed a tree stump and felt suddenly immersed in Itness. I did not call it by that name. I had no need for words. It and I were one." In this world the individual self or ego vanishes. One becomes merged with, one with, the Great Self. Too often, unfortunately, this vision fades with time and is forgotten, its profound significance never penetrated or understood. But when this realization is completely achieved, never again can one feel that one's individual death brings an end to life. One has lived from an endless past and will live into an endless future. The problems of heaven and hell, of individual sin and individual salvation, are ended once and for all. At this very moment one partakes of Eternal Life—blissful, luminous, pure. This experience is salvation in Zen.

It is this world that we wish to enter into when we begin

376

our Zen studies. The first koans given to the Zen student—Joshu's "Mu", Hakuin's "Sound of the Single Hand," the Sixth Patriarch's "Before your father and mother were born, what was your original face?"—these are the koans, penetration into which will lead us through the Gateless Barrier into the Absolute World, the Realm of the Absolute Principle, the *ri hokkai.* But since a first satori is often merely a glimpse into this world, a getting of one's foot inside the gate, as it were, the Zen student studies many koans in order that this world may become a never extinguished reality to him.

But we live and function in the everyday world, the phenomenal world, the world of relativity, the world of separated things. Of this Zen is well aware. So the next step is to bring us to the realization that noumenon and phenomena, the Absolute and the relative, are but two aspects of one Reality. Therefore, when the Zen student has thoroughly realized the *ri hokkai,* the world as the Realm of the Absolute, he is asked, *standing in the Absolute,* to look again at the relative, phenomenal world which he previously believed to be the only world.

This, the third way of viewing the universe, is that known as the realization of the universe as the *riji muge hokkai,* that is, the world in which the Absolute and the particular, the noumenal and the phenomenal, the Principle and the manifested are realized to be completely harmonized and united. The particular, the relative, the phenomenal, the manifested, are but the aspect under which we observe the noumenon, the Absolute, the Principle. The actual words *riji muge hokkai* translated literally mean: *ri* "Principle", *ji* "things", *mu* "without", *ge* "hindrance" or "obstruction". That is, the Absolute and the relative completely interpenetrate one another without any obstruction or hindrance. Or, to use another term, they are completely united. In truth, they are one and the same thing.

When we attain this realization we come to know everything in the world about us, every tree, every rock, every star, every bit of dust and dirt, every insect, every animal, every person, including ourselves, *as they are* to be a manifestation of the Absolute, and every function performed by every one of these as the functioning of the Absolute. Every existing thing, sentient or nonsentient, is holy in essence. From this realization arises the certainty that everything and everyone, no matter how lowly or how depraved, intrinsically is Buddha, is destined for salvation, will ultimately realize Buddhahood.

But there is a still more profound realization to be attained. This is known as the *jiji muge hokkai,* the realization of the realm of the completely harmonious and unobstructed interpenetration and interconvertibility of all things with one another. *Ji,* we know, means "things", so *jiji* means "things and things;" *muge* means "without hindrance," "without obstruction." So *jiji muge hokkai* is the realm in which all things, which we have already come to realize as the Absolute manifested, together form one complete and total whole by means of harmonious and unobstructed penetration, interconvertibility, and identification with each other. The realization of the *jiji muge hokkai* is the realization that everything in the universe is constantly and continuously, freely and harmoniously interpenetrating, interconverting itself with every other thing. It is the realization of the universe as the expression of the eternal self-recreating play of the Absolute. Thus experienced, the universe is seen to be one in time and one in space, or, rather, to be timeless and spaceless.

When my teacher was speaking to me about this he said:

Now think about yourself. You think you are a separate and independent individual. But you are not. Without your father and mother you would not be. Without their fathers and mothers they would not have been and you would not be. And without their fathers and mothers, your fathers and mothers would not have been. And so we can go back endlessly to the origin of the human race and before that and before that. You, at this moment, are the apex of the great triangle formed by all these previous individual lives. In you they all exist today. They live in you today as truly as they lived individually in what we call time.

But, in addition, just as you live today by virtue of all the other individuals and existences in the world at this moment—your body is sustained by the food cultivated and processed by innumerable persons throughout the present world, your body is covered by clothing produced by innumerable persons throughout the present world, your activities are conditioned by the activities of innumerable persons living in the present world, your thinking is conditioned by the thinking of innumerable persons living in the present world—so the bodies, the actions, the thinking of all your ancestors who form the great triangle of which you are the present apex, have in their turn been dependent upon and conditioned by the innumerable persons existing in the world at the time they individually lived. So, if we consider that all past time is concentrated in you at this moment, we must also consider that all past space is also concentrated in you at this moment. Therefore you and every other being in the world at this instant actually each stand at the apex of a great cone rather than a triangle.

But this is not all. From you will come your children and their children's children; from your actions will come the results of your actions and the results of those results; and from your thoughts will come the future thinking and the thinking resulting from that thinking, *ad infinitum*. You hold within yourself the seed from which the future will spring. Just as much as you at this moment are the entirety of past time, so you are the entirety of future time. Just as you at this moment represent the concentration of all past space, so you at this moment represent the concentration of all space in the future. And this is true for each sentient or non-sentient existence in the universe. In you and in each one of them at this moment is all time and all space. In other words, this moment is all.

Kegon and Zen each have their own symbols for illustrating this *jiji muge hokkai*. In Kegon the symbol used is known as Indra's Net. It is described as being a great net extending throughout the universe, vertically to represent time, horizontally to represent space. At each point where the threads of the net cross one another is a crystal bead, the symbol of a single existence. Each crystal bead reflects on its shining surface not only every other bead in the net but every reflection of every reflection of every other bead upon each individual bead —countless, endless reflections of one another.

For the Zen sect, when Shakyamuni held up the single lotus flower before the assembly he was showing the *jiji muge hokkai,* he was manifesting the totality of the universe in time and space, he was illustrating the complete and harmonious interpenetration of all things with each other, he was expounding his complete teaching in its minutest detail and demonstrating its most profound and mysterious principle: that each single existence is the totality of Life, beginningless, endless, ever self-creating, Infinite Life.

That, is what we are. That is what you are, that is what I am, that is what everything in the universe is—beginningless, endless Life, infinite, boundless, eternal Life. This is what we must realize. And to this realization Zen practice leads us step by step. This is the aim of Zen. This is true satori.

When we first enter the great and wondrous world of the *Dharmadhatu* we are like babies who open their eyes for the first time to the world they are to live in. In the beginning they can distinguish little, but gradually their eyes make out the form of the mother's breast, the bed, the room, the playthings. Just so, when with our first awakening we push open the gate and enter the Absolute World, we can at first distinguish little about it. But gradually, with our Dharma-eye, as it is called in Zen, we come to see more and more clearly. That is why a first satori is not enough, why Zen study must continue, and continue. And though our formal Zen study may reach its conclusion, real Zen study never ends. For Zen study is the ever continuing and deepening realization of this one ever-renewing-itself Eternal Life.

As a matter of fact, Zen goes one step farther than the realization of the fourth view of Kegon. The last step in Zen is what may be called "the return to the natural." Though we may have realized the *jiji muge hokkai,* we must now demonstrate our realization in the practice of our everyday life, whatever that everyday life may be. If we must wash dishes, we wash dishes; if we must be the president of a country, we are the president of a country; if we must teach, we teach; if we must be students, we are students. But as we wash dishes, as we act as president, as we teach, as we study, we know that this act is a holy act, an act indispensable to the total universe; upon its being done and done when and as it must be done the entire future of all existences depends. Then, as our realization becomes deeper and more profound, when we have thoroughly digested and assimilated it, as it were, we do not need to think about the philosophic or religious implications of our activities. Naturally and spontaneously we respond to the moment. Without thinking about anything we naturally act. This is the "freedom" of Zen. This is also what is known as "having no thing in the mind and no mind in things." This is the ultimate in the Zen way of life.

*Ruth Fuller Sasaki*

*Robert Godet with Jamyang Khyentse Chökyi Lodrö*

## QUART-DE-SOMMEIL

Gurdjieff had a few students who did not work with others in groups. They tended to be more wealthy and independent individuals. Those who fell into this category include Arnold Keyserling, Dr Pierre Joseph Aboulker and Robert J. Godet. But it would be a mistake to think that Gurdjieff only used them for their money or regarded them any less of a student, especially in the case of Robert Godet. Gurdjieff gave of himself to all and in doing so considered how each would be most receptive to what he had to offer. These soloists were still invited to Gurdjieff's table—a place where group identities were forgotten—and made friends in the Work through that environment.

In the text of "On Tibetan Soil" which follows, Godet refers to Gurdjieff as "my teacher and friend." He also seems to be speaking of his relationship with Gurdjieff in *L'Age de Soleil*—written shortly after his teacher died—where he says, "Dead Milarepa sends this final message to his heart disciple: 'At the borders of Spirit and Matter. Knowledge created by oneself is the big culprit... Stand on the firm ground of the non-objectivity of things.'"[1] A particularly good Work friend of Robert and Babette Godet, Yahne Le Toumelin, also describes Godet as having been Gurdjieff's "heart disciple."[2]

Certainly Godet was more a friend to Gurdjieff than other students of the time. François Grunwald said as much:

...I was waiting with many others on a platform at Saint Lazare station for the Atlantic train from Cherbourg. Monsieur Gurdjieff appeared at the door of the car, wearing a black chapka, his eyes beaming and laughing. At the sight of him, Madame H. was moved to tears. We surrounded him in a large circle which he scanned with his calm gaze before giving his assessment: "Always only eat, not much work!" Then he grabbed the arm of young Robert Godet who brought him home. Robert Godet knew how to employ the freedom of loons and shared with Mr G. a complicity such as that exchanged between friends rather than a master and his pupil.[3]

Solange Claustres, apparently talking about Godet in her book *Becoming Conscious with G.I. Gurdjieff*, mentions Gurdjieff youthfully hopping on the back of his motorcycle and taking off with him. Although this individual is not mentioned by name, the relationship exemplified by this episode, along with her stating that he had the same profession as Godet, describing him as a dinner guest rather than a group member, and describing an emotional disposition which is how Grunwald also portrays Godet, all together makes it fairly clear she is speaking of Godet. Claustres also says that Gurdjieff gave him the nickname Quart-de-sommeil (Quarter-Asleep). If that is to imply a meaning of being three quarters awake, that is quite an honorific to be bestowed upon by Gurdjieff.

Professionally, Godet occupied most of his time as a book publisher, primarily of poetry supplemented with elegant illustrations, as well as an author in his own right. He was also a fifth degree black belt in judo, an authority on the subject, and founder of the International Judo Federation. But he actually acquired his wealth working for and having stock in Forex Drilling, a corporation serving the fossil fuel industry that was founded by his father. However, his involvement in Forex was actually minimal. Godet had other interests that he was pursuing, another being his support for the French Resistance during World War II, which was provided by gun-running. It was his judo skills that made him particularly effective taking on such covert operations. All three of these interests seem

384

to be different ways that his magnetic center expressed itself. The arts, politics and the martial arts are all entryways to an authentic spiritual search. The martial arts in particular may also explain something of Godet's competitive nature in the following tale he told Grunwald, which Gurdjieff evidently needed to repeatedly crush.

"It's still an enigma for me today. Why did I always fall into Mr Gurdjieff's trap and almost always in the same way? We didn't gamble for fun, the stakes were often high and when we started discussing and arranging the bet, I inevitably felt like I was cheating. For everyone, I had to win; it was obvious. However, he managed to introduce an execution clause which, although seemed minor and very acceptable to me, proved to be decisive for his victory."

For example, Godet boasted of owning one of the fastest cars in Paris, a very recent Bugatti model, which could reach two hundred kilometers an hour, in front of Mr Gurdjieff who himself drove an old Citroën 15CV, known for its heaviness, robustness and slowness. He challenged Godet:

"I bet two cases of Celtic cigarettes, me and my car win against you in a hundred kilometer race."

He smoked these Celtic, hard to get on the black market. Godet laughed at him:

"You and your old Rosalie against me and my Bugatti? The best thing is if you give me the two cases of cigarettes straight away; you will save yourself a lot of trouble!"

Then he added with a disgusted air: "To make a bet where it is absolutely sure to win is not worthy of a gentleman."

Mr Gurdjieff was keen on it. They discussed and worked out the conditions. The race was to take place on a fairly steep road between Lyon and Clermont-Ferrand. Mr G. demanded that the course be divided into two sections of about fifty kilometers, and that during the first part of the race, Godet be forced to follow twenty meters behind him. The real race would then begin. The immense advantage his car possessed led Godet to accept all handicaps.

"I got into my Bugatti," he said, "quite sure of winning this time. Nothing could stop me. But in less than two hundred yards, I knew I was going to lose again. During the first fifty kilometers, Mr G. drove at about ten kilometers per

385

hour. His old, robust motor supported it, mine was breaking down. My Bugatti, built for high speeds, was heating up considerably. The engine did not give up completely but arrived ruined at the end of the first stage. During the second, Mr G. took incredible risks on this road, pushing his 15CV to the maximum. I couldn't overtake it with my damaged engine. Sacred man, he knew the mechanics!"

Godet was afraid to be afraid. This was his main trait which pushed him towards the most impossible adventures —to prove himself tirelessly that fear did not affect him. But there are different qualities of fear and he experienced several times that of being kicked out for good by Mr Gurdjieff when his fantasies were beyond acceptable. He then knelt down and begged with touching fervor to be granted permission to stay, and Mr G. always gave in, often much to the regret of Madame de S. and many others. Godet sincerely loved Mr Gurdjieff, and this was his weakness, or perhaps his strength.[4]

Godet had begun the practice of judo sometime before World War II with Mikinosuke Kawaishi, who was responsible for introducing judo to Europe. Kawaishi had begun teaching judo in London in 1928 and in Paris in 1935. It is significant that in the process of teaching judo, Kawaishi was teaching the fundamentals of Zen. This would be a big influence on Godet. After acquiring his black belt, Godet opened his own judo club in which he also taught the art as a form of spiritual practice. As well, he wrote two books on Judo and a poetic commentary on the Zen classic, *Ten Oxherding Pictures,* which featured his own illustrations.

In 1939 at the age of 18, Godet began studying law and was soon active in the Resistance and the underground Communist party.

After the war he traveled to the Americas and was captivated in particular by the ancient Mayan civilization.

Interestingly, Godet had more than one teacher-friend. Another was Sun Wu Kung. But Sun Wu Kung did not have any sort of group that he taught. He was what might be described as an enlightened tramp. He was a Kashgar native who spent his youth in a Tibetan monastery and later wandered Europe.

It was with Sun Wu Kung who Godet initially studied Tibetan Buddhism.

On an occasion when Godet got together with Sun Wu Kung and Grunwald, Godet mentioned to Grunwald that he had introduced Sun Wu Kung to Gurdjieff in 1948. When Grunwald asked what they spoke about, Godet replied that they did not exchange a word. Grunwald then turned to Sun Wu Kung incredulously asking how that was possible, whereupon Sun Wu Kung replied, "Who talks to a mirror?"

Godet appears to have met Gurdjieff in 1946. In the meeting transcript of 9 December of that year Godet is found asking an insignificant question and subsequently being reprimanded by Gurdjieff for only coming once every three months. In 1948 his commentary of the Zen classic *Ten Oxherding Pictures* was published. Although likely inspired by his work with Kawaishi, this text may have also been inspired in part by Sun Wu Kung who clearly studied Zen as well as Tibetan Buddhism. This account illustrating Sun Wu Kung's understanding of Zen comes from an article by Serge Beucler:

> One day, after reading Suzuki, I told Sun about a koan that struck me, roughly in these terms: A Zen master summons a disciple and to gauge him abruptly asks him: "What is Zen?" After greatly concentrating, the disciple exclaims to the master, "It is Zen!" I found this anecdote quite admirable, which for me reflected the purest spirit of Tao and Chan. After a rather heavy silence, Sun took my arm and said, "This story is incomplete, and I will tell it to you in earnest. Here it is:
>
> "A Zen master summons a disciple and to gauge him fiercely asks him, 'What is Zen?' After greatly concentrating, the disciple, thinking to reflect the purest spirit of Tao and Chan, exclaims to the master, 'It is Zen!'
>
> "The master then sadly looks at the disciple and says to him, 'Talkative!'"[5]

Towards the end of Gurdjieff's life, Godet, sensing his teacher's time was limited, asked him where he could find another teacher. In response, Gurdjieff suggested that he go to Tibet. Although it was not possible for Westerners to enter Tibet at the time, Godet thought to journey to Sikkim, whose people are ethnic Tibetan and where there is a large Tibetan Buddhist population. Between 1951 and his untimely death in 1960, Godet traveled regularly to Sikkim, often staying for long periods.

In 1954 Godet embarked on a road trip with his second wife Marguerite Batigne to Asia to visit the monasteries and sacred sites of various traditions and meet the teachers associated with them. Such a trip was quite a feat at the time. Although his main interest was finding a Tibetan Buddhist teacher, he evidently wanted to also make contact with some of the other traditions that Gurdjieff encountered. This journey resulted in two books—*En 2CV vers les Hauts Lieux d'Asie* (*In a Citroën 2CV to the Highlands of Asia*) and *A travers les Sanctuaires de l'Inde* (*Through the Sanctuaries of India*). It is in the second volume that he speaks of his time in Sikkim. A third book, *Les contes de la Valmourani*, a collection of poetic essays influenced by his travels, was also published.

On this trip, Godet met Sikkim's prince and princess, and together with Princess Kukula established the Sikkim Relief and Rehabilitation Committee for Tibetan Refugees. Making himself the committee's chairman enabled him to enter Sikkim regularly and remain there for long periods. Princess Kukula succeeded Godet as chairman when he died.

There are a few things that are interesting about Godet's account of his time in Sikkim. One is that he associates Gurdjieff's idea of conscious labor to the Kagyupa sect in particular by making note of Milarepa's great labors—something he had intuited before making the journey. He also speaks about the *Bardo Thödol* which has significance for Gurdjieffians. And he speaks about Tibetan Buddhism as "the way of conscience," which is how Gurdjieff defined his own teaching. It seems as though he understood that Gurdjieff's idea of conscience is the equivalent of the idea of buddha-nature—a comparison that will be discussed later. He also talks about his friend Sun Wu Kung in his conversation with a lama. No doubt Sun Wu Kung was another inspiration for the journey.

It was sometime in 1956 that Jamyang Khyentse Chökyi Lodrö arrived in Sikkim. The previous year he had witnessed

388

the beginning of Chinese aggression in Tibet and foresaw that things would get much worse. Most others did not see the coming occupation so early. He spent about a year on pilgrimage in Tibet before leaving for Sikkim to begin a tour of the holy sites of India. It was while in Sikkim that he was invited by the royal family to stay. This became his home for the rest of his life.

Shortly after Chökyi Lodrö's arrival he and Godet first met. They were apparently introduced to one another by the royal family. Thereafter Godet remained his student.

It is interesting that Jamyang Khyentse Chökyi Lodrö was Godet's teacher for a couple of reasons. Firstly, he was also one of the teachers of the Sixth Shechen Rabjam—the rinpoche who was likely Gurdjieff's son. Secondly, it is interesting that Chökyi Lodrö was a teacher for all but one of the Tibetan Buddhist teachers with whom direct students of Gurdjieff had studied. Not that there is any direct connection with either of these facts; more that these sincere individuals had the good karma to meet someone in the same lineages that Gurdjieff himself was involved in. Babette Bridault's teacher, Sogyal Rinpoche, was Jamyang Khyentse Chökyi Lodrö's nephew and *very* close to him. Paul Anderson's two main Buddhist teachers, Chögyal Namkhai Norbu and Dodrupchen Rinpoche, were both his students. Chöyam Trungpa Rinpoche, who was a teacher-friend of Lord Pentland, was his student. The two main Tibetan teachers that William Segal met with, Chatral Rinpoche and Dudjom Rinpoche, were his students. Madame de Salzmann met with many of these teachers too. The only one who was not a student of Jamyang Khyentse Chökyi Lodrö was Yahne Le Toumelin's teacher, Kangyur Rinpoche. Even so, Kangyur Rinpoche was in the same lineage. In fact, his third son, Jigme Khyentse Rinpoche, was recognized as Jamyang Khyentse Chökyi Lodrö's reincarnation. But let us talk about Jamyang Khyentse Chökyi Lodrö himself.

Jamyang Khyentse Chökyi Lodrö was considered one of the greatest teachers of his time. He was something of a teacher's teacher. The above is but a fraction of the many tulkus he gave teachings to. A list on the wiki of Rigpa—the sangha founded by Sogyal Rinpoche—currently contains 93 entries and appears to be missing some.

He was born in 1893 and recognized by Jamgon Kongtrul the Great as the activity incarnation of Jamyang Khyentse Wangpo. (Remember that Jamyang Khyentse Wangpo was a teacher of both Tersey Tsewang Norbu and the Fifth Dzogchen Rinpoche, two of Gurdjieff's likely teachers.) Thus he was enthroned at Katok Monastery. At Katok's monastic college he studied the treasuries compiled by the Great Kongtrul. These treasuries are a collection of the great teachings of all the Tibetan Buddhist lineages, as well as of the Hinayana and pre-Tibetan Mahayana, and form the basis of the nonsectarian Rimé movement.

However, because the First Khyentse Tulku, the body incarnation of Jamyang Khyentse Wangpo and abbot of Dzongsar Monastery, became ill while receiving a teaching from the Fifth Dzogchen Rinpoche and suddenly died, Jamyang Khyentse Chökyi Lodrö was installed at Dzongsar as the monastery head. This is why he is also known as Dzongsar Khyentse Chökyi Lodrö.

He studied with many great teachers of his time. I will just note those associated with teachers previously mentioned. From Chögyam Trungpa's predecessor, the Tenth Surmang Trungpa, he studied the Kagyu teachings of Marpa, Chakrasamvara and Mahamudra. Shechen Kongtrul, Chögyam Trungpa's root teacher, transmitted to him the complete works of the Second Shechen Rabjam. And the Third Dodrupchen Rinpoche gave him Dzogchen teachings and was one of his primary Nyingmapa teachers.

Little is known about Godet's time with Chökyi Lodrö. However, Yahne le Toumelin mentions that Godet was present when Chökyi Lodrö gave Rimé transmission to his nephew and attendant Sogyal Rinpoche. So, he too would have learned something of this important teaching.

Godet, along with his friend Prince Peter of Greece, were responsible for enabling the Dalai Lama's escape from Tibet to India in 1959. Later that year he would meet the Dalai Lama in person when he came through Sikkim.

That year is also when Chökyi Lodrö died. He was not very happy in Sikkim and this may have affected his health. Godet had tried to convince him to move to France, but if he was unhappy in Sikkim he certainly was not going to be happy in a country even stranger than his homeland. Yet Godet's proposal may have planted the seed of Sogyal Rinpoche's interest in moving to France.

Godet stayed on in Sikkim despite his teacher's death, continuing his work with Sikkim Relief and Rehabilitation Committee for Tibetan Refugees. He was also planning a trip to Japan thinking that there he would find a Zen master to guide him along the next phase of his spiritual journey. Sadly, his plan never materialized. Godet met an untimely death himself on March 23, 1960. Shortly after his plane departed Benares that day, it caught fire and crashed on the banks of the Ganges. He was returning to Sikkim with a load of arms to deliver to Tibetan revolutionaries. Although an investigation of the crash was inconclusive, many suspect the plane was sabotaged by the Chinese. He was only 39 years old.

But Godet's mission did not die with him. He influenced two others in particular who continued his work and established the dharma in France. His first wife, Babette, having also been a student of Gurdjieff, will be discussed separately. Here I would just like to say a few words about his brother Gérard.

Gérard likely saw continuing his brother's work promoting Buddhism not only as a way to honor his brother's legacy, but also as a way to address the suffering of such a personal loss. His mourning also led him to befriending his brother's friend, filmmaker Arnaud Desjardins. Robert had introduced Desjardins to Madame de Salzmann in 1948, but she did not place him in a group until the following year and he never had the opportunity to meet Gurdjieff before he died. Desjardins was also a friend of Yahne Le Toumelin, and it was probably both her and Robert Godet who got him interested in Tibetan Buddhism.

It was through Desjardins' film *Message of the Tibetans* that Gérard became aware of Kangyur Rinpoche and subsequently traveled to Darjeeling in the late 1960s to become his student. He gave significant material assistance to both Kangyur Rinpoche and the Centre d'Études de Chanteloube—a retreat center in Dordogne. Gérard too had acquired something of his father's wealth. Besides Kangyur Rinpoche, Gérard invited many other rinpoches to France. These included Dudjom Rinpoche, Dilgo Khyentse Rinpoche, the Sixteenth Karmapa, Nenang Pawo Rinpoche, Trulshik Rinpoche, and Nyoshul Khen Rinpoche.

Gérard himself died in 2011 at the age of 87 after devoting over 40 years to spreading the buddhadharma in France.

It was already mentioned what is interesting about Godet's account of his time in Sikkim. A much-edited version of that chapter from his book follows. Two additional texts of interest are also offered—a poem of Godet's from a short cycle called *La voie abrupte* (*The Abrupt Way*), and a Dzogchen text by Jamyang Khyentse Chökyi Lodrö. "The Abrupt Way" is clearly an allusion to Dzogchen, no doubt influenced by Chökyi Lodrö, yet Gurdjieff's teaching as well as Zen can also be considered such a path. Certainly Godet recognized that affinity between the three. (For more on this subject, see the chapter "Haida!")

[1] Robert J. Godet, *L'Age de Soleil* (Paris: Robert J. Godet, 1950), 76.
[2] Private correspondence.
[3] François Grunwald, *Un chemin hors de l'exil, de Freud à Gurdjieff* (Paris: Originel Antoni, 2017), 522.
[4] Ibid., 559–60.
[5] Serge Beucler; "Sun: Un Maître Errant," *Le Nouveau Planète* no. 23 (l'Été 1971), 136.

## On Tibetan Soil

The reader must not be misled by this title. I have never set foot in the political country known as Tibet. Sikkim is an independent kingdom under the aegis of India, and Kalimpong, where I stayed even longer, is in Indian territory. But countries such as Sikkim are historically and geographically Tibetan. The inhabitants are overwhelmingly of Tibetan race, the usual language is Tibetan, and the religion is the Lamaist Buddhist religion directly dependent on Shigatse and Lhasa. In this sense, and although I have in no way satisfied my desire (even greater since this trip) to know Upper Tibet, I can nevertheless say that I went and lived in a Tibetan country.

### Sikkim

Sikkim, the distant goal of our journey, into which we finally entered, is a small kingdom one hundred and thirty kilometers long (between India and communist-occupied Tibet) and eighty kilometers wide between the kingdom of Nepal, which is under Indian influence, and the very independent kingdom of Bhutan, to which anyone—whether Chinese, English, Indian, or whatever—better not venture if they care about their existence. Let us say in passing that, according to what I have been told, there is no comparison between the way in which Sikkim or Tibet are prohibited and Bhutan. The first two, in fact, are only closed as a result of foreign intervention—Chinese or Indian as the case may be—while Bhutan seems to be hostile to any foreigner. This hostility is far-reaching, since the Indian resident in Sikkim, who is also a Political Officer for Bhutan, has, it seems, never been able to reach the capital of this fierce kingdom. How different from the Tibetans of Sikkim, so quick to assail you with questions and so eager to trade!

Geographically, Sikkim is a country of steep forested "hills" between 1,500 and 3,000 meters high to the south, and high mountains of ice and snow in the west, north and east. To the west stands the Kangchenjunga, which marks the border of Nepal like a gigantic milestone of eight thousand and six hundred meters. The passes to Nepal are already at a good altitude (more than 5,000 meters at Kang-La), but towards Tibet it is worse (16,900 feet at Kongralama-La, 18,131 feet at Donkya-La, and 17,000 feet at Ghora-La) according to the most recent maps. (*La* means "pass" in Tibetan.) Nature itself therefore wanted to make Sikkim an independent country, and, in fact, for many years only common religion, language and origin created a link with Lhasa. But times are no longer so acceptable and, for fear of Scylla, Sikkim must now come to terms with Charybdis.

According to the very official *Murray's Guide*, there are only 528 villages and 14,777 occupied houses in Sikkim. If that's true, the country must be a horrible desert, because in the little I've traveled, I've felt like I've seen three-quarters of it! I will not venture to discuss such precise data, but will confine myself to advising my readers to go without fear to visit Sikkim, which is the most beautiful and pleasant of all the countries that I have seen. For beauty, only a few Afghan landscapes can compare to it. As for pleasure, it offers a set of conditions able to make the life of the cultivated person quite happy: suitable climate (one can easily flee the torrential rains of the south by going up to Gangtok or Tumlong), total comfort, proud but welcoming people, grand sites, interesting customs and religion of incomparable depth, and, for those who are traders, the virtually unlimited possibility of making a fortune in this market which unites rather than separates

394

the Asian and European worlds.

For us, Sikkim offered an additional charm: that of the royal family and its leader, the reigning Maharajah. With him, his son, the charming Maharaj-Kumar (who together with my cousin Michel de Cabourg resembled two peas in a pod), his daughters and sons-in-law, and his private secretary, my precious friend Tseten Tashi, it was simply a pleasant meal, washed down with the best Bordeaux I've had since France, and friendly discussion on all subjects that fascinate men in general and Tibetans in particular—war, women, politics and philosophy. Even the Prime Minister, J. Lal, was to prove to be an exquisite companion, as well as the Political Officer, Mr Kapur, a protege of Nehru who seemed to me to have a great political future in India. There were only feasts and banquets, and I needed all my courage and the solid friendship of Tseten Tashi to go, after the banquets, to study the lamaic texts or to photograph the *gompas* (lamaseries) that the protection of the maharajah opened wide to us.

## Lamaism: The Religion of Sikkim

There is no question of summarizing in one paragraph what could be the subject of several volumes. I will therefore hardly go into historical detail, endeavoring to show the spiritual origins of Lamaism as well as the essential points of its doctrine. Nor will I speak in this passage of the thousand and one forms of sorcery and superstition that flourish in Tibet, but will report the essentials of what I learned from long and in-depth conversations with very cultured lamas, one of whom, the Minister of Religious Affairs of Sikkim and uncle of my friend Tseten Tashi, is a valuable philosopher.

The letter of the Buddha's teaching has undergone considerable modification in what is called the Mahayana, meaning "great vehicle." This great vehicle is a metaphysical interpretation of the Buddha's teaching developed late after his death by two great Hindu sages—Nagarjuna, who is from the second century AD, and Asanga, who is from the fifth century AD and is known as Tokmé in Tibetan.

This metaphysical doctrine under the name of Mahayana

is opposed to the orthodoxy of the Hinayana (or "small vehicle") which sticks to the very letter of Gautama's words without any interpretation. The Hinayana dominates in Ceylon, Siam and Indonesia, while the Mahayana has conquered the North: Tibet, Mongolia, China and Japan.

In fact, the religion of Tibet is the fruit of a marriage between philosophy (that of Mahayana) and magic (Tantrist magic). Hence the flowering of gods, demons and spirits that are both symbols and energies. How was this marriage possible? Thanks to the fact that Tibetan philosophy and magic both agree on a fundamental point, namely that, in essence, the world is empty and that all the forms we see in it are only the illusory projections of our *namshés*.[1]

It was therefore admissible to represent in the form of terrifying or beneficent divinities the various components of our "soul", infinitely better named by the Tibetans consciousnesses/energies (in the plural). Although a notion understood with ease by psychoanalysts who have just "discovered" it, the terrifying gods are none other than the beneficent gods simply seen from another angle. When the total body-consciousnesses/energies emerges from ignorance, the deities (forces) which had appeared formidable to him take on a new, usable and beneficent purpose. The opposite is also true: The man who creates monsters and taboos out of things that could otherwise be very useful to him will degenerate, or "involute". The Tibetans, as we can see, did not wait for Freud to dissect the subconscious and its "mysteries".

It is interesting to note that the two generative paths of Lamaism—the philosophical and the magical—continue to this day to teach their methods separately. The philosophical path, that of the yellow hats, whose main school is at the monastery of Tashilumpo in the Tsang province city of Shigatse, advocates the notion of impermanence and the fallacy and emptiness of the self. Meditation on emptiness (*shunyata*) is, for the adherents of this sect, the direct path to liberation.

On the contrary, the magical way of the red hats, of which in Sikkim the Maharajah is great initiate and master, focuses on the agglomerating consciousnesses/energies which form our so-called "soul" or "spirit". One wonders if it is not possible to consciously agglomerate more and more energy until reaching levels of consciousness attributed only to the gods, with whose intelligence the world would appear completely different and could thereby begin to be understood. Their argument, which is the only one to hold against the yellow sect (and well at that), is that if nothing really exists except in the spirit which perceives it, the first thing to do is to improve this spirit by conscious accumulation of energy.

As always, a third way, a third doctrine, emerged from what was most valuable in the yellow sect and in the red sect. This is the doctrine of the Kagyupa, or sect of the white hats. It is interesting to note here the origin of this word Kagyupa, about which I had a very interesting conversation with Prince Peter.

Kagyupa is written in Tibetan bka' brgyud pa, but is pronounced kagyupa. There are, therefore, two possible interpretations of this word, one suggesting that it relates to the white color (*khar*) in which they are clothed, the other to the word "speech" (*kha*), implying the meaning "sect of the oral tradition." I believe, for my part, that both interpretations are admissible, the white sect having always and everywhere esoterically signified knights of the absolute, while, on the other hand, the Kagyupa sect is the Tibetan form of this unwritten teaching, which the Buddha transmitted to Kasyapa before dying and now flourishes in China under the name of Chan and in Japan under the name of Zen.

These ways (Kagyupa, Chan and Zen), one in their spirit and in their means, indeed admit the absolute position of Mahayana, for which all is empty, without 'I', illusory, "like a cloud soon dispersed by the wind." Yet they have also adopted the Tantrist view that "conscious labor" is necessary to raise the level of being of that agglomerate which forms our "soul". The Kagyupas, on this tantrist side, extracted the necessity of "conscious labor and intentional suffering." It suffices to be convinced of this to read Marpa's admirable explanatory statement by which the great root guru of Milarepa explains why he overwhelmed his disciple with so much work.

For me it is the complete unity of path and conduct of my teacher and friend Gurdjieff with that of the purest Kagyupa tradition that confirmed what I always knew instinctively: that it was by this "single way"—that of Kasyapa, Marpa and Huang-po—that he had attained liberation. As for the assertions of Mrs Alexandra David-Neel, according to which a real lama does not drink alcohol and does not eat meat, I have to wonder if it was really necessary to convey such heroism, steadfastness of effort and study, and often of intelligence and timing, to arrive—after years spent wandering with a monastery lama in a *gompa* in the most secret heart of Tibet—at such an obvious untruth.

It is enough to refer to the most sacred texts of the Kagyupas, throughout which can be read things such as, "The holy lama (Marpa), having drunk too much beer, fell asleep heavily," or else: "'Woman,' said the lama (who was married), 'slaughter the sheep and brew the beer; I want to prepare a great feast for my faithful followers who come from beyond the mountains to see me.'" Is it possible that her adopted son, the lama Yongden, did not reveal to his mother the mystical aspect of certain tantric meals, which are strangely close to the Last Supper (eat, this is my body; drink, this is my blood), except that it is a very subtle form of the consciousnesses/energies of the master that we share? Or did Alexandra David-Neel not want to talk about it? Considering that the assault she delivers to her bigoted and prudish European readers fundamentally makes her books excellent, it is quite possible. But it was unnecessary to distort; it would have sufficed not to have informed.

### The Monk Refrained from Refraining

It is also certain that many lamas use and abuse these mystical excuses to feast and revel. Peter of Greece told us that in a monastery in Ladakh, which lies between the border of western Tibet and Kashmir, he had seen a great lama, truly reincarnated, drinking excessively while devouring large chunks of meat and cheerfully groping two or three beautiful Tibetan neighbors who were, moreover, very consenting. Peter of Greece, being astonished by this monastic lama, exclaimed:

"Say, your rinpoche, he eats meat!"

"Ah! Yes," said the other, his throat tight with emotion, "it is so good!"

"I don't mind," said Peter of Greece, "but he drinks like a hole."

"Yes, yes," continued the lama in ecstasy, "I tell you, he wants the good of all creatures."

"And particularly that of the young girls who eat and drink with him," replied the prince.

Suddenly understanding the astonishment of his host, the lama continues:

"Ah! Yes, lord, it is so good; see: he refrains all the time."

"He is refraining?" asks Prince Peter.

"Of course! Yes, he refrains; he refrains all the time."

"But how?" exclaimed my bewildered friend.

"It's very simple," replied the other. "The rinpoche is so holy, so perfect, so far along the natural incline of the bodhisattvas, that if he did not constantly slow down by committing forbidden acts, well, he would become Buddha and leave us immediately. But his kindness exceeds all measure, and to stay with us... Ho! See how he slows down!"

In fact, the rinpoche's hand had plunged into the *ambag*[2] of one of the young girls—presumably to search for relics there—while his wine spilled all around him.

Happy country that one, where critical intelligence, against all odds, does not prevent its childlike faith from giving reason for life.

*The Bardo*

But the Lamaist religion was not made only for heroes who, by total conscious labor and intentional suffering, manage to escape from the endless cycle of death and rebirth in a single existence.

On the contrary, it devotes most of its attention to guiding the consciousnesses/energies forming our individuality so that they do not allow themselves to be led astray by fear or ignorance, whether in this life, the next, or the interval between them. This interval, the *bardo*, or rather the *bardos* (because there are five of them) have been the subject of an in-depth anatomical and psychological study ranging from the first approaches to death to the reincarnation of the consciousnesses/ energies in another body. All of these studies form the *Bardo Thödol*, or book of the *bardo*.

Having consistently devoted myself to this particular interest in studying the problems of the *bardo* has gradually led me to consider it not so much as a manual to use while in this limbo, as a kind of Michelin Guide of Transmigration, but rather like an initiatory teaching to be applied in fact to our current condition. For truly what we call life is in reality only an illusory passage through a limbo of suffering. Without discussing the application of this text to our daily life, however, let us see how it studies the process which separates death from the new birth.

As soon as the breath is extinguished, the consciousnesses/ energies tend to leave the body in which they had taken up residence. If it is the body of an initiate or a man who has looked into these issues, he will try to hold these various energies together and bring them out through the *brahmarandhra*, our window to the infinite located at the posterior fontanel on the top of the occiput. If he is a non-initiate, an assistant will have to stand near him and give him the necessary advice, precisely contained in the *Bardo Thödol*.

Freed from the chains of the flesh, the conscious "everything" is indeed nine times more intelligent than in its earthly envelope. This is fortunate, because one's atavisms, instincts, habits, inhibitions, in short one's acquired character, will act powerfully on one in this new and mysterious domain in which one finds oneself. It is against the weight of this karma, which presents itself in terrible forms as various enemies, yet in reality are none other than the projections of one's own mind, that the reading of the *Bardo Thödol* provides help. It says everyone at the moment of death and for a rather short time after (twenty minutes at the most), sees a dazzling white light, so luminous and radiant, unlike anything ever imagined. If, full of confidence, one allows oneself to be absorbed by it, one will not be reborn again, one will have been melted into the bosom of Abraham, one will have joined God, to use Christian terminology. If, on the other hand, seized with terror, one flees and seeks refuge in darker places—"where a pale whitish glow reigns"—the first *bardo* ends and a second begins. Then likewise a third, a fourth and a fifth; each time the appearances are more formal—less metaphysical, if you like—and, instead of being pure essence of light, will gradually become beneficent gods, terrifying gods, monsters and ghouls of all kinds, until the culmination where, surrounded by one's own projections, the agglomeration of consciousnesses/energies (the self) will seek refuge by plunging into a womb, and that will be reincarnation.

Let us note that this last moment is underlined by a trait which still clearly marks the profound psychology of the authors of this text—a trait confirmed by contemporary psychoanalysis: The soul which prefers the father will incarnate as daughter and hate her mother, and the one which prefers the mother will incarnate as a son and hate his father. Only already evolved consciousnesses escape this general rule.

### The Gods and the Worlds

Gods and worlds, nirvana and samsara, its opposite, are ultimately illusory. This becomes evident to initiates who will have arrived by the union of their subconsciousness and waking consciousness in the state of unity which allows them to consider the common origin of things. By recognizing one's own essence through the beneficent or terrifying apparitions of death, as a waking man sees that his dreams and his nightmares were all woven from the same illusory web, one reaches the state called "the end of suffering." Also, the extensive attention given by the text to the appearance of the various gods of the Lamaist religion is explained, above all, by the intention of showing us in symbols the main characteristics of our spiritual and material functions.

"The full development of the powers of the Dhyani Buddhas, which each personifies," writes Evans-Wentz, "leads to liberation and the state of Buddha. Partial development leads to

401

rebirth in a happier state."³ Likewise, stagnation or regression leads to rebirth into a more miserable state for the soul.

These states or realms are six in number and are called *lokas*. They are: *devaloka* (the god realm), *asuraloka* (the jealous god realm), *manakaloka* (the human realm), *tiryaka-loka* (the animal realm), *pretaloka* (the hungry ghost realm), and *narakaloka* (the hell realm).

As a general rule, the Buddha state can be attained, suddenly, from any world, but rebirth in a world other than *manaka-loka*, the world in which we live, would tend to delay access to liberation.

Regarding incarnate teachers, let us note with interest that while Dipankara, Gautama and Padmasambhava have already lived, and Christ, through his teaching of love, seems to have filled the role of Maitreya (the future Buddha announced by Gautama), the name of the fifth teacher is yet to be filled. This will come down to whose teaching will be based on conscience.

## The Way of Conscience

"How is it that you embraced us like this? After just three days, it feels like we're part of your family!"

My friend Tseten Tashi smiled as he continued walking. At the age of forty, this educated lama, relative of the Dalai Lama, personal secretary to the King of Sikkim, reminds us of a young athlete from our country: an athlete who has not only developed his muscles. Tseten Tashi is one of the best living photographers: he combines, in this art already long-established in Tibet, the rapidity of the journalist's glance, the breadth of the artist's gaze, and the depth of vision of the wise. His technical knowledge and business acumen led him to opening a photo shop in Kalimpong. Thus, dealing with politics, commerce, technology and religion with equal happiness, he is the very type of accomplished Tibetan who knows how to play many more notes on the keyboard of human possibilities than we do.

We walk while a thousand meters below us the valley of the Rani unfolds its tropical splendors and the Kangchenjunga, one and a half times the altitude of Mont Blanc and engulfing the expanse, dominates us. My friend finally responds with precision, equally serious and amusing, that he puts into each of his sentences:

"What you are looking for, we are also looking for. In any case, if a lama went to your country and arrived there after overcoming all the difficulties and triumphing over the same dangers that you must have encountered on your way, I am sure that he would be given a triumphant welcome. And if, moreover, he wanted to learn about the mysteries of your religion, there is no doubt that your monks would open their doors to him. But that's not all. You have already rid yourself of most of what prevents contact."

He is silent and my thoughts try to adjust to this form of mental activity, peculiar to Tibetans, which is based neither on logic nor on feeling, but on a cosmic substratum—on an ever-present vision of the interdependence of things, beings, worlds and gods. The individual, as seemingly revealed by certain esoteric teachings, would automatically secrete "anti-souls" in his astral body, just as "anti-bodies" circulate in his blood. It is the antibodies in the blood that prevent unions between animals and humans, or between animals of different species. They are how the blood determines not to accept any other blood. Ultimately, it is they who protect our individuality, who form its most entrenched barriers, who are the guardians of the self.

Similarly, secreted by the *namshés*, these "circulating-energies-intentionally-grouped-in-conscience", or "anti-souls", would oppose the rape of our mind by thoughts or mental energies that risk causing it to lose its individuality.

For the unified man, the game consisting of a set of material, emotional, mental and spiritual energies would then consist in knowing which anti-souls to destroy and which to keep. Indeed, the fear of thinking differently, reactions to new ideas, the difficulty of putting oneself in the place of others, all such limitations are conditioned by our anti-souls, which are modifiable by suggestion, hypnosis, prayer, meditation, music, living environment, food, dating, reading, etc. Drugs and perfumes are also known agents, as is an alluring individual.

403

Alas! Most often this union for the common march towards more light that must be marriage is only the association of two groups of anti-souls, in other words the reunion of two egoisms.

But to destroy the anti-souls all at once would be to deliver the conscience, of which they are the natural defense, to the mercy of all the devouring powers, of all the forces of dispersion. Excess thorns add nothing to the beauty of the rose, but thornless breeds of roses do not propagate well. As with everything in this relative world, the problem is therefore one right proportions, and the guru intervenes here as a doctor of souls, who purges them of their moods or, on the contrary, strengthens their characteristics, as the case may require.

I tear myself away from these reflections and answer the lama:

"Well! I have a good friend in Paris who was born in Kashgar in Xinjiang, on the western border of Tibet. He came to Europe on foot; he is one of the finest minds I know. However, no one gives him any consideration."

"Your friend is undoubtedly a great sage, who knows how to stay hidden in the middle of the crowd. This is the true power of making oneself invisible."

Such reflection opens the mind to the highest meaning of magic: The ring of Gyges, which renders invisible in the world, is humility. The *dorje*, the lightning that illuminates the worlds, is direct understanding, as opposed to discursive knowledge. The sword of Siegfried, which makes you invincible and makes everything bend before you, is kindness, infinite compassion, which, according to the wish of Amitabha Buddha, wants the liberation of all creatures. The elixir of life which makes one immortal is the poetic sense which discovers the eternal in every perishable thing. Finally, the philosopher's stone, which changes everything to gold, is objective consciousness, the supreme achievement of the man who lives in detachment.

This explains the final sentence of the fundamental text of the direct path (also called *dhyana*, or the way of conscience):

"There is no need for the miraculous power of the gods;

a single gesture of his hand discloses the dead trees covered with flowers."

*Robert Godet*

---

[1] Namshés means "aggregating energies of consciousness." (RG)

[2] A pocket that Tibetan women wear on the front of their dress. (RG)

[3] This is a translation of the French text as I was unable to find the quote in the English edition of *The Tibetan Book of the Dead.* Perhaps it comes from another Tibetan text that Evans-Wetnz translated. (LN)

"On Tibetan Soil" is an automated translation, edited by the author, of an abridged version of "En Pays Tibetain," Chapter 6 of *A travers les sanctuaires de L'Inde: De Khyber au Tibet* by Robert J. Godet (Paris: Amiot-Dumont, 1955).

## The Abrupt Way

This is the devil's Gift Route

The iron circle of the vicious paradox

Seven times you will expose yourself to failure

And the seventh one will make you dust or star.

Failure in each time what you believe is your being

In your possessions, your friends, your wife, your ambitions
you introduce it yourself in what you shape

In the slow passage from your flower to your fruit.

You follow the way of the I, and the I is a mirage

To abandon it or to pursue it, it is to do the same act

Failure in your destiny, in your disciples,
in all your being dedicated to the pursuit
of what you are

Suffering expected, accepted although unnecessary

And stupid as much as the necessary
construction of the Self

Indispensable before any abandonment of the Self.

He gives up cheaply, the one
who has nothing to abandon

But what madness inscribed in the order of the universe

That one must first create to be able to give up

Thus the world turns: nobody abandons it

Who has not been part of it. It's a solar lunch.

But very few are able to digest the sun.

*Robert Godet*

"The Abrupt Way," an untitled poem from *La Voie Abrupte* by Robert J. Godet (Paris: Robert J. Godet, 1954), was translated for the author from the French by Jacques Doyon.

## SPONTANEOUSLY WRITTEN SONG OF EXPERIENCE

Aho!
The Great Perfection of primordial freedom,
Which all sentient beings possess,
Does not need to be sought elsewhere.
The original state of things, primordial purity,
The way in which the natural condition abides—
To recognise this alone is sufficient.
Mentally created contrivance is pointless.
Untainted by the phenomena of intellectual speculation,
Clinging to notions of alertness, relaxation and the like,
No matter whether the mind is active or at rest,
It is none other than rigpa's creative expression.
Saṃsāra does not make it worse;
Nirvāṇa does not make it better.

Within the vast, all-pervasive realm of reality (*dharmadhatu*),
In the expanse of the single, all-encompassing sphere,
All thoughts involving the duality of perceiver and perceived
Are equal, without any basis for distinction or exclusion.

When this is realized through the guru's kindness,
There and then, in that very moment,
There is freedom.

This is the special feature of Ati Dzogpa Chenpo,
The secret pith instruction on clear light.
There is no swifter, profounder path than this
In any of the sutras or tantras.
To encounter it puts the mind at ease.

So that the child may follow the father's lead,
Omniscient guru, grant your blessings!

*This was written spontaneously.*

*Jamyang Khyentse Chökyi Lodrö*

*Babette Bridault and Khandro Tsering Chödrön, the wife of Jamyang Khyentse Chökyi Lodrö*

## BABETTE

Elisabeth "Babette" Bridault was the first wife and publishing partner of Robert Godet, attended dinners at Gurdjieff's flat with him, and was occasionally invited to join Gurdjieff on his frequent automobile excursions. She was also a close friend of Yahne Le Toumelin, another student of Gurdjieff. Although they had divorced by the time Godet made his first journey to Sikkim, she too understood that Gurdjieff recommended going to Tibet to find another teacher. But she did not need to go to Tibet or one of the other Tibetan Buddhist countries herself. The Tibetan exodus had already begun, connections were established by Godet, and she only needed to offer them refuge in France. Sogyal Rinpoche, his sister Dechen Lakar, and his aunt (the wife of Jamyang Khyentse Chökyi Lodrö) Khandro Tsering Chödrön, all came to live with her in her Paris home on Rue de Fleurus.

In 1978, when Bridault inherited her father's home on Rue Burq in Paris, she loaned it to Dudjom Rinpoche, and this became the first Tibetan Buddhist meditation center in Paris. Later, after Dudjom's death in 1987, it became the central center of Sogyal Rinpoche's Rigpa organization.

Bridault also had a vacation home in the south of France that began to be used as a retreat center in 1981. Their first retreat had over 100 participants.

These three homes also hosted other Tibetan rinpoches

and dignitaries when they visited Paris. Two that can be mentioned are Kalu Rinpoche and Chögyal Namkhai Norbu.

Bridault transcribed all the teachings that she hosted, and is also acknowledged for her assistance in the publication of many books by the Tibetan masters she befriended. In short, she played a major role in establishing the Tibetan buddhadharma in France. As Sogyal Rinpoche himself states in his *Tibetan Book of Living and Dying:*

> No mention of my work in France could be complete if I did not express my deep gratitude to Elisabeth Bridault. Her unique vision, her generosity and her consistency, which never failed to move me, have played a prominent role in all aspects of my activities. She has dedicated a significant part of her life to supporting me, and to supporting Buddhism and the Tibetan cause. My connection to her and her family actually goes back more than thirty years; I remember meeting her husband Robert Godet—one of the first Westerners who studied Tibetan Buddhism—when he was in Sikkim to receive teachings from my teacher Jamyang Khyentse.[1]

Bridault also served as the treasurer of Rigpa for a period of time. Interestingly, despite being such a steadfast member of Rigpa and advocate of the buddhadharma, her granddaughter, who Bridault had raised, does not recall her grandmother ever having taken refuge vows with Dudjom Rinpoche or Sogyal Rinpoche. She also mentions that, "My grandmother always kept a photo of Mr Gurdjieff on her nightstand."[2] As much as Bridault valued Tibetan Buddhism and the guidance she received from her Tibetan teachers, it appears that she was unable to commit herself to any teacher other than Gurdjieff.

Of the many Tibetan masters she received teachings from, the one most prominent in her life was clearly Sogyal Rinpoche. So, let us take a brief look at his life.

Sogyal Rinpoche was born in 1947. His father was a nephew of Dilgo Khyentse Rinpoche. When he was six months old, his uncle Jamyang Khyentse Chökyi Lodrö recognized him as the incarnation of Lerab Lingpa Tertön Sogyal, who was a teacher of the Thirteenth Dalai Lama. Chökyi Lodrö was Sogyal's root teacher and Sogyal began serving as Chökyi Lodrö's attendant when but a young boy. The two were very close.

Following Chökyi Lodrö, Sogyal left Tibet and settled in Sikkim in 1956. There he continued to study and practice closely with Chökyi Lodrö until his uncle's death in 1959, after which Khenpo Appey took over responsibility for the young tulku's education, as requested by Chökyi Lodrö. Young Sogyal also attended a Catholic school in Kalimpong, which is just across Sikkim's Border with West Bengal.

When a young man, Sogyal first attended college in Delhi. Later, in 1971, Sogyal received a grant to study comparative religion at Cambridge University and thus moved to England. After his studies, in 1974, he established a meditation center in London called Dzogchen Orgyen Chöling and began realizing his role as a teacher.

In 1978, Dudjom Rinpoche, for whom Sogyal Rinpoche had been serving as translator while in Kalimpong, invited him to take over his role as head teacher at his unnamed meditation center located in Bridault's Rue Burq home. A year later he gave the sangha the name Rigpa, which is a Tibetan word used to denote the wisdom aspect of primordial awareness in the Dzogchen teachings. Since then Rigpa has expanded to include over 100 centers in 23 countries.

Sogyal Rinpoche's book *Tibetan Book of Living and Dying*, quoted from earlier, was published in 1992 to great acclaim. He retired from teaching in 2017 and passed away two years later. Babette, as Bridault was affectionately known, left this world herself in 2013.

The text that follows, "Awakening the Mind, Opening the Heart," is a transcript of a talk that Sogyal Rinpoche gave to J. G. Bennett's Claymont Society in 1984. The subject of the talk is *lojong*, which is a practice that "purifies" the conditioned mind. In the same way that Gurdjieff taught that the lower centers need to be balanced so they do not obscure the functioning of higher centers, Tibetan Buddhism says that conditioned mind needs to be purified so it will not obscure enlightened mind. Thus purification and balancing might be regarded as the same thing, although in practice the technique is different.

[1] Sogyal Rinpoche, *Le livre tibétain de la vie et de la mort* (Paris: Éditions de la Table ronde, 1993), 546.

[2] Private correspondence.

## Awakening the Mind, Opening the Heart

The title of this talk is "Awakening the Mind, Opening the Heart," but the traditional teaching that this talk will be based on is called *lojong*. The Tibetan word *lo* means "mind". But we can distinguish several kinds of mind. For example, there is the mind called *yi* in Tibetan, which is the "perceiving mind." Then there is *rigpa*, "intelligence" or sometimes "the nature of mind," and there is *sem*, the "thinking mind."

The Tibetan word *lo* means a mind that is the result of conditioning—you could call it "the conditioned mind," or the mind that has been conditioned by our conditioning. It's that conditioning of ours that obstructs the manifestation of our true buddha-mind.

*Jong* means "to purify," so we could translate *lojong* as "purifying the conditioned mind," or "training the mind." *Lojong* practice is concerned with how to transform and change our character, and how to transform our mind from an ordinary conditioned mind into free spirit, so to speak.

In the Buddhist tradition of Tibet, *lojong* is a very well-known and much loved teaching. Over the centuries there have been many instructions on *lojong* given by generations of great masters, but there was one master in particular called Atisha, from West Bengal in India, who brought these teachings to Tibet. His main instructions were written down by his disciples, and then classified into seven points known as The

Seven Points of Training the Mind. This teaching is the heart of the Buddhist practice of compassion.

In Tibetan Buddhist training, if you really want to follow the practice, dedicate your life to it and become enlightened, then one of the recommended steps towards that is to go into a three-year retreat. You seclude yourself completely from the world outside and practice for three years. The first year is spent on a lot of purification practice, while the second year is the time to work with the *lojong* practice, so as to bring about a change in your heart. One of the most important practices for His Holiness the Dalai Lama is *lojong*, and when he teaches lojong in a public setting, he always uses the famous text called *The Eight Verses Of Training The Mind*, which he says is the teaching that has made him what he is today. When he was fifteen years old he memorized these eight verses, and from then on, whenever he had time, he would recite them in his mind and reflect and meditate on them and that, he said, helped him to develop compassion.

*The Seven Points of Training the Mind* can be a very vast teaching. It can take months to explain, and so what I'm going to do is present the first point of this *lojong* text. The teachings on the seven points have been arranged into fifty-nine "slogans", and these slogans are extremely useful and helpful. Just remembering one or two in your everyday life will suddenly bring the teaching vividly to mind.

The first of the seven points is called "The Preliminaries to Mind Training" and has two parts: "How to Develop Inner Generosity" and "How to Develop Discipline."

The preliminaries prepare our mind so that we become more available. A lot of the time the problem with us is that we're not easily available, we're closed. There is something within us that is not available—to us. And what prevents us from being available, and obstructs us from becoming enlightened in fact, is not some being with two horns, but our own ignorance. When we are fully open and available, that is called enlightenment. In some ways enlightenment is quite simple to attain, but it takes a very long time.

If you were to simplify the main point and purpose of the

preliminaries, it is to change your heart. The preliminaries prepare us for the main part of the text, the training in bodhichitta—"the heart of the awakened mind."

The first part of the preliminaries consists of contemplation, and the second part meditation. What are these for? Our conditioning is rooted in the various influences we receive: what we hear, what we see, and what we are taught to think. Human beings are very impressionable, especially when they don't know the nature of their own mind. In fact, humans have few strengths and little character: we're mostly just a bundle of conditioning!

So the practice of contemplation works against the gross distractions of life, to help us become clearer in our thinking. The second practice, meditation, works to dissolve the subtle distractions of deeper neuroses and mental and emotional knots.

The practice of contemplation has four points known as "the four causes of renunciation," or "the four thoughts that turn the mind away from samsara." If you're able to think and train your mind in line with these four thoughts, then you will be less attached to life, freer and able to see life itself more clearly.

The first thought is to recognize that this human life is very precious. It is not only precious because it's our life, but because we are here for a reason, and that reason is to understand our true nature. Understanding our true nature, or buddha-being you could say, really is the purpose of life. As human beings we are gifted with the greatest of faculties, the potential to become enlightened, thanks to two qualities we possess: we can understand the truth, and we can communicate it. Since we have the ability to understand, when we have a teaching explained to us we can understand it, and that fundamental quality of understanding is wisdom.

The Buddha taught that we all have "buddha-nature", meaning that we all possess the same potential to become a buddha. If you were to ask the question: "Well, if we're supposed to become buddhas, what is it in me exactly that is the buddha? What is it in me that belongs to the buddha family,

419

or has buddha essence, buddha qualities, buddha-nature, or buddha-mind?"

The answer is "awareness". You can try this out. If you just keep your mind open, quietly, without being occupied with thoughts, you will find that your mind is tremendously spacious and clear. This is the awareness that is the raw material of enlightenment. So the main reason why this life is precious is because we have the potential for enlightenment within us.

The second thought is that, even though we have the potential for enlightenment in this life, death may come at any time. We could lose this precious opportunity very quickly, and there is no guarantee that we will regain a human birth.

Sometimes people believe in reincarnation as an excuse for just being lazy. They think: "In this life, I think I'll just relax. Since I believe in reincarnation, I can put off making an effort till the next life." It just doesn't work like that at all. Reincarnation is intimately linked to what we do right now. As the Buddha said: "What you are is what you have been, what you will be is what you do now." What you do now designs your future life.

It is very important to see that this life really is it. This life is it! We really need to live a full and meaningful life now. But there's also an urgency, because death can come at any time. Then, there are some who will say, "All right, but actually I'm not afraid of dying. I'm really not." It's wonderful that you don't feel afraid at the moment, but when you are facing death and about to die, you might find it's very different.

Put it this way: are you afraid sometimes, do you never feel fear? Maybe you do. Well, at the moment of death, that fear becomes even stronger, because fear is due to the absence of knowledge. So the main point is that we should practice and try to know and understand our mind.

There is another point related to the second thought, which is that everything in this life changes. Everything is always changing, so it is futile to grasp. Everything is impermanent, so don't hold onto it, because holding on will only bring pain. Just let go, because things are always changing, and that is just how things are. There is a very famous Buddhist example:

420

trying to hold onto change is like trying to wash the same dirty hand twice in the same river. It's impossible. The fact that everything is always changing is very, very important to realize. And it also helps us develop a sense of humor!

So the first thought is that this human life is precious, and the second is that death can come at any time, and everything is impermanent and subject to change. The third thought is: whatever we do is very important, because our actions have an effect that comes along with the action. Even if we don't see the result of what we do at the time, the result is still there, latent within the action. It will bear fruit at the appropriate time.

We don't always know the reason why fascinating and wonderful things happen to us in life. It is because they are the results of our past actions. But without a clear memory of our past actions, we can't identify the exact cause of what's currently happening to us. Especially in the West, one thing that needs to be understood better is karma. In some ways, to be a spiritual person is to understand karma. If we do, we will take responsibility for what we do, say and think.

What is karma? The word karma means "action". When we do something good, the result is good; if we do something negative, the result is negative. And the result is already there when we do something; it is registered in the action itself. It is powerful. When we do something harmful, it harms other people and, what is more, it harms us. The harm may not be immediate, but it will arrive sooner or later. Similarly, when we do something good, it benefits others and benefits ourselves.

The fourth thought is the suffering of samsara, samsara being "the cycle of conditioned existence," and the kind of life we lead. We tend to live rather meaninglessly. If we look at our lives, we seem to be always in the same place. We think we are going somewhere, but we are not really going anywhere at all. All that happens is that we are getting older, getting nearer to death and not really achieving anything.

And death can come at any time. I heard that someone who was nearing the point of death once said they felt as if

421

they were sitting in a railway station. They knew their train was going to come, but it had no fixed schedule. They were gripped by a deep anxiety that their bags were not packed and they were not ready.

What the fourth thought is saying is that we have to change our life, and not just go round in circles, getting nowhere and creating more pain. The problem with us is that although we do everything in this life for happiness, the way we go about it brings suffering. We don't want suffering, but we do the very things that bring suffering; so there's a fundamental contradiction in our lives.

We really have to become wiser and contemplate these four thoughts so that we will not be overpowered by the temptations and distractions of life. If we contemplate the four thoughts, we will become stronger and have a clearer perspective, and greater common sense. These four thoughts are a teaching that all the traditional Buddhist masters will teach again and again.

The second part of the preliminaries is to work with deeper, subtler distractions through meditation practice. In Buddhism there are two practices of meditation. One is called shamatha, a practice for developing peace and calmness. The other is vipassana, a practice for developing insight. Of course, vipassana practice is quite popular in the West; it is called "insight meditation."

Shamatha is a Sanskrit word that means "to calm the mind," to calm the thinking mind, or to remain in the state of peace. The purpose of calming the mind is to cut through and dissolve the sense of 'I', the ego, and to develop mindfulness, relaxation and peace.

Sometimes we can be very confused and try to use our head to find the way out of our confusion, but it doesn't work. We just become more confused. What we need to do is just stop right there. Confusion has no beginning and no end, so don't imagine you can end confusion by thinking your way out of it.

The only thing to do is to leave it. Drop it, drop the confusion and just do something extremely simple, like watching the breath. Breathe out, ease yourself, and then place your attention very lightly on your breath. Consider that as you breathe out it is cleansing you, creating more space inside you and a supportive environment around you.

What happens when we are mindful and we place our attention on our breath is that it purifies and filters the process of our thoughts. It is the same mind that previously was confused but now, by being mindful, thought and emotion are filtered. Becoming mindful is like making coffee with a filter. When the water goes through the coffee filter, it makes very good coffee. We need the filter of mindfulness to process emotions and thoughts, so as to reveal our buddha-nature.

What happens when we watch the breath? Slowly our ego, the sense of 'I', gets purified and somewhat dissolved. When we are confused, the 'I' is strong and aggressive. Ego functions like a bodyguard. A lot of passion, desire and anger is aroused when we are confused. But when we are mindful and follow the breath, the intensity, struggle and tension behind the confusion ease away, and we find relaxation and peace instead. The struggle is no longer there.

In fact, the first teaching the Buddha gave, the four noble truths, is about achieving peace. The Buddha's first truth is that there is suffering and there is pain.

Second, what causes pain is ignorance and confusion. When we look for a way to free ourselves from this ignorance and confusion, like a spiritual path or a particular direction in our lives, what happens? At first the way ahead looks quite clear, but then after a while our path itself starts to get confused, because that ignorance and confusion take over very easily. They are the cause of our pain, and that's the second noble truth.

The third noble truth is cessation. We can put an end to our suffering. There is a way out; there is an exit. We don't have to go round in circles all the time.

The fourth noble truth is the method for getting out of the cycle of suffering. The method is to give up the struggle, to give up fighting. If we give up the struggle and tensions inside, we find the way to peace. Ego and confusion only exist when

423

there is a struggle, and without it, the 'I' dissolves. Then we discover mindfulness, relaxation and an even, equanimous peace—not the kind of pleasure we experience from the senses, passion or samsaric joys.

So the first practice is mindfulness. In fact, to cut this whole explanation short, everything I have said so far is only to convince you of the importance of the practice of mindfulness. The main point, you can say, is that whenever we're aware that we are confused, we just quietly sit and watch our breathing, and that will create peace.

Once peace prevails, the next step is called vipassana, meaning "insight meditation," or "panoramic vision." With vipassana practice, our desire, passion and anger are cut through. First the 'I' is quietened by mindfulness, and then our ambition is quietened by vipassana. Instead of ambition, we experience awareness, space, totality, and gentleness. And when shamatha and vipassana are put together, we develop the magnifying glass of *prajña*, or "discriminating wisdom." We are able to see clearly, to see what is good and what is not good, not in a dualistic way but in the truest sense. We see what is truly good, and consequently what to cultivate and what to leave behind.

*Prajña* gives birth to our empty, warm, "soft spot," and to glimpses of our enlightened essence. Then we become inspired and more available, more charitable and willing to work with the world and with ourselves. There is more willingness because we begin to taste a little bit of our own fundamental goodness.

So this teaching is called lojong, the training of the mind in compassion, and its main purpose is to change our heart. And the four causes of renunciation are to contemplate deeply on: the preciousness of human life; the fact that death can come at any time and everything is always changing; karma—the cause and effect of our action; and the cycle of suffering that is samsara.

*Sogyal Rinpoche*

424

*Hugh Ripman*

## Leader of the Washington Group

Hugh Ripman, together with his sister Daphne, joined Ouspensky's London group in 1934. In 1939 he married Mildred Geiger who was also a group member. Mildred was an American working at the U.S.A. Embassy who had been introduced to the group by her friend Janet Collin Smith. They remained in London during the war and continued participating in the group which had come under the leadership of Francis Roles with the Ouspenskys having moved to the U.S.A.

In 1946 Ripmam accepted a position at the British Embassy in Washington, D.C., and moved there with his wife. But the following year he left the embassy to accept a position at the World Bank—an opportunity which enabled him to meet spiritual teachers of a variety of traditions during the travels required of him.

During their first years in Washington they commuted regularly to Mendham to participate in group work being conducted by Madame Ouspensky. As well, they were able to spend time with Daphne who was now living there. Most importantly, it was at Madame Ouspensky's encouragement that the Ripmans spent time with Gurdjieff during his 1948 trip to New York.

Their meeting Gurdjieff motivated them to start a group in Washington, which they were hoping to introduce to Gurdjieff during the visit he was planning for the following year. Unfortunately, Gurdjieff died before he could realize that trip and the meeting never took place. Still, that group was the beginning of the Gurdjieff Society of Washington D.C.

During his years with the Ouspenskys, Ripman read the sacred works of many different traditions, and after Gurdjieff's death he made contact with various of their contemporary masters. Two Buddhist texts he specifically mentions having read in his autobiography are *Dialogues of the Buddha,* and *The Tibetan Book of the Dead.* However, his later practical explorations of Buddhism were limited to the Zen sect. Ripman discusses his meetings with four teachers of that tradition in particular. So, Zen appears to have been the most serious of these pursuits. Regarding his interest in meetings with these teachers, he says:

> I was not led to seek out these Zen masters by any feeling that the way I was following was not right for me. But my own reading and my friend's reports had convinced me that the Zen monks were trying to climb by another route the same symbolic mountain up which my own path led. I was interested to find out whether I might learn something useful about their climbing techniques. I had often discovered in texts of other traditions a symbol or a formulation that crystallised an understanding towards which I had been groping. I was not disappointed in my hope that the same thing would happen if I could make personal contacts with those who were following the Zen road.[1]

It was on a trip to Hong Kong in 1961 that he met with author Charles Luk. Before the trip Ripman had read one of Luk's books on Zen and wrote to him through his publisher about his plan to visit. Besides getting guidance from Luk on zazen and qi gong, they also discussed certain Tibetan Buddhist visualization and yoga practices that Luk had learned from his first teacher, the Khutuktu of Xikang. When Ripman asked if there was anything on the law of seven in any of the traditions he was familiar with, Luk also talked a little about *The Tibetan Book of the Dead.* According to the text, the time between death and the conception of one's next birth is divided into seven periods of seven days, or 49 days total.

428

On the same trip to Hong Kong, Ripman was able to meet with the Venerable Yin Shun. Yin Shun was a prolific writer, but at the time of Ripman's visit none of his books were available in English yet. Probably Ripman was referred to Yin Shun by Luk. Of the various subjects they discussed, perhaps the most interesting is on satori in which Yin Shun describes the three stages: "The first stage is when satori comes and goes, without any control... The second stage is to learn the functions of satori, when it is necessary, and what it can do. The third stage is to become able to enter and leave satori at will in whatever circumstances one is in."[2]

Ripman also made several trips to Japan. In the chapter "A Barrier as Thin as Paper" in his autobiography, he discusses his meetings with two Zen abbots but does not identify them for some reason. Even so, their identities are apparent.

The second is clearly Ruth Sasaki. Appendix III of the book, which was added by the editor and not part of the original manuscript, contains various texts relating to her, and a footnote on the first text included, which is on their first meeting, says that the text served as the basis for "A Barrier as Thin as Paper." However, the editor appears to be mistaken in believing that Ripman's account of his first meeting with Sasaki was the basis for that chapter. Most of the chapter is devoted to the first abbot who is referred to with the pronoun "he" and the second is not given as much attention. When relating his encounter with this second abbot, Ripman cleverly avoids using pronouns entirely. Clearly the second abbot is Sasaki. Also suggesting this is that both the second abbot of the chapter and Sasaki (in the appendix mentioned) discuss koan practice with Ripman.

Regarding the first abbot, the two photos that Ripman took of him included in the book give away his identity as Asahina Roshi.

Considering that William Segal also met with these two abbots, that in the quote above Ripman says he was motivated by his "friend's reports" of the efficacy of Zen to make his own investigations, and that the two men undoubtedly knew one another from Franklin Farms, it might be concluded that it was Segal who provided Ripman with the introductions needed.

According to the same footnote in the appendix on Sasaki, their first meeting was in 1959. Although Ripman's encounter with her is not given as much attention as his encounters with Asahina Roshi, her influence must not be underestimated. They maintained correspondence for a number of years.

Even so, Ripman gives the most attention to Ashina Roshi, likely for good reason. William Segal thought Asahina was "one of the few real men I have met."[3] Ripman did not think quite as highly of him, but still concluded, "From such a man one could learn much."[4] So, let us talk a little about his background.

Sogen Asahina lost his mother when he was five and his father when he was seven. As a result he became interested in spiritual matters. By the time he was twelve he had become a monk at Seikenji, a temple in the Rinzai sect whose abbot was Sakagami Shinjo Roshi.

At the age of 17 Asahina moved to Myoshinji, another Rinzai temple, to begin meditation practice under the guidance of its abbot, Ikegami Shozan Roshi. Asahina had heard Shozan Roshi give a talk when he was 13 and was greatly impressed. He remained with Shozan Roshi until his death seven years later.

About a year later Asahina decided to go into seclusion for intensive meditation practice. Having felt that he achieved his aim, he ended this solitary retreat after 104 days, whereupon he enrolled himself in Engakuji, yet another Rinzai temple. A few years later, at the age of 29, Asahina received dharma transmission from its abbot, Jodo Furukawa Roshi. (Dharma transmission is the ceremony that elevates a priest to the level of Roshi.) Eventually Asahina took over as abbot of Engakuji, which is not only a temple but a subsect of Rinzai. Thus he became the head of the entire Engakuji subsect as well.

Asahina was also a professor at Komazawa University, a renowned calligrapher and a prolific writer. However, only one short title of his was ever printed in a Japanese/English bilingual edition. Although he also provided the introduction to an English edition of the calligraphy of Sengai Gibon, and First Zen Institute included a transcript of a talk he gave the sangha when he visited New York in 1954 in their newsletter *Zen Notes* of that July, and an autobiographical sketch in the following month's issue.

Besides the Gurdjieffians mentioned here, Asahina is known to have been a teacher to one degree or another to many Westerners during the U.S. occupation of Japan. He hardly spoke English himself, but had translators available to assist him, and was often able to get a certain point across without a translator. For example, the time he was walking with Ripman through Engakuji and suddenly stopped at a Buddha statue and said, "That Buddha image. Where true Buddha, real Buddha?"[5] This is something of a koan that the reader may also wish to ponder.

What follows is a poem of Ripman's demonstrating Zen influence, and a much condensed and consolidated version of the first three chapters of Asahina Roshi's booklet, *Zen*. There are a few things in Asahina's text that correspond to some aspect of Gurdjieff's teaching. In the same way that Gurdjieff says the fourth way is the source of all other teachings, Asahina says that Zen is the source of all other Buddhist sects. "Enlightening the darkness," as Asahina refers to it, corresponds to impartial observation. "True nature" or "original nature" corresponds to Real 'I'. The use of the "*Katsu!*" shout corresponds to the shock method Gurdjieff employed in various ways. And doubt corresponds to the need to have a critical mind.

---

[1] Hugh Brockwill Ripman, *Search for Truth* (Washington: Forthway Center Palisades Press, 1999), 91.

[2] Ibid., 215.

[3] William Segal & Marielle Bancou-Segal, *A Voice at the Borders of Silence: An Intimate View of the Gurdjieff Work, Zen Buddhism, and Art* (New York: Overlook Press, 2003), 106.

[4] Hugh Brockwill Ripman, *Search for Truth* (Washington: Forthway Center Palisades Press, 1999), 78.

[5] Ibid., 85.

## STILLNESS IS ALWAYS HERE

Only in a still place can peace exist.

But where is stillness to be found?

At first it cannot be found.

At first it may depend upon circumstance. But a stillness which depends upon circumstance can be disturbed by circumstance, so the way to stillness is the way to independence.

In division there is no stillness, so the way to stillness is the way to a unity which encompasses division.

At the same time the way to stillness is not a way which leads from here to there, from now to then, but a way which returns from there to here, from then to now.

In time there is no stillness, so the way to stillness leads out of time.

For these things, stillness and peace, are of the nature of eternity, not of time.

Stillness is always here.
It always has been.
It always will be.

Peace is always here.
It always has been.
It always will be.

*Hugh Ripman*

434

*Hugh Ripman's photograph of Sogen Asahina*

## An Introduction to Zen

Zen teaches the basically Buddhist discipline which Sakyamuni himself followed. It strives to achieve the very experience of enlightenment which Sakyamuni himself experienced. Hence there are some Zen priests in ancient times who declared Zen to be the source and origin of all Buddhist sects, and I think they were correct.

It was Bodhidharma who gave the first typically Zen exposition of Buddhism, the like of which no one had heard before. It was Bodhidharma who showed that there was in Zen a method of training and a way of life different from those of other sects. He showed clearly how wondrous was the Zen method of sitting in meditation (*zazen*) and the wisdom which such practice brought. He showed that by enlightening the darkness of human delusion and suffering and revealing these to be without real substance, the human mind could be emancipated and realized as completely free, pure and tranquil.

Zen has clear and simple doctrines and a highly practical method of spiritual training. It was not only a religion which solved the problem of life and death. It also released man from the various bondages of his mind, showing him his true nature and enabling him to return to a state of absolute freedom.

If you were to ask what exactly Zen is, we should answer that it is knowing your original nature. Knowing your original nature means knowing your true nature. It means knowing by experience that from the very first the mind of man is free from sin, impurity, delusion and suffering—and indeed is magnificently pure, clear and free.

One of the basic articles of faith in Buddhism is the precept, "All beings without exception possess buddha-nature." This buddha-nature is none other than the "original mind" of man. The word Buddha in Sanskrit means one who has awakening, one who is enlightened. Thus we have come to call the original mind of man the buddha-nature.

Shakyamuni, trying to describe the wondrous world of the original mind, said that in time it was "infinite life" and in space "infinite light." This is a very good description. In this world there is no death. There is simply the great life of eternity. This great life stretches in time from the inconceivably remote past to the far realms of the future. And in space there is nothing outside the mind. Amida Buddha, on whose help and grace certain sects rely for their salvation, is simply a symbol and image of Amitayus (infinite life) and Amitabha (infinite light). The world of this mind is the enlightened world.

The efforts of the student engaged on the quest "What is my own mind?" must be entirely his own. Nothing can be done for him from outside. Hence practitioners of Zen do not use theoretical and systematic methods of expressing the enlightenment they have experienced. They choose rather ways which are direct and super-rational. For example, Rinzai had a habit of answering all his pupils' questions with a single loud shout "*Katsu!*" This Chinese word "*Katsu!*" is simply a sound, without any meaning. If it had had any meaning or logical implication, Rinzai would not have used it. It was because it was an utterly meaningless sound that it was suitable to evoke the superconscious, super-rational world.

In the world of common sense all things that are born must die. But in the World of those students of Zen who have found their original mind, even death is transcended.

You might imagine that to "seek for your original mind" would mean to study the writings of the ancient Zen masters, and to use your faculties of reasoning and discursive thought to decide that your own mind would be thus and thus. But

438

the Zen way of thinking is not like this. As I have said before, everyone without exception possesses this wondrous original mind, but they do not realize it. They do not realize it because of their faculties of reasoning and discursive thought. So that now at this point we must abandon completely our conscious efforts to think in any particular way.

In order to accomplish this we have two methods. First, Dogen's method of sitting correctly "stopping all the activities of discursive thought and meditating in a world transcending all such mental functions." And second, the method whereby the student is given a special subject for meditation called a *koan*. Both these methods have their strong points.

The sitting position is undoubtedly very efficacious, but it is at first fairly painful. But as the old saying goes, "Enlightenment comes through the mind, not through sitting," and the fundamental aim of Zen is to see into one's original mind. Whether we are lying or sitting on chairs, we must never relax for a moment our efforts to concentrate and purify the mind, and if we can increase our efforts in this way we shall certainly attain enlightenment. Gudo attained enlightenment by lying down, and Bankei reached it when critically ill. In cases like this, bodily posture was of no importance.

There are two Zen sayings—"Great enlightenment comes from great doubt," and "with much clay you can make a large Buddha." These words mean that the strength and depth of experience of enlightenment we attain will be proportionate to the degree of effort we put into our training. In Zen training there are some people who are blessed with natural talent and genius. But even these people will not succeed if they neglect to make any effort. Often such people end up by showing none of the brilliance which they first seemed to promise. And conversely there are many examples of people who at first appear relatively dull and stupid but who, through firm resolve and unremitting effort, succeed in attaining a really deep enlightenment and becoming great religious figures with many disciples.

Here arises a problem—is it useless to start training in Zen unless we can be sure of attaining enlightenment? Even if we do not reach this goal we can reap rewards in proportion to what sitting we have done. When the student of Zen sits correctly for half an hour or an hour, for that period the clouds and mists will clear and the original light will shine through. As proof of this we find that restless people become calmer, narrow-minded people become more broad and tolerant, rough-minded people become gentler, and weak and feeble people gain strength. All this is in no way miraculous. It happens for the simple reason that man's original mind is like that. Thus correct sitting will always bring its due results, whether or not you sit for a long time.

*Sogen Asahina*

Photograph of Sogen Asahina, taken by Hugh Ripman, copyright © Christopher Hugh Ripman, Forthway Center Palisades Press, and The Gurdjieff Society of Washington, D.C., is reproduced here with their permission.

"An Introduction to Zen" was adapted from *Zen* by Sogen Asahina, (Tokyo: Sakane Printing, 1954).

*Young Henry Sinclair and sister Peggy in India*

## The Electric Lord

Born into British nobility, Henry John Sinclair obtained the title Second Baron Pentland from his father who was the First Baron Pentland. Because his father was the Governor General of Madras, he had spent seven years of his childhood in India. This experience likely helped to develop his magnetic center and eventually bring him to Ouspensky.

It was in 1937 at the age of 30 that Pentland attended a talk by P.D. Ouspensky and joined his group. Pentland was one of two people—the other being J.G. Bennett—who Ouspensky assigned to answer questions and read pre-written lectures at meetings at Colet House. He also was a regular participant of group work conducted at Lyne Place.

When World War II broke out, Pentland successfully avoided battle by securing a much-in-demand engineering position. Along with the other members of Ouspensky's close circle, he was also tasked to maintain and oversee group work at Lyne Place when the Ouspenskys set sail for the U.S.A. in the beginning of 1941. Later that year he married Lucy Elisabeth Babington Smith who acquired the title Lady as a result and also joined the Ouspensky group.

In 1944 Pentland acquired a position in Washington, D.C. with the Combined Production and Resources Board—a cooperative effort of the U.S.A., U.K. and France. He thus moved with Lady Pentland and their two-year old daughter Mary to Franklin Farms—the Ouspensky Work residence in New Jersey—and commuted to Washington for work. Whereas in London Pentland was close to Mr Ouspensky, in New Jersey he became close with Mme Ouspensky. As he says, "For many of us, she was the senior teacher."[1]

So, when Ouspensky returned to London early in 1947, the Pentlands remained at Franklin Farms. However, Lord Pentland did arrange a business trip to London that spring to try to make sense of the ensuing chaos in the London group rumored as a result of Ouspensky having abandoned the system. Ouspensky had left Franklin Farms in chaos too with his sudden departure and Pentland was questioning his continuance in the Work, as were many others. When Ouspensky died later that year Pentland went to India for a few months to try to figure things out for himself. Besides being the place of his youth, he also wanted to visit a friend from the London group who was now living in Sri Lanka. This friend introduced him to a Buddhist teacher who gave him some advice. Upon Pentland's return to New Jersey, he learned of Madame Ouspensky's advice to make contact with Gurdjieff but hesitated.

In September of 1948 he finally made the trip to Paris with family in tow. Here he describes his first interactions with the master:

> One day I wormed my way into having lunch with Mr Gurdjieff and some others, though I had not been invited. Mr Gurdjieff said nothing at the time, but the following day he took me to a Turkish bathhouse on the outskirts of Paris. The sense was that this was a reward for something I had done that had been in his eyes especially praiseworthy. I was, of course, elated. While I undressed, Mr Gurdjieff took the owner of the bathhouse aside to whisper something but, in fact, he spoke quite loudly, telling the man that his "special friend" was to be given "the best treatment." Thereupon, a masseur was summoned, a huge man, who proceeded to beat me to a pulp while of course Mr Gurdjieff looked on, not being above showing a certain sly satisfaction. Afterward, on the way back to the apartment, a policeman stopped him

and he blamed me to the policeman for distracting him. Can you believe it?[2]

Pentland remained in Paris until Gurdjieff's departure for New York three months later, sailed with him on the journey, and remained with him in New York until his return in February. Had Gurdjieff not put him in charge of getting *In Search of the Miraculous* and *Beelzebub's Tales* published, he probably would have returned to Paris with him. Even so, the task he was given kept them in communication. More significantly, Gurdjieff had also tasked Pentland to be his representative in America.

In August of 1949 Pentland saw Gurdjieff alive for the last time. He had made another trip to Paris to spend some time with his teacher. Knowing his end was near, Gurdjieff said to Pentland at the time, "You are like Paul; you must spread my ideas."[3] Gurdjieff died on October 29th. But eight days prior he had received and approved the proofs for *Beelzebub's Tales*. Pentland immediately returned to Paris for the funeral.

As a result of having been assigned by Gurdjieff to be his American representative, Pentland became President of the Gurdjieff Foundation when it was established in 1953 in New York. Two years later he established a Foundation branch in California, and over the course of his three-decade presidency other branches were established as well. Yet the only significance Pentland gives his presidency is the opportunity the role provided him for self-work. As he says:

> ...the way [Gurdjieff] left things, it made it perfectly easy for me to have to really enter into a position of responsibility as such. So it made it essentially easy for me to try to understand more deeply what he'd shown me.[4]

His professional life was advancing at this time as well. In 1954 Pentland founded the American British Electric Corporation. (Judging by the memoirs of his students, his style of teaching was becoming electric too. He was becoming adept at providing his students with shocks that enabled them to see themselves more clearly.) His position with the Combined Production and Resources Board was only a means of immigrating to the U.S.A. to be near the Ouspenskys and was not providing all that much income. Now that he had been in the country for ten years it would be easier for him to start his own business.

Shortly after Tassajara Zen Monastery opened in 1967, Pentland spent some time there. Besides meeting Suzuki Roshi, he also met Richard Baker Roshi who became Suzuki's successor and would be a lifelong friend. Pentland was interested in promoting mutual appreciation between the Gurdjieff tradition and others and developing various sorts of exchanges with them. This he did by befriending their teachers. Baker was but one of those teachers. At the time, the spiritual scene was really taking off in the San Francisco Bay area and Pentland was spending much of his time at the San Francisco Branch of the Gurdjieff Foundation.

In 1968 he established Far West Institute, a non-profit disseminator of esotericism and book publisher. At their third lecture series, held in San Francisco in 1978, one of the discussions was led by Baker Roshi and Gurdjieff group leader Jacob Needleman. A transcription of the talk is included in Needleman's book *Speaking of My Life*.

A more significant project they initiated, however, was the publication of Lobsang Lhalungpa's translation of *The Life of Milarepa*. Lhalungpa was another friend Pentland had made, and it was Pentland who arranged the translation work as a collaboration between Lhalungpa and the Institute. Much of this work was done at St. Elmo—a sort of Gurdjieffian retreat center owned by the San Francisco branch of the Foundation— by a team headed by Jacob Needleman. Pentland himself was also involved in the translation and often referred to various aspects of the tale in his talks.

It is uncertain, but he may have been inspired to translate this book in particular as a result of his relationship with Chögyam Trungpa Rincoche. Milarepa was the founder of the Kagyupa sect which Trungpa represented. Jeremy Hayward, a former Gurdjieffian who had become a student of Trungpa remembers Pentland's attendance at his first retreat with Trungpa:

446

Lord Pentland, the head of the Gurdjieff movement in America, was attending this seminar ["The Battle of the Ego," Christmas 1970] along with several other senior Gudjieffians. I sat down next to him one evening in front of the fire, and said, "If it's all really so simple as Trungpa Rinpoche is presenting, why is the Gurdjieff work so complicated?" Lord Pentland replied, in his very upper class Scottish accent, "I think it is because we are so complicated." This was helpful. He went on to say that it is ego that is complicated, and therefore the teachings have to be complicated even though, ultimately, it may be simple. Later on, I was to find out that Buddhist doctrine can also be highly complicated, for the same reason—there are said to be as many different teachings as there are beings.[5]

It is difficult to know how Pentland became interested in Trungpa. He may have learned of him from Madame de Salzmann who had met him in 1967. He may also have learned about Trungpa meeting Suzuki and giving a talk to San Francisco Zen Center in 1970 through Richard Baker. Being Scotch, Pentland may also have been aware of Samye Ling—the Tibetan Buddhist monastery that Trungpa Rinpoche and Akong Rinpoche established in Scotland in 1967. Either way, they would meet a few more times over the years.

The next occasion that Lord Pentland is known to have met with Trungpa Rinpoche is 1974. That year Trungpa was establishing Naropa Institute (now Naropa University) and he had invited the Gurdjieff Foundation to give classes as part of its program. He was particularly interested in having the movements taught there. Although his request was declined, Lord Pentland and other senior people in the Foundation met with Trungpa, evidently with ulterior motives. Here Jeremy Hayward elaborates:

> That summer ('74), Rinpoche suggested that we invite the Gurdjieff group to offer courses at Naropa Institute, which I did. I received a reply from Lord Pentland to the effect that "We don't make these teachings public." A short while later all the sangha people in Boulder who had studied with G. were invited to a Gurdjieff meeting up in the Rocky Mountains somewhere. (There were quite a lot of

Gurdjieffians who had joined Rinpoche). It was a very strange meeting, seeming to be specifically designed to tell us that we were mistaken in leaving the Work and joining Rinpoche. Lord Pentland and Jacob Needleman were both there as well as a number of other senior Gurdjieffians. One of them gave a talk on how the Asian traditions such as Tibetan Buddhism were not appropriate for the West, and another talked about the importance of Gurdjieff's teachings for the West, and there was another talk on similar lines. Altogether, it really put me off...[6]

Those who left the Work to study with Trungpa came from a variety of groups. The following year the Nyland group had invited Trungpa to give a talk at their property in Warwick, New York. Trungpa proposed giving the talk in New York City instead. After Willem Nyland, who was one Gurdjieff's main proponents, died in 1975, his group invited Trungpa to give a talk knowing that their group leader had viewed him favorably. Nyland had once watched an interview with Trungpa on Vermont television and was much impressed. He commented, "How amazing! He never lost himself once."[7] After the talk, a few group members would leave to work with Trungpa. Despite the Foundation's concerns, there was nothing they could do to stop Trungpa's influence.

Pema Chödrön is another who was in the Gurdjieff Work before becoming a student of Trungpa Rinpoche. She and her second husband, Magnus Wechsler, were in Basil Tilley's London group when their interest in Tibetan Buddhism and friendship with Trungpa Rinpoche began to grow. Regarding the similarities of the two teachers, she says, "My heroes are Gurdjieff and Chogyam Trungpa Rinpoche and Machig Labrum, the mad yogi of Bhutan. I like the wild ones."[8]

In 1976 Pentland suffered a heart attack, requiring him to withdraw from group activities for much of that year in order to recuperate. No doubt the event also fueled his own inner work.

The next known occasion in which Pentland met with Trungpa was during the annual three-month seminary of 1980, held at Lake Louise in Alberta that year. During a private dinner between Pentland, Trungpa, and some former

448

Gurdjieffians invited, Pentland asked Trungpa how many close students he had. Trungpa had to ask one of his attendants how many *sadhakas* he had for an accurate reply. After the reply of 300 came back, Pentland asked how he was able to give attention to so many. Trungpa then replied that his students were like a mountainside full of pine trees. At first just one or two catch spark, but before you know it the entire mountainside is ablaze. It was also during this dinner that the infant who Trungpa recognized as Gurdjieff's tulku was introduced to Lord Pentland. She was asleep at the time. Meeting the infant may have been one of Pentland's interests in seeing Trungpa this particular time. Trungpa had had a letter declaring the recognition hand-delivered to the Gurdjieff Foundation.

Trungpa also had great appreciation for Pentland. Their relationship was not entirely one way; they were more like friends. Trungpa thought highly of Gurdjieff and recognized something of value in those he knew who had previously or currently been involved in the Work, such as Pentland. Regarding Pentland specifically, Trungpa thought that he was very disciplined and kind. And when Trungpa held a *sukhavati* ceremony on February 18, 1984 for people close to his sangha who had died recently, including Pentland who had died four days earlier, he said that Pentland "...has been an excellent friend of ours. He could be helped because his beliefs are not theistic and the teachings of Gurdjieff. A very decent English man." The ceremony ended with Trungpa saying, "Let us wish that those who died will return and be reborn in the kingdom of Shambhala."

Also indicative of their mutual appreciation is that Trungpa had once accepted an invitation from Pentland to attend a dinner at St. Elmo with Group One (the senior group). Pentland sometimes enjoyed recounting how when Trungpa dropped his keys while the group was seeing him out, he snatched them up himself before anyone else could, despite his drunken state and paralyzed leg. As David Hykes recalls, Pentland said, "He beat us all to it, with incredible agility."[9] It was also at St. Elmo where Trungpa had observed movements practice.

449

Trungpa's appraisal of Pentland should not be taken lightly either. He was no doubt one of the great spiritual teachers of this time. Trungpa was considered as such by great masters in all the Tibetan Buddhist sects, as well as by great masters in other traditions.

Chögyam Trungpa was the 11$^{th}$ Trungpa tulku. He was born in 1940 in Geje, a nomadic encampment in northern Kham, and given the name Dorje Dradul Mukpo. The Trungpa tulkus are traditionally recognized by the Karmapa—the head of the Kagyupa sect—and it was the 16$^{th}$ Karmapa who recognized the 11$^{th}$ Trungpa. As head of all the Surmang monasteries, the Trungpa tulku was a highly respected seat. His root teacher was Jamgön Kongtrül of Shechen, who in turn was a disciple of the 10$^{th}$ Trungpa tulku. The Karmapa was also one of his teachers, as were Khenpo Gangshar, Dilgo Khyentse, and the Sixth Shechen Rabjam, all of whom also had great renown.

Because Jamgön Kongtrül was a Nyimgmapa, Trungpa learned the texts and practices of the Nyingmapa sect in addition to the Kagyupa. Similarly, Jamgön Kongtrül, having been a disciple of the 10$^{th}$ Trungpa tulku, also had a complete education in both lineages. The teaching that Trungpa would later formulate for his Western students was something of a synthesis of the two.

By the age of 18, after nine years of rigorous study, Trungpa had completed his *khenpo* degree. By this time the presence of the Chinese was beginning to turn violent, and about a year later, in 1959, he fled Tibet with 14 monks in his immediate party and some 300 others following.

The escape was quite an ordeal. Not everyone survived. It took nine months altogether, the final leg of which was made through the winter cold and snow, the terrain traveled was often perilous, and the Chinese army was on their tail. The intuition that Trungpa so often displayed enabling his party to evade danger was quite remarkable. A parallel might be drawn with the intuition that Gurdjieff displayed while guiding his own party to safety during the Russian Revolution.

In India the Dalai Lama appointed Trungpa spiritual advisor of the Young Lamas Home School. In 1954, while still in

Tibet, the Karmapa told Trungpa that he would one day bring the dharma to the West. At the time he was unable to envision this himself, but now his path became clear to him. Trungpa thus befriended two British Tibetophiles living in India to teach him the English language and European culture. With their help he was able to obtain a Spalding scholarship to attend Oxford University and left for England in 1963.

In addition to his studies at Oxford, Trungpa also taught meditation and worked on his autobiography, *Born in Tibet*, which was published in 1966.

In 1967, Trungpa and Akong Rinpoche, who was working in a hospital to support Trungpa, were invited to be co-directors of Johnstone House—a Buddhist center in Scotland —after having led a retreat there. As the first Tibetan Buddhist monastery in the West, they renamed the center Samye Ling after Samye Gompa—Tibet's first Buddhist monastery, which was founded in 779 CE.

It may also be interesting to note that it was in the summer of 1967 that Carol George, the first wife of Canadian ambassador James George, met Trungpa Rinpoche in London. This is probably when Trungpa learned about Gurdjieff and subsequently became fascinated by the man and his teaching.

In London, Trungpa had already started behaving more like a crazy wisdom yogi than a monk by drinking alcohol and having sex. After all, crazy wisdom was one of the teachings that he had mastered. Although he is often criticized for this behavior (and receiving criticism to prevent being idolized is one of the purposes of the practice), and although it would not be appropriate in today's culture, it seems as though he realized that he could better fit in and teach the emerging counterculture as a *ngakpa* (or yogi) than as an ascetic. Buddhism is intended to be adaptable this way, utilizing appropriate teachings and approaches for the time and place. In Tibet, he had no reason to make crazy wisdom (or *drubnyon*) a regular practice and did not. At any rate, Trungpa's relationship with Akong Rinpoche, who had a very traditional approach, was becoming more and more strained, and the monastery was becoming divided as a result.

Although the direction that Trungpa needed to take as a teacher was becoming more clear to him, the division of his sangha gave him doubts. So, he took advantage of an invitation he received from the royal family of Bhutan to visit so that he could go on retreat and meditate on the subject while there. In 1968 he took his heart disciple Richard Arthure with him and they retreated at Taktsang for ten days. Taktsang is a meditation cabin built as a sort of antechamber to the cave where, according to legend, Phadmasambhava dispelled the evil spirits that were preventing Buddhism from taking root in Tibet. Trungpa found the clarity he sought in the form of a mind *terma* which he titled *The Sadhana of Mahamudra*. It took him two days to channel the text which Arthure helped to render into English. The text speaks of the seemingly wrathful strength that is needed to remain unaffected by a world of confusion, decadence and materialism. That is, how to avoid getting depressed living in such a world, and especially how to prevent materialism from entering one's spiritual practice. In Gurdjieffian terms, the mind of *mahamudra* wherein this strength is found can be looked at as the subconsciousness, and the use of spiritual practice for material gain is a particular form of wiseacring (or self-deception). The *sadhana* became the foundation of what Trungpa would later call "Shambhala Buddhism"—a lay form of Tibetan Buddhism intended for Westerners.

Although Trungpa had gained clarity as to *what* to teach his Western students, he was not yet clear as to *how* to actualize that teaching. But that understanding came a few months after his return to Samye Ling in 1969 when a car accident which left him partially paralyzed the remainder of his life provided a shock which indicated how to proceed. What he came to understand was that he could no longer hide behind his monk's robes and keep aspects of his life private—that he needed to be completely open about every aspect of his life. Thus, in 1970, he renounced his monastic vows and took off his robes. Shortly after that he married a sixteen-year-old student of his. The environment at Samye Ling stirred even more. Consulting the I-Ching indicated that he should cross the ocean. Fortunately, upon his return from Bhutan, Trungpa received approval of his application for British citizenship.

Some of his American students at Samye Ling departed for the U.S.A. to prepare for his arrival. They purchased property in Vermont they called Tail of the Tiger with the intention of establishing it as a monastery. At the same time, Trungpa received an invitation to teach at the University of Colorado, Boulder. So he and his wife Diana left for Montreal where they waited a few weeks while their visas got sorted out. Entering the U.S.A., Trungpa began teaching not only at Tail of the Tiger, but all around the country. 1970 was also significant as being the year that Trungpa Rinpoche and Shunryu Suzuki met. They bonded immediately.

In 1971 Trungpa began teaching at the University of Colorado and established Rocky Mountain Dharma Center (now Shambhala Mountain Center), another monastery. Meditation centers under his guidance began to open in other U.S.A. cities and in 1973 he incorporated Vajradhatu as an umbrella organization for them all. The following year he founded Naropa Institute (now Naropa University) in Boulder. His teaching was spreading rapidly and thrived throughout the '70s and '80s.

Some aspects of Trungpa's appreciation for Gurdjieff were mentioned earlier—that he kept a photo of Gurdjieff on his altar and that he recognised Gurdjieff's current incarnation. In addition, he knew his teaching so well that "[he] could cite passages and references to his books,"[10] and thought Gurdjieff was "the best"[11] teacher to come to the U.S.A. in his time. According to Steve Roth, when he asked Trungpa what he thought of Gurdjieff, he received the reply, "Oh, he's fantastic, amazing, almost total crazy wisdom."[12]

Yet Trungpa felt that Gurdjieff had failed in assuring the perpetuation of his teaching. In the talk he gave to the Nyland group (some excerpts from which follow), he repeated the necessity for lineage and heritage and his concern that none of Gurdjieff's students were able to pick up his mantle to establish a lineage. Despite Trungpa's view, which he expressed to Pentland, and Pentland's view that Buddhism was too foreign of a teaching to be appropriate for Western culture, which Jeremy Hayward or other former Gurdjieffians no doubt made Trungpa aware of if Pentland did not tell him so himself, the two men clearly had great respect and admiration for one another.

But the transcript of the talk is mainly interesting for Trungpa responding to questions posed from a Gurdjieffian perspective with his classical Buddhist understanding, and thus showing something of the relationship between the two teachings. Some of the questioners seem to have understood his replies while others had a more difficult time. Still, Trungpa gave them all his full attention.

But first are two appended excerpts from an interview with Lord Pentland which go into more detail on subjects discussed here.

---

[1] William Patrick Patterson, *Georgi Ivanovitch Gurdjieff: The Man, the Teaching, His Mission* (Fairfax: Arete Communications, 2014) 401.

[2] Ibid., 448–49.

[3] J.G. Bennett, *Witness: The Story of a Search* (London: Hodder and Stoughton, 1962), 270.

[4] "Transmission: An Interview with Lord Pentland," in *Gurdjieff: Essays and Reflections on the Man and His Teaching*, eds. Jacob Needleman & George Baker (New York: Continuum Publishing, 1996), 383.

[5] Jeremy Hayward, *Warrior King of Shambhala: Remembering Chögyam Trungpa* (Boston: Wisdom Publications, 2008), 29–30.

[6] Private correspondence.

[7] Private correspondence from a student of Nyland and Trungpa who wishes to remain anonymous.

[8] "No Right, No Wrong: An Interview with Pema Chödrön," *Tricycle Magazine* 3, no. 1 (Fall 1993), 21.

[9] Private correspondence.

[10] Private correspondence from Lee Weingrad.

[11] Private correspondence from an anonymous student.

[12] Steve Roth, "Three Spiritual Icons of the Early 20th Century," by Steve Roth; The Chronicles of Chögyam Trungpa Rinpoche, www.chronicleproject.com/a-conversation-with-trungpa-rinpoche-bout-three-spiritual-icons-of-the-early-20th-century/.

Photograph of Henry and Peggy Sinclair provided by the Department of Special Collections, Stanford University Libraries.

## VENTURES WITH BUDDHISM

Did I tell you I was in India before I met Gurdjieff? And I also visited Ceylon. And when I was in Ceylon with one of Ouspensky's pupils who had moved there, a Singhalese teacher of Buddhism, he took me to meet three learned men who were visiting together from the Himalayas. And one of them was very old, the other was in the middle, and the other was young. The old one was said to be somewhere around one hundred and twenty, the middle one said to be eighty, and the younger one said to be forty. And we sat in the sun in a little garden in a modest villa in Colombo, and of course this man could not speak English, but my friend, quite an expert, could, and he sat down, and the conversation began. He gave us an apple, and after he had given us each an apple the conversation began. And at one point I said to him, how did he recognize a real teacher? Do you follow?... which was my question then, as I explained earlier, he said, "You know." I think that's a good answer.

You know Richard Baker Roshi who I keep in touch with, who considers himself a good friend of mine. I met him as one of the first visitors to Tassajara. And I met him with Suzuki Roshi and had conversations with them both in May of the year that Tassajara opened. And also, one of my acquaintances, a good friend, is a Tibetan, Lobsang Lhalumpa, who helped us here to translate *The Life of Milarepa* from the Tibetan.

And so, it's a better English translation than the one by [W.Y.] Evans-Wentz.

When we published *The Life of Milarepa* and were talking over what to put on the cover of the paperback, Lhalungpa suggested we put on the cover a particular Tibetan symbol, a Tibetan symbol which in one symbol brings together all the aspects of Tibetan Buddhism, which is a very complicated system of metaphysics and psychology. And I was reminded of this today because a man came to my room; he had just got back here from Nepal, and he said he'd like to give us, give me, a picture that he had got there, which happens to be a representation of this same symbol, I forget what it's called, which brings together, in one symbol, all the hundreds of different theories, principles, and aspects of Tibetan Buddhism.

Now, that's what I think Gurdjieff managed to do with the ideas, which were recorded by Ouspensky as well as in Gurdjieff's own movement—not as a symbol, because Gurdjieff didn't work with the visualizing capacity emphasized in Tibetan Buddhism, but as a system of ideas. And probably Gurdjieff thought that it could be, and was right, that this is the best way of bringing a teaching in the West, even though obviously Zen Buddhism and Tibetan Buddhism have made enormous impact all over the West. So much so that you could say the headquarters of Tibetan Buddhism is pretty nearly in America now, and something like that is going on with Zen Buddhism. But this isn't an oriental country; this isn't a milieu perhaps where the practices that had been traditional in the East could be introduced directly. So I don't think Zen Buddhism or Tibetan Buddhism will develop here in the same forms. I think that certainly in Tibet and in Zen these traditions have had an extraordinary longevity which is connected with the teacher, before he dies, in some way transmitting his teaching to the leader, selecting the leader, whereas in the West you find no examples of this.

*John Pentland*

456

"Ventures with Buddhism," is two appended excerpts from "Transmission: An Interview with Lord Pentland," in *Gurdjieff: Essays and Reflections on the Man and His Teaching,* edited by Jacob Needleman and George Baker (New York: Continuum Publishing, 1996). Per Bloomsbury, who acquired Continuum, "Unfortunately, we inherited incomplete records for this title when Continuum Publishing joined Bloomsbury so we are not able to confirm the subsidiary rights, which include quotation rights. However, we are happy to say that we have no objection to this use."

457

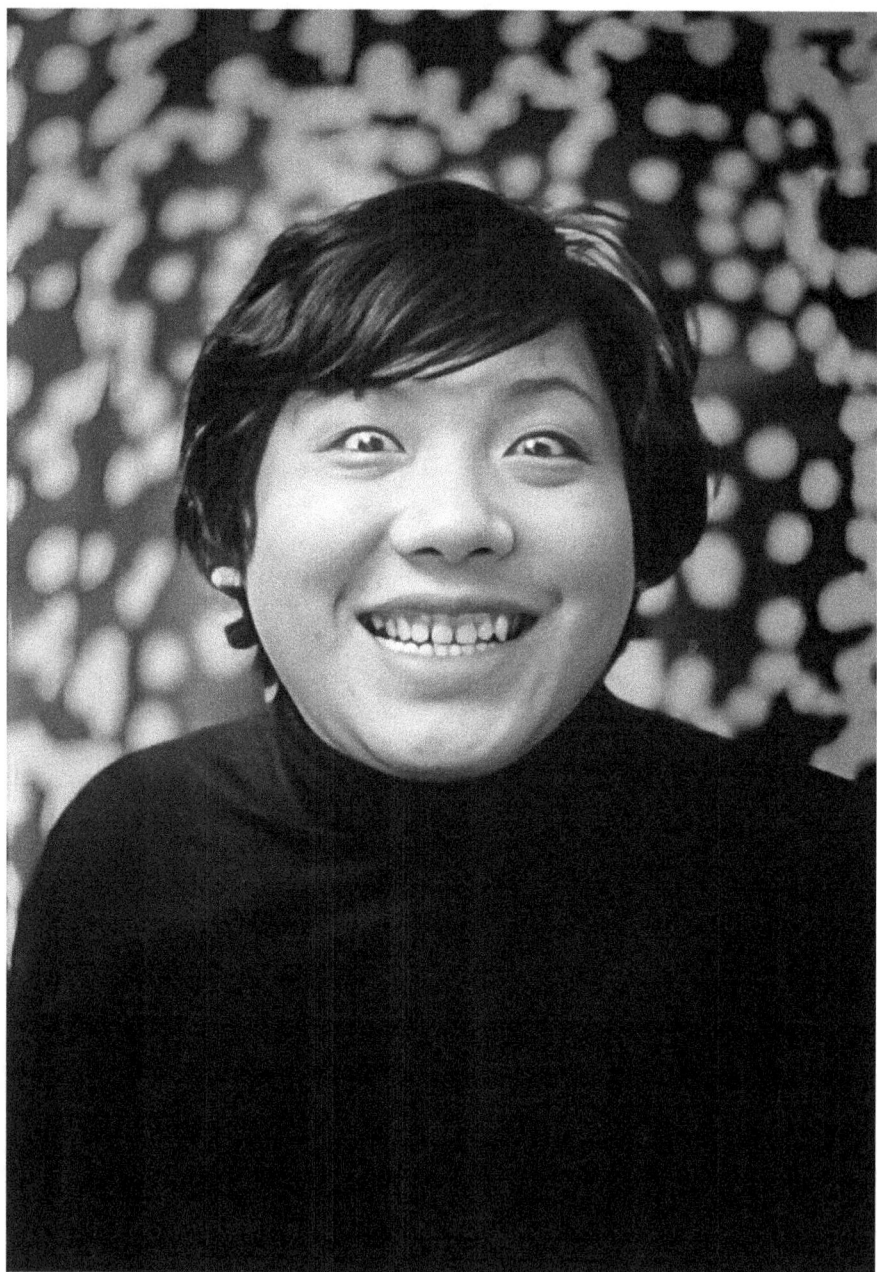

*Chögyam Trungpa Rinpoche*

QUESTION: How much do you know about Gurdjieff's teaching?

TRUNGPA RINPOCHE: Well, not [a] great deal to be expert on it, but I think my friends who came from Gurdjieff's Work taught me a great deal; and the product of Gurdjieff's Work, I met anyway, before. I think I have a fair amount of ideas, you know. But it's not particularly scholarly, chronologically, you know, what year and what date... [But] I was in connection with Gurdjieff's students in London and, you know, I've been in connection with since then. So I think we have altogether by now about ten years connected.

QUESTION: What about a situation like ours? We are in a weak position. Mr Nyland taught us about eight years. And suddenly he's gone. It's a very difficult period for a group like ours with a lot of uncertainty.

TRUNGPA RINPOCHE: Well, we talked about a sense of lineage, a sense of heritage, which is very important. And I have met some of the Foundation people. I spoke about that to John Pentland as well. But there's [a] need for heritage, pride, rather than trying to make Gurdjieff's teaching valid, which seems to be starting from a weaker angle. When he is already there.

He taught it, and there's all evidence of what he did, with people. We don't have to prove, particularly. And we don't try to prove that Buddha was *right*, we just try to teach what Buddha *said*. So, I think the sense of lineage and heritage is important. Without that then you become a freelance something-or-other, and you begin to pollute the teachings. You know, that's what happened with the history of the churches in the past too. That people think they could do [a] better job than their predecessors, and they begin to create churches of all kinds. And the result is a complete mess.

QUESTION: Ego is something that I understand from what you said. Essence is something that I feel, from what Gurdjieff has taught. But in your teachings there doesn't seem to be that concept. Does essence exist in Buddhism?

TRUNGPA RINPOCHE: Well, it depends how you look at it. It seems that the whole thing is a matter of personal journey. Sometimes the essence is called ego, and sometimes essence is called enlightenment. But from the point of view of ego, there seems to be a great deal of essence; there seems to be a self-centeredness, [an] egomaniac sort of thing. But from the point of view of enlightenment, it could be called essence sometimes. If the essence is used purely as [a] reference point to one's ego-centered enlightenment, then it becomes [an] obstacle. Whereas essence [itself] is like space; it doesn't have a center or fringe. Everywhere you look. The terminology in Buddhism is "buddha-nature" which is nature, essence. But it's everywhere.

QUESTION: Rinpoche, Ian and I had a discussion once about whether or not basically the practice of mindfulness and observation were the same thing. And I felt that in some sense they were the same activity but viewed within a different context, so that the words to describe them were different.

TRUNGPA RINPOCHE: Well, mindfulness is a practice, naturally. But it is not regarded as particularly a training process; it is regarded as purely a way of life. And I suppose we have a linguistic problem there, you know. Observation could be that way too. But in the Buddhist context mindfulness is not necessarily [to] watch yourself or to observe yourself, but to *be*, simply. And it's not watching yourself to do things.

QUESTION: That's not how we understand observation, though. [It's] an attempt to be aware rather than...

TRUNGPA RINPOCHE: ...than to be, yeah. You know, even awareness, it comes much later; you're right, mindfulness comes first. First there is [a] sense of learn[ing] how to *be*. We lost that kind of sharpness for a long time through our confusion. That tries to recapture the wakeful quality. Like, if you are awake during the day, you don't have to [be] remind[ed] that you are not asleep. But you [are] already awake and you carry on your daily business. So it is a question of *being*. And that is unconditional. It doesn't have any moralistic implication behind it, that we have to be careful, or trying to come out *right*, necessarily. And it becomes total life. And after that, slowly, the sense of awareness comes. That awareness, again in this case not so much of being careful, but the environment that you've created by *being* can be felt and experienced, which is awareness. So you have basic beingness. Then beyond that extends [a] radius that's created by the basic beingness, [an] environment that's created by basic beingness.

Photograph of Trungpa Rinpoche, copyright © Shambhala Archives, is reproduced here with their permission.

"Excerpts from a Talk Given to the Nyland Group March 8, 1976," taken from a recording and a verbatim transcript in the collection of the Chogyam Trungpa Institute at Naropa University. The excerpts have been lightly edited by Layne Negrin. Copyright © Diana J. Mukpo. Used by permission.

# PART THREE

# PONDERINGS OF A GRANDCHILD

## INTRODUCTION TO PART THREE

I want to be clear that I'm not a teacher, leader or guide of any sort. The intention of this section is not to teach. It is merely a collection of personal ponderings on some correlations between Gurdjieff's teaching and Mahayana and Vajrayana Buddhism. Furthermore, this is not a comprehensive collection of comparative studies; it is just the more obvious correlations. Perhaps in the future I'll expand this section or write another work that's more comprehensive.

The reason for including them is twofold. Firstly, they suggest what aspects of Gurdjieff's teaching were *likely* influenced by Tibetan Buddhism. Gurdjieff was influenced by many teachings, and it is impossible to know for certain which teaching was the primary influence of each of Gurdjieff's ideas. Even so, the correlations offered here seem rather likely and worthy of your consideration.

Secondly, I hope they will inspire you to ponder the subjects discussed yourself. That is, to ponder these ideas based on your experience and make correlations of your own. And by doing so, to discover the center of the circle that various spiritual paths approach from different directions.

## The Sly Buddha

Gurdjieff said, "The fourth way is sometimes called *the way of the sly man*."[1] This was said after describing the three traditional ways—that of the fakir (the physical approach), the monk (the emotional approach) and the yogi (the intellectual approach). The idea is somewhat related to his previous discussion about center of gravity, or the three dispositions a man may have—moving-instinctive, emotional and intellectual. Similarly, he says that there is an additional, albeit artificial, center of gravity one may acquire—one in which one is predominantly concerned with work on oneself. A man with such a center of gravity he calls man number four and is said to be on the way to becoming a conscious or enlightened man. With this understanding, a sly man might be considered man number four. Such cleverness is beyond that of the intellectual man. The intellectual man is conceptual or theoretical whereas the sly man is practical. His intelligence is more of a spontaneous nature. The sly man has a sense of how to use any situation to his advantage—that is, as an opportunity for work on oneself. The sly man always makes a profit. Even if he apparently fails, he profits so long as he learns from his experience.

Obviously, *the way of the sly man* is a definition of the fourth way. Significantly, there is an important Buddhist concept known as "skillful means" and Buddhism as a whole is viewed as such a means. What makes the various means skillful very much relates to what was said about the cleverness a sly man possesses. Yet the idea of skillful means explains the cleverness of work on oneself in ways beyond the practical element as well. These other ways will at once be clear to the fourth way practitioner although Gurdjieff did not speak of them in the same context.

Somewhat related to the idea that the cleverness of the sly man is practical is the understanding of the word "skillful" in its most common meaning as a synonym for "adept" or "proficient." The means used are skillful because they are mastered through diligence no different from the skills developed in learning any craft.

Another way in which these means are considered skillful is that they are practiced without attachment. In Tibetan Buddhism, while there are stable practices such as shamatha meditation, one is constantly learning new practices. Likewise, in the fourth way, there is constant experimentation. These approaches help one to refrain from taking the means as dogma, to retain a fresh relationship to them, and remain unattached. In Tibetan Buddhism, the emphasis to practice the means one uses without thought of personal gain also helps one to remain unattached to them. Perhaps an equivalent to this in the fourth way are the so-called second and third lines of work—making efforts for the sake of others in one's group and the teaching itself respectively.

(What was just said about experimentation and change may seem to contradict what was said earlier about diligence and mastery, but in fact they work together. Mastery is what enables one to improvise.)

One reason Buddhism as a whole is considered a skillful means is because of its adaptability. The expression and practices of Buddhism change according to the culture and era in which it finds itself so those who encounter it can best relate. Gurdjieff said exactly the same of the fourth way. As Buddhism spread through India it took on aspects of the Hindu culture, when it entered Tibet it took on aspects of the Bön religion, when it entered China it took on aspects of Taoism, when it

468

entered Japan it took on aspects of Shinto. Likewise, Gurdjieff gave the fourth way a façade that would better appeal to the scientific, rational Westerner.

Another way in which the means of work on oneself is skillful is that they are considered to be tricks. Here we see the aspect of slyness more clearly in the Buddhist concept. Perhaps they are tricks in part because the material that is worked with is the products of the mind. Especially skillful is that one is taught to make use of one's "negativity". As Gurdjieff taught, everything can potentially be material for work, that shit in fact makes good fertilizer. Or, as Thich Nhat Hanh poetically and succinctly said, "No mud, no lotus."

It also makes sense that, as described in *The Heart Sutra* for one place, skillful means is equated with bodhisattva practice—working for the benefit of others. And perhaps this is why such work is the final of Gurdjieff's five obligonian strivings—because it requires the most skill. In fact, both teachings speak of benefiting *all* beings, not only humans. To be able to provide such extensive care indeed requires skill.

---

[1] P.D. Ouspensky, *In Search of the Miraculous:Fragments of an Unknown Teaching* (New York: Harcourt, Brace & Co., 1949), 50.

# Haida!

Another way that Gurdjieff referred to his teaching is as Haida Yoga. "Haida" is a Turkish exclamation meaning "hurry" that was imported into Russian and understood by Gurdjieff's Russian students. Thus Haida Yoga connotes a quick way. Perhaps it also connotes a way in which shock plays a part as a shout of "Haida!" is intended to jolt someone.

The name may have been inspired by Dzogchen, a Tibetan teaching that literally means "Great Perfection" and is also known as Atiyoga, meaning "Utmost Yoga." Dzogchen is known for its methods of facilitating the spontaneous arousal of "luminous presence." It is also considered an accelerated path in that Dzogchenpas believe that complete spiritual realization can be achieved by their practices within a single lifetime compared to other teachings which require multiple lifetimes.

The aim of Dzogchen is to discover one's innate primordial awareness and keep it at the fore rather than buried. This is achieved by a variety of practices including some in which shocks of one sort or another are employed to interrupt the stream of thoughts and allow one's primordial awareness (or primordial ground as it is also referred) to surface. Shocks are at times given by the teacher, but these alone cannot be relied upon. It is necessary to learn to shock oneself. In one particular practice, one repeatedly shouts "Phat!" as an effort to dumbfound the mind and reveal one's "natural state." The word is said to have special qualities that actualize the effect. As Lama Lena explains:

> So, there's a syllable. A seed syllable. Seed syllables. English equivalent would be magic word. That is comprised of the union of the letters of method and wisdom. Pha and Tra. And it spells 'phat' [pronunciation: 'phet']. "Pheeet!" ...A very, very powerful seed syllable. In this case though, it has to be done with certain characteristics. It has to be done suddenly. It has to be done sharply. It has to be done fiercely. And it has to be done quickly. So, in this case, a little wimpy "peeet" won't do diddly squat. You have to say it hard, fast, and sharp. Almost sneaking up on yourself. Phat![1]

Significantly, Lama Lena describes the practice as "quick glancing."

There's an account given by Thomas de Hartmann that's relevant for a couple of reasons. He says:

> Another Sunday came when Ouspensky lectured. During the tea break Mr Gurdjieff was approached by an elderly man with a long beard. He asked about yogas. This man was the type who has a superficial interest in Hindu teachings. Mr Gurdjieff pretended that he had never even heard the names of the various yoga methods. Then this intellectual began self-importantly to explain hatha yoga and so on, but Mr Gurdjieff interrupted him quickly and said: "Well, and my yoga is called haida yoga." I don't need to say how astonished the intellectual was to hear about a new yoga. He understood nothing. Mr Gurdjieff, however, had expressed in this way an idea full of meaning, if he could have grasped it.[2]

Here Gurdjieff not only defines his teaching as Haida Yoga, but attempts to employ the shock method in the process. In perceiving the humor of the incident, it is easy to miss the intention of Gurdjieff's response. Clearly he dumbfounded the old gent. Unfortunately, although the old man likely got a taste of his primordial awareness, he was simply too full of himself to see the significance.

In Gurdjieff's teaching, the primordial ground is referred to as the subconsciousness, and in the same way that Dzogchen regards the primordial ground as the natural state, Gurdjieff says that the subconsciousness "ought to be in my opinion the real human consciousness."[3] Early on in his teaching, Gurdjieff experimented with using hypnosis methods to access the subconsciousness but abandoned that approach after a couple of years. Mostly he employed various shock methods. Those he implemented as teacher included the creative, spontaneous sort such as the example that de Hartmann gives, as well as certain exercises such as his infamous stop exercise where in the middle of some group activity he would shout "Stop!"—an instruction for everyone to freeze in whatever posture one is in at that moment.

Endurance exercises he led, which have the intention to tap into what he called the "main accumulator," that is, one's main reservoir of energy, and experience what is often referred to as "second wind," might be regarded as a similar sort of shock method.

These examples may in part be what James George means by Gurdjieff's "oral teaching" when he says, "His essential teaching, his oral teaching (as distinct from what he wrote in his books) was all about what you would call Dzogchen and I would call awareness or presence in this moment."[4] Elsewhere George says, "From all that I have been able to learn from my Tibetan teachers, my best guess is that Mr Gurdjieff was thoroughly familiar with Dzogchen practices, as transmitted by the Nyingmapa Lamas."[5]

But as with Dzogchen, there are also exercises Gurdjieff gave whereby one shocks oneself. For example, one might be given an aim to remember oneself whenever something in particular occurs during one's day, such as walking through a doorway, hearing a certain expression, or encountering something in particular. The realization that one hasn't been remembering oneself specifically is what serves as the shock.

Besides James George, there seem to be a couple of others who recognized an affinity between Gurdjieff's teaching and Dzogchen. Consider that Robert Godet, who was a student of both Gurdjieff and Jamyang Khyentse Chokyi Lodro, wrote a cycle of 26 poems called *La voie abrupte* (*The Abrupt Way*). It is likely that both teachings inspired his work. The references to "radiant light," which appear in three of the poems, is an obvious allusion to Dzogchen. Spontaneous presence (*lhündrup* in Tibetan) is also often rendered as "luminous clarity" and is described as the mind of "clear light" (*odsal*). The allusions to Gurdjieff include two poems that mention effort as well as some more subtle references.

No doubt Paul Anderson, who handed over the guidance of his Gurdjieff group to Dzogchen master Chögyal Namkhai Norbu, also recognized some relationship between the two teachings. The impression he gave his students is that although different on the surface, the cores of the two teachings are essentially the same, and this enabled Dzogchen to serve as a natural progression of the foundation established in his group by Gurdjieff's teaching.

Also consider that Gurdjieff apparently advised Yahne Le Toumelin to become acquainted with *Yeshe Lama*, a classic Dzogchen text by Jigme Lingpa.[6]

Although Dzogchen is largely taught by the Nyingmapa sect, it is recognized to predate Buddhism and even the 18,000 year old Bön tradition from which the teaching was imported. It is in fact believed to be older than humanity itself. This is interesting in that Gurdjieff too describes his teaching as being ageless.

---

[1] Lama Lena, "Dzogchen for All Levels: Beginner, Intermediate, & Advanced," Lama Lena Teachings, lamalenateachings.com/dzogchen-levels-beginner-intermediate-advanced.

[2] Thomas & Olga de Hartmann, *Our Life with Mr Gurdjieff* (Sandpoint: Sandpoint Press, 2008), 68.

[3] G. Gurdjieff, *All and Everything: First Series: Beelzebub's Tales to His Grandson* (New York: Harcourt, Brace & Co., 1950) 24.

[4] "Interview with James George," www.chronicleproject.com/interview-with-james-george

[5] William C. Segal, *Meetings with Three Tibetan Masters* (Brattleboro: Green River Press, 1993), 3.

[6] See the chapter "Mademoiselle Pourquoi."

## THE SCIENTIFIC PATH

Buddhism originally was not a religion. It was more of a psychological method practiced by the followers of the various religions of northern India of the time. The language used was very technical and the meanings of the terms very specific. Some of the language was borrowed from Hinduism, but these early Buddhists largely gave these terms somewhat different meanings, often focusing on some other nuance of their definitions in the Prakrit languages spoken by Buddha Shakyamuni and his followers. In contrast, most other religions use a more allegorical language. Most significant in showing Buddhism's nonreligious origins, however, is that there are no deities in Buddhism; it is considered a nontheistic religion. Figures such as Avalokiteshvara are understood to be metaphoric representations of some aspect of enlightened mind rather than deities (which is how they are often described in English) having some heavenly existence, and were only later introduced into Buddhism; Buddha Shakyamuni did not talk about such figures himself.

The same can be said of Gurdjieff's teaching. The overall psychological map used by Gurdjieff may be different from Buddhism, but he too considered his teaching a psychological method, employed technical language, did not speak of deities, and welcomed practitioners of all religions. It may be too soon to know for certain that Gurdjieff's teaching will eventually become more of a religious practice, but there are already signs that it is heading in that direction.

No doubt there will be readers who disagree with two things said thus far. Firstly, in mentioning that most religions use a more allegorical than technical language, the intention was not to suggest that Gurdjieff did not use allegory. His writings are filled with allegory. However, he seems to have only started using allegorical language after realizing that his teaching was not going to spread as quickly as initially anticipated. Sensing that his students would not be prepared for his more advanced teachings, he hid them allegorically for future generations to discover. This is indicated in the commentaries of Gurdjieff's writings by his direct pupils, none of whom appear to have understood the various metaphors pertaining to nonduality that Gurdjieff conceived.

Secondly, there are no doubt readers who, in interpreting Gurdjieff's teaching through their familial religion, interpret it theistically. In the interpretation offered here no disrespect is intended to these readers. One does not invalidate the other and progress is very much possible utilizing both interpretations. Here the nontheistic interpretation is being emphasized for those who are somewhere between both views. The point here being that Gurdjieff rarely spoke of God. In the early Russian phase of his teaching he used the term "the Absolute" to refer to the highest of the seven cosmoses. While some may equate the term with the God of monotheism, it is largely intended as a scientific term as part of an illustration depicting the structure and interconnectedness of the universe. As well, his use of the term Endlessness in *Beelzebub's Tales*, while largely interpreted as a denomination for God, suggests something somewhat different. This will be discussed in detail in the chapter "Empty and Endless."

In sum, like Buddha Shakyamuni, Gurdjieff derived a non-religious teaching that could be understood and practiced by people with a wide range of beliefs.

## RECOLLECTION

Many teachers and scholars of Buddhism have pointed out that the Sanskrit word *smrti*, which is usually translated to "mindfulness" in English, literally means "recollection". Chögyam Trungpa Rinpoche, who is often mentioned in this book, is one such teacher. Although it is a Sanskrit term, as used in the Hindu tradition, it seems to have a different meaning; it refers to certain religious texts committed to memory. But in the Buddhist tradition it refers to the recollected mind and is thus used to connote mindfulness.

Very likely this explains, at least in part, the term "self-remembering" as Gurdjieff used it. Gurdjieff had a way of taking words and phrases from ordinary language—often formulations which had lost their original meaning—and, by giving them very specific meanings, used them to explain concepts related to his method of work on oneself. The term "self-remembering" is one such example. In the Russian language (the language he first taught in), as well as in English, the command "Remember yourself!" is used as a shock to calm someone who is upset, someone who has "lost it" in some way. In common usage it is used much the same way as the command "Pull yourself together!" This phrase too connotes some sort of "recollection". Although Gurdjieff's usage is obviously related, he explains self-remembering more specifically as a matter of identification—of identifying consciousness as one's self rather than the ever-changing *arisings* in consciousness (thoughts, emotions, sensations) as one ordinarily does. To put it more simply, self-remembering means remembering who one is. Very likely, this was the original meaning of the phrase in common usage. Although very similar, in common usage we seem to have lost the understanding of what this self to be remembered actually is.

Another way to express this connotation of remembering one's true identity, inferred by both *smrti* and self-remembering, is the recollecting, or making whole, of one's attention. In other words, instead of one's attention being pulled from one thing to the next, one's attention is made whole, is recollected, is diffused amongst all impressions, internal and external, as opposed to being seized by one, then the next.

*Smrti* has several other meanings as well, and there's one other in particular which may indicate another connotation or nuance of the Buddhist usage as mindfulness. This is its meaning as "wish". According to Gurdjieff, wish, distinct from desire which is a manifestation of one of man's lower centers and prone to identification (or attachment), is an "impulse" of the Self (or consciousness). Thus when one is recollected the impulse of wish is present, is an aspect of that presence.

In summary, of all the traditional ways of expressing mindfulness, Gurdjieff's formulation "self-remembering" seems to come closest of all to the Buddhist concept of *smrti*. This is not to say that the ways in which other traditions express or practice mindfulness do not relate—mindfulness is mindfulness however it is described—only that the *verbal presentation* of self-remembering seems most similar to the Buddhist presentation of *smrti*.

## SLEEP IS IGNORANCE

In Buddhist thought, the chief cause of our various forms of suffering is denoted by the Sanskrit word *avidya*, meaning not *vidya*, or not seeing or knowing. Similarly, the Tibetans translate *avidya* as *marigpa*, meaning not *rigpa*, or non-awareness or -wisdom. In English, *avidya* is most commonly translated as ignorance. What we are ignorant of, what we fail to see, is our inherent unity and interdependence. If we were able to perceive this reality, we would better care for one another and our surroundings, because the world would be part of us, would actually be our identity. We would also better care for our *selves* so we could be best of service. But as things are, living in ignorance, in the world or *samsara*, we get angry, we get offended, we worry, get sad, etc.

Gurdjieff approached the subject of interdependence differently than Buddhism does. His Ray of Creation diagram explains how each of the seven cosmoses contains the cosmos below, and thus how all fits into the design of the Absolute, the underlying unity. He also speaks of the unity that this interdependence illustrates in *Lecture on Symbolism* where he says, "Everything in the world is One and is governed by uniform laws, and for that reason the *Emerald Tablets of Hermes Trismegistus* put it: 'As above, so below.' All the laws of the cosmos we shall find in the atom, and in any phenomenon existing as something complete according to laws. The knowledge of the laws of the plurality of the One was always based on the similitude of the microcosm to the macrocosm, of man to the universe, and vice versa."[1]

In Gurdjieff's teaching he mainly speaks of ignorance as sleep. He uses the concept in exactly the same way—as the antithesis of wakefulness. Sleep is just another way of describing the lack of awareness or consciousness or conscience that *avidya* points to.

Yet Gurdjieff does at times use the word ignorance instead. For example, Ouspensky quotes him as saying, "The first reason for man's inner slavery is his ignorance, and above all, his ignorance of himself."[2]

Whether one calls it *avidya* or *marigpa* or ignorance or sleep, this is our chief fault; it is what is behind all our vices and the suffering that these vices bring.

Yet this fault cannot be addressed with aggression. Ignorance cannot be addressed with ignorance. This is a common trap. Only compassion and care can bring about a transformation.

---

[1] G.I. Gurdjieff, *Lecture on Symbolism* (McMinnville: Stopinder Books, 2002), 2.

[2] P.D. Ouspensky, *In Search of the Miraculous:Fragments of an Unknown Teaching* (New York: Harcourt, Brace & Co., 1949), 104.

## Empty and Endless

In Chapter 18 of *Beelzebub's Tales*, "The Arch-preposter-ous," Beelzebub describes the time Gornahoor Harharkh, his feathered friend from Saturn, demonstrated an elaborate experiment he was working on which analyzed the conditions of a pure vacuum. The scene described is an obvious metaphor of the Buddhist concept of *shunyata*, or "emptiness" as it is commonly translated into English. In particular, it is a metaphor for the Mahayana view of emptiness, for the Theravada view is somewhat different. But "emptiness" fails to convey the full meaning of *shunyata* which includes the connotation of "boundlessness". The concept is not intended to suggest that nothing is real, a frequent misinterpretation of its translation to "emptiness". Rather, it points to the fact that the individuation of things, which is necessitated by language, is purely conceptual and has no inherent reality—that nothing is separate from anything else, and that no being has an inherent self; that everything existing is part of a boundless unity. Gurdjieff alludes to this through the conclusion of Harharkh's experiment, which is that empty space is composed of "omnipresent-okidanokh". Saying that empty space has an omnipresent component is how he describes emptiness as being all-pervading.

By describing empty space as omnipresent, Gurdjieff also appears to be equating the concept of *shunyata* with the concept of God, specifically the pantheistic view which regards the entire universe as God. He does this elsewhere as well—namely, by referring to God as His Endlessness throughout *Beelzebub's Tales*. Again, *shunyata* does not merely mean emptiness; it includes the connotation of boundlessness or endlessness. Gurdjieff is equally speaking of *shunyata* whenever he speaks of His Endlessness. He recognized that all spiritual teachings are different ways of looking at the same truth, and this is one example of him equating seemingly unrelated ideas from different traditions. The only difference is in the approach to the subject. In the monotheistic religions God is glorified, whereas in the nontheistic religions *shunyata* is to be regarded as "nothing special." (That is, one is taught not to be identified with the experience.) But both approaches lead to oneness.

## The Embryo

The Sanskrit word *tathagatagarbha*, which literally means buddha embryo, is commonly translated as buddha-nature. In Tibetan it is rendered as *degshegs snyingpo*, which literally means embryonic essence or kernel. Although Buddhism advocates the idea of no-self, buddha-nature is sometimes interpreted as being the equivalent of a soul.

Gurdjieff had a similar view of the soul, and at the same time recognized that soul was not quite the right word; it was just the closest word in Western languages for what he was trying to convey. As Olga de Hartmann notes, "In general, in his discussions with us Mr Gurdjieff never used the word 'soul'. He referred only to a 'something'. However, in his discussion with these new people, it was necessary for him to use words that they would understand and for that reason he used the word 'soul'."[1] Also consider this exchange that Dorothy Caruso had with Gurdjieff:

> We sat in silence. Finally I said, "Mr Gurdjieff... the 'I' which I am trying to develop—is this the soul that survives after death?"
>
> He waited so long that I wondered whether he had heard me. Then he said, "How long have you been with me?"
>
> "Almost two years," I said.
>
> "Too short the time. You not able to understand yet..."[2]

Like Buddhism, Gurdjieff too regarded this indescribable

something as embryonic. As aphorism 29 states, "Blessed is he who has a soul, blessed is he who has none, but woe and grief to him who has it in embryo."

Coming closer yet to the idea of soul in Tibetan Buddhism is the *zhentong* interpretation of *shunyata* (or emptiness). *Zhentong* is a concept that originated in India and was maintained and elaborated upon by the Jonangpa sect. Unlike the traditional view of *shunyata* (which they refer to as *rangtong*) which views all as empty, the *zhentong* view states that all is empty *but* buddha-nature. This was heretical because it implies an essential self whereas Buddhism professes the idea of no-self. *Zhentong* too regards buddha-nature as being embryonic, but it differs from *rangtong* by stating that it is an embryo *of an enlightened being*, that is, of an individual. According to the common view of *tathagatagarbha*, buddha-nature is actually fully developed; it only appears embryonic because delusion obscures it and prevents it from manifesting. So, what might be viewed as the growth of an embryo is actually the gradual dissolution of delusion.

As well, buddha-nature does not appear to belong to the individual. It is more something impersonal or universal that we all share. To understand this it is useful to equate buddha-nature with conscience, which Gurdjieff likewise says is fully developed and only need be unburied. Whether acquainted with one term or the other, it can be observed that it always manifests with regard to the welfare of others; it never manifests for personal benefit. Trungpa defines buddha-nature as "basic goodness." It is the instantaneous response one makes to assist someone in need. If someone you are near was unaware that a car was about to hit them, you would instantaneously pull them out of the way without thinking about it. Consciousness itself initiates the action. Whether you prefer to call it basic goodness, buddha-nature, or conscience, it is the wisdom aspect of consciousness that knows how to act in any situation for the benefit of others.

Yet the *zhentong* view has its merits. Indeed pure awareness does not appear to change. It neither ages nor changes in any other way; pure awareness appears the same whenever

484

it surfaces and comes to our attention. The outer and inner impressions falling on awareness during each manifestation may differ, but pure awareness itself is unchanging.

It is interesting that in Tibetan *tathagatagarbha* is rendered as *degshegs snyingpo*, meaning embryonic kernel. Kernel is another word Gurdjieff used to describe this something. In this case he was speaking of 'I', or what he calls Real 'I' elsewhere. Namely, in the third series he says, "...the possibility is also foreseen for beings to acquire the kernel of their essence, that is to say, their own I..." According to Gurdjieff, this 'I' is what survives death. Note that here Gurdjieff appears to be using the word essence more in the sense of its Buddhist meaning in comparison to the meaning he gave essence in his early teaching—that is, as that aspect of the lower self that is one's genuine nature in contrast to personality which is acquired. His teaching changed somewhat when he began writing. In this quote Gurdjieff is clearly speaking of the higher self rather than the lower. Another meaning of the word part *garbha* (in *tathagatagarbha*) is essence. As used in Buddhism it always refers to the essence of something higher. Other examples are *vajragharba* (indestructible essence) and *guhyagarbha* (secret essence). If correct about Gurdjieff's meaning, the essence also survives death, not just its kernel.

The essence and its kernel appears to be another way of speaking about the two finer bodies that both Gurdjieff and Buddhism say we contain. While in his earliest teaching Gurdjieff utilized the four-body model (the physical body plus three finer bodies) used by both esoteric Christianity and Theosophy, when he put his teaching into writing and refined it he settled upon the three-body model (which contains two finer bodies) used by Buddhism (and Hinduism). So, here we have yet another example of a teaching refinement that Gurdjieff made.

Buddhism calls these non-physical bodies the subtle body and the very subtle body. The subtle body is composed of the subtle energies flowing through the body's channels. These energies are worked with during various yoga practices. The very subtle body is said to be the seed of the subtle and physical bodies and resides in the center of the heart chakra.

Gurdjieff calls these non-physical bodies the body kesdjan and the highest being-body. The body kesdjan is the body of feeling and the neologism *kesdjan* means "vessel of the soul." The physical body might be regarded as the body of sensation and Gurdjieff teaches that sensation is the doorway to feeling. It is the highest being-body that he describes as the "body of the soul." In his earlier teaching these higher being-bodies are equated with what he calls higher emotional center and higher intellectual center. It is easy to see how a body of feeling equates to the higher emotional center. The soul, or highest being-body, relates to the higher intellectual center in that it is the wisdom aspect of consciousness spoken about when discussing conscience (or buddha-nature) above. The body kesdjan is merely a vessel for the soul; it is not the soul itself.

So the body kesdjan, or body of feeling, relates to the subtle body of Buddhism, or the body of energy channels. I tend to view various feelings as energies. When I am not consumed by them and can better perceive them, they just appear as energies of various qualities.

The highest being body, or wisdom body (if I may call it that), relates to the very subtle body of Buddhism, which is considered the seed of the physical and subtle bodies that resides in the heart chakra. It might seem as if the feeling body should reside in the heart chakra but consider that wisdom is based on compassion according to Buddhism.

Returning again to the meaning of the neologism *kesdjan* as "vessel of the soul," it is also interesting that another meaning of the word part *garbha* is "womb", which is another way of describing a vessel. This womb or vessel or essence is what nourishes the seed or kernel or embryo within. And this vessel of feeling continues to carry the seed of wisdom through the threshold of death and beyond.

But does this seed negate the Buddhist idea of no-self, or is it actually not a greater self or soul? In all likelihood both views are valid but only focus on one aspect of something that is paradoxical in nature. Perhaps this is why Gurdjieff had difficulty using the word "soul". While there is no doubt that

486

we possess some sort of seed that has an unchanging nature, it appears to belong to the universal rather than the individual; it is something universal that is carried by the individual. A particle of Omniscient Endlessness. Is it right to say that this particle is one's own? From the Buddhist perspective, no; from the Gurdjieffian perspective, yes.

One thing that may be difficult to reconcile is the idea of multiple bodies with the idea of unity. Where is the unity in this model of multiplicity? What may help is to envision these bodies as coexisting concentrically, as each existing within the next. Although the higher can theoretically exist without the lower, they are a unity when they coexist. At the same time that the body kesdjan is the vessel of the highest being-body, it is also a manifestation of the highest being-body. At the same time that the physical body is the vessel of the body kesdjan, it is also a manifestation of the body kesdjan. But one's center of gravity needs to be in the higher to realize this experientially.

---

[1] Thomas & Olga de Hartmann, *Our Life with Mr Gurdjieff* (Sandpoint: Sandpoint Press, 2008), 183.

[2] Dorothy Caruso, *A Personal History* (New York: Hermitage House, 1952), 186.

## TRIAMAZIKAMNO OR TRIKAYA

One of the interesting aspects of Gurdjieff's teaching is the law of three (or triamazikamno as he calls it in *Beelzebub's Tales*). The idea can be found in one form or another in virtually every spiritual tradition, but none describes its three components in quite the same way—as affirming, denying and reconciling forces. Yet the Buddhist idea of the *trikaya* (or three *kayas*) seems to come close. The *trikaya* is generally understood as the three bodies of the Buddha, but in its esoteric sense refers to buddha-*nature*—that is, one's inner buddha. Rather than provide textbook definitions of each *kaya* (which only gives their exoteric meaning), I think it will be more useful to refer to Chögyam Trungpa's poetic description:

> The totality aspect of the *dharmakaya* is like the ocean, and the *sambhogakaya* aspect is like the waves of that ocean, which make the statement that that ocean does exist. The *nirmanakaya* aspect is like a ship on the ocean, which makes the whole situation into a pragmatic and workable one—you can sail across the ocean.[1]

*Sambhogakaya* corresponds to what Gurdjieff called denying force. *Sambhogakaya* are all the thoughts, feelings and sensations arising in awareness with which ego identifies and thereby denies one's true identity—the totality of awareness. But these waves are not separate from the totality, which is a common misconception. They are part of the ocean and, as Trungpa says, make the ocean observable. That is, without objects to be conscious of it would not be possible to recognize the existence of consciousness. Really it is not these inner impressions that are obstacles; rather it is the tendency to identify with them.

*Nirmanakaya* corresponds to what Gurdjieff called the affirming force. *Nirmanakaya* are all the methods one uses to ride the waves of *sambhogakaya*. By remaining on the surface rather than being pulled under, one is able to affirm the totality.

*Dharmakaya* equates to the reconciling force. It is when awareness realizes its existence (or when it self-remembers as Gurdjieff puts it). It is this sudden *realization*, rather than the consequence of some action, that Gurdjieff means when he describes reconciling force as the result. *Nirmanakaya*, or affirmation, does not actually cause anything to happen; it just creates the conditions so that realization or remembrance can happen naturally on its own. One cannot cause memory; it just happens.

Of course, the totality of awareness exists whether or not it is self-aware. In this sense that it is always there, it can also be understood as the *potential*. Every manifestation first exists as potential before it even happens. This is how reconciling force is both the energy behind a manifestation and the manifestation itself. Potential neither affirms nor denies. It is innate but it still has energy (or force).

The neologism triamazikamno is made of three Greek elements—*tria*, meaning three; *mazi*, meaning together; and *kamno*, meaning labor. Thus triamazikamno literally means three laboring together. Although *trikaya* literally means three bodies, the understanding that the three *kayas* work together as one can also be understood from Trungpa's description.

---

[1] Chögyam Trungpa, *The Collected Works of Chögyam Trungpa: Volume 5* (Boston: Shambhala Publications, 2004), 30–31. (*Crazy Wisdom*, Chapter 3.)

## A NEW ORGAN

Probably the most significant message in *Beelzebub's Tales* is its conclusion in which Gurdjieff suggests that the "sole means" of saving the Earth beings would be to implant in them a new organ which would make one ever aware of one's impermanence, as well as the impermanence of all who one perceives. Obviously he is saying that the only way to save oneself from one's own self-deception is to practice some method which would make one continuously aware of impermanence.

Knowing the intentions of each of Gurdjieff's three series of writings, one would expect that this method would have been revealed in the third. Unfortunately, such a method is not described in the published version. Some suggest that Gurdjieff never completed the third series while others believe the complete text is being suppressed. However, also possible is that Gurdjieff came to regard the manuscript that was published as complete although it does not satisfy his original intentions.

Be that as it may, Gurdjieff practitioners have been left to their own devices on this subject. One obvious source of guidance in this area has been traditional Buddhist contemplative meditation on impermanence. (On this note, it is worth mentioning that E.J. Gold's rendering of this meditation, called "The Last Hour of Life," has been distributed amongst Gurdjieff practitioners for years being misattributed as a talk from Gurdjieff himself, due to the fact that Gold signed his work "Mr G.") I myself have experimented with using a continual awareness of my breath, and thus awareness of life, as such a reminder, and found it to be very effective.

Certainly there are many traditions which advocate some sort of contemplation on the subject of impermanence. In the Buddhist tradition impermanence is one of the four "reminders", the other three being the preciousness of human birth, karma and samsara. The most frequent that the four reminders are practiced would be daily as part of one's daily morning practice. Yet the intention of these contemplations is to help remember them throughout one's day, not just during the practice itself.

In Tibetan Buddhism, further inspiration to develop a continual awareness of death is found in the story of Padmasambhava, the tradition's founder. Specifically, his life story relates that when Padmasambhava was banished from Uddiyana he made a charnel ground in India his home. A charnel ground is a sort of mass grave. Metaphorically this is understood to mean that he was continually aware of death. Significantly, Padmasambhava was an innocent, playful sort, and the charnel ground was something of a playground for him. This may sound very strange, but certainly the image is meant to relate how contemplation on impermanence should not be a nihilistic one, that it is meant to remind one of the miracle and joy of life—of each and every moment—regardless of the difficult and even terrifying situations one may find oneself in.

Inspired by Padmasambhava, Tibetan Buddhism has many other reminders of impermanence that can be practiced and teachings on death that can be studied. Best known in the West is *The Tibetan Book of the Dead*, but there are many others. As well, there are many reminders in its arts and ritual objects. For example, there are dances in which skeleton costumes are worn and rituals in which a skull cup is utilized. The subject of impermanence has an emphasis in Tibetan Buddhism not found in other Buddhist sects.

## THE GURDJIEFFIAN BOOK OF THE DEAD

Gurdjieff's ideas about the afterlife are different from what Tibetan Buddhism has to say on the subject. And yet "The Holy Planet 'Purgatory'," the chapter in *Beelzebub's Tales* where he talks about these ideas, appears to be loosely based on the *Bardo Thödol*, or *The Tibetan Book of the Dead* as it is more commonly known. Consider the following:

The *Bardo Thödol* teaches how to avoid reincarnation by which yet another life of suffering would be lived. The idea of reincarnation is an understood truth. In Gurdjieff's teaching reincarnation is a very minor subject, but one of the few places where Gurdjieff speaks about it is in "The Holy Planet 'Purgatory'." There he calls it "Okipkhalevnian exchange."

The character Beelzebub spends quite a bit of time speaking about "stopinders", or intervals. He says there are seven of them. The word *bardo* also means interval, and according to Tibetan tradition there are six—three that pertain to life and three that pertain to the space between lives. Admittedly, the way Beelzebub speaks about intervals does not seem to correspond to Tibetan understanding, but the idea of six *bardos* may still have been an inspiration for Gurdjieff's formulation.

"The Holy Planet 'Purgatory'" is also the chapter in which Gurdjieff speaks about the three bodies of man—that is, the physical body and two higher being-bodies. The same model was also imported into Buddhism from Hinduism and is foundational for understanding the *Bardo Thödol* although the text does not discuss the subject directly. The first higher being-body, which Gurdjieff calls the body kesdjan, corresponds to what Buddhism calls the subtle body. Similarly, the highest being-body (as Gurdjieff calls it) corresponds to the very subtle body of Buddhism. The relationship between the two presentations of this three-body model was discussed in further detail earlier in the chapter "The Embryo."

One detail worth repeating here, however, is the idea that the subtle body (or body kesdjan) is composed of the energies flowing through the body's channels, as the nodes of these channels make up the seven *chakras* which is a subject also discussed in "The Holy Planet 'Purgatory'." The names that Beelzebub gives the *chakras* (or, rather the substances produced by the *chakras*) are Protoëhary, Defteroëhary, Tritoëhary, Tetartoëhary, Piandjoëhary, Exioëhary and Resulzarion. (Gurdjieff considers the various energies spoken of in other traditions as substances instead, perhaps thinking that Westerners would better accept these ideas presented as such.) Here too, although the *chakras* are not discussed in the *Bardo Thödol*, an understanding of them is necessary for the accompanying yoga practices. Also interesting, pertaining to this subject, is that the very subtle body (or highest being-body) is said to reside in the heart *chakra* and that in an exercise Gurdjieff gives in the third series he suggests that what he calls there 'real I' resides in the solar plexus.

Specifically regarding Exioëhary, the substance produced by the sexual organs, Beelzebub speaks at length about its use for spiritual development. The same is understood by *chakra* and channel science wherein the substance is called *bindu*.

The *bardo* and the planet Purgatory are both places where higher being-bodies need to spend a certain amount of time. There is a difference, however, in that Buddhism says virtually everyone will traverse the bardo and, according to Gurdjieff, only higher being-bodies that have "crystallized" go to Purgatory. Yet both sources state there are a rare few able to bypass these places.

Robert Thurman, in his edition of *The Tibetan Book of the Dead*, brings up the Buddhist concept of interdependence in relation to the teaching. This is also something discussed in "The Holy Planet 'Purgatory'." Here Gurdjieff calls interdependence Iraniranumange.

One similarity between the two texts may be regarded as coincidence, but given that there are seven identified here, it seems safe to conclude that the *Bardo Thödol* was an influence for Gurdjieff's chapter. Also supporting this idea is the evidence presented earlier in the chapter "Sausage" suggesting that Gurdjieff was familiar with this particular Tibetan teaching.

## MEMORY

The *alaya vijnana* is a concept of Mahayana Buddhism that pertains to memory. It is often translated as "storehouse consciousness." It is considered a latent form of consciousness where all one's knowledge, experiences and impressions are stored. The idea is used to explain how habits manifest and how karmic seeds are created.

Apparently to explain the same idea, Gurdjieff uses a contemporary metaphor. He talks about how knowledge, experiences and impressions are stored on something akin to phonographic rolls (or simply rolls). To those unaware, he is referring here to Edison cylinders, which were the first sound recording media, predating discs. The first phonographs recorded on and played these cylinders rather than discs. They were high tech in his younger years. In *Meetings with Remarkable Men*, Gurdjieff talks about using an Edison phonograph that he modified for use while working as a shoe-shiner in Rome as a young man. So, he was intimately familiar with the technology.

Unlike the Buddhist concept in which all this data is stored in one place, according to Gurdjieff, each of the lower centers has its own set of rolls. Yet he also talks about how a certain amount of data needs to be recorded on these rolls in one's personality in order to begin work on oneself. So, he seems to regard there being a single storage facility at the same time.

Either way, it seems clear enough that Gurdjieff's presentation is an adaptation of the concept of *alaya vijnana*.

## Animate and Inanimate Phenomena

The transcript of the meeting Gurdjieff gave on February 12, 1924 is on the subject of "the animate and the inanimate"—a concept discussed in Buddhism. The talk is Gurdjieff's response to an individual who asked a question on the subject. At the time, Gurdjieff was in New York preparing for the public demonstrations of his sacred movements and giving talks. Considering New York's diverse cultural scene, the questioner must have been someone acquainted with Buddhism whose question was evoked by something Gurdjieff said.

Basically, the Buddhist idea is that all phenomena, whether animate or inanimate, contain energy, therefore sentience of some degree, and relate to one another in various ways. The concept is used to lead into the subjects of interdependence and no-self.

For Tibetans, however, the concept is much more than an intellectual one. As Reginald Ray puts it, "In the traditional Tibetan view… the animate and inanimate phenomena of this world are charged with being, life, and spiritual vitality. These are conceived in terms of various spirits, ancestors, demigods, demons, and so on."[1] This relates somewhat to the discussion on magic where it was mentioned how Tibetans tend to see magic in everything. Gurdjieff himself uses the Christian idea of the Holy Ghost in his response to explain this aspect.

He also alludes to the relationship to interdependence

where he says, "Everything feeds and is fed. Even a stone feeds." An observation that the Seventeenth Karmapa makes may be more accessible: "...I discovered great harmony between Buddhism and the environmental movement. The emphasis on biological diversity, including ecosystems—in particular, the understanding that animate and inanimate beings are parts of a whole—resonates closely with Buddhism's emphasis on interdependence."[2] Interestingly, Gurdjieff seems to imply that the enneagram is a symbol for interdependence. Looking at the symbol, the circle clearly represents the whole, the triangle seems to represent the potential of the inanimate, and the figure of six represents the six activities that animate phenomena may undergo, and how they relate to one another within the whole.

This is the talk that was included in the first edition of *Views from the Real World* and removed from later editions. One wonders if it was removed to conceal the Gurdjieff's Buddhist influences once discovered. Whatever the case may be, it is currently in print within *Gurdjieff's Early Talks,* a volume which was produced independently of the Gurdjieff Foundation.

---

[1] Reginald A. Ray, *Indestructible Truth* (Boston: Shambhala Publications, 2000, 26.

[2] Ogyen Trinley Dorje, "Walking the Path of Environmental Buddhism through Compassion and Emptiness," *Conservation Biology: The Journal of the Society for Conservation Biology* 25, no. 6 (December 2011), 1094.

## Devils and Demons

Gurdjieff advises us to befriend the devil so that he may help us achieve our aims. Of course, he is talking metaphorically here; he is suggesting that we get to know our features (or vices), as he calls them, which Buddhism refers to as "obstacles", and that in doing so they can somehow be put to use. It is quite possible he is alluding to a Tibetan practice called chöd.

In chöd, one visualizes such a feature taking a physical form which is regarded as a demon. Then one enters into dialog with it to learn what its wants and needs are. Once its needs are known one visualizes one's body dissolving into a nectar enriched with the need and feeding it to the demon. After a number of sessions the demon is then transformed into an ally who vows its assistance. Although there is some ritual involved, it is actually a very psychological approach, and very effective in my experience. For a more detailed guide to this practice the reader is referred to *Feeding Your Demons* by Tsultrim Allione.

In the placard for Gurdjieff's Institute designed by Alexandre de Salzmann, the enneagram is flanked by an angel on its left and a devil on its right. The two figures mirror one another, having the same posture and countenance. Although it is usually assumed that the two figures represent two completely different forces, it is worthwhile considering that they may actually be one and the same, representing a demon before and after its transformation into an ally.

Also related to this subject are practices that visualize Dorje Trolö, a demonic yidam representing the crazy wisdom aspect of Padmasambhava that is used in the Kagyupa sect. Dorje Trolö has three bulging eyes, a red complexion, flames emitting from his body, and he rides a pregnant tigress while wielding a *phurba* in one hand and a nine-pointed *vajra* in the other.[1] Although a fierce, uncompromising figure, his anger is said to be devoid of hatred. In other words, he has the spirit of a warrior—he jumps into action swiftly with all his strength—but is driven by wisdom rather than hate. He represents the swift, uncompromising aspect of buddha-nature that does not tolerate the tricks of the neurotic mind. But as Trungpa Rinpoche points out, Dorje Trolö subdues these neuroses by creating chaotic situations that confuse them rather than aggressively suppressing them. This is how crazy wisdom works.

Considering that the West has no equivalent to Dorje Trolö, it is reasonable to suspect that Gurdjieff may have modified Beelzebub's character and given him a new storyline in his first series to emulate Dorje Trolö. Without doubt, Gurdjieff's Beelzebub also has an uncompromising demeanor. And as Gurdjieff states of the first series, its aim is "To destroy, mercilessly, without any compromise whatsoever, in the mentation and feelings of the reader, the beliefs and views, by centuries rooted in him, about everything existing in the world." Also consider how Beelzebub baffles his readers in the same way that Dorje Trolö confuses the neuroses he subdues.

As well, the book is subtitled, "An Objectively Impartial Criticism of the Life of Man." Understanding the need for an impartial approach is important. While the more authentic Gurdjieff groups properly instruct their members to regard one's so-called demons impartially, there are also a number of groups led by misguided, self-appointed individuals who instruct their members to suppress their demons, leading them down a path of spiritual bypassing. This approach is not only very superficial, it is also very egoic. Most importantly, it does not give real results because it does not address the root of the

502

pattern. For there to be real results healing at the root needs to take place. This healing occurs as a result of proper care. Battle never leads to healing. This healing is what Gurdjieff was alluding to when he spoke of repairing the past.

---

[1] A *phurba* and a *vajra* are ritual objects, a *phurba* being a sort of weapon and a *vajra* a sort of tool, both of which symbolize the aspect of consciousness that cuts through ignorance.

## THE SUBCONSCIOUSNESS

Gurdjieff's teaching apparently differs from nondual teachings such as Buddhism because Gurdjieff emphasizes effort whereas nonduality emphasizes surrender.[1] Yet neither does Gurdjieff say to only practice effort nor do nondual teachings say to only practice surrender. These are merely emphases. Nonduality recognizes that effort is needed to discover one's innate expansive awareness, and Gurdjieff recognizes that once one's innate expansive awareness is tapped, it is time to cease effort and rest in that awareness. In short, both practices are necessary.

It might also be considered that whereas in his early teaching Gurdjieff spoke of "effort", in his later teaching he used the phrase "conscious labor and intentional suffering" instead. *Conscious* labor seems to imply an effort of a different quality—an effort without tension, a letting go of sorts. This idea is supported by the fact that he combines the idea of conscious labor together with intentional suffering which entails the letting go of one's reactivity. This letting go is achieved by relaxing the tensions caused by a reaction observed while sensing. Gurdjieff did in fact place much importance on relaxation. Personally, I tend to view relaxation as the antithesis of effort, but there are many in the Work who see it as an effort of sorts. The use of the phrase "conscious labor and intentional suffering" is rather clever as it can be interpreted differently depending upon what approach to inner work one currently has. Which is to say that both interpretations of the phrase are valid.

Consider also that Gurdjieff said all spiritual teachings are intended for a given time and place. His own teaching was clearly intended for the materialistic, egotistic West of the first half of the 20<sup>th</sup> century, and this is clearly why his teaching emphasizes effort. That culture would not have been able to relate to practices of surrender. Yet Gurdjieff surely saw effort merely as the beginning of the path as he said that it is necessary to be an egoist before one can be an altruist. All effort, although needed for the development of being, is egoic; it is self-serving. An altruist does make some self-serving effort, but only as much as is needed to be able to better serve one's community however one wishes to do so. To be an altruist is to be literally selfless—to identify as one's community more so than as one's individuality—which necessitates surrender practice. Today's culture is different from our grandparents'. Surrender and altruism no longer need to be hinted at, disguised or hidden. We get it; we see how materialism has left us empty.

Even so, it seems that there are many in the Work who have not yet discovered its nondual side. Many think that consciousness is something that is developed through attention and do not see that the primary purpose of attention is to discover one's innate expansive awareness—a consciousness that is fully functioning, that is aware of everything that is going on around us. They think that what Gurdjieff calls "divided attention" and "self-remembering" are the same thing when they are different things entirely. The practice of dividing attention is merely an effort that enables one to discover an expansive consciousness (or self) that is underlying the mind stream obscuring it, to discover the self of self-remembering. The remembering of self-remembering is a knowing, it is not an effort. That is, knowing as a direct experience rather than an intellectual understanding. Once the self is known it is necessary to cease whatever attention or sensing practices were used to get there. They are no longer needed. This is where surrender begins. Otherwise ego is perpetuated.

506

Of course, this differs from nondual teachings which suggests that this innate expansive awareness is not individual and cannot be regarded as any sort of self—that it is universal in nature and contains us, we do not contain it. But perhaps this is the difference between Worlds 12 and 6, between the first and second conscious shocks, between self-remembering and the transformation of negative emotions. The consciousness of the two are the same consciousness only they can potentially have two different vibrations, one being more individual and the other being more universal. Consider also how James George views the subject:

> Yes, there is some risk in this "I Am" approach. I am already too habituated to taking everything egoistically. My wounded vanity does not readily forgive. My pretension to understand knows no limits. I can too easily assume that this "I Am" of Gurdjieff's (or of the Bible) is all about *me* and my personal development. It may take years of inner work to come to the realization that this self-centered attitude of mine is the greatest barrier between me and the impersonal highest in me, which he calls "I". And many more years to see that what I am *when I am* is not different from what you are *when you are*. It is not different from the Highest Presence; it is a drop of the same water as the Ocean. For that cosmic Ocean is indeed omnipresent, as is consciousness. Gurdjieff tells us in his Third Series that the difference between how I am when I am and God is "only" one of scale—and, of course, the scale is inconceivably vast. But the vibration that is the real I in me resonates with the same divine seed of life in you and (if I let it) with the Oceanic Consciousness. When, for a moment, I am truly present, I Am rings true on all levels. Then my physical body is the vehicle for a sensation of love that is not of this world, not of this planet. In *this* moment, I am present, no longer bound to the time of change and successiveness, from past to future. Here and now, I can receive a momentary taste of what always and everywhere Is—the changeless, the eternal *I Am*.[2]

In *Beelzebub's Tales,* Gurdjieff refers to this underlying expansive consciousness as the subconsciousness. He borrows the term from Western psychology but gives it a somewhat different meaning. He evidently calls it *sub*consciousness because it is buried, but he is quite clear that it "ought to be in my opinion the real human consciousness."[3] He explains that things we did not realize we were aware of can be accessed through hypnosis, which demonstrates that the subconsciousness is constantly taking in everything going on around us. (This is why nondual teachings say we are already enlightened but do not see it.)

Gurdjieff also mentions that the subconsciousness is where conscience resides, which is in line with what the Dzogchen teachings call *rigpa*—the wisdom aspect of "primordial awareness" as that teaching refers to one's innate expansive awareness. Also note that in Gurdjieff's earlier teaching he refers to the subconsciousness as the higher intellectual center. At any rate, Gurdjieff's teaching is not as opposed to the various nondual teachings as is generally thought, and for our present culture, it would be helpful to bring this aspect of his teaching more to the fore, in my opinion.

---

[1] When I speak of nonduality I'm referring to nondual teachings in general (such as Zen and Advaita Vedanta, not Neo-Advaita specifically, which sees no place for effort and whose practitioners use the term interchangeably with their own teaching. As far as I know, Neo-Advaita is the only nondual teaching that sees no place for effort. By saying this my only intention is to clarify my meaning and not to dismiss that teaching.

[2] James George, "Gurdjieff Heralds the Awakening of Consciousness Now," Gurdjieff International Review, www.gurdjieff.org/george1.htm.

[3] G. Gurdjieff, *All and Everything: First Series: Beelzebub's Tales to His Grandson* (New York: Harcourt, Brace & Co., 1950), 24.

## THE INTELLIGENCE OF NEGATIVITY

So-called "negativity" itself is not something bad. It has an intelligence. It shows one where one needs to heal, or "repair the past" as Gurdjieff would say. The only form of negativity that is harmful is judging oneself for having such manifestations. This is why Gurdjieff emphasizes *impartial* self-observation. The practice of nonexpression of negative emotions that he recommends is much misunderstood. It all too often becomes a form of negation and suppression which kills the possibility of healing. Suppression is an egoic manifestation because what is behind it is some idea about *how one should behave.* So that the practice of nonexpression of negative emotions is not egoic, its motivation must be on how one's manifestations affects others instead; there needs to be a reverberation of compassion or *feeling* in the solar plexus.

Buddhism, of course, addresses this concern for how one affects others via practices to develop *bodhicitta.* Gurdjieff, using a more technical language, apparently so that the idea could be better embraced by the Western culture of his time, addresses the subject in his talks on radiation and emanation. Radiations he says are energies transmitted that are a product of negativity and adversely affect others, while emanations are energies transmitted that are a product of the higher emotions unveiled via "conscious labor and intentional suffering"—that is, being mindful to and nonidentifying with irritations arising as a result of the way manifestations of others affect one, so that one is better able to give one's attention to the individuals one encounters, in effect caring for them, and thus emanate positivity.

Regarding the intelligence of negative emotions, Trungpa Rinpoche and Gurdjieff both discuss this in their unique ways. First Trungpa:

> Basic negativity is very revealing, sharp, and accurate. If we leave it as basic negativity rather than overlaying it with conceptualizations, then we see the nature of its intelligence. Negativity breeds a great deal of energy, which clearly seen becomes intelligence. When we leave the energies as they are with their natural qualities, they are living rather than conceptualized. They strengthen our everyday lives.[1]

Judging oneself for one's negative reactions is one of the forms of conceptualization of which Trungpa is speaking. Another form of conceptualization that he mentions is denying their existence, which is a form of what Gurdjieff calls buffering.

Gurdjieff approaches the subject somewhat differently, yet the essence of meaning is identical. In a paper titled "The Meaning of Life"[2] he says, "All the elements of the psyche of man—perceptions, sensations, conceptions, ideas, emotions, creation, are instruments of knowledge. All emotions, from the simplest to the most complicated—religious, moral, artistic—all are instruments of knowledge..." Further on he adds, "Each sentiment has a reason for being. Certain ones are important for knowledge, others hinder; though theoretically all emotions serve knowledge..."

Interestingly, whereas Trungpa talks of conceptualization diminishing the value of emotions, Gurdjieff speaks of their impurity (as he puts it) as another way. In fact, the original title of his paper was "Pure and Impure Emotions." As he explains, "Personal emotion fools, is partial, unjust. Greater knowledge is in proportion to fewer personal elements. The problem is to feel impersonally..." And further, "A pure emotion is one which is not mixed, which never seeks personal profit. An impure emotion is always mixed, is never one; it is mixed with

510

personal profit, with personal elements; It has sediments of other emotions. An impure emotion does not give knowledge, or gives only confused knowledge. It sheds no light."

Thus there is nothing wrong with being angry or sad about some plight of a group of people, for example. It is the nature of our interconnectedness to have such emotions. These are the sorts of pure, impersonal emotions that Gurdjieff alludes to.

Of course, both Trungpa and Gurdjieff are right. Both conceptualizations and personal elements make one's emotions impure. Perhaps Trungpa would regard the personal elements that Gurdjieff speaks of as another form of conceptualization.

Gurdjieff is not generally known for speaking this way about negative emotions and some may doubt the authenticity of this paper. It must be considered, however, that this was written in 1923—a time when his teaching was still being refined. In all likelihood he had found that his Western students' Judeo-Christian conditioning, egotistically centered on guilt and proper behavior, prevented them from being able to embrace the idea that negativity is intelligent and useful, and abandoned the notion. But we are a different culture today and can better grasp the idea now.

The same can be said of the idea of nonduality, or "oneness" as he called it. It appears his egotistic Western students were unable to grasp the idea that they were merely a particle of some greater being and he buried the idea metaphorically upon seeing their inability to embrace it. This was mentioned previously, but worthwhile repeating here, given that it is a subject touched upon in his paper on pure and impure emotions. As he puts it there, "Our separate lives are the manifestation of some large entity." According to Gurdjieff, the acquisition of knowledge is the function we serve in this entity, and emotion is a major form of the knowledge we provide.

In sum, it is necessary to see the value of one's emotions and not regard them as obstacles. If there is any obstacle it is the disregard of emotions.

[1] Chögyam Trungpa, *The Collected Works of Chögyam Trungpa: Volume 5* (Boston: Shambhala Publications, 2004), 235–36. (*The Myth of Freedom and the Way of Meditation*, Chapter 4.)

[2] G. Gurdjieff, *Gurdjieff's Early Talks 1914–1931: In Moscow, St. Petersburg, Essentuki, Tiflis, Constantinople, Berlin, Paris, London, New York, and Chicago* (London: Book Studio, 2014), 233–36.

## THE THREE JEWELS

In "Taking Refuge in the Work," Paul Anderson indirectly relates what Gurdjieff refers to as "the third line of work" to the second of the three jewels of Buddhism—the dharma. According to Gurdjieff, efforts made for one's own spiritual development is the first line of work, efforts made for the benefit of companions in one's group is the second line of work, and efforts made for the benefit of his teaching is the third line of work. In Buddhism the same idea is expressed but in a more passive way. One seeks refuge along these three lines, surrendering to them, rather than making efforts in them.

Buddhism regards these three lines as "jewels". The first jewel is the Buddha. But the Buddha that one takes refuge in is not external; it is one's own *buddha-nature*, or the Self that one remembers while self-remembering. Thus taking refuge in the Buddha pertains to the first line of work.

The second of the three jewels is the dharma, specifically the *buddhadharma*—the teaching of the Buddha. But considering that the more esoteric sects of various traditions embrace each other's teachings, it can be regarded as spiritual teaching in general, which in fact is the original meaning of dharma. When Anderson talks about taking refuge in the Work it is clear that he is referring to the third line in particular because he talks specifically about taking refuge in Gurdjieff's magnum opus, *All and Everything*.

The third of the three jewels is the sangha—one's spiritual community. Gurdjieff uses the word "group" instead of sangha but the idea is identical. The second line of work pertains to taking refuge in the sangha.

In the Work, although the three lines of work are not referred to as jewels, they are still regarded as precious.

## SECTARIANISM

It may be significant that it is in the chapter "Beelzebub for the First Time in Tibet" that Gurdjieff spends some time talking about sectarianism. It suggests that Gurdjieff was influenced by Rimé—a nonsectarian movement that arose in 19th century Tibet in response to the partisan religious climate of the time. Although historically there had been much openness between the Tibetan Buddhists sects, and openness with other religions too, things had become partisan as a result of the dominant Gelugpa sect. Rimé, which means all-embracing and unlimited, is a return to Tibetan Buddhism's former openness. As Ringu Tulku points out "Shakyamuni Buddha forbade his students to criticize others, even the teachings and teachers of other religions and cultures... True followers of the Buddha cannot help but be Rimé, or nonsectarian, in their approach."[1] Because Rimé promotes openness with other religions as well as other Buddhist sects, it should more accurately be regarded as a universalism movement.

This universalism is also something that Gurdjieff expressed in various ways, and the reader may be interested in returning to the Preface where several examples are given. Of those examples, one is particularly significant—the metaphor of various spiritual traditions being like the multitude of radii on a circle, all of which approach the same center and get closer to one another as they do so. Arnaud Desjardins relates having heard from Chatral Rinpoche the same metaphor in virtually identical language.[2] It seems likely that the metaphor originates from Rimé in particular. Chatral was a Rimé master who studied other religions entirely. Dudjom Lingpa, who Chatral seems to suggest was Gurdjieff's teacher, was also a Rimé advocate. It may well be that Gurdjieff first heard the metaphor from Dudjom Lingpa.

Possibly also influenced by Rimé is Gurdjieff's teaching of what he calls "idiotism"—a teaching intended to make one more humble regarding one's understanding and more appreciative of others. But this is a somewhat different subject; it is more about personal understanding than sectarian understanding. So, continue to the next chapter where it is discussed in greater detail.

---

[1] Ringu Tulku, *The Ri-me Philosophy of Jamgon Kongtrul the Great* (Boston: Shambhala Publications, 2006), 4–5.

[2] Arnaud Desjardins, *The Message of the Tibetans* (London: Stuart & Watkins, 1969), 20–21.

## Idiotism

In Buddhism, it is taught that whatever insight one may have, whatever understanding an insight leads to, it is only a *view* that is subject to change as one progresses further along one's path. This is not to diminish our insights in any way. Each one serves a needed purpose for the time. But it is important to understand that no apparent truth is absolute, that even the understanding of great masters is subject to change, and to have a little humility and openness to the views of others. As well, it is important not to cling to our views, for doing so may inhibit the next insight from coming.

In a certain way, one's views describe not only one's understanding, but one's ignorance as well. And this is not particularly a bad thing as it is said that *samsara* (delusion) and *nirvana* (liberation) are inseparable. In other words, delusion is a necessary ingredient for the experience of liberation. Equally, it can be said that liberation contains some degree of delusion. Liberation is only considered liberation because the mind compares it to delusion. Without this comparison liberation would be regarded as ordinary.

Gurdjieff sought to put teachings such as the above that he likely received at Surmang and elsewhere in Tibet in a form that Westerners would be better able to embrace, in a form which would not be so utterly foreign. The core of his teaching is no different from core of Tibetan Buddhism (or any other authentic spiritual tradition for that matter), but the façade was changed to make it more approachable for the Western culture to which he was bringing it. In this way he borrowed elements of Western esotericism but bent their usage to fit Buddhist ideals. This is why his teaching is often perceived as a synthesis—because the façade contains knowledge from a variety of identifiable sources. But it could be argued that the way he uses the knowledge he incorporates is rather Buddhist.

The teaching on the temporary nature of one's understanding was expressed by Gurdjieff as what he called idiotism. Most readers will be aware of the toasting ritual devised by Gurdjieff which employed idiotism. Briefly, there are 21 types of idiots, everyone is one type of idiot or another, and they each represent a particular phase of spiritual development. J. G. Bennett is not entirely certain, but he seems to recall Gurdjieff having said that he learned about idiotism while he was in Tibet.[1]

While he may have received the underlying understanding of idiotism while in Tibet, the form in which he himself expressed it apparently comes from the Tarot—specifically the major arcana. Note that there are 21 numbered cards of the major arcana. The unnumbered 22$^{nd}$ card, The Fool, appears to be a sort of title card of the set. The 21 numbered cards are all different types of fools, or "idiots" as Gurdjieff preferred to call them. Interestingly, Micheline Stuart, a student of Maurice Nicoll, wrote a book called *The Tarot Path to Self Development* which describes the major arcana cards as representations of the various stages of psychological evolution, but she does not seem to have made the connection to idiotism. But J. G. Bennett relates something about how idiotism expresses this evolution: "About ascending, [Gurdjieff] said that this is automatic for everyone who works. Every two or three years he goes up one stage—Square becomes Round, Round Zigzag and so on. This 'automatic' ascent is the result of life experience, of increasing knowledge. It does not come without effort and sincere striving..."[2] (Square, Round and Zigzag are three of the 21 idiots.) Because there is variation to the numbering of both the major arcana and the system

518

of idiotism, it is somewhat difficult to map every idiot to a fool. Even so, there are still cases where Gurdjieff's naming is clearly a humorous or insightful description of the Tarot card.

The point I want to get to, however, is that idiotism is a means of perceiving impersonal buddha-nature amongst one another. Speaking about these phases or characteristics as idiocies helps both to relate to one's own with humility, to better appreciate the understanding of others, and to approach the subject in a light-hearted way. One particular form of understanding is no better or worse than any other. Thinking this way crushes dualistic thinking which separates, qualifies and judges. Idiotism, although a form of separation, only does so in order to see the underlying unity. So, the source of the knowledge of idiotism may be Western, but its application is entirely Buddhist. To enhance this understanding, idiotism was only discussed during meals while toasting in a community setting which fostered the dissolution of the individual egos collected and the possible evoking of a group consciousness, thus providing a glimpse of some greater Self. Group consciousness is something that performers in particular sometimes experience, and it is essentially a glimpse of nondual awareness (or what Gurdjieff calls the fourth state of consciousness), but its significance is not truly understood until experiencing what Gurdjieff calls a realization of nothingness, or what Buddhism refers to as perceiving the nature of mind.

As mentioned in the chapter "Sleep Is Ignorance," another map that Gurdjieff lays out in order to illustrate an underlying unity is his Ray of Creation diagram. The details of both of these maps are not as important as the unity they illustrate.

Interestingly, Gurdjieff describes the Tarot (and thus idiotism which he had not yet formulated) as such a map where he says, "Then there exists also a *symbology of magic*, a *symbology of alchemy*, and a *symbology of astrology* as well as the system of the symbols of the Tarot which unites them into one whole. Each one of these systems can serve as a means for transmitting the idea of unity."[3]

The idea of idiotism was first introduced in 1922. I have a theory that Gurdjieff introduced it at this time because his

British pupils had misunderstood the idea of mechanicality—that they were using the idea in such a way as to believe that by their efforts they were overcoming their own mechanicality, and as such superior to those who did not. Ouspensky had started the London group in August 1921 and Gurdjieff visited to lecture to the group in March 1922. If I am correct, this misunderstanding would have been introduced by Ouspensky. The fact that Gurdjieff later had Madame Ouspensky return to her husband to better assure his teaching was properly disseminated there lends credence to the theory. Also supporting this theory is *Beelzebub's Tales'* "From the Author," in which Gurdjieff talks about rogue students of his who went on to establish their own institute, and whose own students he regarded as "candidates for lunatic asylums."[4]

While it is true that our tendencies which Gurdjieff called unnecessary suffering feed the ego and inhibit the perception of our true nature, overcoming such tendencies does not equate to becoming any less mechanical. Overcoming these tendencies is only changing the programming—developing different mechanics. The mind and all its functions are mechanical by nature. Gurdjieff is quite clear that what he calls the "steward"—the internal overseer that is developed—is also part of the "machine" (or lower self). These pupils were missing the point of the idea of mechanicality. Their egos had grabbed hold of the idea when its purpose is actually to realize one's nothingness. The right way to understand the idea of mechanicality is to see that absolutely every thought, feeling and instinct that arises in the mind is mechanical. It is all stimulus-response though some responses, such as those which the steward develops, may be more complicated. Seeing one's utter mechanicality is an important factor leading to the "realization of nothingness," which marks the start of a person as an individual number four—that is, someone whose center of gravity is work on oneself rather than the disposition one was born with.

The idea of nothingness is also very Buddhist. Buddhism refers to this idea as emptiness which has been discussed previously. At any rate, idiotism seems to have been a way of correcting this misunderstanding. It puts everyone on equal footing by showing that everyone wishes for fulfillment (though we may perceive different means towards that) and that all approaches are merely different forms of nothingness. One of the reasons I believe that idiotism was developed to correct some misunderstanding of the idea of mechanicality is because this is something I observed in the first Gurdjieff group I was in. We were mistakenly led to believe that intentionality was above mechanicality. As a result we felt aversion towards whatever unintentional mechanics we observed even though Gurdjieff taught to observe them impartially. The compassion Gurdjieff had towards all walks of life was totally lacking. It is difficult to say how prevalent this misunderstanding is today, but it still seems a shame that the ritual of idiotism toast was abandoned after Gurdjieff's death.

---

[1] J.G. Bennett & Elizabeth Bennett, *Idiots in Paris: Diaries of J.G. Bennett and Elizabeth Bennett 1949* (High Burton: Coombe Springs Press, 1980), 8.

[2] "The Science of Idiotism," an unpublished anonymous paper attributed to J.G. Bennett.

[3] P.D. Ouspensky, *In Search of the Miraculous:Fragments of an Unknown Teaching* (New York: Harcourt, Brace & Co., 1949), 283.

[4] My intention in this paragraph is not to belittle Ouspensky. Without his clear overview of Gurdjieff's teaching, *In Search of the Miraculous*, it is unlikely that the Gurdjieff Work would have gained much popularity. Gurdjieff himself acknowledged its significance. All spiritual guides have their strengths and weaknesses. I only point out a specific weakness of one of them here so that readers can avoid a trap created by it—one which I fell into myself.

## Animal Sacrifice

Beelzebub's second descent to our planet was made to address the unbecoming practice of animal sacrifice which had become prevalent throughout Asia. He decides to go to Turkmenistan, which at the time was the most populous region in Asia, and befriend a certain priest there in order to influence him. Although Gurdjieff situated this tale in Turkmenistan, it may have been inspired by the conflict that the Buddhists of Tibet had with the Bönpo—the aboriginal religion of the region. As Trungpa Rinpoche explains:

> In the eighth century when Buddhism first began to spread into Tibet practices such as the worship of nature spirits and animal sacrifice of the Bön religion were forbidden and many Bönpo adherents emigrated to the outlying regions of the Himalayas, both to the Pemakö district and to parts of Nepal, for they could not go to India which at that time was largely Buddhist. However, after Buddhism had become universal in Tibet the inhabitants of the Pemakö area took shelter of the name of Buddhism, though still practicing some of the Bön rites. On the other hand, in the eastern province of Kyungpo the people still call themselves Bönpos, though their practice is Buddhist in effect; they are known as "White Bönpos."[1]

It might also be considered that the Buddhists of Turkmenistan, who were practicing the religion long before the Tibetans were, likely had a similar conflict. When Islam arrived in Turkmenistan, they drove out and converted the Buddhists. The aboriginal religion was eradicated long before.

---

[1] Chögyam Trungpa, *The Collected Works of Chögyam Trungpa: Volume 1* (Boston: Shambhala Publications, 2003), 252. (*Born in Tibet,* Chapter 19.)

## ATLANTIS?

In *Eden in the East*, author Stephen Oppenheimer uses linguistics, genetics and comparative myth to trace man's origin to the sunken southeast Asian continent which the scientific community calls Sundaland. Not once does he refer to "Atlantis" in his magnum opus, but obviously this is what his research indicates. After all, the name "Atlantis" is a result of confusion on the part of the ancient Greeks who got their information from the ancient Egyptians and somehow interpreted that information believing that the sunken landmass existed somewhere in the middle of the Atlantic Ocean. But all earlier sources speaking of such a land indicate that it lied to the east. So "Atlantis" is a misleading name and should be abandoned.

The continent did not actually sink as some might imagine. Rather, the rising of the sea level as a result of the melting of the polar caps after the last ice age blanketed it. This took place 8,000–10,000 years ago. All that remains of the continent are its highest peaks which exist now as the islands of Indonesia.

At any rate, Oppenheimer identifies several migrations out of Sundaland. Interestingly, one of these migrations was to Tibet. But it was not a gradual migration, for linguistic evidence shows that the Tibeto-Burman language phyla radiated out *from* Tibet. Thus it spread from Tibet *to* Southeast Asia rather than vice versa, suggesting that the migration to Tibet from Sundaland did not stop till it reached that destination. On the one hand, such a distant migration seems irrational. Why travel all that distance? On the other hand, it would seem quite logical to seek out the highest place on Earth for refuge if the sea level was quickly rising and it was unknown when the rise would stop. This explains why flood myths are to be found in the Himalayas.

Another migration out of Sundaland that Oppenheimer identifies is to Egypt. This explains how the ancient Egyptians had knowledge of "Atlantis". Oppenheimer also provides evidence that ancient pioneers from Sundaland had settled and established a community in pre-sand Egypt long before the flood. So, Egypt was another choice of migration when the sea began to engulf their home. In *Beelzebub's Tales*, Gurdjieff only speaks about the migration to Egypt from Altantis. He was an authority on ancient Egyptian civilization and no doubt most of his knowledge on Atlantis comes from his Egyptian studies. Again, the source of the Greek myth was Egyptian.

Yet it is not unreasonable to consider that Gurdjieff found additional information on Atlantis from Tibet's indigenous Bön religion who have an 18,000 year old history. Remember the suggestion that Louise March got the idea that *The Egyptian Book of the Dead* and *The Tibetan Book of the Dead* share a common source from Gurdjieff. Significantly, although *The Tibetan Book of the Dead* is attributed to Padmasambhava, the founder of Tibetan Buddhism, March believes that it may have actually originated with the Bön religion. Also worth considering is if Gurdjieff was privy to a conversation between Petrie and Norzunov on the possibilities of a common source of the two civilizations, or intuited such himself based on some conversation of theirs.

Tibetan Buddhism has largely taken Bön ritual and practices and put a Buddhist spin on them. Without having done so it is unlikely Buddhism would have flourished in Tibet. Perhaps not having adapted Buddhism this way is why earlier attempts to establish the religion in Tibet failed. One such practice is the concealment and discovery of *terma* (treasure

526

teachings). These are teachings hidden by a master for a future generation in need of them to discover. There are two types: earth *terma*, which are physical objects concealed in some location, and mind *terma*, teachings concealed in the ether to be channeled at a later time. Gurdjieff speaks of both kinds. Although they are not discussed at the same time, both are described through Beelzebub in relation to Atlantis. Earth *terma* he calls legominisms, and mind *terma* he calls teleoghinooras. Here is what Beelzebub says about the former:

> This word Legominism... is given to one of the means existing there of transmitting from generation to generation information about certain events of long-past ages, through just those three-brained beings who are thought worthy to be and who are called initiates. This means of transmitting information from generation to generation had been devised by the beings of the continent Atlantis.[1]

And here is what he says about teleoghinooras:

> A Teleoghinoora is a materialized idea or thought which after its arising exists almost eternally in the atmosphere of that planet on which it arises. Teleoghinooras can be formed from such a quality of being-contemplation as only those three-brained beings have and can actualize, who have coated their higher being bodies in their presences and who have brought the perfecting of Reason of their higher being part up to the degree of the sacred "Martfotai".[2]

Certainly Gurdjieff encountered some legominisms of Egypt and various other cultures, but only in Tibet would he have had the opportunity to learn about the living tradition of the concealment and interpretation, not only of legominisms, but of teleoghinooras as well. One might think that only rinpoches get such training, but to repeat what was said about instantaneous teachings in "A Conversation with Chatral Rinpoche," "...there are various methods where the disciple gets teachings in an unusual way... in other words, he receives teachings direct from the teachers, the great teachers of the past..." If indeed Dudjom Lingpa was Gurdjieff's root teacher, there is no better teacher from whom Gurdjieff could have received such training. *Beelzebub's Tales*, which was written largely for the benefit of future generations who would unbury its secrets, is regarded as a legominism. Clearly, he learned the practice. It may also be significant that he wrote about these subjects in relation to Atlantis, which could be understood as the origin of the Tibetan people, and that *terma* concealment and discovery is a practice that the Bön could have brought to Tibet from Sundaland. The enneagram may have been a teleoghinoora (or mind *terma*) that Gurdjieff discovered while in Tibet. Supporting this suggestion is that the number nine is something of a sacred number in the Bön tradition, appearing repeatedly in its teachings. Remember also that he brought up the subject of the enneagram in response to a question about the Buddhist idea of the animate and the inanimate.

---

[1] G. Gurdjieff, *All and Everything: First Series: Beelzebub's Tales to His Grandson* (New York: Harcourt, Brace & Co., 1950), 349.

[2] Ibid., 293.

# APPENDICES

## INTERVIEW WITH SOPHIE PERKS

*The following is an email interview I conducted with Sophie Perks, the person who was recognized by Trungpa Rinpoche as the tulku of Gurdjieff. Having been conducted early on in my research (in 2009), I sense a bit of naïveté on my part reading it all these years later. Overall, however, I feel it was a rich and honest discussion worthy of your attention.*

LAYNE: Originally I wasn't so interested in your story of being recognized as Gurdjieff's tulku as I was hopeful that because of this Trungpa Rinpoche may have told you or your parents something he had heard about Gurdjieff's presence in Tibet that he didn't speak about ordinarily. But the more I thought about it the more I felt that the story helps to show a certain bond that exists between Gurdjieff's and Trungpa's teachings. Before my research I didn't realize there was once something of an open exchange happening between the Shambhala sangha and the Gurdjieff Foundation. Perhaps it even suggests something beyond mutual appreciation—some common origin. I find many parallels between the two teachers' missions and their teachings.

SOPHIE: Yes, I have often thought that there were some similarities. I do know that Trungpa Rinpoche held Gurdjieff and his teachings in high regard. I have heard that Trungpa Rinpoche once said that Suzuki Roshi and Gurdjieff were the best teachers to teach in the West before his own teachers, His Holiness the 16ᵗʰ Karmapa and His Holiness Dilgo Khyentse Rinpoche, taught there.

LAYNE: Your recognition as Gurdjieff's tulku also seems to say something of the certainty Trungpa Rinpoche had about Gurdjieff having studied in Tibet. Tibetan masters don't go recognizing tulkus outside their own tradition, do they? And as much of a joker as Trungpa Rinpoche was, my impression is that recognizing a tulku isn't something that would be joked with. Comments?

SOPHIE: No, I don't think they do that very much!
Chögyam Trungpa Rinpoche's actions, and those of all our great teachers, were truly with the one view of benefiting beings. It seems to me that there was never an ordinary action which he engaged in. Every action was expressly executed for the sole purpose of bringing his students the very teaching they most required at that moment to train themselves into kinder, saner human beings. With this in mind, every one of his "joker-like" actions become completely serious methods of teaching. And in the same way, it would also seem that even those times when he seemed to be serious, he was joking with us—perhaps because we took it so seriously. This does not in any way undermine the great teachings he presented to his students. He used whatever method was most appropriate to bring them out of the confines of the shrine room and into everyday life.
I cannot possibly know what his intentions were when he said what he said about me. Perhaps the moment required it but nothing more need become of it.

LAYNE: You seem to be describing something of crazy wisdom. This is a subject I'm currently studying—the possibility that Gurdjieff was familiar with the crazy wisdom tradition that Trungpa Rinpoche acquired from the Nyingma lineage.

SOPHIE: In the West that which we call "crazy wisdom" is, I believe, often misunderstood and/or misused. I have often felt that many of us are more attracted to the crazy aspect and we forget the most important part, the basis, the wisdom. We imitate the outer actions of the "craziness" even to the point of forcing it upon others and then condone our actions by adding the term wisdom. "Crazy wisdom" is a manifestation of the wisdom which is free from the constraints of doubts, hesitations and narrow mindedness which are nothing but aspects of the debilitating clinging to reality which we all suffer from. A teacher manifests the actions, which to the ordinary person are labeled as "crazy", which is most useful in breaking through the walls of belief (foremost being the belief in a solid self) which we have built up over a lifetime of grasping to reality. With this in mind I think that while Gurdjieff may have "acquired" some teaching methods from watching teachers with whom he may have come into contact with, such as Tibetan teachers, or from stories that he listened to, such as those of Mulla Nasreddin, it is also entirely possible that through his own spiritual development the outer appearance of his actions being similar to what we now call "crazy wisdom" may have naturally developed by virtue of nothing other than his view having been influenced by the lessening to the grasping to duality and clinging to the belief of a conditioned self.

I am particularly fond of a story my dad once told me about Gurdjieff. That one day while he was out driving with his students he suddenly stopped and got out of the car. He walked over to something on the ground, picked up an apparently random rock and said "There you are. I've been looking for you everywhere." I believe this is the way the story goes. It seems to be quite indicative of his joker-like character.

LAYNE: Also, I think I was a bit reluctant to use your story because Gurdjieffians (who will be the primary audience of my book) tend to be doubters. Or perhaps it's more that Westerners tend to be doubters and this is what attracts many of us to the Gurdjieff teaching. At least I can say that one of the primary ideas that attracted me personally to the teaching was the idea of verification—that one must not believe anything taught till it has been verified for oneself.

Yet I think it is a mistake to interpret the insistence upon verification as meaning one should doubt something till it has been verified, for doubt is really just another form of belief— the belief that something is not true. So, what verification *should* lead to is a place of openness and emptiness, because when it comes down to it, there isn't a whole lot one can know with certainty. Anyway, this is how I relate to the idea of re-incarnation. It's a subject I will probably never really *know* about, though I'm certain others have had experiences which have made it more than an idea for them.

SOPHIE: Buddhism also has the same tradition of encouraging students to question all aspects of the teachings presented to them as well as the authenticity and conduct of the teacher presenting them. This itself is a method in which the students can strengthen their own views. Although at some point, after having very thoroughly examined the teachings and the teacher, one should come to a point where one no longer needs to question the teachings nor the actions and advice of the teacher. Of course, this process may take many years. One has to come to a point of exhaustion. Also one must understand that questioning is a skillful means to better understand oneself, but one must not use it as an excuse to stop making changes in oneself which are needed but difficult. Sometimes people keep questioning because we just don't want to do the right thing and need reasons not to do it. So I think a proper, honest approach to questioning is imperative.

I feel that we Westerners in general are somewhat wary of anything suggesting that we no longer doubt or question. Perhaps we feel that it is some sort of brainwashing, or not being "true" to ourselves. However, in Buddhism it is important that at some point one must have a great amount of faith in the dharma and the teacher. One must place oneself, take refuge, in the teachings and teacher to guide one correctly along the path. In another point of view, developing complete faith

534

and trust in one's teacher and the process is also a method of slowly letting go of our attachment to our identity of self which we so greatly define by placing so much importance on our beliefs; whether they are profound spiritual beliefs or simply that vegetables are good for you. We get stuck with who we are and make our worlds very small and restricted.

LAYNE: That Buddhism has the same concept of verifying or testing the teaching is one of the many points I make suggesting that Gurdjieff's teaching is derived from Tibetan Buddhism.

Also, I understand you completely about a sort of switch to an approach of faith at some point. It's as if real faith is a natural outgrowth of verification. Verification establishes the trust required for faith to blossom. Gurdjieff doesn't speak much about faith, but he has an aphorism on the subject which says, "Conscious faith is freedom. Emotional faith is slavery. Mechanical faith is foolishness." Of course, we're specifically discussing conscious faith which is something that needs to be developed.

SOPHIE: This is a nice quote. Yes, I think we are talking more about a conscious faith, a faith which has developed from extensive analyzing. In Buddhism they teach about four kinds of faith which are sequential and progressive. It is important to view faith as confidence in the truth which brings about a quality of stark fearlessness and going beyond hesitations and doubts. The first one is "vivid faith" and is the faith one experiences when one first comes into contact with a great teacher, hears the teachings for the first time or sees images of the Buddha, listens to the life stories of great teachers etc. The second is called "eager faith." It is the faith which develops when one is truly struck by the sufferings of the three lower realms and wishes to be free from them, develops an eagerness to engage in positive actions as an accumulation of merit and to avoid accumulating negative actions, which bring suffering. The third faith is "confident faith" and is the faith which develops into a total and complete trust in the three

535

jewels. The fourth type of faith is the ultimate faith called "irreversible faith." With this faith we reach a state of complete trust in oneself and the path and at complete peace with who one is. Khandro Rinpoche speaks of this as "irreversible confidence"—the kind that empowers you to be totally open to all beings and all situations.

LAYNE: Maybe you can help to clear up a particular doubt I personally have about reincarnation. It's related to my understanding and experiences of nonduality (which is very disguised in Gurdjieff's teaching and I didn't come upon till I ventured into Zen). If ultimately we don't exist as individuals—if one's identity is awareness and this awareness turns out to be impersonal in nature—then the idea of reincarnation doesn't make sense. Why would we be reborn if the entire basis of our individuality is an illusory ego? Is there anything individual that is not illusory, that is genuine? The ego certainly isn't what would be reborn. How do you rectify this apparent contradiction between the ideas of nonduality and reincarnation? I think I'm missing something.

SOPHIE: I am really not the person that you should be addressing these questions to. I will answer as best I can, with what little I know, but then it would be good if I could present a few of these questions to my own teacher, Jetsün Khandro Rinpoche. Or if you asked them of another teacher...

As far as I have understood, it is somewhat of a conundrum since if one has realized the true nature of things as they are, then even karma itself is empty and ceases to turn. Reincarnation is no longer an issue as existing or not existing. However, as long as we are bound to the samsaric world and continue to make all things separate in a dualistic manner, then each of our actions create endless and unimaginable streams of karmic results thereby propelling one into future births.

LAYNE: Maybe you can say something about doubts you may have had yourself related to reincarnation, and how you face the obstacle of doubt in general.

536

Sophie: I have never really had any specific doubts about reincarnation as an idea. Perhaps this is due to my upbringing. It was an idea that I grew up with and was an idea which always seemed quite logical and possible to me.

However, doubt as a general topic, I have, of course, experienced. Certainly, when I first started studying with Jetsün Khandro Rinpoche there were some aspects of the philosophy that I questioned heavily and more or less doubted. I think a very practical way of working through doubt, in regards to philosophy, is engaging in some form of analytical meditation. One must examine very thoroughly and come to one's own conclusions. But then at the same time just as one does not personally need to experience every single thing in the world to know that it "exists"... one is constantly relying on the experiences of others to verify one's own ideas, and one does not usually doubt these things even though one has not experienced them for oneself. For instance if I have never seen snow and someone was trying to explain it to me, they would say it is cold and white and falls from the sky etc., they would go on to try to describe it to me, I would trust that what they were telling me was true, based on them having experienced it themselves. In the same way, if I have a teacher, whom I trust completely, or taking it to the very beginning, the Buddha, his teachings, what he experienced, these are things I can no longer doubt.

But then, in Buddhism, there are many, many different ways to look at things. Rebirth is something real sometimes and then sometimes it's not. It's like an onion, the outer layer looks real and solid and is what it is, but then one keeps exploring and peeling it back and it appears different and you keep going until in the end there is nothing. And you don't know why you made such a big deal in the beginning about the onion, but then maybe you should look at it as a process, a method. The Path is very real, it needs to be walked on, and we as ordinary beings cannot just skip over it. So the doubt in the beginning is important. It is not a mistake. But I think it is important to be open to different things and not to become too rigid in one's ideas of how things are.

537

I think I am rambling about something I really don't know much about. Again, it would be good to ask these questions to someone else.

LAYNE: I think that another difficulty is that we don't know how to distinguish between omens and the auspicious signs affirming them—such as those which might affirm the recognition of a tulku—and superstition. Certainly we live in a miraculous universe and at times receive certain indications. For me Jung's idea of synchronicity helps explain this somewhat. And yet it seems that our awareness of the human tendency to see what one wants to see makes us question genuine auspiciousness along with the fabricated indications. How do you see the difference?

SOPHIE: This is something which I have thought about especially in the last year brought on entirely by the parinirvana or passing away of one of the great teachers of our time, His Holiness Mindrolling Trichen last year. For days following his passing, there were many amazing and miraculous things witnessed by everyone. There were moments when I questioned what I witnessed or experienced wondering if I was making something extraordinary out of the ordinary merely due to my desire to see something. I think I even asked the sister of Jetsün Khandro Rinpoche, Jetsun Dechen Paldron, and she said that one has to rely somewhat on one's own discriminating awareness. Discriminating awareness or wisdom is something inherently present in all of us. I think we have to learn to trust it. One thing I have noticed is that Easterners, and especially Tibetans, have a great amount of confidence in themselves and in their discriminating awareness, much more so than most Westerners that I know.

Having said this, my teachers have also always told us that we cannot make too much of these auspicious signs, dreams or miraculous things which we may experience. At least not more than we would ordinary experiences. It might be safe to say that one could rely on them as support if one requires it but if it is a cause for arrogance one should quickly abandon any fascination with such things.

LAYNE: Gurdjieff isn't generally known for making predictions, but there's one account I'd like to mention, both because it shows that he did have the capacity, and because the prediction itself is somewhat related to our discussion. Apparently J.G. Bennett heard him say that after his death a teacher will come from the East to continue his work. What exactly suggested this to him is unknown. Bennett for a while considered the Indonesian Pak Subuh to be that teacher, but eventually left Subuh's teaching to return to the Gurdjieff ideas. The reason I find this interesting is that knowing what I do now, I would think Trungpa Rinpoche was the teacher who Gurdjieff foresaw.

SOPHIE: There are many such similar predictions of the spreading of the dharma to the West. Padmasabhava has many famous predictions and I believe that there were Hopi Native American predictions which foresaw His Holiness the Karmapa's coming to North America. So I think that it is entirely possible that Gurdjieff also made predictions about these things.

LAYNE: Your mother told me that she was in Willem Nyland's Gurdjieff group before meeting Trungpa Rinpoche. To what extent do you think your mother's previous experience in the Gurdjieff Work influenced Trungpa Rinpoche's recognition of her child in particular as Gurdjieff's tulku?

SOPHIE: This could certainly have played a part in it from what I have understood. There were quite a few Gurdjieffians who were studying with Trungpa Rinpoche at that time, so I think it is quite safe to say that their influence on Trungpa Rinpoche led him to say what he did about me.

LAYNE: How did you get the name Sophie? Did you know Gurdjieff had a sister named Sophie? Having the name Sophie makes you seem like part of the family. It's as if he chose the name himself.

SOPHIE: Until I heard it from you, I actually had no idea that Gurdjieff had a sister named Sophie. I really don't know why my parents chose that name. I will have to ask them...

LAYNE: Do you have a Tibetan name? What is it and what does it mean?

SOPHIE: Before I was born I have heard that Trungpa Rinpoche told my parents to give me the middle name Pushpa or Senge. From what I have understood he used to go back and forth between the two. Pushpa is an old-fashioned Sanskrit name/word meaning flower and Senge is a Tibetan boy's name for lion. However, when I was born Trungpa Rinpoche was away teaching and since my parents had to put a name on the birth certificate they ended up, through various miscommunications, choosing Pushpa. Though when Trungpa Rinpoche came back he called me Senge.

LAYNE: I've heard the story before, but I'd prefer if you would say in your own words how Trungpa Rinpoche recognized you as Gurdjieff's tulku. Tell me everything you know about it.

SOPHIE: I don't really know that there is much of a story behind it. From what I know Trungpa Rinpoche said that I was Gurdjieff in my last life, and when questioned further said something along the lines of, "Well she's somebody, she might as well be Gurdjieff."

LAYNE: Your father mentioned to me that Lord Pentland, who was president of the Gurdjieff Foundation at the time, visited you as an infant. I'm curious what he would have thought about your recognition. Have you ever heard anything along those lines? Perhaps the act of the visit itself says enough.

SOPHIE: No, I never did hear anything about what he might have thought. It did surprise me when I first heard that he came to see me. In a way, I was sad to have missed it.

540

LAYNE: And your mother mentioned that Ravi Ravindra, another leader in the Gurdjieff Work, also visited you and offered you a gift. Have you ever heard anything of his impression of you as Gurdjieff's tulku?

SOPHIE: Again, no I don't know what he thought. I am starting to think that I should ask my parents some questions myself! I did hear that he gave my mom a small ivory elephant that used to belong to Gurdjieff to give to me when I was older, but unfortunately it was misplaced. I have often thought of that little elephant and wished that it hadn't been lost. I would have liked to have it, only because it had once belonged to Gurdjieff.

LAYNE: When did you first hear about being Gurdjieff's tulku yourself? How did you first react to it?

SOPHIE: Actually, I have no recollection of first hearing about it. I can't really pinpoint a time before I knew and after.

LAYNE: How were your parents supportive about it?

SOPHIE: Well, this is funny and I don't want to say anything bad about the way my parents raised me but I do think that they were quite supportive, only I am not sure if this was really the best thing for me. I think with their love and confidence in me, they allowed me to get away with perhaps too much and I became quite spoiled.

I have a funny story to tell that even my mother doesn't know. It's a good example of how I used to exploit my recognition. There was one time when I was in my early teens, my mother was listening to some music which Gurdjieff had composed and though I had never heard it before I had heard enough *about* it to know that it was music by him. So I began to hum along with it. I remember my mother watching me from the corner of her eyes while I pretended not to notice and pretended to remember the music... she asked me if I knew who it was by, and of course I feigned ignorance. More or less, I knew that if I played up to the whole thing I could get whatever it was that I wanted from my poor mother…

Needless to say, despite my mother's best efforts, I ended up on Jetsün Khandro Rinpoche's doorstep a very spoiled young person.

LAYNE: Were others supportive of it?

SOPHIE: Within the Shambhala community people were mostly very supportive of it. Again, maybe too much so. I think I got away with a lot of things I shouldn't have. Sometimes it came in the form of people wanting to hear stories and sometimes it came in more dramatic ways. When I was 14, for example, there was a Georgian man who heard and, granted he was a little drunk, he came to me and wouldn't let me go. He kept holding my hands, saying how happy he was and trying to get me to drink straight vodka. He was quite pleased when I attempted to prove my "manliness" by drinking it down without making a face.

Of course, there were some who were less than happy when they found out. I remember one woman who, after she heard, came to read my palm, to see what all the fuss was about, I guess. She proclaimed that I couldn't be Gurdjieff because I had a very normal palm.

LAYNE: You were just a girl when Trungpa Rinpoche died. Did he ever have the opportunity to speak to you directly about it?

SOPHIE: I have a terrible memory and I have to say that I really don't remember much about Trungpa Rinpoche. My little sister has more memories of him than I do.

I have always been greatly attached to Trungpa Rinpoche and in my teens I went through a lot of sadness at losing him. I think that was when I really experienced his passing. I remember feeling so sad and almost angry that he had abandoned all of us, though specifically me. Even now I regret that I was not born even five or ten years earlier.

LAYNE: Have you ever heard anything he said related to Gurdjieff's presence in Tibet, whether it was heard first-hand or second-hand?

SOPHIE: No, I never heard anything about this from Trungpa Rinpoche either directly or indirectly, though I have to say I never did ask. It would probably be best to pose this question to someone who was more conscious at that time.

Having said that, I do remember my mother saying that there was a huge gap in Gurdjieff's memoirs, *Meetings with Remarkable Men*, where he disappears and never explains where he was and that it was generally thought that Gurdjieff had been in Tibet during that time. It's possible that she may have asked Trungpa Rinpoche about this.

LAYNE: Is there anything else Trungpa Rinpoche said or did that stands out in your mind?

SOPHIE: My mother told me that Trungpa Rinpoche had once said to her that she didn't need to worry about me—that I would make the right choices in my life. This has more or less given me some degree of reassurance when I am unsure about the bigger decisions in my life. But I am incredibly lucky to have ended up where I am, to be able to study with Jetsün Khandro Rinpoche and her sister Jetsün Dechen Paldrön that looking back I think he must have been right. Somehow, without knowing it, I have made some good decisions.

LAYNE: Trungpa Rinpoche's children were all recognized as tulkus, but they were recognized by others, weren't they? Are you the only tulku to have been discovered by Trungpa Rinpoche?

SOPHIE: I don't know of anyone else who was recognized by Trungpa Rinpoche, but I think that it is very possible that there were others.

LAYNE: Are there any ways in which you yourself perceive being

Gurdjieff's tulku? For example, I understand that something of one's past life can be expressed in dreams.

SOPHIE: No, I have never had any experiences which might have confirmed to myself that I *was* Gurdjieff in my last life. Unless my love of alcohol counts... I'm joking, of course.

LAYNE: My sense is that amidst Tibetan culture wherein the miraculous is perceived in seemingly ordinary things, the recognition of a tulku, as well as other phenomena we Westerners would bundle under the label of "extrasensory", isn't all that unusual. They are still extraordinary, but no more so than a spectacular view. I wonder what your own relationship is to having been recognized as a tulku. On the one hand you're obviously a Westerner, but on the other hand perhaps having been raised in the Shambhala community gave you an outlook that is somewhat Tibetan-like.

SOPHIE: Growing up in Shambhala did give me a certain amount of familiarity with some amount of Buddhist ethics and ideas, such as rebirth. Otherwise, I do think of myself as entirely Western. I can't even say that maybe I was Tibetan in my previous life...

LAYNE: Most tulkus begin their spiritual education at a very early age. Was that true for you or did you have a more-or-less normal American childhood?

SOPHIE: My education was pretty normal. Though with Buddhist parents I was given meditation instructions when I was quite young, what little I was able to understand. But this was the experience of most of the children of Shambhalian parents.

LAYNE: What was it like growing up in a spiritual community?

SOPHIE: At the time I took it completely for granted, but now looking back, I am so incredibly grateful for the privilege of growing up within a close-knit community. My mother, sister

544

and I were so well taken care of, first by Trungpa Rinpoche, who supported us while my mother went back to university, and then by many members of the sangha later on. It was like having many mothers and fathers and though I found much to criticize when I was a teenager, I am now realizing how much credit and appreciation the previous generation should be given. They gave up everything to work towards attaining the vision of Trungpa Rinpoche. And though we are all abundantly endowed with plenty of faults and imperfections, we still strive to practice and study the dharma while working within the community, often without any credit, and always with a lot of joy. Growing up within the Shambhala community was a very happy experience, people were always very joyful.

LAYNE: One thing I appreciate about Trungpa Rinpoche's teaching is the confidence it gives. Or perhaps it's more accurate to say that his teaching helps to recognize a confidence that's always there. Because the confidence he speaks of is the nature of awareness rather than a particular kind of thought. Is this something you picked up on at all? And did it help in particular to recognize a confidence with regards to fulfilling your role as a tulku?

SOPHIE: Trungpa Rinpoche did teach a lot about confidence, whether directly or indirectly. It seems to be a very important underlying aspect of many of the different meditation methods he introduced to the Shambhala sangha, such as kasung, drill, kyudo, ikebana. My own teachers have spoken about developing a confidence in oneself, stating that at the point that one can be truly confident, which is not arrogant or self-inflated, one can be genuinely kind to others without ever "losing" something of oneself.

LAYNE: At what point did you commit yourself to a spiritual path? Having been recognized as a tulku, did you take it for granted that was your destiny? Or did you embark on your spiritual path regardless of that?
SOPHIE: What Trungpa Rinpoche said about my being Gurdjieff

really had no influence on the decisions I have made in my life.

I remember the first time I really thought about my own death. I must have been eight or nine. I don't know what brought it on, I had never experienced death in my life, except perhaps on TV. Whatever the cause, I remember lying in bed and thinking that one day I would die, that at some point there would be no more me on this earth. I tried to imagine what it would be like. It was terrifying enough to give me a physical reaction. I ran to the comfort of my mother's bed but I was too afraid to even voice my fears. This very tangible fear of death, my own death as well as the death of those I loved and was attached to, has been one of the greatest forces propelling me into a spiritual life... the search that we are all searching for, meaning... truth.

On top of this I knew without a doubt that I would never be able to practice and study Buddhism on my own—that although I rebelled against it, I needed discipline and guidance. For this reason, when I was 17 I entered the youth monastic dathun in Gampo Abbey. In my imagination I saw cell-like rooms, strict schedules and terrifying nuns keeping us on track... it wasn't quite like that, and like usual, I managed to get away with a lot of things I shouldn't have been able to.

I was almost 19 when I first heard Jetsün Khandro Rinpoche teach in France, and although I didn't understand much of what she was teaching, I knew pretty much right away that I had found what I was looking for.

LAYNE: So, you didn't continue participation in the Shambhala sangha as an adult?

SOPHIE: I didn't have much involvement in Shambhala after I left Halifax when I was 17. As much as I love and appreciate most things about the Shambhala community, at the time I really needed to strike out on my own, so to speak. I didn't leave for any negative reasons. I just had to find my own way.

LAYNE: To what extent are you familiar with Gurdjieff's teaching? What's your take on it?

SOPHIE: I am really not very familiar with the teachings of Gurdjieff. I was always afraid that it would influence me too much, so I purposefully didn't read any of his books. I always thought I would study his teachings when I got older.

LAYNE: Are there any other teachings you've had some interest in?

SOPHIE: Honestly, while I do think that almost all philosophies and ancient wisdoms have much to teach and learn from, I have always been satisfied enough with Buddhism that I have not done much looking elsewhere for answers to my questions.

LAYNE: You've mentioned your teacher, Khandro Rinpoche, a few times. I understand that you've been serving as her attendant. How did that opportunity come about? Was it offered to you as part of the education required of a tulku?

SOPHIE: No, not at all. Actually, I have spent much more time attending for Rinpoche's sister Jetsün Dechen Paldrön, who has also been a teacher to me.

Attending is a type of work I have felt more or less predisposed to. Maybe the act of service runs in my blood. Also, I think typically, attendants are not those who are the best students or good practitioners. We are the ones who seem to most require constant observance and the influence of seeing the teachings being put into action constantly by our teachers, since we don't seem to study or learn any other way.

It has been a great learning experience for me, and I am so grateful for the opportunity to serve my teachers in this way.

LAYNE: What is Khandro Rinpoche's attitude regarding your recognition? Is she supportive? In any particular ways? Perhaps this question sounds a little strange. I guess what's behind it is wondering what the Tibetan community thinks about a tulku of a great teacher not generally recognized to be part of their spiritual heritage. So I wonder if the support you get is any less than other tulkus.

SOPHIE: I have had one or two teachers ask me about it, but these were teachers who traveled a lot in the west and had a large base of western (and Shambhalian) students. Otherwise, I don't think that there are many Tibetan teachers who know much about Gurdjieff and his teachings.

As for Jetsün Khandro Rinpoche, she has never treated me any different than the rest of her students, and for that I am very grateful.

LAYNE: Is Khandro Rinpoche acquainted with Gurdjieff's teaching at all? If so, what are her feelings about it?

SOPHIE: Jetsün Khandro Rinpoche has heard of Gurdjieff and holds his teachings in high regard. Rinpoche has often made clear her respect for many different teachers of many different philosophies and traditions. Rinpoche has always maintained that we must develop respect for anyone who is able to teach and bring benefit to beings regardless of whether or not they sit on thrones and wear brocade or come from the East. I believe that anyone whose words and works lead to a more sane life is a great teacher and thus worthy of respect.

LAYNE: Can you say a bit about Khandro Rinpoche's lineage?

SOPHIE: Jetsün Khandro Rinpoche was born to His Holiness Mindrolling Trichen, who was the head of the Nyingma lineage for many years and one of the most renowned masters of Tibetan Buddhism in the last century. The Mindrolling lineage is noted for maintaining the very authentic traditions and for being an authentic source of dharma within the Nyingma or Old Translations School of Tibetan Buddhists. Mindrolling Monastery in Tibet is one of the six major Nyingma monasteries, and was known as a great center for learning.

The Mindrolling Lineage is slightly different from other lineages in that it is a blood lineage and does not rely on the tulku

548

system to find the next throne holder. From Mindrolling's founder, Rigdzin Terdag Lingpa to His Holiness Mindrolling Trichen and now Jetsün Khandro Rinpoche, those born into the lineage have been known to be great visionaries and progressive thinkers. Perhaps because of this, many great female practitioners and teachers are born into the Mindrolling lineage and it is famed for its many great female teachers throughout history.

At the age of two, Jetsün Khandro Rinpoche was recognized by His Holiness the 16th Karmapa as the Great Dakini of Tsurphu, Khandro Ugyen Tsomo, who was one of the most well known female masters of her time. Thus, the present Jetsün Khandro Rinpoche came to hold the lineages of both the Nyingma and Kagyu schools. Rinpoche completed a Western education at St. Joseph's Convent and St. Mary's Convent as well as the traditional Buddhist education given to young tulkus. Rinpoche has been teaching extensively in Europe, North America and Asia since 1987 and travels all over the world for several months every year.

LAYNE: And what are some particular teachings you've studied under her tutelage?

SOPHIE: I have been remarkably fortunate as to have been able to travel with Rinpoche and attend her teachings all over the world. I think of this as one of the lucky perks of being an attendant. As for teachings, Rinpoche has been guiding me just like all her other students along the progressive path of Buddhist training. I feel especially fortunate to have been able to spend a great deal of time in India and attend many teachings and transmissions happening at Mindrolling Monastery and Samten Tse Retreat Center. Someday, I hope I can gather them all in my own practice path and progress as a human being.

LAYNE: Living in India, have you had the opportunity to visit any sacred sites there or in Tibet?

SOPHIE: I have never been to Tibet, though I hope to someday

549

make it there. I have been on quite a few pilgrimages to the sacred places in India, Nepal and Bhutan.

LAYNE: Your father was Trungpa Rinpoche's attendant, wasn't he? Do you feel like you're following in his footsteps at all?

SOPHIE: Yes, he was Trungpa Rinpoche's attendant for many years and I have often felt like I was following in his footsteps. Actually, it has been quite helpful sometimes, since many of his experiences attending have been quite similar to my own.

LAYNE: Are you teaching at all yet? Your mother mentioned that she regards you as a teacher, but maybe that's not the same thing.

SOPHIE: Yes, I suppose, my mother would say something like that! I'm sure she means it in the best of ways, but no I am not at all teaching or anything like that. It is not something I see myself doing in the future at all. There are so many great teachers out there from so many different philosophies, that there is nothing I think I could add or say in any better way.

LAYNE: Well, I wouldn't think you would *want* to teach. People on the path of enlightenment, and therefore egolessness, don't have any *personal* interest in teaching. You may not see yourself as teaching eventually, but, nonetheless, isn't teaching expected of a tulku? Theoretically, doesn't a tulku *choose* rebirth, though no longer necessary, in order to benefit others?

SOPHIE: Within Tibetan Buddhism tulkus are born again and again with the one aspiration to bring benefit to all sentient beings. While this often manifests in the form of teaching the buddhadharma to others, it would be incorrect to assume that teaching is the only means to benefit beings. In fact it is said that bodhisattvas manifest as and when necessary in the form most needed. Yeshe Tsogyal, one of greatest figures in Tibetan Buddhism, makes this famous aspiration saying, "May I be a daughter where a daughter is needed and a father where a

550

father is needed. May I manifest as a cool river to the thirsty and a fire to the ones in need of heat. May I be born in whatever form is needed to fulfill the needs of sentient beings." I have always found this quote most inspirational. Khandro Rinpoche tells stories of His Holiness Mindrolling Trichen, her father, always pointing out that bodhisattvas can be in the most unexpected places as shopkeepers, farmers, butchers, beggars, your next-door neighbor etc., in every conceivable form. That seems to be the very essence of the bodhisattva principle—to go beyond set limits in order to be of benefit. Bodhisattvas undertake the aspiration, truly and completely, to be of benefit to all beings without the inflation of self and ego which most of us are afflicted with. They can actually accomplish whatever it is that is most required by beings at any given time.

For all of us who walk the bodhisattva path, we try to take the example of these bodhisattvas and pray that we too may develop a pure aspiration to truly be of the most benefit to beings in whatever form it is needed.

LAYNE: Do you have any general advice you'd like to offer to practitioners, regardless of the teaching they follow?

SOPHIE: For those seriously on the spiritual path I would say that finding a guide, or teacher, is an incredibly important aspect. That teacher-student relationship, which Gurdjieff himself seemed to have such a great grasp of, cannot be substituted with books or tapes. Personally, I feel one really needs that direct training experience.

Other than this I hope that people on a spiritual path don't lose their sense of humor. All too often I feel practitioners seem to become rigid and take things too seriously. One of the greatest things I have learned is how to laugh at myself (sometimes this is harder than at other times!) and to see how ridiculous I actually am.

LAYNE: Cheers to that!
Thanks for everything, Sophie. All the best to you.

551

SOPHIE: Thank you Layne. It has been interesting for me to try to answer your questions. I am excited to know what you will discover about Gurdjieff and his life. I hope you will keep me updated. Best of luck to you!

**APPRECIATION**

Thanks are due to the following libraries and their staff: Brooklyn Public Library, The Buddhist Digital Resource Center, Deutsche Nationalbibliothek, (especially Sybille Stahl), the library of First Zen Institute (especially Ian Chandler), The Griffith Institute Archive, Latse Library (especially Kristina Dy-Liacco), the library of The Jacques Marchais Museum of Tibetan Art, New York Public Library, Shambhala Archives, Shechen Monastery Archives, the State Library of New South Wales, and the library of the Frank Lloyd Wright Foundation (especially Indira Berndtson).

For providing photos and/or permission to use them, I thank Paula Barry, Sara Burnett, The James George Archive, The Konchok Foundation, Philippe Lelluch, Damon Lindbergh, New York Public Library, ouspenskytoday.org, Matthieu Ricard, Christopher Hugh Ripman, Roger Sherman, Doug Sprei, Stanford University Libraries, tibetantrekking. com, and University of Wisconsin-Milwaukee Library.

For permission to use the texts of others included, I thank Udon Beidler, Éditions de La Table Ronde, Eureka Editions, The First Zen Institute of America, Tsiporah Gottlieb, Sylvia March, Lady Diana Mukpo, Adam S. Pearcey, Jon Pepper, John Reynolds, Christopher Hugh Ripman, Shambhala Publications, Gosung Shin, Lama Surya Das, The Tertön Sogyal Trust, P.L. Travers Will Trust, Wisdom Publications, and Zen Studies Society.

For translating various texts, I thank Dr C. Bruce Boschek, Jacques Doyon, Sara Elliot, Vaillant Gicqueau, Jigme Dorje (Dr Ben Joffe), and Erick Tsiknopoulos.

For engaging in conversations on subjects of interest, whether written or verbal, I thank Daniel Aitken, Akong Rinpoche, Slava Alexakhin, Richard Baker Roshi, Margot Becker, Paul Beekman Taylor, Peter G. Beidler, Udon Beidler, Yosh Beier, Ben Bennett, Gert-Jan Blom, Peter Brook, Roberto Cacciapaglia, Shinge Roko Sherry Chayat, Chögyal Namkhai Norbu, Lyndon Comstock, Alex Daggett, Dagpo Rinpoche, Karl Debreczeny, James Evans, Walter Fordham, John Foster, Ashala Gabriel, Victor Gamolsky, James George, Madeline Gold, Jeremy Hayward, Greg Heffron, James T. Hill, Russell Huff, David Hykes, Sergey Konstantinov, Menpa Kunchog Tseten, Roger Lipsey, Ginny Lipson, Patty de Llosa, Ian MacFarlane, Sylvia March, Efrem Marder, Annabeth McCorkle, Alexandra Mikhalkova, Fran Miller, Yoko Ohashi, Zuzana Ondomišová, William Patrick Patterson, John Perks, Sophie Perks, Greg Quint, John Reynolds, Christopher Hugh Ripman, Allen Roth, Mary Rothenberg, Andrew Phillip Smith, Gosung Shin, John Shirley, Steffan Soule, Doug Sprei, David Stone, Surmang Khenpo, Yahne Le Toumelin, Serge Troude, Dr Scott Williams, How Man Wong, Lee Worley, Zurmang Gharwang Rinpoche, and especially two very helpful individuals who prefer anonymity.

For writing the foreword, I thank David Hykes.

For proofreading my text, I thank James Evans.

For creating and enhancing various images, and designing the dust jacket, I thank Felipe Oliveira.

Finally, for supporting my practice at various phases, I thank John Baker, Fiona Denzey, John Henry Goldman, Ian MacFarlane, Shingetsu Laura O'Loughlin, Russell Schreiber, Shechen Rabjam Rinpoche, Kosen Gregory Snyder, Jerry Toporovsky, and especially my root teacher, Soshin Teah Strozer.

.